Femina
A Work For Every Woman

By

John A. Miller

Femina
A Work For Every Woman
by John A. Miller

Copyright © 2024

All Rights reserved.

ISBN: 978-93-61426-77-3

Published by

DOUBLE 9 BOOKS

2/13-B, Ansari Road
Daryaganj, New Delhi – 110002
info@double9books.com
www.double9books.com
Tel. 011-40042856

ABOUT THE AUTHOR

John A. Miller, a distinguished author and advocate for women's rights, is renowned for his transformative masterpiece "Femina: A Work for Every Woman." In this groundbreaking book, Miller embarks on a journey to empower women of all backgrounds, offering a comprehensive guide to navigate the complexities of modern life with confidence and resilience. Through meticulous research and heartfelt insights, Miller addresses a wide range of topics relevant to women's lives, including career advancement, personal development, relationships, health, and societal challenges. With compassion and clarity, he offers practical advice, inspirational anecdotes, and empowering affirmations, empowering women to embrace their strengths, overcome obstacles, and pursue their dreams. "Femina" stands as a testament to Miller's unwavering commitment to gender equality and social justice. By amplifying women's voices and advocating for their rights, Miller champions a vision of a more inclusive and equitable society where every woman has the opportunity to thrive and fulfill her potential. With its timeless wisdom and universal appeal, "Femina" serves as a beacon of hope and inspiration for women everywhere, guiding them on a path of self-discovery, empowerment, and fulfillment. Through Miller's compassionate guidance, women are encouraged to embrace their unique talents and perspectives, forging a brighter future for themselves and generations to come.

CONTENTS

CHAPTER I
THE REASON WHY

I see a large field of usefulness which has not been covered by competent authorities. I propose, therefore, to offer a plain, simple statement of the most common causes of physical suffering in women, and a simple and reliable method of home or domestic treatment, to be carried out by the patients themselves, which, in the great majority of cases, is easily applied.

The first nine years of my professional life was an untiring and incessant devotion to the arduous demands of a large family practice, after which I decided to go to Europe, and there prosecute such studies in two German universities as my experience as a practitioner had fully convinced me to be of the greatest practical and scientific importance; hence, I offer no excuse or apology for aught I may say on a subject with which I have taken especial pains to familiarize myself. Having in a measure established my identity, I am more fully prepared to proceed in a more congenial way.

In the realm of thought there is no monopoly, and it is, after all, at the bar of public opinion that a final judgment must decide the merits of my course.

The question is not what to teach, but whom to teach. This may seem, at first sight, an easy matter to determine, but a more careful inquiry will show the complexity.

The platform of a medical college is considered by some the only legitimate place from which a medical man may impart his knowledge, but here the opportunity is limited, notwithstanding the abnormally great number of these institutions. This, however, is not the only reason. Medical colleges are becoming so numerous, that they should be discouraged by all honest and high-minded medical men, because in this country they are private institutions, with very few exceptions, and subserve sinister purposes, in furthering the interests of their promoters either as advertising schemes or money-making institutions, or both.

Of course they are incorporated under State laws, which make them *quasi*-public institutions, but the State exercises no authority over them, and their self-constituted professors conduct them to suit their own private ends. They are not limited by law, nor is a *required course* for their students imperative, so that the public have no guarantee of the fitness or competency of their graduates. There is, also, an unhealthy rivalry among our colleges for students, improper material is taken in, and correspondingly poor material is turned out; this in turn causes a rivalry among their graduates in making spoil of the sick.

Every self-respecting and competent medical man has an utter contempt for these doctor mills. This will never be different in this country until we follow the plan of European governments, and make medical colleges State institutions, and their professors officers of the State, with liberal salaries.

The medical press has a comparatively limited opportunity for imparting information to the public, unless the editor of the secular press happens to make a quotation.

The exclusiveness that has characterized the learned professions generally, and the medical profession particularly, is rapidly passing away. Only half a century ago, the medical lectures in Germany were mostly delivered in the Latin language, and, while we now often suffer, in listening to medical lectures in *bad* English, the latter may still be the lesser evil. In fact, so great is the deference to public opinion in favor of diffusing knowledge that medical faculties court popular favor by delivering a course of lectures on medical subjects, and consider these the best-drawing card of the institution.

Information that is not sensational nor untruthful cannot fail to do incalculable good to the class for whom it is intended, namely, our wives, mothers, daughters, and sisters, so that they may avoid errors, that entail suffering and disease; information that will teach them how to cure themselves of the commoner and simpler ailments, and thus avoid running to the doctor, who cannot always afford to tell them the truth. Some would not if they could.

The Darwinian theory is of wider application than to mere animal or plant life; it extends itself to the overcrowded professions, and the increasing "struggle for existence" in the ranks of the profession makes men dishonest and greedy for any opportunity to raise a fee, so that patients are being treated for diseases which are created for them by the cunning and dishonesty of their doctors.

A little common sense and a knowledge of the elementary principles of disease would be the best protection against these deceptions; but, as a rule, sick persons are inclined to throw aside all good sense, and give themselves up entirely to their feelings or to their doctor. This is a very wrong thing to do, and opens the door for all manner of impositions.

The general practitioner of thoughtful and studious habits finds that, in the course of years, a diversified reading on the different diseases which in the routine of his work he is called upon to treat makes him a generally well-informed man, but not a thoroughly exact man, either in theory or in the details of his treatment.

Fifty to sixty years ago the entire field of medicine was comparatively so small that it was easier for a brilliant mind then, to comprehend all that was believed to be known, than it is for the same quality of mind to understand any of the subdivisions of medicine to-day.

Those were the days of doctrines and rules. Little that was absolutely correct or true was then known about disease, otherwise such absurd theories as the "*dynamization* or *spirit-like*" influence, causing disease on the one hand, or that the "great source" of chronic diseases was *psora*, or itch, on the other, as Hahnemann would have them believe, could never have gotten a foothold.

These are the days of scientific deductions from microscopical and physiological research, in laboratories connected with great universities, and the result is, that any of the specialties or subdivisions of medicine is as large and interesting a field as the entire area was some time ago. It thus happens, that some thoughtful persons, after years of general practice, drift almost involuntarily into some one department of medical art and science. To this they become gradually wedded, and in it they grow in knowledge and experience far beyond their previous anticipations. What they read on the subject is better understood, and new ideas are constantly formed, which enlarge the scope of their knowledge. In this manner the writer drifted into the domain of diseases peculiar to women, which was as unhappy on the one hand, as it is interesting on the other, for the phrase "*diseases of women*" has fallen into disrepute because every superficial practitioner professes to know all about them, and it often is but another name for criminal abortion.

But for all that, there is a legitimate and scientific specialty of women's diseases. The time-serving specialist must be exposed in every department of medical science. Whether the pretender is labeled, a professor in a college, or labels himself through glaring newspaper advertisements, one is just as much a catch-penny as the other.

The object of educating the laity cannot be reasonably confined to a few medical truths, but the perversion of the truth must also be understood, so that the false can be detected. It is necessary to point out the dangers and frauds which are the unhealthy outgrowths or excrescences of established truths, and there must be no veneering of the wicked and sinful with ambiguous phrases to shield the guilty; the truthful and innocent require no apologist.

The honest observer can pursue no middle way in a work to which he has devoted the best years of a studious life, and hence he may seem radical in his opinions. While policy often dictates a conservative course, that which conscience and reason dictate to be true is prompted by loftier motives, namely, to subserve the highest purpose of moral integrity.

It has often been said that this is a mechanical age. How true is this even in the furtherance of science! How true is this of the science of astronomy, which was revolutionized by the construction of good telescopes! Mechanical genius has perfected a lens for Mount Hamilton thirty-six inches in diameter, and one is now in course of construction for Mount Wilson, in Southern California, which is to measure forty inches. Through these means scientists hope to decipher the complexion of remote planets.

Microscopic lenses have been equally perfected, and, by means of achromatic condensers and immersion lenses, great magnifying power can be obtained with perfect distinctness. That this mechanical spirit of the age should also have obtained a foothold in medical art and science, is but natural. Surgical and other mechanical methods have entered so boldly into the field of diseases of women that the writer feels constrained to sound a note of alarm. Great strides have been made in a more perfected technique in abdominal operations, and, by favorable recoveries from grave and severe operations, the field of surgical usefulness became enlarged, but this has degenerated into a license for notoriety and personal aggrandizement of not over-scrupulous and selfish surgeons who are over-anxious to operate so as to be able to boast of the great number of their capital operations, or laparotomies.

I was enthusiastic in abdominal and pelvic surgery, but not until I entered the field as a specialist in this department of medicine did I see and hear of daily abuses and misuses of this branch of surgery. In many instances it degenerated into criminal malpractice. It will be instructive information to cite a few cases which occurred under my observation, and present the actual facts to the reader.

It was in the month of February, in the year 1888, that a business trip to the southern part of the State forced an absence of several weeks upon me. Some two months before this time I had been called to see a young woman, who had then been sick for several months. She informed me that she had been married nine years, and, not having had any children, she concluded to see a noted specialist of female diseases. By this physician she was told that her sterility was owing to a closure or contraction of the mouth of the womb. This was obviously a wrong diagnosis, and for these reasons: she had always menstruated regularly and without pain, which excludes a constriction; and, secondly, no physician can honestly call a woman sterile until he has examined her husband, who, in the majority of instances, is the cause of his wife's sterility, because it is he who is sterile. This woman and the doctor agreed, however, on a course of treatment, which was to forcibly open or stretch the mouth and cervical canal of the womb. This by itself is neither a dangerous nor a severe operation, if carefully performed, but care in this case was evidently not exercised, because the young woman was taken with severe inflammation, which caused a pelvic abscess.

I found her after two months of suffering. The discharge had become extremely offensive, her body emaciated, and her strength exhausted.

I enlarged the opening of the abscess, placed a large drainage tube in the cavity, through which it was washed out, by means of an antiseptic solution of bichloride of mercury, 1 part to 2,000 parts of water, and, by further giving her simple, nutritious food, she improved rapidly, so that the day before I left the city she was at my office, and told me that she felt as well as ever, although not thoroughly recovered. I was absent two weeks, and a few days after my return I incidentally met her husband, who told me that a week after I had left, his wife felt unwell and called in one of her former doctors, who, by the way, rides a hobbyhorse on surgery. This man found a few pimples on her body, which can be found on almost any healthy person, these, he said, were signs of blood poisoning from her abscess, and that an operation to extirpate the abscess, with one or both of her ovaries, was of urgent necessity to save her life from blood poisoning. The deceived woman was of course frightened into giving her consent to the operation, which was undertaken immediately, and, as luck would have it, she recovered; but she might have easily died, which she undoubtedly would have done had this *knife-man* got her sooner, or before I had restored to her a splendid physical condition, which withstood the unnecessary butchery to which she was induced to submit.

Some doctors seem to have a perfect mania for cutting operations, just as though the entire science and art of medicine were exhausted in surgery alone. To assume this for an instant is manifestly ridiculous. More lives are annually saved by a scientific application of other methods of cure than the most elaborate and brilliant statistics of surgery can approach. There is science and skill in selecting proper medicines, in the employment of hygiene or the rules of health, in the practice of obstetrics, and in a variety of other ways to demonstrate the triumphs of the art of healing.

The rash and unnecessary resort to the knife has brought surgery into general distrust, so that some patients would rather die, or wait until they are almost dead, before they allow an operation to be performed on them, in cases where surgery is, indeed, the only possible method of cure.

A lady recently called at my office for a consultation. I found her uterus and other pelvic organs in a perfectly healthy condition, although she suffered pain there. This was due to neuralgia from a generally exhausted and debilitated condition. I was not a little surprised to learn, from her own lips, that she had been treated for womb disease, and was about to undergo an operation for a tear in the mouth of her womb. This was manifestly absurd, because no laceration existed at all, and if there had it might not have been necessary, because it is quite natural for women who have borne children to have the scars of old lacerations on the mouths of their wombs, and they are not any the worse for them.

It is important for mothers to know something about themselves and of the common diseases to which they are liable, for then they will not be so easily persuaded to permit the use of caustics, or the cutting, stitching, or scraping of their wombs, which is quite likely to excite complicated inflammations, more serious in their results than the diseases for which these operations were performed. I know of what I write, and there is no one who can successfully deny it.

Dr. William Goodell, who stands as high in the department of diseases of women as any American, had an article in one of the medical journals on "The Abuses of Uterine Treatment." He says: "From a large experience I humbly offer to the reader the following watchwords as broad helps to diagnosis: 1. Always bear in mind what another has pithily said, that 'woman has some organs outside of the pelvis.' 2. Each neurotic case will usually have a tale of fret or grief, of cark and care, of wear and tear. 3. Scant or delayed or suppressed menstruation is far more frequently the result of nerve exhaustion than of uterine disease. 4. Anteflexion of the womb, *per se*, is not a pathological condition. It is so when associated with sterility or painful menstruation, and only then does it need treatment. 5. An irritable bladder is more a nerve symptom than a uterine one. 6. In a large number of cases of supposed or actual uterine disease, which display marked gastric disturbance, if the tongue be clean the essential disease will be found to be neurotic, and it must be treated so. 7. Almost every supposed uterine case, characterized by excess of sensibility and by lack of will-power, is essentially a neurosis. 8. In the vast majority of cases in which the woman takes to her bed, and stays there indefinitely, from some supposed uterine lesion, she is bedridden from her brain and not from her womb. I will go further, and assert that this will be the rule even when the womb is displaced, or it is disordered by a lesion or disease, that is not in itself exacting or dangerous to life. Finally, uterine or womb symptoms are not *always* present in cases of uterine disease, nor, when present and even urgent, do they necessarily come from uterine disease, for they may be merely nerve counterfeits of uterine disease."

There is not a physician of any extended experience in the land who, if he be true to his better judgment, will not indorse every word of Professor Goodell's propositions. But the chances are they will never accomplish the good for which they were intended if the mothers, wives, and daughters are not permitted "a little peep" behind the curtain, and learn for themselves. For those who are wealthy and have plenty of money, doctoring may be a luxury or an amusement, but there the line must be drawn for the benefit of the deserving poor, with whom any treatment is a hardship. Stupidity of the masses is one of the causes of the abuse of surgical treatments, for they always look upon a surgical or bloody operation as one of the greatest achievements of modern medical art. Then there is the cupidity of the professional classes, who trade upon this popular error and delusion, and charge correspondingly large fees, which, as a rule, are exorbitant, particularly when the working classes are the sufferers.

A little cutting or stitching is much more quickly done, and the patient may be dismissed as cured, or left under the impression "that everything was done that could have been done," than a conservative medical or hygienic treatment, which involves more thought, labor, and patience, qualities which are not as eagerly cultivated as the art to wring out a good fee by a little surgery, with less labor and skill.

There is not only too much mischievous doctoring, but there is too much of every kind, whether good, bad, or indifferent. The trouble is there are too many in the ranks of the medical profession; and this is not only true of this country, but is raising a cry of warning in Europe. The struggle for existence is a natural law, and nature is immutable. I do not mean to say, that it is a humane law, or that competition is a virtue; in fact, I believe quite the reverse. But much that is natural from a physical standpoint might not be so from a moral or spiritual plane; thus the two natures are distinct.

It is reasonable to suppose that, if the natural crop of diseases falls short of supplying the demands of those who hunger for an opportunity to treat disease, and it lies within their power to create disease, they will certainly do so. The deficiency must be supplied, or one of two things must be done by the doctor: he must either starve, or go to work at something else. This may be cruel logic, but I know that these are the actual facts.

Now let me ask how many persons who have some sort of a diploma will be self-sacrificing enough or sufficiently unselfish to prefer to starve or honestly work for a living, if they can avoid either, by defrauding someone out of a fee, for pretending to cure some manufactured disease? It seems almost a waste of time to argue such a self-evident proposition. I have known physicians of high standing who treated women for womb diseases which never had a real existence, and surgeons of large incomes to remove the female breast for a "supposed cancer;" and, that being the case, what would you expect from a less fortunate brother practitioner who is eking out a miserable existence?

How many a case of simple sore throat or tonsilitis is being paraded as a case of diphtheria. Why, I know of doctors who built up their reputations in that way. It is quite an easy matter, to call an ordinary, simple case of bronchitis, pneumonia. Harmless swellings, no matter of what sort, are treated and palmed off every day as cancers. The quack cancer doctor is almost ubiquitous. Some would much rather part with the village parson, or their regular old town doctor, than to part with the cancer doctor. Diseases that are conjured up in the minds of susceptible or hypochondriac persons have for them a real existence, because if a person believes he has a certain disease, it becomes a reality, as far as his own state of mind is concerned, and as far as the treatment is concerned to him who created the delusion, it is much more desirable than if the disease were real, because you can cure an imaginary disease, which may be impossible when a real one comes under treatment. This is another method of making a reputation for extraordinary cures that really never occurred.

When I contemplated writing a book, which I hoped to make a *vade mecum* for those who felt interested in the subject, I felt that it would be a duty which I should reluctantly perform, for it would be a criticism on the status of the medical profession of this country. I was convinced that whatever I said that would lower the tone of the profession in the estimation of my countrymen would naturally reflect on me as unfavorably as upon any other member, for I never claimed to be anything else but an American physician, and, as such, I have an ambition to elevate the rank and file to honor and respectability.

There is also a motive that underlies a work of this nature which should appear justifiable to the author. It is absolutely necessary that side-lights should be thrown into dark corners and recesses that are usually screened from public notice. If there is a growing deterioration in methods of proficiency and morals, the public should know it, for who is the greater villain, he who trifles with human life through officious ignorance and venturous operations, or the midnight assassin, who, under cover of darkness, waylays his unwary victim? The title "doctor," from the Latin *doceo*, "I teach," has a halo of learning that it derives from the original significance that was attached to it when it was first sanctioned at Bologna University, about the middle of the twelfth century, where it first passed into the faculty of divinity. It was afterwards introduced into the universities of Northern Europe, and remained ever since a degree of distinction in theology, law, philosophy, and medicine. In the German universities *doctor* implies also a license to teach within the university, as a *privat-docent*.

When we now consider that no person can matriculate in a German university who has not graduated from the gymnasium or high school, it is clear that, under the above conditions, the title "doctor" guarantees that the possessor is an educated person, not only of the high school, but added thereto is the accomplishment in the specialty of which he holds the doctor degree.

What may a "doctor degree" mean in this country? The title of an illiterate and utterly incompetent person, who was by natural environment and occupation a teamster, saloon keeper, barber, tailor, or patent-medicine vender, etc.

If a woman, she may be retraced to an ignorant nurse, midwife, or quacksalver, the conceited wife of a man who indulges her in the freak of "learning to be a doctor," for she had demonstrated her genius for the profession by successfully treating a case of measles, which started the doctor's bee a-buzzing in her bonnet, until she passed through a medical college; last, but not least, are the winsome daughters of the millionaire or successful business man, who imagine themselves too smart to make useful housewives and good mothers.

There is not a medical college in this State, and there are few, if any, in the United States, that would not eagerly take in all of this material, and guarantee to them beforehand, that they can graduate as *medicinæ doctor* in twelve months to three years, a five months' course being considered a year.

The above comparison is a disgraceful commentary on the degree of *doctor* in this country, and the public should learn to know the difference.

"The United States and Its Doctors" is the title of an editorial in the July number of the New York *Medical Record*, and it says: "There is certainly no more curious social phenomenon than that of the extraordinary popularity of the medical profession in this country as a means of securing a livelihood.

"This subject is one that is often dwelt upon, but we doubt if many even yet realize the grotesque misproportion which medicine in the United States holds to other bread-winning occupations. Here are some of the naked facts in the matter:—

"France has 38,000,000 of population, 11,995 doctors, while it graduates 624 medical students in one year. Germany has 45,000,000 of population, about 30,000 doctors, and graduates 935 students in one year. The United States has about 60,000,000 of population, 100,000 doctors, 13,091 medical students, and graduates 3,740 students in one year.

"Germany, which has relatively less than half as many doctors as America, is already groaning over its surplus. When one compares France with this country, the excess of medical men here seems most astonishing.

"A comparison of the United States with European countries, in whatever way it is made, leads one to think that there is something almost alarming in our medical productiveness."

In connection with the above comparison, in which it is shown that Germany has proportionately less than half as many doctors as the United States, it will be interesting to learn the views of the German profession. The Berlin correspondent of the Medical Press writes that the "Deutcher Ærztebund," Society of German physicians, felt it to be their duty to warn the guardians of young men studying in the gymnasiums or high schools, against entering the medical profession, the state of overcrowding being so great as to *insure disastrous* consequences. In glancing over the above figures, there is one very important point which is greatly in favor of the German profession and militates against the Americans. It is the enormous patent-medicine trade and quacking that is done through it in the United States; on the whole, this has been calculated to amount to at least fifty per cent of all the doctoring that is done; that means, that where one hundred doctors now practice for a living, fifty more could make a similar living, were it not for the patent and quack medicine trade, which, in some of the German States, is almost prohibited, and in others I know it is entirely inhibited.

When the Society of German physicians warns the German people that an overcrowding "insures disastrous consequences," what does it mean?

This is a question which, we presume, was answered in Germany, and it is certainly worth our while that we should answer it here, and in this we have decidedly the advantage, because in that country the answer was entirely based upon what was anticipated, while in this we can answer from what we have already realized, namely, disastrous consequences to honor and to integrity on the one side, and to health and security against imposition on the other. To this I have already referred. Everyone competent of judging, and who has lived in that country, knows from study and observation that the arrangements and conveniences there for treating the sick are in a much higher state of perfection than with us. Hospitals and physicians are as accessible to all classes as the most humane and philanthropic heart can desire, and now we learn that if this wholesome state of affairs shall continue with less than half the proportion of doctors that we have here, there must be no further increase of physicians, or it would insure *disaster*. This statement and warning a close and careful observer clearly appreciates. The writer was personally acquainted with a large number of German practitioners while in that country, and knows as an actual fact that while their fees were and are much smaller than anything ever paid in this country, they had not overmuch to do, and were only leisurely employed. This applies to some of the greatest and world-renowned medical professors, as well as to the ordinary general practitioners. But there is a reason for all this, too. These men as a rule are honest, they are no money grabbers, they are thoroughly competent and scientific and manufacture no diseases to suit emergencies nor conjure up complaints that have no real existence. If their number were doubled, if the normal proportion were disturbed, the *disaster* would surely follow, professional demoralization would ensue. So the German profession sounds a timely note of warning ere the canker of selfishness has destroyed the noble altruistic principles of physicians, without which the doctor is as likely to be a messenger from hell as a ministering servant from heaven.

Medical legislation in this country has been nothing less than a farce, partly because the general public is not aware how abased the profession is, and partly that Americans are extremely jealous of what they term personal liberty. It is being attempted to remedy some of the abuses of the medical profession by regulating the practice of medicine by State Examining Boards. Experience has demonstrated that these boards are but the excrescences of the various medical colleges, who are themselves the root of the very evils that are sought to be remedied. The duties of these boards are simply to make themselves officious, and to inquire into the source of the credentials or diplomas of the applicants for a license to practice medicine, and not into the qualifications or competency of the applicants. All that is necessary under such laws is simply to present a diploma of some sort; whether it was stolen, or the diploma of a dead man, or gotten from any of the numerous worthless colleges, is not made the subject of inquiry; and as by far the greatest number of quack-salvers in this country have diplomas, the law falls short of remedying quackery.

There are, usually, enough boards of examiners, representing the different schools, so that the different interests of the diploma manufacturers are well represented. A medical examining authority whose functions and powers do not go higher or beyond the mere granting of licenses, or which does not examine into the qualifications of the persons who possess diplomas, is utterly absurd, because it is no protection against ignorance and imposition. A law that presumes that all persons holding diplomas are qualified and competent to practice medicine, is essentially wrong, or inadequate to fulfill the purpose for which it was designed. I have known graduates from what were considered good colleges who could neither write a safe prescription nor diagnose a case.

There is only one way towards an approach to an efficient and intelligent board of medical examiners, and that is, one single State board in which the different schools may be represented as to their pet theories of prescribing medicines, but in all other departments of medical science and art there must be a uniformity of talent and qualification.

There must be a *standard of excellence* established by the State, which is higher than and above the recognized standard of any medical college, for no medical college is trustworthy in this respect.

The State in its sovereignty must prescribe what shall constitute a medical education, and the requirements should be embodied in the statutes. A license or degree from that source, after a final examination, should be the only legitimate license to practice medicine.

Such a method would establish a system that would clearly define the status of every medical practitioner. The board must have the power, and it must be their duty, to examine each and every applicant for a license, as all candidates for the army medical service are examined. All this noise and talk about a preliminary examination and an extended course of medical study are simply the vaporings of superficial minds. It is neither the preliminary course, nor the length of time that a person consumes in trying to become a doctor, in which the public is interested, but what kind of doctor a person is when he hangs out his shingle and begins to practice, whether he is competent to do that which is expected from him in the hour of sickness or great peril, irrespective of any diploma or any medical college. Foreign graduates should be amenable to the same examination, for behind these, too, belongs the interrogation point. The gushing mediocrity of some of these diploma holders gives rise to the suspicion that their credentials are not genuine.

As an American to the manor born, I would not for a moment deny the humblest citizen an opportunity to elevate himself to the highest professional honors; but why can he not be required to thoroughly equip himself and prove, by oral and written examinations on subjects of preliminary education, that his mind has become disciplined for broader or special studies, irrespective of any course in a college? After the State has satisfied itself of the proficiency of the applicant in scholastic acquirements, it should go further, and examine into the qualifications for a degree of medicine, just as they do in the *U. S. Army*, only with this exception, that no diploma of any medical college should be required from the candidate, and if he has one it should not be recognized.

This would simply incorporate in the State laws the distinctive feature of the University of London, which examines and confers graduation on persons who have received instruction in such institutions at home and in the colonies as have satisfied a Secretary of State with regard to their studies.

This university also has and exercises a power of examining for degrees persons who have not been at any institution. Nothing could be more democratic than for the State to make such a provision for State medical examinations. The German Government does precisely the same thing, with the exception that it makes graduation from the medical department an essential prerequisite. It has a State board of examiners to examine all graduates in medicine of their own universities, to further prove if they are really qualified. A diploma in Germany is of no value; it is the so-called *ærzliche Approbationspruefung, State's examination*, that gives the license to practice legally.

When this is found necessary, notwithstanding the high standard of German medical schools, how much more is this safeguard against incompetency needed with us? I have endeavored to prove from the methods of Germany and the course of the *United States* medical department that diplomas cannot be accepted as *bona-fide* evidence of a medical education. With us a half dozen doctors can get together any time, incorporate a medical college, call themselves professors, and start out advertising themselves and their college for the purpose of manufacturing diplomas and doctors. Why, a diploma under these conditions should not be worth the parchment it is written on, as evidence of a medical education, unless attested by a higher and perfectly independent authority!

If the public once understood that too many doctors are dangerous to the morals and health of society, they would be quite as anxious as the most enthusiastic medical educator to remedy the evil.

The question of too many doctors is one of economical and social science, not of medical science, and, therefore, it can only be intelligently considered from these philosophical standpoints. It is a well-understood and accepted law of political economy that in the industrial pursuits, whether in the manufacturing departments or in agricultural production, the surplus or glut in the market of any of the products of industry, reduces the price and stimulates consumption, which, in the course of time, is regulated by a suspended or reduced production, thus restoring a healthy equilibrium. It would be an absurdity to apply the same rule to a surplus of doctors, because human ills or diseases do not increase in proportion to the surplus of doctors, nor will fees be any less. But the surplus, in order to live, must live on the earnings of the community, and here the disastrous consequences appear.

The credulous, and those who often may imagine that they require medical advice, become the unconscious victims of the unhealthy disproportion, for the doctor seizes the opportunity to make a case, while the normal proportion of cases do not reach around. Thus, it is calculated that at least fifty per cent. of all the diseases for which patients are treated are fictitious as far as actual disease is concerned, and the remaining fifty per cent. are, in the majority of instances, overdosed and overdoctored. For this reason medical legislation would not make a privileged class of physicians, nor throw unusual safeguards around medical practitioners, but medical legislation is to protect the people themselves from imposition and quackery.

The reason for the overcrowded state of the profession is not alone the laxity of medical laws, or the low standard of medical education in most of our colleges, but the general tendency of the country population to drift into the cities. Honest labor has not the dignity which its importance demands, and a radically faulty method of common-school education is another reason. Utilitarian manual methods, in which the hands are educated for useful employment and the minds to habits of industry, are to be wished for. Young men who have acquired a technical education in mechanics and arts will learn to respect labor in every department, and their ambition in life will be greater than to swing a cane or wear a silk tile.

In proportion as the productive employments are made respectable, this questionable ambition to become M. D.'s will fall off.

History tells us that the opulence of Rome was speedily accompanied by a decline of its agriculture, after which came the fall of the Roman Empire, because the country population became too indolent and restless and flocked to the cities for an easier and luxurious living. History in this respect seems to be repeating itself. We are always talking of encouraging the beauty and growth of our cities, but not one word of encouraging agriculture; no one talks of encouraging farm life and making it profitable and attractive, so that men and women would prefer the more independent subsistence in the country to a shabby gentility in the city. Some reader may ask, What has all this to do with doctoring? I say that the answer must already have been apparent; it becomes the duty of everyone to interest himself, that the division of labor shall be apportioned so as to do the greatest good to society.

We have a national characteristic which shows itself in an abnormal conceit for everything American in a degree that is not essential for true patriotism and love of country. But when by comparisons we learn that there are abuses and errors which are destructive to a healthy intellectual and material growth, we must have the honesty and independence to acknowledge them, and busy ourselves to find a remedy for existing evils.

The physician who can assist in the amelioration of society by administering to human ills which are the result of unwise laws, is accomplishing as much good as if he writes prescriptions or *bleeds* patients. The sooner everybody recognizes the fact that the time has come to deflect the current of ambition from the practice of medicine as a means of making a living, the sooner will untold suffering be lessened, and there is no honest-minded physician who does not heartily agree with me. Mercenary persons, and ignorant or unscrupulous doctors who run diploma mills, may criticise severely the honest sentiments here expressed, but the truth is so apparent, that he who runs may see the inevitable consequence of this unhealthy competition. Professors of colleges have a direct interest in the ignorance and incompetency of their graduates, because they are the means of calling them into consultation on every possible occasion in trifling ailments, and if the disease belongs to some specialty, they have the cases entirely turned over to them, because, in the mind of the incompetent and newly-made doctor, the professor who was the means of getting him a diploma, poses as the *beau ideal* of medical wisdom. In this way it becomes exceedingly profitable to be a professor. If there are not enough medical colleges in a community to afford places for the ambitious, it is considered to be one of the best-paying financial investments for a company of physicians to start one, and in most of these concerns it is easier to get a diploma as a doctor than to learn to be a good dressmaker or shoemaker.

Hence there is only one remedy to control the educational aspect of this evil, and that is to take medical colleges entirely out of the hands of private individuals and make the State the only source of the necessary credentials to practice medicine.

An American system of medical education fostered by the State would be productive of grand results, because, under the shadow of our free institutions, the mind transcends the circumscribed sphere of despotism. This has already been proven in numerous instances, notwithstanding unfavorable surroundings.

Forming the galaxy of great names that illumine the milky way of science, there are none brighter than a Gross, a Flint, a Sims, and some others. These were great American authors and physicians, who never pretended anything else; they never dreamt of the Don Quixotic escapade of pretending to be American professors while they appended to their names initials or abbreviations of questionable credit from foreign institutions. The brilliancy of true genius was their only passport to fame.

CHAPTER II
DELUSIONS AS TO THE CURATIVE
VALUE OF DRUGS

Medicines that are sure cures for all the diseases to which humanity is heir, are not the spurious discoveries of the quacksalver and patent-medicine vender alone, but some very intelligent persons believe that if there is not a panacea, there is at least a remedy, for every disease. In cases where the patient does not recover, they believe that either the disease was not thoroughly understood or the medicines which were given were not properly selected.

This is a great error, because there is no such thing as a specific or infallible remedy for any disease, and, on the other hand, it is quite possible that most patients, with proper nursing and diet, would naturally recover without any drugs or medicines whatever. Outside of those drugs, like ether, chloroform, opium, or morphine, that are employed for the purpose of deadening the sensibility of the nerves, so as to render them insensible to pain, there is not another drug that is absolutely sure and true in its medical effects. Some few are very useful at times, but the great bulk of medicines do much more harm than good.

Medicine in its broad sense means a knowledge of the cause, course, treatment and ultimate results of disease. The study of medicine cannot be circumscribed by dogma or theory, nor can it be mastered in a few short years of study at the very best medical schools. It requires a mind adapted by nature for a plodding investigation of her laws, and incessant application, long after the college curriculum is ended. In fact, the student must unlearn much of the stereotyped lessons of the text-books, and this is particularly true of the supposed medicinal effects of drugs, which are always exaggerated. When physicians really have a threatening case, under their observation and care, the attributed therapeutic action of drugs is nearly always disappointing, and very often injurious, and they are forced to let the drugging entirely alone, and bring their skill to bear on measures which support the strength and vitality of the system, so that nature can effect a cure in her own way. This may seem to some simple doctoring, but I can assure the reader that it requires the highest degree of medical skill, notwithstanding the droll sarcasm of Voltaire, that "medical science is the art of amusing the patient while nature performs the cure." There is neither skill nor much learning required to give an ordinary prescription; that the average apothecary could do with the greatest exactness. But science and medical skill can be exhausted in managing and husbanding the resources of nature, in order to effect a cure.

Medicine no longer stands alone as a simple art, based on theoretical deductions, as it was less than a hundred years ago, but it has become a department of natural science, a part of the natural history of the human race.

Disease is as much a vital process as health, only in one case the vital function is perverted, or destructive, while in health it is constructive. The germ theory of disease and cellular pathology are clearly within the domain of biological research, while chemistry has solved many physiological processes. Mental philosophy has been no less serviceable in the department of medicine, by teaching the wonderful influence of thought and emotions on the physiological functions of the organs.

A one-sided education is inadequate to appreciate the subject of healing or teaching. A comprehensive knowledge of all that bears on the subject of health and disease has several important objects in view, namely, it thoroughly acquaints the doctor with all of nature's resources for the amelioration or cure of disease; and it gives him judgment in all cases to avoid irreparably wrong treatment, which places obstacles in the road of nature's efforts to heal spontaneously. The quack or professional imbecile will, in the ordinary course of diseases, be accredited with remarkable cures; in fact, the cures wrought by a quack or an ignorant person are just as welcome and valuable to the patient interested as if they were accomplished under the advice of the most erudite and skillful physician, but the invalid ran the chances of malpractice or bad treatment at the hands of the quack, which might have cost him his life, because the incompetent healer does not know when his method of treatment does mischief. Every method of cure may possess merits of its own, which are beneficial when the disease or conditions for its employment are present, whether this is mind cure, water cure, or anything else that you may name. All that any system of treatment can do is simply to stimulate the curative force of nature, which is the only *first cause* of any cure.

The reparative energy of nature has never been duly recognized, because the selfishness and pride of the doctors will not concede this as often as they ought. The doctor should be the most useful as a monitor to the sick, in guiding and controlling thought and conduct, in harmony with the curative energy of nature. From this point of view the pretensions of anyone effecting this or that cure are only a delusion, because the doctor effects nothing, he only assists, guides, and directs towards effecting a cure. What this curative force is has by no means been understood. Some believe it identical with life or vital action, which manifests itself only in organized substances, but even if we admit this identity, we are balked again, because we do not really know what life is, any more than we know what electricity is. Descartes resolved life into matter and motion; this, however, is rather the phenomena of life and gives us no idea of the real essence of the force that we call life. There is another theory, that all life whenever or wherever found is a spiritual force, ethereal and universal. For our purpose, the discussion of this question has no particular value, were it not for the fact that life, or vital activity, wherever we find it in organized substances, whether in the lowest living thing or in the highest type of physical development, is accompanied by or is endowed with the natural tendency to repair defects or injuries in that in which it is active.

Regeneration, or the curative process of nature, is always the handmaid of vital activity. It is present at the earliest formation and division of a cell, which constitutes the unit of all organisms. Just as one brick is laid on the other with mortar or cement between them, so as to make a whole wall of a building, so are our bodies built up of minute cells, one added to the other, with cement between them, until the entire structure is completed. There is no tissue of the living body which was not at one time during its existence a cell. This curative force is beautifully illustrated in the lower animals, where parts of organs are replaced to a far greater extent than among warm-blooded animals.

Professor L. Landois, in his work on "Human Physiology," says that "when a *hydra* is divided into two parts, each part forms a new individual— nay, if the body of the animal be divided into several parts in a particular way, each part gives rise to a new individual. The *planarians* also show a great capacity for producing lost parts. Spiders and crabs can reproduce lost feelers, limbs, and claws; snails, part of the head, feelers, and eyes, provided the central nervous system is not injured. Many fishes reproduce fins, even the tail fin. Salamanders and lizards can produce an entire tail, including bones, muscles, and even the posterior part of the spinal cord, while the triton reproduces an amputated limb, the lower jaw, and an eye. This reproduction requires that a small stump be left, while total extirpation of the parts prevents reproduction. In amphibians and reptiles the regeneration of organs and tissues, as a whole, takes place after the type of embryonic development, which is by cell division, and the same is true as regards the histological processes which occur in the regenerated tail and other parts of the body of the earth worm." Comparative pathological anatomy clearly demonstrates the inherent curative power of nature, and this is also apparent in the vegetable kingdom, and together they deliver a lecture on the "art of healing" from the stage of creation, in silent and modest language, but eloquently instructive to the thoughtful observer.

The question now naturally arises How far this curative energy of nature operates in warm-blooded animals, and especially in man? The answer must be that, while it falls short of reproducing parts of organs or even tissues in the same degree of perfection as in the lower orders, the innate tendency towards regeneration and recovery from injury and disease is, on certain lines, practically the same. There is not the slightest doubt that ninety per cent. of all cures, whether the invalid took this, that, or the other medicine, or whether the method of treatment was homeopathic, allopathic, or mind cure, are entirely due to this inherent curative energy; and the other ten per cent. may have required some active remedy, but this, too, alone, without nature's healing force, would have been ineffectual.

What is ordinarily termed mind cure is not mind cure in the sense that the term implies, but it is simply the mind toying or playing with the idea of a cure, for while the mind is thus engaged, nature's energy is accomplishing the result or cure. This is the only rational explanation, and corresponds with the cures that nature is continually making in the lower orders of animals. If the recovery of the sick depended entirely upon the caprice and wisdom of the doctor, and not on the reparative forces of nature, the race would soon die out. I fully recognize the fact that the curative force can be stimulated; this may be done through the influence of nourishing food, alcoholic stimulants, a drug or medicine, or through purely mental influences. No physician can estimate how much merit he can accredit to the methods or substances he employs in any particular case that recovers, and how much to the lady physician, Dame Nature. This old lady doctor is ever active, and the most inert drugs, employed or administered with her assistance, have achieved wonderful cures; this the history of medicine confirms. The tar water cure of Bishop Berkeley is an illustration how an inert substance is capable of making for itself an enviable reputation for curing ailments, like pleurisy, pneumonia, erysipelas, asthma, indigestion, hypochondria, and other diseases. This remedy had the vehement indorsement of one of the greatest metaphysicians of the English-speaking world, and that the cures reported by him were genuine no one will doubt for a moment; but the bishop, like many of our day, was determined to have a remedy to cure disease, where none was required, but the mind had to be humored, while nature was actively repairing the disorder. To-day almost everyone is satisfied, that the virtues ascribed to tar water by Berkeley were a delusion, which was shared by all those who believed as he did.

The Weapon Ointment affords another instance where the credulity of the public was supported by abundant facts to prove the efficacy of the remedy, yet it was based on the wildest superstition. This ointment was employed for the healing of wounds, but instead of being applied to them, the weapon with which the wound was inflicted was carefully anointed and hung up in a corner, and the wound was washed and bandaged without the salve being allowed to touch it. This ointment created such a furor that eminent medical men indorsed its virtues as a healing agent. Another example of superstition and charlatanry was the equally famous Sympathetic Powder, which, when applied to the blood-stained garments of wounded persons, cured their injuries even when miles away. That dukes and knights vied with each other to obtain the secret of its preparation and ingredients is a matter of history. Instances of delusions on medical subjects could be multiplied a thousand fold, but they prove nothing but ignorance and superstition on the one side, and the inherent all-powerful curative force of nature on the other. While I wish to avoid wounding the fastidious and sensitive in the matter of their faith in their cherished system of cure, I cannot refrain from classing homeopathy as a similar delusion.

I am glad to admit at the outset that I have read Hahnemann's "Organon of the Art of Healing" with a great deal of interest and some profit. I am convinced that his theory of infinitesimal dilutions is as absurd and ridiculous as either the Weapon Ointment or the Sympathetic Powder treatment already referred to.

If we consider the harsh, or, preferably-termed, *heroic* treatments, then in vogue, we need not be surprised that the pendulum of medication should have swung in the opposite extreme. Blood was drawn from the already enfeebled body, emaciated by disease; emetics were administered to sensitive and inflamed stomachs, and only aggravated into greater disorder; blisters, or the burning moxa, scorched into greater agony the suffering mortal, while large doses of drastic cathartics depleted the waning forces of nature. There was a tendency of the medical profession about that time to entirely ignore the *curative forces* of nature, and to attack disease as you would a midnight marauder, with the most powerful and dangerous weapons at command; and there is no doubt that with these powerful expedients, disease was destroyed, but life also. Under these conditions Hahnemann appeared on the scene, and I am frank to admit that he rendered suffering humanity invaluable service by espousing a system of cure which had the merit of being harmless. If we take into account that physiological studies were then in their infancy, and that the word "Biologie," from the Greek words which signify a discourse upon life and living things, was made use of for the first time by Lamarck, in a work published in 1801, it will not seem altogether strange that even learned men were mystified into beliefs which, in the light of our present knowledge of the subject, appear preposterous. This was a most opportune time to fasten on the healing art any doctrine or dogma, however absurd, and on this tide of ignorance and superstition, the doctrine of infinitesimal dilutions floated into popularity. Homeopathy affords us one of the most striking illustrations of the uselessness of drugs in ordinary ailments, and conclusively proves that nature possesses inherent curative powers. Cases treated under this system make splendid recoveries, and often much better than when the powers of nature are opposed or weakened with nauseating drugs and poisonous doses, prescribed by incompetent persons.

Hahnemann truthfully observed that existing diseases are liable to become aggravated, complicated or replaced by *drug diseases*.

There is no doubt of the truth of this statement where drugs are heedlessly administered. When I was a student I was told that *calomel* was par excellence a babies' medicine without any qualification. I was credulous enough to believe it and prescribed it for my own children for its purgative effect whenever it was deemed necessary. In later childhood, when the second dentition set in, the germs of the permanent teeth were so injured, evidently from the calomel that had been absorbed into the system, that the teeth were ragged and defective. The glands of the neck were also inclined to swell and suppurate, and there is no doubt in my mind that a great deal of what is generally supposed to be scrofula in young children, is nothing more nor less than a "drug disease." I believe that Hahnemann was cognizant of the potency of nature under ordinary circumstances to cure disease. I believe that he absorbed this view of the philosophy of healing from the writings of Paracelsus, which he had studied, and from which he drew his inspiration, but he also appreciated the practical necessity that success depended on satisfying the superstitious belief of the times, and that consisted in offering some tangible remedy. Hahnemann proved himself equal to the emergency by formulating his doctrine of potentizing drugs or medicinal substances by reducing them to a wonderful degree of minuteness.

The preparation of these dilutions was directed to be carried out in a ceremonial sort of way. Chalk from an oyster shell, sulphur, charcoal, or any other substance, was potentized by taking one grain of the drug and mixing it with one hundred grains of sugar of milk. Of this mixture one grain was taken and mixed in the same manner with another hundred grains sugar of milk. This gave the ten-thousandth of a grain of the drug. Take one grain of this with another hundred grains of sugar of milk and the powder will contain the millionth of a grain of the substance, or the first potency, which forms the bases of other dilutions. This is reducing the doses of any drug to an absurdity, and Hahnemann was too brilliant a mind not to know this. It might be mentioned in connection with these dilutions, that if one grain of the most powerful drug, strychnine, aconitin, arsenic, or any other chemical that is known, is mixed with six hundred grains of sugar of milk, one grain of this powder, or the one six-hundredth of a grain of this substance, cannot be detected by any test or chemical reagent; or, in other words, the quantity of the drug or chemical contained is so small that the most delicate chemical test fails to show it; yet, in homeopathy, the dilutions are carried to the decillionth of a grain, from which important medical effects are expected.

Drugs are physical agents, and if they are diluted so as to destroy their chemical or physical properties, it is sheer nonsense to expect any physical result from them on the system. Chemical and physical facts conclusively prove the utter inertness of certain drugs either in themselves or in the manner in which they are employed, and the indisputable evidence of biological science demonstrates the natural curative tendency of nature observable in the lowest living thing to the highest, so that we should stultify our reason were we to arrive at any other conclusion than that the doctrine of this therapeutic creed is one of the most irrational delusions that ever befogged the mental horizon of a thinking being.

The supposed cures effected through the employment of the Weapon Ointment, the Sympathetic Powders, the endless dilutions of the Hahnemann system, and, indeed, most other remedial agents from any school or source, whether offensive powders, mixtures, or patent medicines, or the more agreeable and tasteless pellets, have but *one role to play*, that is, to assuage the apprehensions of the mind while nature is performing the cure; that is, to engage the mind with the thought or idea that something tangible is being done to bring about a certain result.

If the patient has pinned his faith to the curative value of mind alone, the mind is for the time being engaged with idea that *mind* is performing the cure. This is a delusion quite similar to the previous one, in which medicines are taken, with only this difference, that while you pin your faith on drugs in the one case, you pin it to mind cure in the other.

CHAPTER III
WHAT IS MIND CURE?

This subject has given rise to an endless variety of contradictory discussions, and while it has won for itself fanatical devotees on one side, it has been ridiculed on the other. This is not at all surprising, when an inquiry is made into the competency of the parties to the controversy. To be informed in metaphysical philosophy, or fully equipped in scriptural lore, but without a practical study in the art and theory of medical science, precludes the possibility of presenting the theme in a logical manner, or establishing a relevancy between medical science and mind cure. A medical education that is based on strictly physical characteristics of disease, as they are studied at the bedside, or in a microscopical laboratory, is equally inadequate; for the question of mind cure goes beyond the physical into the metaphysical, and not until the operations of the mind have been closely followed to the bodily or organic functions, can the intimacy of their relations be thoroughly appreciated. Medical men betray their incapacity for observation if they contemptuously dismiss the subject of mind cure by some superficial, disparaging illustration, for there is much more in the subject than is dreamt of, even in the mind of the average college professor.

"The mind," says Dr. W. F. Evans, "can be made the plastic or formative principle of the body, and that thought can retard, pervert, or stimulate and correct the different functions of the human organism." The relation of spirit and matter is very intimate, and some very clever thinkers resolve all matter into spirit, in its ultimate analysis.

Bishop Berkeley affirms this in his "Principles of Human Knowledge." In section seven he says "there is not any other substance than spirit."

If we view nature from a materialistic standpoint, we see only one-half of what we think we do, and even that must be very imperfectly judged by our senses. Friedrich Wilhelm Joseph Schelling states the relation of matter and spirit, in very simple and plain words, so that a child can understand what he says: "Nature is spirit visible, and spirit, is invisible nature." This may be illustrated in physical science from what chemistry teaches of the physical properties of the *diamond*, whose atoms or molecules are so perfectly continuous and closely aggregated that it forms one of the hardest substances known to physicists. These atoms of pure carbon may be made to repel each other, so that the diamond assumes a gaseous state, which is imperceptible to our senses.

I am aware that the definition of a gas is not that which metaphysicians would accept as applicable to spirit, and yet it illustrates the idea from a physical standpoint. It is much better to illustrate a question with something with which people are generally familiar. The body and every organ and tissue forming a constituent part of it, is simply the plain ordinary matter in motion, vitalized by what we call life, and this life principle is a mystery, and what is true of the diamond is true of the human body in its entirety. If placed in a crematory, it is reduced to a few ounces of bone ash, and, with the addition of a little acid, this too would soon disappear into invisible gases, so that the doctrine of philosophers, that matter is spirit, is, after all, not so far removed from physical evidence.

Physiological science gives abundant proof that the mind has a powerful influence over the body. By mind is meant all that class of mental phenomena called reason, and the emotions and passions. Doctor Evans says "the body is included in the being of the mind," or, in other words, that matter is included in the being of spirit.

The thinking quality of the mind is undoubtedly the mainspring of its action, of which the formation of ideas is the highest kind of mental activity. These originate either within the mind or are brought within its sphere by transformed impressions from without, but through the power of the Will these are more or less modified, and may, indeed, be entirely suspended, so that the mind may become entirely passive and not think of anything. It is the exercise of this Will power which may make the operations of thought conducive to health or disease.

Cogito ergo sum, "I think, therefore I am," is a maxim of Descartes. What we think and give shape to in thought has for us a real existence, and we have it in our power to create thoughts that will have either a painful or pleasurable sensation. Painful sensations have occurred to persons by the conviction of the existence of a cause which would, when present, have produced certain results. Of this several examples are given in W. B. Carpenter's physiology: "A clergyman told me that some time ago suspicions were entertained in his parish of a woman who was supposed to have poisoned her newly-born infant. The coffin was exhumed, and the coroner, who attended with the medical men to examine the body, declared that he already perceived the oder of decomposition, which made him feel faint, and in consequence he withdrew. But on opening the coffin it was found to be empty, and it was afterwards ascertained that no child had been born, and consequently no murder committed." The second case is yet more remarkable: "A butcher was brought into the drug store of Mr. Macfarlan, from the market-place opposite, laboring under a terrible accident. The man, on trying to hook up a heavy piece of meat above his head, slipped, and the sharp hook penetrated his arm, so that he himself was suspended. On being examined he was pale, almost pulseless, and expressed himself as suffering acute agony. The arm could not be moved without causing excessive pain, and in cutting off the sleeve he frequently cried out. Yet when the arm was exposed, it was found to be quite uninjured, the hook having only traversed the sleeve of his coat." In this, and similar cases, the sensation was perfectly real to the individual who experienced it, but it originated in the mind by an impression through the nerves of *internal sensation* which created the idea or image in the brain, and the *external senses* to which it was referred had nothing to do in causing the feeling. Diseases are thus created every day, either by ourselves or by those to whom we go for advice. I call to mind a lady who had gone to a distinguished practitioner for a supposed womb disease for some six months. She experienced no change for the better, but kept on growing continually worse, so that she no longer had a refreshing sleep, and her appetite for food was entirely gone. On examination I found her womb entirely healthy, in fact, exceptionally so, thanks to her attending physician, because, after a certain amount of useless doctoring, the rule is quite the other way. I told this lady of her error or delusion respecting her womb, and prescribed a quieting mixture for the night and a tonic for the day. She began at once to improve, and when I saw her again, six weeks afterwards, she had so fleshed up that I failed to recognize in her traces of her former delusion. The disease of which this woman was suffering was imaginary, and had no real existence for anyone outside of herself. She was the victim of the harrowing symptoms which her mind conjured into shape, and an attempt to brush aside the disease, with the flippant remark that "there was nothing the matter with her," would have been cruel, unscientific, and absurd. The ailment which she thought she had, had as much an existence as though the most malignant disease was destroying her life; for her imaginary disease was doing the same thing, only in a different way.

Imagination is the most powerful function of the human brain. Associated with thought, it constitutes the empire of the soul, which recognizes neither time nor space. With it we are brought into communion with everything that is grand and beautiful in nature. Imagination is the architect of our souls; it continually creates and projects into the beyond; it enlarges the sphere of our thought in building up artificial structures for our pleasure and entertainment. When it becomes perverted and abnormal from false impressions, either through the nerves of internal sensation or through the nerves of external sense, or, what quite often occurs, from morbid thoughts or ideas received from others, it becomes equally potent in causing misery and disease.

Expectation or attention influences, in a remarkable degree, the bodily functions. There are a great many persons who keep themselves in misery and disease by always thinking of their imaginary or real sickness. I had a profitable experience some years ago in my own case, which conclusively proved to my mind the aggravating tendency which constant attention has on disease. I had contracted an ordinary catarrh of the pharynx, or what is generally called a sore throat. At first I did not mind it, but in the course of time, from continued exposure in all kinds of inclement weather, at all hours of the day or night, it fastened itself upon me so that it was at times very annoying by its dryness and pain. I do not know of anything that I did not use, but, after a trial of several years, I was convinced that the more I looked at it and the more I treated it with sprays, gargles, etc., the worse it became, so that one day I resolved to let it alone, and not think about it. I took a teasponful of glycerine once in a while when it became too dry. For years I have not looked at it, and for all I know, it is perfectly well. I stopped bundling up my neck, used light bedcovering, so as not to sweat, and by this simple method accomplished what the very best selected drugs utterly failed to do.

The great English authority, Daniel Hack Tuke, in his work, "The Influence of the Mind on the Body in Health and Disease," quotes from Unzer's work, published in Germany in the year 1771: "Expectation of the action of a remedy often causes us to experience its operation beforehand." And John Hunter said as early as 1786: "I am confident that I can fix my attention to any part until I have a sensation in that part." A great number of cases are recorded where complete insensibility to bodily pain has been induced without the use of drugs. The intention of administering a certain drug was made known in this manner. Bread pills have acted as decided cathartics, and an empty chloroform or ether bottle put the sensitive into a profound stupor or insensibility.

Dr. Woodhouse Braine, of the Charing Cross Hospital, writes: "During the year 1862 I was called upon to give chloroform to a very nervous and highly hysterical girl, who was about to have two fatty tumors of the scalp removed. On going into the operating room, it was found that the bottle containing the chloroform had been removed to the dispensary, and on testing the Snow's inhaler, which at that time I was in the habit of using, I found it to be quite devoid of even any smell of chloroform. Then, having sent for the bottle, in order to accustom the girl to the face-piece, I applied it to her face, and she at once began to breathe rapidly through it. When she had done this for about half a minute, she said, 'Oh, I feel it, I feel I am going off,' and as the chloroform bottle had not arrived, she was told to go on breathing quietly. At this time her hand, which had been resting across her chest, slipped down by her side, and as she did not replace it, I thought I would pinch her arm gently to see the amount of discomfort her hysterical state would induce her to bear. She did not notice a gentle pinch, and so I pinched her harder, and then as hard as I could, and to my surprise I found that she did not feel at all. Finding this was the case, I asked the operator to begin, and he incised one of the tumors, and then, as the cyst was only slightly adherent, peeled it away. At this time I had removed the face-piece, and, wishing to see the effect of her imagination, I said to the operator, who was going to remove the second tumor, 'Wait a minute; she seems to be coming round.' Instantly her respiration, which had been quite quiet, altered in character, becoming rapid as when I first applied the inhaler, and she commenced moving her arms about. I then replaced the face-piece, and her breathing again became quiet, and she submitted to the second operation without moving a muscle. When the water dressing and bandages were applied, in answer to the question as to whether she had felt anything, she said, 'No; I was quite unconscious of all that was done.'" The mental phenomenon that we observe in this case clearly shows how completely the sensation of the patient was suspended by the imaginary chloroform, which existed only in her mind, yet the real drug could not have been more potent in its effects.

Phenomena of the same mental process, like the different colors of the solar spectrum coming from one source, constitute the different stages or degrees of what is generally called mesmerism or somnambulism, until the sensitive arrives at that condition of complete double consciousness now commonly called hypnotism, in which state the will power of the person becomes entirely suspended, so that he acts only from suggestions of another person, regardless of propriety or consequences. When a subject who has been completely hypnotized is restored to his normal condition, he remembers nothing of what has transpired during the somnambulistic state. We all have acquaintances of whom we speak as being easily led; by that we mean that they have no will or mind of their own. These persons are truly unfortunate, because they are at the complete mercy of every designing person or cunning rogue. They constitute the large army of dupes who support the great number of idle women and lazy men, who claim to be clairvoyants, life readers and fortune tellers. In sickness they are equally as credulous, and when they are a little out of sorts, they would a great deal rather be told that some dangerous or severe illness has hold of them than to hear the truth that, outside of not eating properly, or clothing themselves improperly, or being out late at nights when they should be in their beds, there is nothing the matter with them.

These are the dupes who fill up the chairs in the doctor's waiting rooms, on regular days, for local or special treatment for diseases which could be much better treated by themselves at home, if they only were fortunate enough to fall into a physician's hands who had the honesty to tell them so. This can be further illustrated by an experience of which every one of us has been a victim at least once in our lives. When we were trying on a pair of new shoes, we felt that they pinched, or were too short and generally uncomfortable; but the salesman insisted that they were a "perfect fit" and that after a little wearing they would surely suit. The shoes were bought, and we were convinced, after a few days, that our impression of the smallness of the shoes was correct, because they continued to pinch us; but we were for the time mesmerized or psychologized by the clerk into buying what we were satisfied in our own minds to be not what we wanted. This should be constantly guarded against, and our conscious will power should always be exercised on all occasions.

Parents should take particular pains to cultivate the will power of their children, in the right direction, of course. To stifle the will of children, when the exercise of it entails no bad consequences, is wrong, because it weakens their character, and makes them the prey of the wicked and selfish when they are grown to adult age. This influence which one person may exercise over another is not due to any particular force or magnetism, as was supposed by Mesmer, and which is yet claimed by ignorant frauds and pretenders, but it is simply a suspension of your own *will*, or a sacrifice of force of character. Dr. J. M. Charcot, of France, has lately taken up this subject, and has given it a great deal of attention. His researches have confirmed the experiments and conclusions of Braid, an English surgeon of Manchester, who, in 1841, showed that, in order to produce artificial somnambulism, there was no need of any extraneous influence, and that any person of moderate sensibility can easily produce in himself the "magnetic sleep" without any aid or act of another.

Braid discovered that to simply fix the eyes for a few minutes on some shining object, placed a little higher than the ordinary plane of vision, and five or six inches from the eyes, caused that total abstraction which Doctor Braid called "hypnotism," and which now, in honor of the experimenter, is often called "Braidism." This Doctor Charcot calls "impersonal" sleep, artificially produced by mechanical means. He remarks: "The psychic characteristic of the state of somnambulism is an absolute trust, a boundless credulity on the part of the subject toward the one who has hypnotized him.

Take one example from among a thousand: I present to a woman patient in the hypnotic state a blank leaf of paper, and say to her: 'Here is my portrait; what do you think of it? Is it a good likeness?' After a moment's hesitation she answers, 'Yes, indeed; your photograph! Will you give it to me?' The image being now fixed in her mind, I take the leaf of paper, with a private mark, and mix it with a score of other leaves precisely like it. I then hand the whole pack to the patient, bidding her to go over them and let me know whether she finds among them anything she has seen before. She begins to look at the leaves one after another, and as soon as her eyes fall upon the one first shown, she exclaims, 'Look! your portrait!'" This is the latest phenomenon, and proves how the mind may print an image on a substance, as the sun prints on a negative.

For persons of casual thought or reading, hypnotism may at first appear complicated and mysterious, but if you will only bear in mind that the different mental processes operating between two persons always resolve themselves into a *weaker* will power *yielding* and a *stronger* will power *controlling*, you have a key which unlocks the different manifestations of minds in their relations one with the other. This does not relate to action alone, but to the creation and meaning of our thoughts.

The cures effected by the royal touch, which prevailed in England from the time of Edward, the confessor, to Queen Anne, were but a disguised hypnotism, or a sort of mind cure. Soothsayers, or magnetic healers, who claim a healing magnetism, are either knaves or fools, and often both. They undoubtedly can report cures, but these are due to the natural tendency of some diseases to get well, and to the hopeful thoughts which these persons inspire by their promises of a cure; sometimes these hopes are heightened by the different movements or passes which the healer makes. The greatest healer of whom we have any reliable record never claimed any abnormal power or force. Christ healed by the Word, that means by the thought or mind. Faith in anything creates a curative or healing thought in the mind of the patient, which stimulates the reparative or healing force of nature, and in this manner wonderful cures are effected.

The faith, or confidence, which you have in a physician stimulates you at once into a better or stronger feeling. This has been the experience of every sick person, but this is not due to any power or force that this person possesses, which departs from him and goes over to you, but is entirely due to the confidence, which stimulates your own nerve centers, and especially the brain. The soothing and quieting influence which the "Weapon Ointment" had on the injured person was not due to any virtue of this ointment, because it was never applied to the wound, but to the weapon or implement which caused the wound. Its operations were entirely mental or psychical. It pacified the excited and anxious mind into the faith or belief that the best possible thing to do was being done, and nature went on triumphantly and effected the cure, for which, of course, she never got any credit. When a doctor or healer enters the chamber of the sick, putting on a wise air, or indulges in affectation, and when he succeeds in making a good impression, that alone assuages the pain. But if, on the other hand, he impresses his patients unfavorably, the sooner he gets out of their sight, the better they feel, because his presence has inspired neither confidence nor hope.

Hysteria constitutes a peculiar group of diseases which belong to that class of nervous ailments that are included among functional affections; they are oftener amenable to faith or mind cures than to drugs. A great number of diseases of women belong to this class and these poor deluded creatures never had anything real or serious the matter with them, until they went to some doctor who began to apply irritating drugs to their delicate organs, which made them ever afterwards habitues of doctors' offices.

Functional diseases have a wide range. As their name implies, they are characterized by a disturbance of the function of an organ or system, without any visible alteration of its tissue or texture; there are no pathological or histological changes, which the most careful microscopic examination can detect. They constitute a scapegoat for our ignorance; it appears to be in the majority of instances a disturbance between the psychic or spiritual forces as they operate on the tissues. The normal and harmonious relations between the mind and the body or any particular organ are disarranged. Such are the hysterical convulsions or spasms which we see in women who have suffered great mental strain, especially grief, and often it is due to pure "cussedness," or unbridled passion. In men there is also a hysteria; it was formerly believed that this peculiar nervous derangement was confined to women only, hence the name, but this was an error. I was once called to attend a physician of more than average ability, who located in this city for the purpose of enlarging his field of labor and usefulness; from where he came he had been very successful. His reputation as a surgeon was enviable and deservedly so, but here, in this city, among strangers and strange customs, he was a failure. This preyed on his mind so that he became despondent and gloomy. He failed in flesh and strength. I found him in his room convulsively sobbing, which shortly turned into a paroxysm of laughter. I prevailed upon him to return to his former residence among his friends and admirers, which he did, and he told me afterwards that from the moment he struck his "old stamping-ground" he felt stronger and better, and shortly recovered his former mirth and healthfulness.

Girls show this abnormal nervous function in different ways. I have known a case where a sensitive girl accidentally saw another girl in an epileptic fit; the contortions became so real and fixed in her mind, or imagination, that they were transmuted into motions or epileptic fits. I tried remedies but without any beneficial results. The parents afterwards went the rounds of the "fits doctors," but with the same negative results. A Christian scientist or faith healer cured her, by cultivating or strengthening her will power.

There is a class of these faith healers, composed of silly, loquacious women and men, who know nothing at all of the principle governing their cures, and they glibly tell their patients, "You must say or think there is no disease, or I have no pain, or there is no body; all is well; all is good," and a great deal of similar nonsense. All is not good, and all is not well by any means. I would say, Indeed there is pain, disease, and a body, but by striving to live a healthful moral life, and thinking healthful thoughts, of the good, the pure, and the beautiful, the curative energy of nature will become stimulated to repair the defects, to harmonize the functions and dissipate disease.

A person who is troubled with dyspepsia cannot get well if he thinks of nothing but an acid or sour stomach, or feels the food disagreeing with him before he has it in his mouth. He must have thoughts quite remote from these, and the chances are nine out of ten he will not feel what he eats. There is the same state of mind about "catching cold." Some persons are forever on the alert to catch a cold, and why should they not, when they are always watching out for it? If you dress so that you do not sweat, and do not use too thick bedcovering, and are not constantly on the catch or lookout, I assure you you will not catch cold, nor will it catch you.

Terror or fright causes or cures diseases. Dr. Toad reports the case of a boy, in Tuke's work, nine years of age, who was frightened into chorea, or St. Vitus' dance, by his sister, who had covered herself with a white sheet and appeared before him unexpectedly, while he was in bed. I know, also, a case of functional bladder weakness of a child who wet his bed at night during sleep. There appeared no signs of any local disease, nor was any remedy which I employed of the slightest advantage. The father of the child, becoming exasperated, gave the child a severe thrashing one morning. The mother remonstrated at what she considered cruel and useless chastisement. But, strange yet true, that child never wet the bed after that; it was entirely cured by fright.

Sympathy will often make persons sick; of this I had in my own experience an opportunity for a very interesting observation. It was the husband of a woman who had been retching and vomiting incident to the early months of her pregnancy. So great was the sympathy of her husband that he retched and vomited exactly like his wife, not only when in her presence, but when separated from her, the impressions or thought exciting the *excito-motor* nerves of the stomach. This sympathetic sickness lasted as long as that of his wife.

Dr. H. C. Sawyer, author of "Nerve Waste," has kindly shown the writer another form of functional or hysterical disorder, which was, or is even yet, considered by many general practitioners a scrofulous enlargement of the joints; but the doctor discovered the peculiarity of *metastasis*, which means a sudden or complete removal of a disease from one part to another. This gave the disease what he termed a hysterical or functional character. It would be the swelling of the elbow of one arm and the knee of the opposite side at one time; and in the course of a few weeks or months these would feel and appear entirely well, while the disease had located itself in other joints. This case the doctor considered could be only reached through the mind, or some faith cure. He further believed that many of these enlarged and swollen joints among the wealthier classes were due to a nervous trouble. Indeed, it would be an easy matter to cite case after case, from my own experience, or quote cases from the highest medical authorities, illustrating in every conceivable manner how the mind, the imagination, the emotions, or the different passions, are continually causing disease and suffering.

It must naturally follow that what is potent to induce diseases will, under different conditions, be a means of curing them.

A serious question now arises with reference to the selection of cases suitable to *mind-cure* treatment. Bigoted fanaticism is quite incompetent, so are the great majority of spiritual healers, owing to their absolute ignorance of the scientific aspects of disease. The first prerequisite for intelligent and proper treatment is to establish the precise nature of the disease under consideration. It must be distinctly grouped or classed, whether it be a functional or hysterical disease, or a zymotic or contagious affection.

In diphtheria or typhoid fever mind cure subserves no purpose; the treatment must be avowedly antiseptic and stimulating.

If it be a physical injury, say a fractured bone, it must be treated on mechanical principles.

A woman suffering in the pangs of labor, which is being delayed from some abnormal position or some other physical obstruction, can only be delivered through mechanical methods; and here the enthusiastic mind healer may commit serious errors, sacrificing limb and life by unnecessary delay. So I would lay down this broad maxim, that the mind healer must either be a competent, educated physician, or a physician should be a competent metaphysician.

Note.—In the year 1887 Mrs. A. C. Hurrell was a healthy, middle-aged woman and the mother of two children. When the youngest was ten months old she contracted a severe cold. The coughing spells "took her breath," and from these exaggerated expiratory paroxysms she drifted into *spasmodic asthma*, at least that was the diagnosis of prominent medical men of Sacramento and of this city. Change of climate was advised and tried, so were also the different drugs which experience had taught to be useful, even operations were performed on her nasal passages by enterprising specialists, but all to no purpose. Morphine was prescribed by the first medical attendant, and when her suffering became unbearable she had to fall back on this drug for relief. In May, 1890, I was consulted, but a most careful examination revealed nothing which I could assign as a cause and upon which to base a hopeful treatment.

In October, 1891, she was persuaded to take treatment from a lady who claimed to cure through Christian Science (a mind healer). The treatment commenced on a Thursday afternoon. The lady impressed on her that the morphine, of which she now consumed, hypodermically, the enormous quantity of ninety grains a week, was injurious, and that if she made up her mind that there was no disease the asthma would leave her. Friday night the patient was in great agony, both from the withdrawal of the drug and the asthmatic attack, and this double pressure weakened the faith of both patient and healer, but the husband stood firm and insisted that she have no morphine. The struggle for breath and the narcotic continued until four o'clock Sunday morning, when she began to get easier; the improvement continued, and in ten days she had "outgrown" both. I saw her two months later, entirely recovered, and the most brilliant specimen of the efficiency of mind cure that one could wish to see.

CHAPTER IV
GENERAL CAUSES OF UTERINE AND PELVIC DISEASES OF WOMEN

Why are womb diseases so prevalent? is a question which we are not infrequently called upon to answer. At first sight this would strike one as a casual or commonplace remark, but a moment's reflection makes it one of vital interest, for a truthful and intelligent reply lays bare the causes which undermine the health, strength and character of the mothers of our citizens, and when a disease of this sort becomes common, it threatens the morality, health and life of our nation.

The causes which operate in producing these diseases of the female differ widely in their origin; some are due to ordinary imprudence, while others are deeply rooted in moral depravity and marital abuses and for this reason I consider it convenient to arrange them into three distinct classes or groups.

The first class is characterized by comprising those causes which are for the most part accidental. They are peculiar to confinement and motherhood, and may be in a great degree controlled or averted by the skillful and competent accoucheur. They have principally a scientific interest, and do not fall within the scope of the non-professional reader.

The second class is entirely beyond anyone's control. The causes belonging to this category are innate to the human organism; they induce those numerous afflictions which here and there sprout up in previously healthy persons, and are, in all probability, due to some specific hereditary taint. They are to be attributed to the natural imperfections of humanity, and are a constant reminder that the body is simply the transient abode of the soul, or spiritual man, and as such only perfect in its imperfections. Like the causes of the first class, these, too, have principally a scientific interest.

The third class of causes of uterine diseases constitutes a very large group, and has a popular or general interest. For this reason it should be freely discussed, because the causes of this class are *avoidable*.

They are entirely within the control of the average sensible person, and for that reason should be known and understood by everyone. These causes superinduce inflammatory diseases, which are not confined to the womb alone but take in the entire pelvic *appendages*, the Fallopian tubes and ovaries. They are the greatest source of revenue to the doctors, and vary in symptoms in different persons, from a slight casual reminder of something wrong to harassing pains and physical suffering; and that these all are brought about through ignorance, wanton carelessness, or sinful disrespect of nature's or God's law, is the characteristic feature of the causes under investigation.

Exercise in the open air is so essential in strengthening the nervous and muscular systems that where this is neglected it predisposes to womb disease. I consider the differently-devised indoor or room calisthenics or exercises as totally inadequate and no substitute whatever for healthful outdoor movement, and for the following reason: that while it irritates the muscular and nerve fibers, it lacks the stimulating and tonic influence of pure oxygen-laden air, so that the blood becomes still more deteriorated and overloaded by excessive waste material, which is not thrown off. If a person exercise at all with a view of deriving physical benefits, let it always be in the open air. Like walking, riding, rowing, to which bicycling should be added as one of the very best of outdoor exercises, the mind can then be engaged at the same time, though it must not be overstrained. The great obstacle nowadays arises from a fashionable and morbid desire to cultivate an appearance of delicacy; if, instead, recreations which required muscular exertions were more fashionable, the results in developing strong and hardy women would be astonishing.

No exercise can be profitable which is not interesting to the person who practices it.

It is not the bodily exertion alone which can profit a person, but the happy associations, the abandonment of self thought, the mental relaxation, and the pleasure which accompanies it. With one or two companions we can have a jolly time, while taking a swimming bath or floundering in the surf, but alone it soon becomes tiresome. If we take a stroll with an agreeable companion, we can walk a distance which, when undertaken alone, would fatigue and tire us completely out, while, when with an associate or friend, we cover the same distance refreshed and invigorated, because the mind is entertained while the body is exercised. This must have been the experience of everyone, and if it teaches anything worth remembering, it teaches that monotonous exercises should be avoided and entertaining ones sought and practiced. Walks over hills in small, friendly groups is one of the best modes of exercise I know of. And then there remain the many outdoor games. The pernicious systems of training which are observed in some female seminaries often plant the seeds for future disease. All the school hours are employed in reading, drawing, music, and other brain work, while the evenings are devoted to preparing lessons for the following day. This is very injurious, and should never be permitted.

After school hours the mind should have complete respite from study, so that the forces can recuperate themselves for the next day.

Nervousness or neurasthenia is often a result of this excessive mental application. Where the mind is constantly engaged in intellectual pursuits, the result often is a too rapid development of the brain and nervous system.

When the thoughts and memory of girls of tender age are too long and too laboriously engaged, there will be an abnormal development of the nervous centers; they will grow or develop beyond the muscular or physical strength, and a morbid impressibility, great feebleness of the muscular system, and a marked tendency to disease of the pelvic organs, is established. Parents may refer with pride to the precocious talents, the refined and cultivated tastes, of their daughters, as qualities to be admired and appreciated, but without a physical substratum it is a dreamy delusion. It would be much better for the children if their parents took more pride in rotund figures and robust constitutions, for these would ever be a source of joy, while the cultivated talents, especially at the expense of their health, will not only be of little practical value to them in after years, but often incapacitate them for wives and mothers, by making them restless, discontented, and physically unfit for maternal functions.

There is entirely too much scholastic education imparted to our girls, and not enough domestic education. I believe that the most favored should not have too much of one and not enough of the other, because if parents do not prepare girls for household duties in early life, they run desperate chances of laying the foundation for a failure in the remote future.

Children must be constantly reminded that they are in this world to serve a useful purpose, and that co-equal with every accomplishment is a utilitarian training.

We take a pride if our boys trade pocketknives, especially when our own gets the better one of the two, because we appreciate the natural business trait. He will be no less a good candidate for some of the learned professions, and, indeed, it has come to this, that material success in the professions depends as much on shrewd business tact as it does upon proficiency in professional attainments.

The knowledge or even wisdom of a person is of no earthly use to himself or the world if he or she do not possess the faculty of letting the people know of this superior wisdom; and that is why some persons often become more celebrated and even renowned than others, who are intellectually their superiors, because the former possess the faculty and cunning to make people believe in their superiority. By this I simply desire to impress upon parents not to be over-anxious about their daughters standing *first* in their class room, but, rather, to be very anxious that they attain a healthy and vigorous growth, and that sufficient practical knowledge of domestic affairs be imparted to them so that they can creditably fill their mother's places some day. This I consider the best legacy.

The time to commence to train mothers is from the moment they are born. The minds of parents should be disabused of the false delicacy about this aspect of a girl, and while no one expects daily lectures to be given to children or young girls upon the responsibilities which await them, such information should not be studiously avoided. I insist that this important fact should not be lost sight of, motherhood is the ultimatum of feminine existence.

Mistaken conceptions of woman's education, in pinning girls to a life of close mental application, is often productive of uterine disease, by lowering the tone of the nervous system; while others who are ambitious to acquire a professional education in later life, fall by the wayside as hopeless invalids.

I do not disparage her capacity to study with equal proficiency the arts and sciences, often with more ardor and closer application, than her male colleagues, but she is simply striving to accomplish that which the men can and do willingly accomplish for her, while at the same time she is neglecting the education of those qualities which are the sole inheritance of her sex, and which man could not usurp if he would.

This class of uterine diseases develops in a few years into melancholy, which closes the windows of the soul to the sunlight of hope, and gradually drags the sufferer into a decline, that nothing but an entire change in the habits and thoughts of the patient will ameliorate or cure.

I would have our girls as independent of our boys as the latter are of our girls. I would have it understood that each, in their specialty for which God and nature has ordained them, is as honorable and important in the social and industrial conditions of mankind as the other. I would give woman the right, and deem it her privilege, to frankly and unrestrainedly profess her fondness or desire to marry the man who she believes would make her a desirable husband, because woman's intuition transcends man's reason.

A reform in this direction would, indeed, elevate the woman to man's estate, where she belongs. A little less sentiment and more sense is a wholesome panacea for some of the abuses of the marital contract.

I fully subscribe to the view that a woman shall at all times receive the same wages for her mental and physical labor that men receive for the same work, but I am entirely opposed to that modern tendency and false social philosophy which is constantly striving to make a man out of a woman. There is something so grossly absurd and unnatural in this artificial readjustment of the natural duties of the sexes, in their industrial and social relations, that it has degenerated in many instances into fanaticism.

Women are organizing everywhere for the purpose of increasing the facilities of their sisters in the studies of science and philosophy. Large sums are offered to the faculties of universities to gain admission to female students on an equal footing with the male students, for the purpose of studying some of the already overcrowded professions. In the main, all this abnormal rivalry does not contribute a single advantage to either sex.

There was a time in the history of civilized nations, and that time is not more than twenty or twenty-five years ago, when an academical education gave an immense advantage to its possessor over his less-informed contemporary, but this is not true in our time, because there is now an overproduction of college-bred men. The man who can decline a Greek noun or conjugate a Latin verb is no longer a rarity, because the sons of European tradesmen and American farmers have deserted the pursuits of their progenitors—which, in the case of the American farmers, is to be deplored—and obtained a collegiate education, that is no longer the inheritance of the privileged few, so that in our time and day an academical education has run to seed among the men. And now the attempt is being made, under the guise of social progress, to burden our girls with the same wisdom that has incapacitated many of our boys from making an honest and independent living. It would be much better for the State if two-thirds of our universities or high schools were changed into manual training schools or polytechnical colleges, where the foundations for the industrial pursuits may be laid, so that labor will be made not only respectable but intelligent.

We would then hear of educated mechanics or artisans, and scientific farmers, which, to my mind, requires the same order of intelligence to excel, that it does in the professions generally qualified as "learned."

Why crowd our girls, then, into the professions for which they are not only unsuited by nature, but which are already demoralized by the keen competition within their ranks? It is, certainly, an open secret, in the profession to which I have now devoted the best years of my life, that the methods in vogue to get business have descended to the level of the "confidence trickster," and that, no matter what ability or merit a person may possess, without the natural instincts and elements of the quack and charlatan he can gain neither a livelihood nor fame. This theatrical demeanor of the profession, this aping the gaudy display of European aristocrats by riding in closed coaches, driven by liveried coachmen, is but the outward symptom of the internal disease of contention for notoriety and success.

If, instead of all this false and demoralizing philosophy, termed "woman's rights"—which is more appropriately designated "woman's wrongs"—we turn the thoughts and ambitions of women towards domestic economy and domestic virtue, which alone should be and ever will be the *ideal* of noble womanhood, there will be, then, much less disease, more happiness, and less discontent. There is enough on God's earth for all of his children to eat, wear, and work, if the labor and the subsistence are fairly and wisely apportioned.

The growing sentiment, which is as vicious as it is absurd, is that a girl, to be educated or accomplished, must be either a teacher, lawyer, or doctor, or anything else except an accomplished housekeeper, just as though it required less talent or ability to raise a child, cook a wholesome or digestible meal, and cut or sew a garment.

Why, there is much more thought and judgment required in making an angel mother than in administering or prescribing a dose of medicine and filing a legal brief, and there is not a lawyer or doctor who has given sufficient thought to the duties and requirements of maternity who disputes it for a moment. If our strong-minded women would preach this doctrine, which would tend to make household duties respectable, they would be benefactors instead of mischief makers, and then our comely girls would prefer to cultivate habits of domesticity, which should and would become as honorable an occupation as that of a doctoress or lawyeress.

Improprieties of dress are to be found in excessive or deficient clothing, in an improper adjustment, and in an inherent defect of the undergarments. I will reserve some of my views on these questions, for the chapter that is devoted to hygienic measures. In the main, the custom or manner of dressing women in Christian countries does not deserve that sweeping denunciation that some radical dress reformers make. I would not, if I could, change the very becoming and graceful modern female dress, for it possesses the merit of displaying the beauties of the figure in a modestly delicate manner, and it hides its defects from the vulgar gaze.

As a rule, there is too much pressure on the abdomen, from the weight of heavy skirts that are suspended from the hips, and not sufficient room for the chest to expand, so as to accommodate the respiring movements of the lungs. In the absence of shoulder bands, to which the skirts should all be fastened, the much-decried corset has its redeeming qualities, for it serves the purpose of a yoke or support for the different undergarments, and when not tightly laced is rather a benefit than an injury, and if the corset had a shoulder strap fastened to it over both shoulders so as to keep the garments from dragging on the hips, there could then be no objection to it whatever. The corset must always be so loosely worn as to permit the wearer's hands to be easily passed between it and the waist. It then becomes a useful brace to a weakly woman and entirely harmless to a strong or healthy one. We can imagine how a tightly-fitting corset will cause mischief by compressing the ribs and abdominal walls, and that this absurd fettering will prevent the lateral expansion of the chest, and also injuriously press upon the internal organs, but this is not due to an inherent property of the corset itself, but to an abuse of it. One might as well advocate a return to the Roman sandal, on the ground that some persons are foolish and vain enough to wear shoes altogether too small for their feet, thereby causing deformities and corns. For my part, I admire a nice, well-shaped, healthy foot, incased in a low, broad-heeled, comfortable shoe, even if its size were one or two numbers larger than a pinched-up, deformed one. But no one would be enthusiastic enough on the question of healthy feet to have us all wear sandals again.

Warmth of the lower extremities is a very important point in a female's apparel, and of more importance than all the other questions raised on this subject. The exposures endured by women, from ignorance or indifference to this fact, is, in my experience, a fruitful source of disease. The chilling blast which sweeps under the skirts must be mitigated and the moist vapor arising from a damp and cold earth neutralized. If the limbs are only protected by thin cotton fabrics, they are insufficiently clad to avoid the evils above mentioned. It is of the greatest importance that the limbs of women should be incased in flannel drawers, and these can be worn underneath the white muslin or linen ones, and the hose, especially in cold or damp weather, should be made of woolen material; the soles of the shoes should be sufficiently heavy so as not to be permeable by the moisture from the ground, and in wet or rainy weather rubber overshoes are always a necessity. When the feet and lower limbs are kept warm, the whole body is more or less protected against cold.

Superfluous or too warm garments are the cause of an endless variety of diseases. The rule is this, that any garment which by its weight or thickness excites perspiration when the wearer sits quietly or exercises moderately, is either superfluous or too thick or heavy, and, as perspiration relaxes and softens the skin, it makes one susceptible to take cold. It is reported on good authority that sealskin wraps cause more deaths among those who wear them than typhoid fever and for the reason above mentioned. Loosely-woven woolen goods make the best wraps and the best underwear.

If we were called upon to state a single proposition which we considered of the greatest importance in preventing disease, we would frankly say that, next to an irregular and unwholesome diet, excessive clothing is the most mischievous factor in causing or predisposing to disease.

The same rule applies to bedcovering; if it be so heavy as to make the sleeper sweat during the night, he is almost sure to take cold from the sudden change, from a warm, moist bed to the cool room or comparatively chilled clothing.

Imprudence during menstruation. A heedless disregard, ignorance, or carelessness of the precautions above referred to is, during the catamenial days, quite sure to lay the foundation for disease. Every practitioner has met with a great number of cases where the disease originated during menstruation from some indiscretion, and it ran on for years, until a condition of affairs was developed which was well-nigh incurable.

The female organism is particularly sensitive about this time and much easier affected than at any other.

During this period the ovaries and uterus are intensely congested, and the Fallopian tubes which connect the former with the latter share this condition, and if a cold should suddenly check or interfere with the natural functions of these organs, it might result in inflammation of the ovaries or in a catarrh of the tubes and womb. Any one of these conditions is painful and often troublesome to cure, but when all these organs are complicated in the diseased process, which we frequently find to be the case, it may entail serious consequences.

Dysmenorrhea, or painful menstruation, will be a prominent symptom, if any of the above organs have suffered from imprudence, during this period, and I have known of cases which gave me no end of trouble before they were restored to health.

Measurements of the healthy uterus. In a grown person the average length is three inches, two inches in breadth and an inch in thickness. It weighs from an ounce to an ounce and a half. The size of the uterus is an important guide to the physician in establishing the presence or absence of certain diseases.

In the child-bearing period measurements and weight change, because the organ grows correspondingly large to accommodate the growth of the child.

Growth of the uterus from the moment of conception is one of the most interesting physiological studies. All its tissues, muscles, nerves, vessels, and lymphatics are increased in bulk and multiplied in number. The human ovum is an extremely minute microscopic cell, from one two-hundred-and-fortieth to one one-hundred-and-twentieth of an inch in diameter. This grows so rapidly that at the end of nine months we often have the average nine-pound baby. The growth of the muscular fibers of the womb is truly remarkable. They grow eleven times longer and twice to four times thicker, so that the growth of the womb keeps pace with that of the child.

Changes immediately after confinement. Women as a rule, and their husbands also, are wofully ignorant of the condition of the womb just after confinement, and at this point it will be opportune to impart the necessary information illustrating that it is one of the most critical periods of the entire process, because the pelvic organs are again very sensitive, somewhat akin to the menstrual condition, namely, one of engorgement, or congestion.

After the child is in the world, the uterus usually contracts to about the size of a cocoanut; its measurements and weight as compared with what it was before pregnancy have materially increased.

The diameter is now about four inches, and its weight a little over two pounds. If we now stop to reflect that its weight was formerly an ounce to an ounce and a half, to which size and weight it must again return, we can readily appreciate the important changes that must take place to accomplish this object. The scientific world has only learned how this is effected within the last thirty years. It was a very important discovery. The superfluous or excessive tissues are converted into fat—the process is called *fatty degeneration*—and as fat the tissues are absorbed into the blood and disposed of, and thus gradually is the superabundant substance removed, until its measurements are as they were formerly and its weight as it was before.

Involution is the name given to this process by medical writers. It signifies a rolling back of the size and substance of the womb to where it was before pregnancy. It is the physiological activity in the tissues of the organ to restore it to its former size and healthfulness. The time usually required for nature to accomplish this remodeling varies in different individuals from six weeks to three months.

Subinvolution is a term employed to designate a partial or complete cessation of this restorative action. The prefix *sub* means always *under*; in this case the same thing is meant, *under-involution* or *incomplete* involution.

When, in six weeks to three months after confinement, the womb has not returned to its previous healthy size, weight and state, or if the enlargement of the womb incident to pregnancy lasts longer than already specified, we have the disease termed subinvolution. It generally becomes complicated with inflammation of either the cavity of the womb or of its entire substance, and often the inflammation extends to all the other organs and tissues in the pelvis.

Indiscretion in getting up too soon may cause this state of affairs. Taking cold and excessive exertion should be guarded against.

A mother who has just been delivered must gradually feel her way as to how much and what she may or can do without jeopardizing her recovery. Pains in the pelvis, back, and thighs, or a heavy, dragging sensation after getting up, indicate a subinvolution. These symptoms should be attended to, because the longer they last the more obstinate the disease becomes.

Lying on the back after confinement for ten or twelve days is not only injurious but an unnecessary hardship for every mother. It is one of the most fruitful causes of an abnormal position or falling back of the womb, and very often this excites diseases which greatly complicate the improper location of the organ.

Retroversion and retroflexion of the womb will be considered more minutely later on. It is generally caused by this common error of nurses and physicians, who allow the delivered woman to lie and often insist on her lying on the back. Thus the womb gradually sinks backwards, instead of falling forwards, where it belongs: see Plate IV.

Women will not generally feel that anything is wrong until some time after they are up and around. The first few weeks or months after confinement, persons are inclined to attribute their weakness, pains in the back or thighs, and other disagreeable sensations, to the natural consequences of what they have gone through. But after weeks roll into months, and their former strength and health do not return, then they seek the advice of a doctor, who will disclose to them the cause of their suffering. This can be avoided every time by changing the positions of lying, from one side to the other, and from the back to the stomach for a change; then naturally the womb will gradually resume its normal position, which is inclined forward and rests with its body over and on the bladder. All of these displacements should receive early and prompt attention.

Antiseptic precautions. Only a few years ago this phrase was entirely unknown. It originated with the modern antiseptic treatment of wounds, and from the domain of surgery it has been transplanted into the department of obstetrics, in which the application of antiseptic principles has achieved the most brilliant triumphs. From this conception has sprung the germ theory of disease, which is now, beyond doubt, an established fact.

I never can forget my first case of *childbed fever*. It is only fourteen years ago, and then there was as yet no one who could give a scientifically truthful interpretation of the disease. My patient was a young mother, who was being rapidly consumed by a fever, but beyond that science had not unlocked the causes lurking in the organism, which had doomed the young woman, on the threshold of motherhood, to a premature grave.

Thousands of lives were yearly destroyed by *puerperal fever*. Volumes of literature had been written on the subject, but as yet no one had deciphered its origin.

Now the whole scene has shifted; we know that the fever is essentially a blood poison, a septic infection of the patient, precisely similar to a wound infection anywhere else on the body. The act of parturition causes wounds or abrasions; these, then, place the woman in imminent danger of infection of every sort, and it is this infection which it is now possible to avoid. There is the greatest precaution necessary on her part and on the part of her attendants, that she be not contaminated by suspicious-looking finger nails, or dirty hands, or soiled linen, or unhealthy and unclean surroundings.

The German Government has a compulsory law for a system of antiseptic precautions, which is incumbent upon all who attend lying-in women. The importance of a rule to guide midwives and others in carrying out strictly antiseptic measures was recognized in that country some ten years ago, and the statistics show a remarkable diminution of diseases peculiar to the childbed period. The sources of these infectious micro-organisms are very different. They may be derived from the body of another person, sick or having died from an infectious disease, from suppurating wounds and even from the secretions of healthy lying-in patients. The patient or person herself may have improperly bathed or neglected cleanliness and ablutions, but the greatest danger arises from the neglected and unclean hands and sleeves of the midwives and physicians, and from the instruments usually employed under these circumstances, like forceps, catheters, or the nozzle of a syringe. The law above referred to requires all these instruments to be thoroughly scalded, washed, and brushed every time they have been used, and by such a complete system of disinfection, the chances of infection are reduced to the minimum. I hope some day our legislators will be wise enough to give us similar laws.

CHAPTER V
UNCLEANLINESS AS A CAUSE
OF DISEASES IN WOMEN

The custom of washing and bathing has existed from the earliest times. Among the Egyptians it was a part of their religious worship. Among the Jews it formed part of the ceremony of purification prescribed by Moses. The Greeks considered it a sanitary expedient, and among the Romans it was instituted for similar purposes. All virtues when carried to extremes degenerate into folly or vice, so bathing in the days of the Roman Empire, became immoderate and degenerated into enervating luxury and unbridled debauchery, in which indiscriminate bathing of both sexes was one of the demoralizing features.

The bath was usually taken after exercise and before the principal meal, which rule holds good to-day, as the very best and proper time. The gorgeous splendor of the *Thermæ*, which was a palatial edifice constructed by Agrippa, was adorned with beautiful statues and fine paintings, while luxuriant green foliage of great variety formed enchanting bowers of fairy splendor. This was thronged by the Roman citizens for the pleasures of gymnastic exercises and bathing.

In those countries which have adopted the religion of the Arabian prophet, Mohammed, people bathe as a part of their devotions, and a religion which has for a part of its ritual the washing of the body, goes a great way towards cleansing the spirit.

Among the Northern nations the introduction of the bath dates back to the period of the Crusaders, although *Tacitus* speaks of the river bathing of the Germans, which was one of the strengthening methods employed by the early Saxons. That filth and dirt generate crime and moral depravity seems to be apparent, where squalid misery has dulled the sensitiveness to unwholesome surroundings.

Sanitary science has also demonstrated that filth is the most fruitful source of diseases that are called infectious, because their origin is due to germs of the lowest forms of vegetable life. The brightest page in the medical history of the nineteenth century is that which records the discovery of these micro-organisms as the cause of such diseases as septicæmia or blood poisoning, pyæmia, diphtheria, tuberculosis or consumption and others. All forms of fermentation and putrefaction are due to the presence of some germs, and upon this fact antiseptic surgery bases its scientific premises.

The germ theory of disease, like every new discovery, which supplants the accustomed and deeply-rooted theories of the speculative philosophers, met with opposition, criticism, ridicule and misconstruction, but the brilliant achievements of Lister and Koch have established its founders upon a pinnacle of fame, which promises to be an immortal monument to their genius, and not only in surgery has its beneficial influence been exerted, but the entire field of medicine has been enriched by the germ theory, which plays so formidable a part in the causation of many diseases.

The great boon that medical science will confer upon humanity, in the future, will not be so much in improved methods of treatment, as in the means and methods which medical science will devise for preventing disease. One ounce of prevention will always be worth a pound of cure. When we look back fifteen or twenty years, we must even now acknowledge that preventive medicine has accomplished greater results than curative measures, because the former can be made in the very nature of things *absolute*, while curative agents are only relative. Puerperal, or childbed fever, which is an *infectious disease*, was at times a pestilence, which destroyed women by the score, in maternity hospitals, or in certain neighborhoods, by the infection being carried by midwives or accoucheurs from house to house, yet no one had the least suspicion that it was possible to carry the germs of this disease under the fingernails of the attendant, or on the clothing or a syringe, or on some other little instrument, from one patient to another, and, indeed, there are a great many to-day who are practicing midwifery who are still ignorant of the importance of refined cleanliness.

But for this ignorance, there is no longer an excuse, because the infectiousness of this and other diseases is so positively established, and even the physical characteristics of the micro-organisms have become familiar to the microscopists. This knowledge of the causation of puerperal fever has been applied to the employment of preventive measures, so that this dreadful malady is becoming a rarity, particularly in countries where scrupulous care and cleanliness are enforced by governmental rules and regulations. I refer to this particular *fever*, because it is, to my mind, one of the most brilliant illustrations of the efficacy of preventive or antiseptic medicine.

There is a gynecological hygiene with which women should become familiar; it is based on the principle of antiseptic precautions applied to the daily lives of their sex. The object of this is to keep the body and reproductive organs that are exposed to contamination or infection from the outer world in the most refined and scrupulous cleanliness. The vaginal douche or syringe is as important an auxiliary to a refined woman's toilet case as her tooth brush, because the cleanliness of the genitals is as essential to the preservation of health and comfort, as the possession of a sweet breath and the preservation of the teeth. I am therefore convinced of the hygienic value of familiarizing little children with washing or sponging their external genitals; in a few years this will have become second nature, and they are thus protected for all future time from contracting diseases which have their origin in personal uncleanness. It behooves mothers to avoid all delicacy on this subject, so that their little ones may grow up with the sentiment that to the pure in heart all things are pure. It is false modesty and ignorance which degenerate into vice and excesses; the scientific truth is always pure and holy, because it is based on reason, while abnormal delicacy is only emotional, and is quite likely to shoot into the other extreme, namely, licentiousness.

As the world grows wiser, the physiology of the reproductive organs should form a part of its wisdom, and in proportion to this knowledge, will their functions become questions of sense, instead of sentiment and nonsense.

The vagina is a membranous canal. It is situated in the cavity of the pelvis, below and behind the bladder, and in front and above the rectum. Its direction is curved from before backwards and a little upwards; its walls are flattened and ordinarily in contact with each other. Its length is about four inches along its anterior wall, and an inch or two longer along its posterior wall. In introducing a nozzle of a syringe it must always be remembered, that the tube is to be introduced directly backward on a horizontal plane with the body in the erect posture; by attempting to introduce it directly upwards, you meet with resistance from the anterior wall of the vagina.

In this cavity the secretion is susceptible of decomposition, owing to the accessibility of air laden with germs, which excite fermentation. A day or two after the cessation of the menstrual flow, there still lingers a little blood in the cavity of the vagina; this becoming infected with the germs in the vagina, a decomposition is the result, which is recognized by an offensive smell. The naturally soothing and harmless secretion is now changed into an acrid, irritating fluid, which not only may cause an inflammation of the membrane of the vagina, but also excoriate the skin at the orifice of the canal.

Leucorrhœa, or what is commonly called *whites*, is the most distressing symptom of this condition. In the course of months or in some instances a few years, the inflammation spreads from the vagina to the mouth and lining membrane of the uterus. Inflammation of the endometrium or lining of the womb will excite another complication, the so-called ulceration, but more correctly termed *erosion*. Who will deny the usefulness of any advice that will teach girls or women to avoid all these diseases? It is all contained in the simple phrase, *Keep clean*. Young girls must be taught by their mothers or guardians, not only the necessity of keeping the external genitals clean by daily ablutions, but a few days after menstruation, upon the slightest indication of offensiveness, she must resort to the employment of the vaginal douche or syringe, so as to wash out the seeds of disease, that are rapidly multiplying themselves, and if allowed to remain will entail the consequences to which I have already referred.

As an antiseptic wash, there is nothing so simple, efficacious and healing, as a solution of borax in previously boiled water, that has been allowed to cool to the proper temperature, which is between 103 and 106 degrees Fahr., one teaspoonful of the powdered article to the half gallon of water, to be used as a rinsing for each time.

Directions for administering vaginal douches will be given elsewhere. The proper time of the day for the employment of the wash is always at bedtime; and once or twice a week is quite often enough in the majority of instances.

Married women are more exposed to infectious contamination than single ones, because they are constantly liable to have infectious microbes introduced into the vagina during the ordinary course of marital relations. Men, as a rule, are neither cleanly nor careful in their habits, and approach their wives without any thought of serious consequences in their sexual relations. I had a married woman under treatment for an offensive discharge from her vagina which I traced to her husband, thence to a suppurating wound on his horse, which the husband had under his treatment. This can happen, of course, only through carelessness. By getting some of the matter or pus on the fingers, which incidentally contaminates his person, or not washing and brushing the finger nails, the husband may directly convey the infection to his wife, and thus inaugurate, unconsciously, an inflammation of the vagina, which becomes complicated, as the primary disease is neglected, leading to inflammation of the womb and ovaries, and often to abscesses, that compromise not only the health but the life of the sufferer.

To preclude the possibility of *innocent* infection, between husband and wife, there is only one means of prevention, and that is a careful *toilet*, which thoroughly cleanses the bodies in general and the genitals in particular.

Another fruitful source of disease of women, in this country and to an alarming extent in Europe, to which the elder Martin of Berlin called the attention of the profession over thirty years ago, is the specific or gonorrhœal infection of wives by their unfaithful husbands. The number of poor women whose health has been irretrievably ruined, by their husbands having had illicit relations with lewd, diseased women, is only known to those who have made this class of diseases a special object of inquiry. I have nothing to do with the moral aspect of this question, but only with the physical suffering that such men inflict upon their innocent wives and the mothers of their children, for the brief indulgence of libidinous pleasure. To think that any man would take the chances of making his wife a suffering and perhaps incurable invalid, just for the purpose of gratifying temporary animal passions, is to place him beneath the brute creation, which has not the intelligence to reason on the fearful consequences. No man who has been guilty of illicit relations should return to his wife until seven days have elapsed, and even not then until he has repeatedly washed himself by means of a syringe with some cleansing or disinfecting fluid, like borax water, or, what is preferable, a weak solution of the bichloride of mercury.

The wife and mother who entertains the slightest suspicion, must insist upon these precautions, and then not neglect to thoroughly wash and cleanse herself in the manner previously referred to. It is the height of hypocrisy to be mealy mouthed on this subject; the wives and mothers who are fortunate to have husbands beyond suspicion, should learn that some of their sisters have dangers to encounter and heartaches to suffer, with which their own lives are not marred, but perhaps the lives of their daughters may be; for the unhappy woman who becomes the wife of the blear-eyed sensualist, there is only one relief, and that is education in these subjects.

I know of no disease in which a correct and early diagnosis or recognition is of greater importance to avoid the frightful consequence and serious complications, than this one. It begins with a mild vaginal catarrh, which, when it is as yet locally confined to the vagina, can be easily cured. In course of time it spreads itself along the vaginal tract to the cavity of the womb. When it gets there, the treatment becomes more complicated, and for this reason; in order to reach the disease now, the cavity of the womb must be dilated, and this is an operation which the average physician can only accomplish in a bungling and imperfect manner. But even in this stage of the disease, in the hands of a skillful physician, the course of the disease can be checked and the patient readily cured. When the disease gets beyond the womb, when it invades the Fallopian tubes and the ovaries, the picture has entirely changed.

The organs affected are then inaccessible to local treatment, so that the disease invariably continues until the organs are more or less destroyed by inflammation, which results in the tissues breaking down into an abscess. In this stage of the disease it has become quite the fashion to operate in this class of cases, offering as an excuse a sure and speedy cure. Here I would interpose a word of warning to sufferers belonging to this class, not to be too willing to comply with surgical methods, because I know from careful observations, that promises of this nature end often in disappointment and death, while an intelligent conservative treatment can only disappoint but never kill, and with patience and perseverance in the application of electricity and hygienic rules of health, a cure is almost certain. The sick in body and mind are often beguiled into operations of a very serious nature, which are entirely unnecessary, because better results can be accomplished by other methods of cure, in which the possibility of a fatal termination is excluded.

Some women feel tired and languid from morning until night; they feel as tired in the morning when they get up as they were in the evening when they retired. If we tell them that it is entirely due to negligence of their own persons in not using vaginal washings regularly, they will undoubtedly feel surprised. In the great majority of these cases, this is owing to putrefactive changes going on in the cavity of the vagina. In the process of fermentative decomposition, the so-called *ptomaines* are developed; these are chemical poisons, which are absorbed into the blood, and by their depressing influences on the nervous system are the cause of the weakness and tired feeling. There are no remedies which, when taken into the stomach, will do the slightest good for this condition, and it is a waste of both time and money to expect relief from drugs.

This can easily be remedied by cleanliness, so that the secretions are not long enough retained in the vagina, to decompose and develop these ptomaine poisons.

During and after confinement is another important time for the employment of vaginal washes. The *lochial discharge*, which is one of the ordinary accompaniments of the newly-delivered woman, is a discharge from the uterus, which continues for several days, growing less and less, for a few weeks, when, in a normally healthy state of affairs, it should cease entirely. The lochia is the oozing from the mouths of the blood-vessels of the womb where the placenta or afterbirth was attached, together with the passing off of the old lining membrane of the womb, while the organ is returning to its original condition. At first the discharge is bloody, and it may retain this character for two or more days after delivery; then the color is changed, partaking more or less of a watery nature and presenting a yellowish hue; it then becomes whitish and ultimately ceases altogether. After the first four or five days the lochial discharge often becomes very offensive; this is a sign of putrescence or decomposition, and the only remedy in this, as in all other similar instances, is to wash the vagina thoroughly with borax water, or with a preparation for which a prescription will be given further on.

In every case of delivery, the mouth of the womb is more or less torn or lacerated; this is unavoidable, and it is generally harmless. One of the surgical humbugs is to sew or stitch, or attempt to stitch, these little harmless tears together, not of course for the good it will do the patient, because she is more likely to be injured by this meddlesome surgery, but to make a business and a fee. The common practice of these and kindred surgical expedients is one of the crying evils of an overcrowded profession which is trying to keep itself employed at all hazards.

The vagina also receives more or less injury during an ordinary confinement; if the midwife or the doctor is too meddlesome or in too big a hurry to get through, he will use the forceps, which simply means, to pull the child out and through the vagina, before nature has had time to dilate or stretch the parts sufficiently, to allow the child to pass through the maternal organs without injuring them. As a result of this brutal haste, frightful lacerations are incurred, which require immediate attention, but small lacerations heal without any further treatment than to keep clean.

After every confinement there is considerable sore or raw surface, with which the offensive discharge comes in contact, to become readily absorbed or taken up into the system, giving rise to fevers or inflammations of the womb and other pelvic organs. If one has a wound on any part of the body, the first thought would, or rather should, be to keep it clean; exactly the same treatment is required for wounds of the womb and vagina.

When the discharge becomes offensive, it also becomes dangerous and poisonous, and the only and proper thing to do is to thoroughly wash out the entire vaginal cavity until all offensive smell has disappeared. The only sure sign that anyone can have of the completeness and thoroughness of the vaginal washings, is that there is no longer any fetid or offensive smell perceptible.

It requires no particularly trained nurse or expert to administer a cleansing vaginal injection, yet it is more likely to be done in a bungling, inefficient manner than in a proper workmanlike manner; for this reason, it would be well to remember a few of the necessary details of carrying out the douching. In the first place, the room in which the vaginal douche is administered must be comfortably warm, so as to preclude the possibility of chilling the patient; the windows or any other opening liable to cause draft must be closed. The nozzle of the syringe, whether it be a fountain or a family syringe, must have been thoroughly brushed and cleansed with soap water, before and after each use; if the instrument is old, or has been used for questionable purposes, or, perchance, made the rounds of the neighborhood, it had better be thrown into the ash barrel, and an entirely new syringe, the "Alpha," be employed, which, by its sure and continuous stream, I consider the most suitable female syringe. The bulb of a syringe must be compressed in the palm of the hand slowly and deliberately.

The position of the patient is of considerable importance; a vessel is placed under her, which is carefully adjusted, so as not to tip too far backwards, otherwise it will overflow and drench the bed or the patient's clothing. Beneath the small of her back a few extra pillows are placed, and thus she comfortably reclines on her back, while the attendant manages the disinfecting wash and syringe, placed in a basin between her thighs. Half a gallon of the fluid is usually sufficient. The temperature of the wash is very important and may range between 103 and 106 degrees Fahrenheit.

The recumbent position is only intended for women who are confined to their beds; others, who are around and about on their feet, can sit comfortably over a chamber, on the edge of a low chair, having the vessel underneath them, and the wash of course in a separate basin. In the course of my experience I have been called to mothers, five to eight days after delivery, who were in a raging fever, presumably from the ptomaines which had developed in the vagina and poisoned the blood. After a few vaginal injections, sometimes after the first, the fever subsided entirely. These remarkable results we owe to the *antiseptic* treatment of disease, and when it once becomes generally known that this is only another word for cleanliness, infectious diseases will grow correspondingly less, and the cure for those that exist will be less experimental and more reliable.

CHAPTER VI
MARITAL EXCESSES AND
PREVENTION OF CONCEPTION

In a previous chapter, the physiology of conception was explained, and it was shown to be an organic function, independent of and remote from the sexual act, and over which the parties to the act have no control. From this scientific statement of the actual fact, it becomes at once apparent that conception or pregnancy may result without natural sexual congress, by simply injecting the sperm of the male, by means of a uterine syringe, into the womb of the female, while she is in a state of unconsciousness. It is also quite probable that a criminal conspiracy of this nature could be carried out, without any violation to the delicate anatomy that is involved in the natural process; a detailed account of all the probabilities which the ingenuity of a scientifically-trained mind could devise, belongs more properly to the department of medical jurisprudence. It is, however, of sufficient general importance that the reader should have at least an idea of the door that has been unlocked through physiological researches.

What we are at present endeavoring to make clear is, the great distinction and difference between *coition* and fecundation or conception; while one is but the result of the natural instinct aroused by the senses, the other reaches out into the realm of the Creator. When man undertakes to destroy the product of conception, he has interfered with the prerogative of God and is guilty of murder.

The question may now naturally arise in the minds of pure and morally-disposed persons, whether there is any time, without doing violence to God's law, that the children of men have the moral right to control, or regulate, the procreation of the human race? If I answer the question in the affirmative, I will then proceed to inquire into the ways and means to that end, and also into the pernicious methods that are employed, to accomplish this result.

It is true, that the Divine command was to be fruitful and multiply, but before this command was given, man was a free agent and a reasoning being, which implies that he is after all to be the judge as to the degree in which this command is to be carried out. That is, that there are mitigating and qualifying circumstances, which man has not only a right to consider, but which he is expected to take into account in propagating the species, by virtue of his reasoning faculties.

If this command were absolute and universal, chaste celibacy would be a cardinal sin, yet it has always been held by the canons of spiritual growth and morality, to be a Divine virtue, and even the loving Jesus knew not woman, because the forces that are thus expended will exert their power in other directions and towards developing powers of a higher order.

I believe that a moral code, which is too exacting to be observed by the average person, fails to accomplish the restraint or reform that is desired, so that, after all, it becomes essential to lay down such rules as the average men or women can follow as guides for their actions. A reformer, who starts out with the broad declaration that it is immoral to take human life, and a murderous act to destroy a half-formed human being in its mother's womb, and that it is equally murderous to prevent the recent products of the sexual act from becoming a viable being, fails to make the impression he desires. The first half of the proposition neutralizes the second of its sacred essence, in placing on the same level the organic function of conception and the animal function of the sexual act.

This view is so manifestly absurd to the person of even ordinary perception, that I feel assured, that it would neither lessen feticide nor sexual excess.

Spermatozoa on the one hand, and the ova of the female on the other, are, even in the natural and uninterrupted course of nature, destined for destruction, for whenever the female menstruates, these ova are discharged, and whenever the male copulates, hundreds of spermatozoa are found swimming in the spermatic fluid, which in case there be no ripened ovum are nothing more than so much waste secretion. Both are a means to an end, and that end is the reproduction of the species. It appears to me a flight of fancy, from the sublime to the ridiculous, to assign to the sexual act the same importance as to the passive function of conception, and I believe that doctrines of this nature lack not only the least scientific support, but weaken any argument in favor of the moral or spiritual aspect, which alone raises the question of feticide from a social evil to a mortal sin.

Man is prompted by a powerful instinctive desire for the use of the sexual organs, that draws him involuntarily to the opposite sex, not for the continuance of the race, because the passion arises much oftener without the remotest thoughts of any fruitful results. I have the greatest regard for the life of the unborn child, yet I am far from agreeing with those who would stamp as libidinous every thought of the sexual instinct, that has not as its stimulus the procreation of the species. While the average man is in the flesh, he is an animal man, and there is no use of trying to make a spiritual saint out of flesh and blood, and when we do find that, we have a very exceptional and remarkable person. But what, as reasonable beings, we should do, is to bridle the animal passions with moral reins, so that we can stand up, in full-statured manhood, with the respectful approval of our own conscience, able to rise above the mere animal appetites, to the dignity of reasonable beings. This instinct, like other propensities, is excited by sensations, and these may originate either in the sexual organs themselves, or may be excited through the organs of special sense. In man the passion is most powerfully aroused by impressions conveyed through the sight or the touch. It often happens that localized sensations will excite the sexual desire of either sex, so that many cases of excessive sexual desire can be traced to some local disease of the genital apparatus: chief among the numerous causes that may be cited, is pruritus or local itch, erythema and active congestion of the womb and ovaries.

"This tendency cannot be regarded," says Dr. Carpenter, "as a simple passion or emotion, since it is the result of the combined operations of the reason, the imagination, and the moral feelings: it is in this engraftment of the physical or spiritual attachment upon the more corporeal instinct, that a difference exists between the sexual relations of man and those of the lower animals. In proportion as the human being makes the temporary gratification of the mere sexual appetites his chief object, and overlooks the happiness arising from spiritual communion, which is not only purer but more permanent, and of which a renewal may be anticipated in another world,—does he degrade himself to a level with the brutes that perish. Yet how lamentably frequent is this degradation." This quotation gives the entire physical and spiritual aspect of the question, by one of the most eminent physiologists of our time, so that in the natural course of our investigation we are led to inquire into the currents of thought, which would tend towards developing *moral restraint.*

Moral restraint means the restraint of the animal man by his spiritual or higher self; the *will* must possess its due predominance to exercise its determining power in curbing the passions of the one, and directing the course of the thought in the other.

The cold, calculating materialist, whose ideal is circumscribed by the laws that have been deduced from the phenomena of the material world, can scarcely appreciate the higher sentiments that are involved in this investigation, unless he becomes changed in thought and feeling to the things that are about him. To accomplish this result is hardly within the scope of this work. With the average man as we find him, my observation has taught me that it makes, after all, little difference, whether he believes in a spiritual nature or is avowedly materialistic. The great majority of men and women live, so to say, in the turbulent waters of their own passions, wafted hither and thither by the impulses of emotional excitement and instinctive desires. There is little or no hope for reform, if they have not sufficient force of character to cry halt, and stop to think a little upon questions which are to them of the greatest importance.

Marital excesses are the mainspring of so much disease, that ordinarily is attributed to quite different causes, that this chapter would be very deficient were I to omit to call the attention of my readers to this fact. The men on the whole are oftener the victims of the ill effects of unbridled lust than the women, which shows itself by violent and uncontrollable temper, in the one case, and stupid docility in the other: by a lean, hungry, nervous appearance, or a brutish, sanguineous obesity; extremes of the different temperaments and habits are but the natural outgrowth of the constitution inherent in each individual case.

Women, as a rule, are more passive, less amorous and more chaste in thought and feeling than men, and if we define emotion as an *idea* associated with pleasurable or painful feelings, women are, as far as appertains to their sexual nature, contrary to the generally-accepted opinion, much less *emotional* than men. Continence, among the unmarried women, is the rule, while among the men it is the rare exception; this is because her *will* is by nature stronger, while her *reason* is weaker, she intuitively arrives at conclusions that are her guide and saviour.

It is a prevalent idea among men that the marriage ceremony removes all restraint from the exercise of the sexual function; this not only neutralizes and destroys all sentiment of true love, which seeks for the happiness of the object it loves, but breeds hatred and contempt. To be permanently happy and mutually respectful, there must be love beyond the pleasure of gratifying the mere sexual instinct, there must be love in the realm of thought and a spiritual communion above the instincts of the flesh.

"Any warning against sexual dangers," says Dr. Acton, "would be very incomplete if it did not extend to the excesses so often committed by married persons in ignorance of their ill effects. Too frequent emissions of the seminal fluid, and too frequent excitement of the nervous system, are in themselves most destructive. The result is the same within the marriage bond as without it. The married man and woman who think that because they are married, they can commit no excesses, however often the act of sexual congress is repeated, will suffer as certainly and as seriously as the unmarried debauchee, who acts on the same principle in his indulgences—

perhaps more certainly, from their very ignorance, and from their not taking those precautions and following those rules which a career of vice is apt to teach the sensualist. Many a man has, until his marriage, lived a most continent life; so has his wife. As soon as they are wedded, intercourse is indulged in night after night, neither party having an idea that these repeated sexual acts are excesses which the system of neither can bear, and which to the man, at least, is absolute ruin and to the woman a source of disease. The practice is continued till health is impaired, sometimes permanently, and when a patient is at last obliged to seek medical advice, he is thunderstruck at learning that his sufferings arise from excesses unwittingly committed. Married people appear to think that connection may be repeated as regularly and almost as often as their meals. Till they are told of their danger, the idea never enters their heads that they are guilty of great and almost criminal excess; nor is this to be wondered at, since the possibility of such a cause of disease is seldom hinted at by the medical man they consult. Some go so far as to believe that indulgence may increase these powers, just as gymnastic exercises augment the force of the muscles. This is a popular error, and requires correction. Such patients should be told that the shock to the system, each time connection is indulged in, is very powerful, and that the expenditure of seminal fluid must be particularly injurious to organs previously debilitated. It is by this and similar excesses that premature old age and complaints of the generative organs are brought on."

Wives of men of great vital force are not long before they become delicate, sickly and nervous, and, entirely ignorant of the real cause Of their feebleness, seek relief by taking "a good iron tonic," which does them about as much good as if they had left it alone, the tonic effect of iron being entirely overestimated, but the delusion is created by associating the word iron with the idea strength. After the different *tonics* have been tried, the patient consults a physician, who, on general principles and after a hasty examination, informs her that she has "womb disease." These two words for the time being settle the question; she now begins "to doctor," and from the general or family doctor she finds her way to the *female* specialists, who, as a rule, belong to the recognized magnifiers and humbugs of the day. Here she becomes one of the regular habitues of the specialist's waiting room, disappointed and not a little discouraged. She makes the rounds of the most prominent of them, until she has been doctored out of her dear patience and her still dearer money. Hope is often a forlorn consolation, and if by chance she now takes a trip to the country or undertakes a long visit at some distance, to her folks, which gives the poor woman respite from the "marital rights" of her Lord and Master, she recovers her former health, strength and buoyancy. Of course everybody congratulates her upon the wonderful effect of the climate, when the climate had no more to do with her recovery than the moon. The remarkable change was owing to having been let alone by husband and doctor.

That the attempt to call attention to these flagrant abuses of the dishonesty and ignorance of the one and the blind animal instinct of the other will be decried and stigmatized as "cranky," I know beforehand, but I know also, that those who criticise these sentiments are fully convinced of the truth of the statement. The diseases that belong to this class are, like most uterine diseases, of an inflammatory nature, and for that reason *rest* is one of the most essential features in the treatment. But as this class belongs to the avoidable causes, prevention is much better than cure. I therefore advise, as of first importance, to abandon the American custom of man and wife occupying the same bed, which is only customary among the poorer classes of Europe, who cannot afford to have separate beds or chambers. The advantage of the European custom in segregating one's self on retirement, to avoid the sexual instincts being unduly excited, can be borne out by remembering the physiology of the instinct, which we were told is excited by sight and feeling. Besides these, there is the possible undue familiarity, which the joint occupancy of the chamber or bed of man and wife may engender, and that, too, is likely to lead to excessive relations.

All efforts to exercise voluntary control, by prolonging the sexual act or extending the venereal orgasm, are fraught with the most pernicious results to the nerves, terminating in a partial or complete paralysis of the different organs of the body, or a low grade of inflammation is excited, which offers a fruitful soil for the development of various diseases.

A man who has become the husband of a woman should never cease to be a gentleman on that account, nor should he become lost to a consideration of those delicacies of refinement, which smooth the common relations in the exercise of daily duties.

Continence is the complete restraint from sexual indulgence, which in its fullest sense does not apply to the married state, but it comes within the scope of every married life to cultivate and practice it as one of its virtues. Every married couple should be continent for days and weeks at a time, and when one or the other is not feeling well, abstinence should be practiced, as the rule, not only to avoid a nervous shock, which may have serious results, but because conception in an abnormal physical condition, will perpetuate itself in the child, which is quite likely to inherit a nervous or sickly constitution. When pregnancy supervenes, undue sexual excitement of the mother often has the most serious consequences to the fetus, and may result in its death, or induce abortion.

Diet is to be regulated, to assist a firm determination to lead a chaste and purer life. Stimulating and highly-seasoned food, and alcoholic beverages, are not to be used, because they increase the circulation of the blood and stimulate the nerves to inflammatory activity. Meat should be eaten only once a day, and the supper should be bland and light.

Nature has set a time during which continence should be practiced for the purpose of preserving the health and controlling the reproductive function, that is, the menstrual period. Menstruation in women corresponds to the ripening and discharge of the human ovule. The aptitude for impregnation is a day or two before and six to eight days after the courses cease. This is a rule which applies to the great majority of women, and if the sexual relations are suspended from a few days before the onset of the menses until six or eight days after the flow has ceased, the chances for pregnancy are reduced to the minimum. This physiological relation of the organic function of conception to the sexual act is to be recommended as the most wholesome check to reproduction in early married life, although I believe that there is no time better calculated to raise a family than while you are young and hopeful.

Children are common objects of love and hope for both parents. Life and health are ever changing the relations of our surroundings, and when newly-married people put off to the dim future the hopes of rearing a family, they are often doomed to everlasting disappointment. Nature is capricious and jealous of her prerogatives, and those who trifle with her functions must expect to be frustrated in the end, and have no one but themselves to blame if she fails to respond to their capricious wishes. Children make trouble of course, so were we as troublesome in our time, but there is also a great deal of pleasure in watching them grow from day to day in bodily strength and mental perception, which no amount of selfish enjoyment can compensate.

The diseases that are brought upon women by the different practices and mechanical devices to prevent conception are too numerous to mention in a work of this character. Some of the methods are absolutely loathesome to all sense of decency and reduce sexual intercourse much below the instinctive indulgence of the brute; these debauches of the conjugal bed not only sap the vitality of the participants, but must lower or destroy all mutual respect, and ultimate in dissension and strife, which the divorce court will finally assuage.

Referring to the practice of conjugal onanism or interrupted or incomplete coitus, Dr. Franklin Devay says: "However, it is not difficult to conceive the degree of perturbation that a like practice should exert upon the genital system of woman by provoking desires which are not gratified; a profound stimulation is felt through the entire apparatus; the uterus, Fallopian tubes and ovaries enter into a state of orgasm, a storm which is not appeased by the natural crisis; a nervous super-excitation persists. There occurs, then, what would take place if, presenting food to a famished man, one should snatch it from his mouth after having thus violently excited his appetite. The sensibilities of the womb and the entire reproductive system are teased for no purpose. It is to this cause, too often repeated, that we should attribute the multiple *neuroses*, those strange affections which originate in the genital system of women. Our conviction respecting them is based upon a great number of observations. Furthermore, the normal relations existing between the married couple undergo unfortunate changes; this affection, formed upon reciprocal esteem, is little by little effaced by the repetition of an act which pollutes the marriage bed; from thence proceed certain hard feelings, certain deep impressions, which, gradually growing, eventuate in the scandalous ruptures of which the community rarely know the real motive." This is in every respect as hurtful as the vicious practice of solitary vice, although that is comparatively less common among young virgins than among those of the opposite sex. Nevertheless, this is a frequent cause of hysterical symptoms and uterine disease. Stop it at once; there is no burden that a large family of children can impose upon you, be it even poverty and want, as great as the inevitable results of these unnatural habits.

The use of caps or tissue coverings, made of thin rubber or gold-beater's skin, are not only suggestive of the licentiousness of the brothel but their employment causes physical lesions from their irritating friction to the walls of the vagina. I have had under my treatment obstinate ulcerations of the vagina which were due to their use, and in one instance it degenerated into cancer. The use of the "womb veil," which originated in France, has been denounced as a fruitful source of ulceration of the womb, by modern French writers, who are more familiar with their indiscriminate employment than Americans. There has been also a plug or stem pessary employed for the purpose "of sealing up the womb," which is partly introduced into the mouth and cervical canal of the organ; this obviously adds insult to injury, by also irritating the cavity of the womb and exciting inflammation of its lining membrane. There are other devices for a similar purpose, that have the same tendency of irritating and wounding the genitals of the female.

There is nothing that could be said, to intimidate some women, by forewarning them of the danger of their preventive measures; they will continue to make business for the specialists, and drain the purses of their husbands, but there is a great majority of good, noble, matronly women who are pure in heart and mind, that appreciate the value of the information that I impart. What I desire to further suggest, is a preventive measure that is entirely harmless and consistent with chastity and cleanliness, for I believe that within certain bounds, a woman has a moral right to limit or control the conception of her womb. But right here the option ceases. If she pushes her measures beyond the portals of the womb, if she employs medicines or mechanical devices to bring around her courses, when she suspects pregnancy or conception, she becomes a murderess in the eyes of the Creator. The bowl of tanzy tea, or any of the many quack nostrums, advertised in the public prints, are as much an instrument of murder as the *probe* of the abortionist. It would be the height of sophistry to make a distinction between the embryo of an hour or a day old, and that of any future period. The potentiality of a human being is established at the moment of conception, and the destruction of this, at any period, is homicide. No one can deny less importance to the cause, which is conception, than to the effect, which is the human embryo, for without the one, the other is impossible.

Hence, not to bear a child implies not to conceive a child, for if once conceived, it must be born.

The reasons that may exist for limiting the progeny of each particular pair cannot be formulated into a code, for these are questions of conscience, between the individuals and their Creator, on the one hand, and on the other, they should be influenced by economic conditions and physical or constitutional taints of the progenitors. I do not believe in the truth of the law of Malthus, that there is a tendency for population to increase faster than the means of subsistence, but I am inclined to the view held by John Stuart Mill, that "no one has a right to bring children into life to be supported by other people." But when the same eminent authority designates the procreative act as brute instinct, I think he is in great error, for that is not so. Conjugal affection and the sentiment of love spring from the reproductive systems, through the reflex action of the brain, and these have their moral significance, and should not be branded as brutal, for upon their normal functions depends the perpetuation of the race, and as it was so ordained by the Creator, it cannot be an unholy passion.

To be physically strong and well are the prerequisites for happiness, and if we cannot transmit to our offspring this essential quality, it would be much better for society if we were not instrumental in bringing defective children into the world. The competitive struggle for existence is hard enough for the vigorous and robust; how much greater must it be for the constitutionally infirm? When these conditions of infirmity exist, they should influence our course as progenitors; this appears to me self-evident, and I trust in the wisdom that is innate to the human soul, that only the best ends will be subserved.

An expedient that is to accomplish the object in view, must be in the nature of a wholesome sanitary measure, that violates no law of nature. The inordinate use of any preventive, coupled with excessive indulgence, cannot be without ill effects. Excesses must be studiously avoided, so as not to incur the diseases of which mention has already been made. The employment of a vaginal douche of the proper temperature, medicated with a little pure alcohol, is not injurious and is the most reliable of all preventives, provided it is intelligently used and without delay. The quantity of fluid to be used is a *quart* of warm water, of 103 to 105 degrees Fahr., to which two tablespoonfuls of alcohol is added; of this, three-fourths or all is to be douched through the vagina.

The vaginal irrigation is to be undertaken immediately after the act; if sufficient time is allowed to pass, the spermatozoa will have entered the mouth of the womb; then they are clearly beyond the reach of the wash. The warm water and the necessary paraphernalia are to be held in readiness so as to lose no time in making the toilet, nor should there be unnecessary exposure to the danger of catching cold. The nozzle of the syringe should always be of hard rubber, because that is not likely to rust or corrode. The syringe is to be kept scrupulously clean by means of occasional brushings in soapy water. Vaginal injections should never be taken in the morning, if the person is required to exercise on her feet, and for the same reason, should any husband have marital relations with his wife before rising in the morning, the wife is likely to suffer all day, either by soreness or pain or by a dragging sensation of the womb and vagina.

The same rule is to be followed in vaginal irrigation as for other purposes, the main point being to throw the fluid well up into the vagina, and that can only be done if the nozzle is carried directly backward and not upwards. No violence or force is to be used, under any circumstance.

CHAPTER VII
CRIMINAL ABORTION OR FETICIDE

I have so far endeavored to give a cursory description of *avoidable* causes, which were inadvertantly or thoughtlessly encouraged, and it is to be hoped that my friendly reproof and counsel will incite my readers to modify their pernicious habits and direct the currents of their thoughts into channels more or less in harmony with the hygiene that I have been at liberty to suggest.

There are few persons, if any, who would voluntarily act and think in a manner that would be prejudicial to their physical or moral welfare, if they were educated to a standard of knowledge that gave them an insight into the evil consequences. The law of *self-preservation* is innate in our natures, so that we are ready to cultivate the good and useful and shun that which may do harm.

Among the avoidable causes there is none so prolific of disease as that which is traced to the premature expulsion of the ovum or fetus from the mother's womb.

This appears self-evident, when we stop to consider that the function of reproduction is at once by far the most complicated of the physiological processes of the female economy, so that its sudden interruption will naturally induce any one or all of the physical or pelvic ailments which we are called upon to discuss.

For our purpose it will not be sufficient to consider the subject from a medical standpoint alone, because the thoughts drift involuntarily, as it were, from the physical into the metaphysical, from the material into the spiritual part of our nature.

It is not within the scope of this work to enter upon an inquiry into the scientific evidence of the existence of the soul or advance any argument whatever in support of that doctrine, but I assume the existence of an immortal soul to be a fact.

What I will endeavor to explain is when and where this mystic union of the soul with the body takes place? Here the speculations of the medical philosophers have been contradictory, on account of attributing to the fetus different kinds of life, that is, an organic or vegetating existence attached to the mother's womb, and as such not possessed of sentient principle, until the real or spiritual life imbues the fetus, when it becomes a living soul.

Hippocrates, the most famous physician of antiquity, who, even in the light of the nineteenth century, looms up as one of the most brilliant intellects that the world ever had, lent the weight of his judgment to this very unreasonable doctrine.

He supposed that animation occurred from thirty to forty-two days after conception.

The Stoics went still further and maintained that there was no vitality until after birth and the establishment of respiration.

The Academicians were of the opinion, that life was imparted to the fetus during the period in which the mother carried it in the womb, but they could not agree on the time when it began. Even the Roman Church, which, in the main, is right on this question, speaks of *animate* and *inanimate* fetuses. When it is remembered that there was no scientific physiology upon which the ancients based their opinions, it is not at all surprising that, in the light of modern research, they are shown to be all wrong.

There is no time during the child's sojourn in the mother's womb that life is less active than at another, and any opinion to the contrary is manifestly absurd and unscientific.

I appreciate the distinction between *physical life,* or vital activity, and spiritual life, but the one must necessarily be in the other.

A central fountain of physical force is consistent with scientific deductions, and physicists are inclined to admit such a source. Many of the phenomena of the material world are explained upon this hypothesis. The sun is supposed to be that central fountain of physical force which inspires activity in matter on this planet. Matter in itself is inert and motionless; the globe we inhabit has no energy in itself which could keep it in motion, but the forces playing on and around it impart to it its motive power.

The life of any complex organism, such as that of man, is in fact the aggregate of the vital activity of all its component parts, and each elementary part of the fabric has its own independent power of growth and development. If we contemplate the history of the life of a plant, we perceive that it grows from a germ or seed to a fabric, sometimes of gigantic size,—it multiplies its species, by the production of germs similar to that from which it originated. This it performs without feeling or thinking or any effort of its own. All the functions of which its life is composed are grouped together under the general designation of organic functions, or vegetative life.

In the building up of the animal structure we have precisely the same operations taking place, one minute cell added to the other, like the stone mason running up a brick wall, each brick representing a cell, until the structure is completed.

The question that we are particularly interested in is whether this "animal life" which stimulates the growth of the fetus from its first inception, can be any the less sacred at one time than at another?

There is a general impression among a large portion of the community that the fetus first becomes endowed with life at the period of quickening, which is between the fourth and fifth month of pregnancy. The time when the mother first feels the motion is considered the period when the child becomes animated, that is, when it receives its spiritual nature into union with its human nature.

The English law recognized the truth of this infamous doctrine, in varying the punishment of an attempt to procure abortion according to whether the woman be "quick with child or not," and in delaying execution when a woman can be proved to be so, though the execution is made to proceed, if she be not "quick," even if she be unquestionably pregnant. This was a most barbarous penal provision and hardly excusable in a savage nation, much less among a Christian people, because it is contrary to all fact, to all analogy, to reason, and at variance with biological science.

If the embryo or fetus is simply an animal growing in the mother's womb, until the period of quickening or birth, it would not be a crime to procure an abortion, at any time, before these events take place. No sacrifice of a human life would be involved, so that the act would be simply a "misdemeanor" regulated by the degree of injury which the mother sustained as a result of the operation. This was the prevailing opinion for many centuries, until, in the year 692, the Roman Empire so amended its law that the procuring of an abortion at any time during the period of gestation was *homicide*, murder, to be punished with death.

France patterned after the Roman law for a time and made criminal abortion punishable by inflicting the death penalty; during the French revolution this law was amended by imprisonment for life; and later, under Napoleon, in 1810, the law was again changed, and the punishment lessened.

In England there has been a gradually growing moral sentiment to protect the defenseless child in its mother's womb, so that to-day England has so amended her law that the fetus has the same protection in the uterus before as after quickening, so that a conviction for the procurement of criminal abortion at any time during gestation from conception until birth is *felony* and punished by imprisonment or transportation.

In Germany the law makes abortion a State prison offense, and public opinion is in such a healthy state there that anyone justly accused of this crime is quite sure to meet with a punishment.

In America legislation on this subject differs widely in the different States. In Massachusetts the barbarous distinction, "before quickening and after," was still recognized a few years ago, so that the crime of abortion before quickening was not an indictable offense. In some of the States the laws are stringent and conform with the physiological facts of fetal life, but, like most of our "good laws," they are. observed only in the breach.

The essential peculiarity in the process of reproduction is the absorption of a small cell of the male, the spermatozoon, by another small cell of the female, the ovum. This coalescence of the two, *male* and *female* cells, is the fertilization of the ovum, and constitutes *conception*.

The spermatic fluid of the male holds in suspension a large number of very small bodies, or cells, which, from their usually remaining in active motion for some time after they have quitted the human body, have been erroneously considered animalcules. A more thorough familiarity with these bodies, and careful microscopic examinations, can distinguish nothing in the nature of structure within them. They are simply little oval, flattened, transparent cells between the one-six-hundredth and one-eight-hundredth of an inch in length, having a little thread-like "tail," gradually tapering to a fine point.

These measurements make the spermatozoa considerably larger than the average red blood-corpuscle, which is one-thirty-two-hundredths of an inch in diameter.

The spermatic fluid of a single emission of a healthy male contains thousands of these little ciliated cells, the cilia or tails of which are seen in an active vibratile undulatory motion, in the field of the microscope, wriggling hither and thither, like a school of frightened fishes. This lashing motion is continued for hours, and under favorable circumstances for days. In the cases of microscopical examinations of vaginal secretions of married women, for causes of sterility, I was able to establish their activity thirty-six hours after marital relations.

Through this peculiar lashing motion the ciliated cells are propelled onward and upward, through the mouth and cervix of the womb, thence along its body to the openings of the Fallopian tubes, along which they migrate to the ovaries of the female. In a healthy condition of the female generative organs, hundreds of spermatozoa arrive at the ovaries about the same time, a few hours or days after copulation, but as the ova ripen and are discharged only at regular intervals, the hundreds of ciliated bodies that travel thither are doomed to disappointment, and gradually lose their vitality, and perhaps are removed by absorption.

Of all these hundreds of germs it requires only a single one to combine with an ovum, or a similar little cell of the female, to constitute conception. When this combination has been accomplished, a new being is inaugurated, another human soul is started out, by the magic wand of nature, to go through the different spheres of evolution, of whose ultimatum we can have no clear conception, but this is perfectly clear, that after this coalescence of the two germs, the die is cast and the female becomes then only the vehicle in which the creative forces are effecting their elaboration.

Coition and conception are widely different processes, and require to be separately analyzed to be understood.

Coition is always a physical act, a gratification of the senses, and, like many other human passions, is often abused by excessive indulgence, degenerating into lust.

Conception, on the other hand, is purely passive, an organic function, without consciousness on the part of the female.

Thus far there is a similarity in the organic processes of conception in all mammalia, so that their embryos cannot be classified and assigned to their respective species in the early stages of their development. Physiologists are unable to say whether the one belongs to and will ultimately develop into a brute animal or a human being, yet one has the attributes of mental force, the elements of a soul, while the other is to follow a blind instinct, without the possibility of spiritual perception. Conception, in the one case, is simply a vegetative or organic function, while in the other there is, in addition, a spiritual effort to individualize a human soul.

The creative energy of nature is separate and independent of the sexual act, for it does not take place during copulation of the sexes, nor immediately after it, but hours or days after the act is accomplished.

I am often called upon to say when and where the human soul becomes associated with the human body?

There is a divine life, or spiritual energy, that animates the soul from the spiritual realm. It is the correspondency of the physical force that animates the physical body.

The term or phrase which I employ to designate this force is of less importance than the definition which is given to it, and upon this, of course, we must agree. I recognize in such an energy or power, the primal cause or force, behind and beyond the phenomena of nature. This force must be universal and omnipresent, hence *spiritual*; it must be the central source of supply for all spiritual things, so that the doctrine of Paul is scientifically in harmony with a rationalistic view of the subject, when he says "in Him we live and move and have our being."

The science of the *conservation of forces* teaches, that forces are never lost, that they are indestructible and eternal. We derive our spiritual existence from this central spiritual sun and inherit the quality of eternity with it. Mind is spirit and the soul is mind; this is the view of Spinoza, who, in the second part of his work "Ethics," employs the terms synonymously throughout the chapter "Of the Nature and Origin of the Mind or Soul." Mind differentiates man from the inferior animal creations, and can make him what he will.

Professor Carpenter in his "Principles of Human Physiology," tells us, that when we first discern the primordial cell, which is to evolve itself into the human organism, we can trace nothing that essentially distinguishes it from that which might give origin to any other form of organic structure. The earliest stages of its development consist in simple multiplication of cells by "duplicative subdivision," so that a mass of cells comes to be produced, amidst the several components, of which no difference can be traced; and this also finds its parallel among the simpler organisms of both kingdoms. There is nothing at this period to distinguish the germs of man from that of any other vertebrated animal, yet in the course of nine short months a human being is developed possessing all the faculties of its progenitor, and how could all this come to pass, if not instituted at the moment of conception?

It is at this time and moment, that an *atom* of the universal spirit becomes separated and individualized, and the germ of a human soul is implanted, deep in the dark recesses of nature's laboratory. The ovum of the female and the germ of the male coalesce, imbued by the incarnation of the immortal spirit, and no time can be more opportune for that union than at the very inception of our being, because the soul and the body must interact, one on the other.

In the reproduction of man, there is a higher purpose than simply to multiply the species. The Creator can only manifest Himself, if he has intelligent souls or spirits as his creatures, and the reproduction of the human species is the natural means of bringing this about.

The mystic union is accomplished at the time and moment of conception, when a *unit* of the universal spirit becomes *individualized* into a human soul. In the dark recesses of the mother's womb the ovum of the female and the germ of the male, imbued by the immortal spirit, begin their growth and development together, this constitutes the *triune* of nature, from which the evolutions of body and soul take their beginning.

Sexual instinct is not an unholy and depraved action of the human mind, but the necessary means to an end, a finite instrumentality of the Divine mind to procreate the body, as an abode for the human soul. One of the attributes of the Creator is, in the very nature of things, *to create*, and he has thus endowed us, His creatures, for the manifestation of His creative power. He perpetually and eternally creates, and this has no reference to time, place or space: just as in the beginning, God created all things, so we recognize the supreme hand, now, to-day, and forever, ever active in His natural element.

The operation of nature's law may be contravened by the selfish, sordid, criminal acts of the human heart, but it cannot be frustrated. No one can console himself, that the invincible law of evolution is at the capricious behest of finite man, and can be neutralized and obstructed at will; that would place a limitation on the Creator; it would contradict the omnipotence of the Divine mind; it would place every life or soul at the mercy of the sordid conscienceless abortionist, and it would reduce the Divine origin of man and the soul's immortality to an absurdity.

After the fetus is murdered, its soul continues to grow in the spiritual realm, an undying witness of the criminal infamy which deprived it of that earthly experience which nature intended for the children of men. It is the greatest crime against nature to kill off a human fetus, and prematurely hurl into eternity a human soul, which has the same right to human experience as those already born, and, in the eyes of God, it is no less a crime than the murder of an adult.

> "Dust thou art, to dust returnest,
> Was not spoken of the soul."

The meaning of the term abortion is etymologically not to be born or not to be carried out, or, in other words, the premature expulsion of the fetus from its mother's womb, which is any time before it is capable of independent existence. This is according to the construction of the law of France, which means any time previous to the termination of the sixth month of pregnancy. Abortion may be accidental, that is, it may be due to a casualty which was entirely beyond the control of the person suffering or going through an abortion, or it may be due to disease affecting either the embryo or the mother.

The word "miscarriage" is generally preferred to that of "abortion" under the misconception that only the latter implies criminal culpability; this, of course, is an error, because each word means exactly the same thing, with this difference, that one is of Latin origin, while the other is a plain Anglo-Saxon term. An abortion that is brought about, from other than natural causes, for the deliberate and avowed purpose of escaping from the inconvenience, privation, and cares of maternity, is always qualified by the adjective *criminal*.

In the early months of pregnancy, it very seldom, though it occasionally does happen, that complications arise which place the life of the mother in imminent danger; that the embryo shares this danger in a corresponding degree is self-evident, because the fetus is unable to live independently of the mother any time before the expiration of the sixth month of gestation, so that the death of the mother means death to the fetus also.

Through a fall, heavy lifting, or a sudden jar, a partial detachment is liable to occur between the placenta of the fetus and the wall of the mother's womb, that being the place where the blood of the one is exchanged into the blood of the other; from this, a hemorrhage may result, which will not yield to rest nor to other means which experience has taught to be useful. This loss of blood may be so great that, if it continues, the life of both will be sacrificed.

In some women pregnancy may become complicated with convulsions; these may be so violent, and recur so often, as to threaten life, and they are obstinate to all medicinal resources.

Contingencies of the above nature evoked the scientific inquiry, whether abortions are ever justifiable. The answer must invariably be, that when it is clearly seen that the mother will surely die, and her fetus with her, an induced abortion becomes a justifiable obstetric resource, and under these circumstances it is not a crime nor even a sacrifice of the embryo, which would have perished with the mother.

This rule of practice has been endorsed by the very highest authority in obstetric science, and the competent conscientious physician will readily draw the line between cases where so radical a measure becomes necessary, and where milder conservative measures will save the life of both mother and child.

This cannot be a license for crime, except that the sordidly depraved time server may often try to stretch the threatening danger, but when this is done it is no less a crime of murder in the eyes of God, than if he had premeditatedly and willfully slain a fellow-being.

Such persons would not shrink from the perpetration of any crime, be it ever so heinous and black. These wretches are too cowardly to thrust a poniard into their victims on the highway, but ever ready to operate in secrecy in the abortion chamber, which is hidden from the eyes of man. I have known abortions being sought and abortions being committed, upon the flimsy pretext of being too weak, or too sick at the stomach. These are shallow subterfuges, that should not be countenanced by any conscientious practitioner.

Many reasons are either imaginary or pretended, and I have often proved the fallacy of pretensions of an inability to carry a child, after women had gone through the abortion mills, by persuading them to become reconciled, for the time being, and that I would see them through to a happy end, and in no case were their fears justified by subsequent developments. There is a great deal in controlling the minds of these women, and directing them into wholesome channels of thought, and after that they become much happier and contented than ever before in their married lives.

If the proposition is generally accepted, that abortions are justifiable as a therapeutical expedient, you open the door to the criminally inclined. Wily women will impose upon inexperienced practitioners by feigning physical suffering as a result of pregnancy, for the purpose of getting rid of their fetuses. There is a certain amount of hardship and discomfort associated with the average pregnancy for a part of the period at least, but this should be suffered with a mother's fortitude.

The testimony of the early canons of the Catholic Church is very decisive on the crime of abortion, namely, "that the destruction of the fetus in the womb of its parent, at any period from the first moment of conception, is a crime equal in turpitude to murder."

In Protestant countries abortions are on the increase, and in America it is one of the crying crimes of society, which has so thoroughly tainted and defiled the moral sense of American communities, that it has become next to impossible to get a jury of twelve men who will agree on a verdict to punish this dastardly foul crime of murder, and the abortionist is thus encouraged in his iniquitous vocation.

Professor J. Taber Johnson, of Maryland, stated in his annual oration before the State Medical Society: "The difficulty of conviction for producing abortion is shown in the statement of the Attorney-General of Massachusetts, that of thirty-two arrests and trials of abortionists in that State, in a period of eight years, not a single conviction resulted; and this fact is equally true of other States." This is indeed a sad commentary on the jury system, which often degenerates into a farce or travesty on justice.

The practice of abortion is on the increase. This is not due to a single cause, but to a number, operating separately or co-operating jointly to the same end. Boarding-house or hotel life exercises a pernicious influence on the habits and morals of women. They sit all day in their apartments with indifferent occupations, or walk the streets between meal hours, without the inspiring thoughts which a cozy home alone can inspire. The maternal instinct languishes or dies completely out, and if women become pregnant while transiently domiciled, they scruple not against committing this great crime, because their surroundings and accommodations may not be suitable for the changed relations which motherhood brings about. If these people had their own little homes, were they ever so humble, their minds would run in different grooves, their lives would be much happier and offspring longingly desired, to fill the nooks in the little household.

Want of domestic training in childhood lays the foundation for this crime. The American girl is trained with a view to display so-called refined accomplishments. This is done by totally ignoring domestic duties; these are to be shunned as menial and degrading; and when girls grow into womanhood and are married, they naturally look upon the ordinary household duties as drudgery, and quite unbecoming a woman of their attainments. There is nothing in their bosoms to arouse a pride in their homes; quite the reverse; that principle has never been inculcated in their youth, so that it is quite natural, that they hie to a boarding-house; here they patronize the abortionist, or acquire proficiency in that art themselves, from lack of nobler occupation.

Changed relations of the sexes destroy the maternal instinct. A man in a man's place, and a woman in the sphere for which God and nature intended her, is for the best interests of society. There is useful and profitable work for everyone, but each should labor in his or her respective field of natural adaptability, in which there is plenty to do. There is, in the very nature of things, never anything gained by a woman doing a man's work, because there are always plenty of men around to do that, but while a woman is doing a man's work, she is necessarily neglecting a woman's, which it is physically impossible for any man to do for her. There is, consequently, an irretrievable loss to society from misapplied labor. When the great Napoleon was asked by Madam de Stael whom he considered the greatest woman in France, his curt reply was, "She who bore the largest number of children." This is a tribute to motherhood, which no one can ridicule, for whom should we honor and respect more than the faithful, loving mother, who makes her life subservient to that of her children? There is no comparison between the self-denial of parental devotion and the devotee to amusements and fashion, or the slothful wife, who imposes sterility upon herself for the sake of pandering to depraved appetites and frivolous pleasures.

Depraved associates pave the way to feticide. Some married women are so brazen and callous, that they have no delicacy in narrating their exploits of child murder with a triumphant air, whenever their acquaintances are patient and foolish enough to listen to them. These gadding persons often contaminate the minds of newly-married women, who had never for a moment entertained the thought of such an awful crime, and who would have made happy and contented mothers, were it not for the seeds of discontent and crime which were sown in their early matrimonial career. I have known mothers who had lost the delicate maternal instincts, without which a mother becomes a monster, advise their daughters and encourage them in the perpetration of this crime.

Women of this type should be avoided like the dreaded mancanilla tree, for they poison the body and soul of pure, virtuous women, with whom they come in close contact; they should be shunned by the young housewife like a pestilence, because their hands are scarlet with the blood of their own children.

Unprincipled physicians are too often instrumental in abetting criminal abortions, and this for two reasons, namely, for the immediate lucre which is to them in hand paid, and also for ingratiating themselves into the confidence of their patrons, so that they may become their physician in other ailments. These are the pariahs of the profession, but, viewed from a business standpoint, they are very successful. It is through the looseness with which medical colleges are conducted in this country, many of them not deserving the name of college, but more properly denominated a rendezvous of self-constituted professors and ingenious advertising sharps, that the ranks of the profession are overcrowded, because there is no scrutiny of moral character or professional attainments. These once labeled M. D.'s are determined to make a professional living, and nothing deters them from becoming *particeps criminis*, but owing to the corrupt and depraved jury system such a thing as punishing a physician for feticide is hardly ever heard of. I would advise my readers to shun each and every one of these criminal monsters as they would a pestilence. In general, "female specialist" is but another name for abortionist, for the great majority of these self-constituted specialists do not know the rudiments of the science of gynecology; and women should exercise great precaution in whose hands they place themselves, or, rather, their lives. I know of no calling that is capable of rendering more good to humanity than the profession which I have made my own.

The honorable physician occupies a position where he can do a great deal to improve the tone and morality of the community. He can do more than the pulpit in preventing feticide, because he can depict the physical dangers and the moral turpitude, for it is to him that the deluded woman first goes for advice. It is with him to become an oracle of heaven; in the great majority of instances he can be instrumental in saving human life and prevent the mother from murdering her own child.

Maternity is the function of Divinity in human nature. Who can look upon a newly-born babe without seeing something truly Divine, a manifestation of the Divine mind to create in his image, through the instrumentality of man, an innocent human flower, planted upon this earth to enjoy the fullness thereof, and what miscreant shall deny it its inheritance?

That husbands are often the instigators of this crime is a fact well known to every physician of experience. I have known of a number of cases where wives came to my office with a woeful tale of discontent on the part of their husbands, who did not want an "*increase.*" Such men are not worthy the name of father or husband. They should have been emasculated before they ever approached the marriage altar, for they are below the brute creation and have no claim on human affections. The luxuries of life should not be considered as weighing against the birth of children, nor the expense of maintaining a large family considered as an excuse for feticide; expenses had better be reduced and economized in other directions, so as to meet the little extra increase, which the little stranger may cause. It is a fact, that among thrifty people, large families are no barrier to material success, for the blessedness of heaven rests upon them.

I invariably solicit an interview with the recalcitrant spouse, and take the opportunity to tell him of the responsibilities which married life imposes upon married couples; that the simple gratification of the carnal senses is lust, which can and should be controlled by every person, and more in particular by married men. Matrimonial relations based only on libidinous pleasure are transient and evanescent; incompatabilities arise, which cause conflict and dissension, ultimating in estrangement and divorces, but when soul is wedded to soul, then they are in harmony with the music of the spheres, and children constitute the cement of an eternal wedlock which no man can rend asunder.

Abrupt termination of pregnancy constitutes in itself a diseased process in the tissues of the womb. We have already learned of the gradual growth of the body of the womb to accommodate the growth of the child; when abortion takes place there is a sudden check to this growth in the tissues of the womb, and a low grade of inflammation invades the entire structure. This inflammatory process fixes or hardens the womb so that this acquired enlargement often becomes permanent. The result is, that women can often trace the beginning of a long series of complaints and a shattered constitution to a so-called miscarriage. For this reason, the after-treatment of an abortion is of much greater importance, than after a regular normal delivery.

After the close of a natural gestation, the child is born, and nature immediately sets to work to restore the womb to its healthy normal size. No violence having been done to the organ, there is no extra effort necessary on the part of nature to restore it. In a premature expulsion of the fetus, it is altogether different, the cell growth and the necessary physiological action to build up the womb, to house the rapidly-developing fetus, was suddenly interfered with, and the shock which the vital activity sustains, diverts their energies into a diseased process. Inflammation is to be guarded against, for it constitutes the root of all pathological conditions; chief among them is its prevention of fatty degeneration and absorption of the superfluous tissues of the organ, so that the womb remains heavy and enlarged. This entails a series of consequences; its size and weight may force it to occupy an unnatural and painful position, such as a falling of the womb or *procidentia*, or it may turn or even bend on itself into abnormal positions, called *versions and flexions*; these become obstinate to treatment in proportion to the time which elapses from the occurrence of the disease to the time when they fall under proper treatment.

Inflammations are limited sometimes to only portions of the organ; this may be to the lining mucous membrane of either the body or neck. It may also invade the entire organ and even extend to the neighboring tissues and ligaments. From the uterus along the Fallopian tubes to the ovaries inflammation may spread itself, causing abscesses in its wake and other complications which may require surgical skill of a special nature to give permanent relief.

Sterility is often the result of disease caused by abortion, and this should be another warning to thoughtless, giddy women, who desire no children in their early married life, because it would interfere with their regular pleasure rounds, and so resort to abortions, which will, in all probability, make them entirely unfit to ever become pregnant or bear children. I have made an attempt to impress on the reader two things; one of these is the flagrant violation of ordinary and simple rules of health, the other the enormity of the crime of induced abortions, and to accomplish this I have avoided screening the subject by employing ambiguous or finely-selected phrases, but have used plain terms which will not shock the pure or noble in heart and mind, but may the hypocritical, under the gauze of a false modesty.

PLATE I.

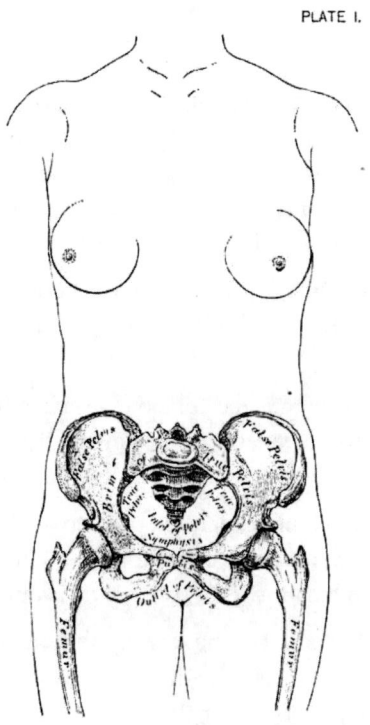

CHAPTER VIII
ANATOMY OF THE FEMALE ORGANS

The bony part of the skeleton which is of particular interest to women, is the pelvis, so called, because it forms a basin or cavity which contains the most important female organs of generation.

All the organs that are liable to the diseases of women, bear certain anatomical relations to the pelvis, so that the phrase, *pelvic diseases of women*, is often employed instead of the phrase, *diseases of women*, and pelvic surgery means also, surgical procedures, that may be employed for the relief or cure of these diseases.

In confinement, the pelvis again comes into more or less prominence, for when the diameters of the pelvic canal have not their normal measurements, there is likely to be an obstruction to the passage of the child into the world, so that mechanical means must be employed to overcome the obstacle. A broad pelvis in a woman is always a guarantee that there will be no insurmountable difficulty in the parturient act.

Plate I shows the shape and locality of the bone in the human body, and gives also an approximate idea of the relation of the pelvis to the rest of the body.

While the pelvis was referred to above as a basin or cavity, this is only partly true, for it is also a canal or passageway, through which the child is born. The pelvis is divided by a prominent line into the false and true pelvis.

The False Pelvis is all that expanded portion of the pelvic cavity which is above the rim or line that forms a circular ridge, which marks the beginning of the bony canal to which the term true pelvis is applied.

The True Pelvis constitutes the lower subdivision of the pelvic cavity. The circular ridge, which marks the division, constitutes also the *inlet* of the true pelvis, which is much smaller than the upper or false pelvis. Its walls are more perfect and their lower circumference is very irregular and forms what is called the *outlet*. Between the *inlet* and the *outlet* we have what is called the true pelvic cavity, in which the internal female generative organs are contained.

These organs are located in the following order from before backwards: first, behind the pubis there is the bladder, and behind this is the uterus, and thirdly and a little to the left is the rectum.

On each side of the womb, but also in the small or true pelvis, are the Fallopian tubes and ovaries.

In this order the anatomical relations are easily remembered, and I believe that every woman should make it an object to learn at least as much of her own anatomy as I have laid down; because there is just little enough, so as not to make it tiresome, and quite enough to insure intelligent reading in the subsequent chapters.

The points of differences between the male and female pelvis are entirely on the principle of adaptation to natural functions. The female pelvis has a broadness or greater prominence of the hips and a correspondingly greater pelvic cavity, while that of the male is altogether more massive.

Its cavity is deeper and narrower, and the muscular eminences and impressions on the surfaces of the bones are much stronger marked.

Plate II. This illustrates a cut or section, through the middle of the pelvis, from before backwards, so as to give a side view of the capacity of the true pelvis and of the organs that it contains. A careful study of this plate will permanently fix the anatomy in the reader's mind.

PLATE II.

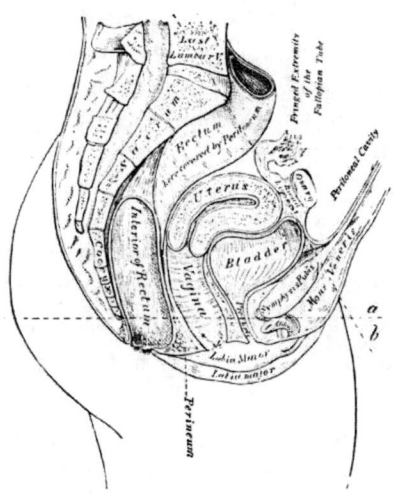

A Median Section of the female Pelvis and of the Organs that are centrally located.

This plate is anatomically correct; the uterus resting normally on and being elevated by the distended bladder.

The lines *a* and *b* show the planes of the inlet and outlet of the true pelvis, and it will be seen that within these lines the most important organs of the female are located.

THE BLADDER.

The bladder is situated at the anterior part of the pelvis. It is in relation, *in front* with the *symphysis pubis*, behind with the womb, some convolutions of the small intestines being interposed; its base lies in contact with the neck of the uterus and with the anterior wall of the vagina. The bladder is said to be larger in the female than in the male, and is very broad in its transverse diameter.

THE URETHRA.

The urethra is a narrow membranous canal, about an inch and a half in length, extending from the neck of the bladder to the external orifice. It is placed beneath the symphysis pubis, embedded in the anterior wall of the vagina, and its direction is obliquely downwards and forwards. Its diameter, when undilated, is about a quarter of an inch; behind the bladder and urethra, there is in regular order the uterus and vagina, and behind both of these, the rectum.

THE PERINEUM.

The Perineum is the muscular triangular body between the vagina and rectum; it constitutes a segment of the female pelvic floor; it is the *prop* for all the pelvic organs, and for that reason every woman should know precisely what it is, and study the plate carefully until she understands it. The skin covering it is of a dark color, thin and freely movable over the underlying parts. There is no part of the pelvic anatomy so vulnerable, because in confinement during the passage of the child's head into the world, the perineum is put on a great stretch, and if the delivery progresses too quickly or is hurried, then the tissues have no time to stretch themselves so as to accommodate the child's head, and they must naturally tear.

The awkward and officious use of instruments will do the same thing. I have seen the perineum torn asunder from this cause, from the vagina and back into the rectum.

Plate III is one of the most instructive drawings that I could devise. It gives the reader a practical illustration of the internal generative organs and their anatomical relations to each other. This was a drawing from my own dissection, and the clearness and artistic reproduction is due to the skill of the engraver, Mr. H. X. Van de Casteele, of this city.

THE VAGINA.

The vagina is a membranous canal, extending from the vulva or *introitus* to the uterus. It is situated in the cavity of the pelvis, between the bladder in front and the rectum behind; its direction is not in a straight line, but curved from below backwards and upwards. When distended it is cylindrical in shape, but naturally it is flattened from before backwards, so that its walls are ordinarily in contact with each other. In length it averages about four inches in its anterior wall, while its posterior wall describes a segment of a larger circle, that makes it between one and two inches longer. At its commencement it is constricted, and at its upper extremity, where it is attached to the womb, it is dilated, so as to surround the vaginal portion of the neck of the womb (*see* Plate III, *c*) this is a short distance above the mouth of the womb. The attachment extends higher up on the posterior than on the anterior wall of the womb, which makes the posterior lip of the womb longer than the anterior.

The mucous membrane is continuous above with that covering the vaginal portion of the uterus; below it begins at the vulva. Running longitudinally along the anterior and posterior walls are distinct ridges or raphe; these are the columns of the vagina.

The relations of the vagina to the neighboring organs can be studied to better advantage by referring to Plate I.

PLATE III

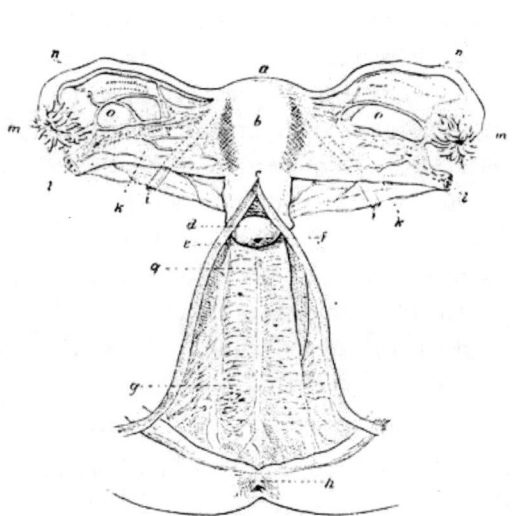

The Vagina slit open to the neck or Cervix of the Uterus, showing the insertion of the latter into the former.

From the author's own design, beautifully illustrating:—

a.	Fundus (or Base) of the Uterus.	*ii.*	Round Ligaments.
b.	Uterus' Body.	*kk.*	Broad Ligaments.
c.	Cervix, or Neck.	*ll.*	Uterine Vessels and Nerves.
de.	Vaginal part, forming the Anterior and Posterior Lips.	*mm.*	Fringed Extremity of the Fallopian Tubes.
f.	Mouth of the Womb.	*nn.*	Fallopian Tubes.
gg.	Interior of Vagina, illustrating the Vaginal Folds.	*oo.*	Ovaries.
h.	Perineum.		

Its anterior surface is concave, and is in relation with the base of the bladder and with the urethra. Its posterior surface is convex and connected to the anterior wall of the rectum for the lower three-fourths of its extent, the upper fourth being separated from the tube by a fold of the peritoneum, the *recto-uterine fold*, which forms a *cul-de-sac* between the vagina and rectum. Its sides give attachment superiorily to the broad ligaments, and inferiorily to the Levatores Ani muscles and recto-vesical fascia.

THE UTERUS OR WOMB.

The uterus is the organ of gestation, receiving the fecundated ovum in its cavity, retaining and supporting it during the development of the fetus, and becoming the principal agent in its expulsion at the time of parturition. In the virgin state it is *pear-shaped*, flattened from before backwards, and situated in the cavity of the pelvis, between the bladder and the rectum. It is retained in its position by the round and broad ligaments (Plate III, *ii* and *kk*) on each side, but *also by virtue of its anteverted position, and by the vagina and perineum*. Its upper end or base (*a*) is directed upwards and forwards; its lower end, or apex, is directed downwards and backwards in the line of the axes of the inlet of the pelvis. It therefore forms an angle with the vagina. The uterus measures about three inches in length, two in breadth at its upper part, and an inch in thickness, and it weighs from an ounce to one and a half ounces in its healthy condition.

The fundus or base is the upper broad extremity of the organ (*a*); it is convex, covered by peritoneum, and placed on a line below the level of the brim of the pelvis.

The body (*b*) gradually narrows from the fundus to the neck. Its anterior surface is flattened, covered by peritoneum in the upper three-fourths of its extent, and separated from the bladder by some coils of the small intestines; the lower fourth is connected with the bladder.

The posterior surface of the body is convex, covered by peritoneum throughout, and separated from the rectum by some convolutions of the intestines.

Its lateral margins are concave and give attachment to the Fallopian tubes (*n*), above.

The round ligaments (*i*) are attached below and in front of these, while the ligaments of the ovaries (*o*) are attached behind and below these structures.

The cervix or neck of the womb (*c d e*) is the lower rounded and constricted portion of the uterus; around its circumference is attached the upper end of the vagina, which extends upwards a greater distance behind than in front.

At the vaginal extremity of the uterus is, in the virgin womb, a round, but after childbirth a transverse aperture, the *os uteri* or mouth of the womb, bounded by two lips, the anterior of which is thick, the posterior narrow and long.

THE FALLOPIAN TUBES.

The Fallopian tubes, or oviducts (*n*) convey the ova from the ovaries to the cavity of the uterus. They are two in number, one on each side, situated in the free margin of the broad ligament, extending from each superior angle of the uterus to the ovaries. Each tube is about four inches in length; its canal is exceedingly minute, and commences at the superior angle of the womb by a minute orifice, the *ostium internum,* or internal mouth, which will hardly admit a fine bristle; it continues narrow along the inner half of the tube, and then gradually widens into a trumpet-shaped extremity, which becomes contracted at its termination. This opening is called the *ostium abdominale,* or abdominal mouth, because it communicates freely with the abdominal cavity. The margins of this extremity are surrounded by a series of fringe-like processes, termed *fimbriæ,* and one of these processes is connected with the outer end of the ovary. This part of the Fallopian tube is called the fimbriated or fringed extremity (*m*).

THE OVARIES.

The ovaries are analogous to the testes in the male. They are two oblong flattened and oval bodies, situated one on each side of the uterus, in the posterior part of the broad ligament behind and below the Fallopian tubes. Each ovary is connected, by its anterior margin, to the broad ligament, by its inner extremity to the uterus by a proper ligament of the ovary, and by its outer end to the fimbriated extremity of the Fallopian tube by a short ligamentous cord. The ovaries are of a whitish color, and present either a smooth or a puckered uneven surface. They are each about an inch and a half in length, three-quarters of an inch in width, and about a third of an inch thick, and weigh from one to two drams.

CHAPTER IX
MENSTRUATION AND
MENSTRUAL DISORDERS

The first appearance of the menses marks an epoch in the life of the girl which ushers in womanhood. It is the harbinger of the fruitfulness of the maiden, whose limbs now become rounder, and her hips widen out, while the breasts increase in size and the entire aspect undergoes peculiar changes, which all point to the approaching condition of maturity.

The term is derived from the *Latin* plural *menses*, meaning month, from moon, and it is an actual fact that the lunar forces seem to influence this physiological function, inasmuch as it recurs every four weeks; most women menstruate during the first quarter, and only a very few during the new or full moon.

During infancy and childhood, the sexual system of the female is inactive. The menstruation begins, in a temperate climate, about the fourteenth or fifteenth year of life, and ceases at the age of forty-five or a little later.

The climate exerts a marked influence in determinating the first appearance of menstruation, which is further influenced by the conditions of life and society in which the child is brought up.

The diversity in the ages at which children menstruate in different countries cannot be laid to any constitutional peculiarities of the races. Observation has established that, when children of the same race and family are brought from a hot to a colder climate, the advent of the first menstruation changes. These girls menstruate not so young as their older sisters, but begin about at the same age as those who are born in the colder climate.

In hot countries, for instance in Africa, the negroes and girls in East India begin to have their periods at the age of ten to twelve years. In Sweden and Norway the average age for the first menstruation is sixteen, while further north, in Lapland, the ages vary from eighteen to twenty years. Next in order of importance, influencing the menstrual epoch, are the surroundings and food.

In the same climate there are differences in the ages of children that are entirely due to these causes. Children who are pampered and who are nurtured in ease and luxury menstruate earlier than those of the poor or even of the middle class, who are brought up in habits of industry.

We observe again a difference in the ages between those who are reared in the country or rural districts and the dwellers in the cities, whether it be in luxurious apartments or in tenement houses. The former grow older and stronger than the latter before the *show* begins.

The temperament also greatly influences the development of the function; children who are nervous, irritable, and of a sanguineous temperament, menstruate earlier than those of sedate habits.

The color of the hair and complexion are also indices of the respective appearance of the menses in the *brunette* and *blonde*. It has been observed that the dark-complexioned girls menstruate sooner under similar conditions than the blondes. Weakly children, who are delicate from some constitutional habit, or whose organism has suffered from disturbances of indigestion or suffered severely from teething in early childhood, menstruate earlier than their stronger and robust sisters.

The quantity of the natural menstrual discharge, as well as the time or duration, varies greatly in health with different individuals. We first notice a slimy discharge, which soon becomes tinged with blood, and after one or two days it is almost of pure blood. The flow generally lasts three or four days, very seldom only one day, and sometimes a week to ten days.

The monthly recurrence of the menstrual periods averages thirty years; in temperate climates it may overreach this figure a little, while in hot climates it comes much below this average.

It does not follow as a rule that because a woman began to menstruate quite young, the change of life will take place earlier. This also depends much upon temperament, habit and mode of life.

Physiologists have established, by carefully-prepared statistics, that the average period of menstruation for women who began to menstruate early is thirty-three years, while those who commenced late have an average of only twenty-seven years.

When a woman is forty-five years of age, we may, however, as a rule, look for the change of life to set in; if she goes beyond this age, she may be taken as the exception.

The cavity of the womb is the principal source from which the blood comes; while the ovaries and tubes are also greatly congested with blood, the amount that comes from them must be very small.

The blood that comes from the womb is not different from blood coming from any other source; the changes and peculiarity of the menstrual show are due to its passage through the vagina, where it becomes contaminated with vaginal secretions.

It is supplied from the blood-vessels of the womb, oozing through the mucous membrane of that organ, just as in a case of nosebleed. The entire womb is more or less swollen, and more especially the mucous lining, so that it corresponds, in many instances, to an inflammatory process, and for that very reason, a sudden check of the menstrual flow will often result in a regular subacute or acute inflammation of the womb. If the discharge of blood from the uterus is in small quantities and a gradual, steady flow, it becomes so altered by the secretions in its passage through the vagina that it does not coagulate, but when it is poured out more rapidly or in larger quantities, the menstrual blood coagulates or congeals in the same manner as if it were derived from other sources.

If a woman becomes pregnant, the menses as a rule are suspended during the child-bearing period, and usually remain absent after the child is born so long as the woman nurses the child. I have known one woman who menstruated during her entire pregnancy, and another who had had eight children and never menstruated in her life, yet she was, and always had been, in perfectly good health: thus we see, that there is no rule without exceptions.

An essential part of the menstrual function is that in which the ova or female germ cells ripen and are expelled from the ovary. The menstruation is only a reflex or side issue, to a more important part that is going on in the female generative system; this is termed *ovulation,* or the ripening and expulsion of the human egg from the tissues of the ovaries. In the physiological process that operates in the economy of nature for reproduction, the *ovaries* are the principal organs. The other organs are simply accessory, and indeed many of the lower animals have no other organs than the ovaries for the perpetuation of their species.

In the human female, the ovaries consist of a tough fibrous tissue, between whose meshes are little cysts, which are called *Graafian vesicles,* and these little vesicles serve as the nests in which the ova or little germ cells mature.

These ova which are imbedded in the Graafian vesicles are so small that they can only be seen by a high magnifying power.

The activity of the ovaries begins at puberty, and ceases with the change of life, or menopause.

The approach of the menses is signalized by a certain group of symptoms, which clearly indicate a congestion of the pelvic organs.

There is generally a drawing sensation in the back and thighs, and a sensitiveness upon pressure in the regions of the ovaries and the womb. There is a feeling of lassitude and weakness of the limbs, sometimes hot flushes changing off with chills, and often a feverish condition, which will last until the flow is fully established.

Professor Dalton says: "In many birds, for example, the plumage assumes at this period more varied and brilliant colors; and in the common fowl the comb or 'crest' enlarges, and becomes red vascular. In the American deer, the coat which, during the first year is mottled with white, becomes in the second year of a uniform tawny or reddish tinge. In nearly all species, the limbs become more compact and the body more rounded; and the whole external appearance is so altered, as to indicate, that the animal has arrived at the period of puberty, and is capable for reproduction."

In the human subject, the child now becomes conscious of the sexual instinct, however chaste or virtuous her mind, for we must not dull our intelligence with the idea that the sexual function is unholy; it is no more so than to say our prayers; so that an additional duty is now incumbent upon mother or guardian.

The child must be made to know that she must be more reserved and guarded in her relations with the male sex; that she no longer can romp or play on the knees of male friends or visitors, and that it is dangerous and unbecoming to be left alone with them. A little later on, she must be apprised that she too may become a *mother*, and that that would be a great disgrace for one so young and not married. The child thus learns to protect herself against the insidious smiles and snares of the seducer, for he is ever abroad, and often family friend and trusted adviser.

There are beings who are men in form only, but at heart are black villains, and selfish brutes. When the mischief is done, then it is too late to repent of a mother's negligence, or to bewail a child's disgrace and man's perfidy; the three combined make one of the most distressing scenes that it has ever been my misfortune to behold.

Successive crops of eggs ripen, and are discharged by the adult female at each menstrual period.

I have already said that the ovum is contained in the Graafian vesicle, in which it grows and matures, as the fruit ripens on a tree, so the Graafian vesicle gradually ripens for the expulsion of the ovum, which gradually makes its way to the surface of the ovary. Within the Graafian vesicle the serous fluid accumulates, so that it ruptures and discharges its little ovum, which is taken up by the fringed extremity of the Fallopian tube, and carried along the oviduct into the womb, from which it escapes into the vagina, and is lost, provided conception has not taken place.

Investigations have been made as to the number of ova certain mammalia discharge, and it has been found to correspond with the number of young that the animal produces at birth. Where a litter consists of from three to twenty, as in the bitch and the sow, a similar number of eggs ripen, and are discharged at the period of œstruation.

In the cow or mare, and in the human female, as a rule, only one egg is discharged at each period of ovulation.

The discharge of ripened ova does, however, occur in exceptional cases without any sign of the menstrual show, and the person may be susceptible to conception, so that we may reasonably infer, that ovulation constitutes the most important function of the menstrual period.

MENSTRUAL DISORDERS.

These are designated by different terms, not because each name signifies a particular disease, but simply an indefinite symptom of a diseased condition. In other cases menstrual disorder may produce symptoms that are common to widely different diseases. In other words, the phrase menstrual disorder, without being qualified as to its particular cause, means, from a practical standpoint nothing upon which a treatment can be intelligently based. Not any more than a cough which is simply an irritation of the bronchial nerves, and may be due to a bronchitis or pneumonia, or it may not be due to any pulmonary affection at all, as, for instance, in the case where an aneurismal tumor presses on the bronchial nerves, and excites severe paroxysms of coughing. A great many menstrual disorders are due, not to any disease of the generative organs, but to an affection of the nervous system.

Menstruation may be precocious in some girls, and if the discharge is not accompanied with the usual symptoms of backache and some of the other symptoms that characterize the normal appearance of the menses, or if the girl is otherwise not fully developed, and has in this climate not reached her twelfth or fourteenth year, it constitutes a sign of a disease. If, however, the show recurs at certain intervals, it is not to be considered with the same degree of apprehension that it would be if it recurred at irregular intervals.

The sanguineous discharge which shows itself at the genitals during an acute attack of an infectious disease, has no relation whatever with the menstrual function; this may take place in children at any early age.

We often see girls who are not yet thirteen, who still wear short clothes and go to school, that menstruate regularly, but with this precocious menstruation there is also a corresponding development of the body which gives them a womanly appearance. Such girls should not be permitted to expose themselves to the inclemency of the weather, because they are much more liable to take cold, which may result in inflammations, than girls in whom the menses have not appeared.

Girls of a scrofulous taint or other hereditary habits of constitution, often begin to menstruate prematurely; outdoor exercise and cod liver oil with cold sponging on retiring at night are the proper resources for building them up.

AMENORRHŒA.

This term is employed for the purpose of designating an absence of the menstrual flow in persons who are old enough to menstruate, and in whom there is no physiological reason for its suppression, such as being too young, after the change of life, or during pregnancy and while nursing the child on the breasts.

We find this disorder of the natural function of menstruation more among the women of the rich and affluent whose lives are spent in indolence and luxury; this is to be ascribed to lack of sufficient exercise to stimulate the nervous and sanguineous systems to the performance of their healthy functions.

The amenorrhœa, or a retarded menstruation in young girls, is oftener the result of a general debility than of a disease of either the womb or ovaries. We have here again about the same causes playing their pernicious role as in precocious menstruation in weakly children; that is, that the same causes produce directly opposite results. The scrofulous and hereditary taints always interfere with the proper and healthy development of the system; in amenorrhœa they appear to be a hindrance to the formation and growth of the red blood corpuscles. In some girls the suppression of the courses appears to be a wise conservative provision of nature, because the girls are already so weak and bloodless that even the loss of a very small amount would only increase the anæmia, so that in these cases it is not so much a question of "bringing on the courses" as of building up the constitution, and enriching the blood in order to bring about the desired result.

Chlorosis, or the green sickness, is not simply an anæmia or a bloodlessness, but a physiological incapacity of the system to prepare the required blood cells for the sanguineous fluid, and this is, indeed, the most frequent cause of the disorder under consideration. Chlorosis is a disease that is peculiar to the female sex, beginning as a rule at the age of approaching puberty, between the fourteenth and twentieth year, so that there appears to be a physiological relation between the blood genesis on the one hand, and the development of womanhood on the other.

In some cases we can trace the impoverished condition of the blood to unhealthy dwellings, impure air, want of exercise, improper diet, nervousness, the reading of exciting, amorous novels, and the practice of masturbation or self-abuse. On the contrary, the disease is often developed under the most moral and exacting discipline and hygienic surroundings.

I have known girls who lived in the country, enjoyed horseback riding, ate nutritious and wholesome food, and whose solitary moments were beyond suspicion, yet at the age of puberty they commenced to fade in color, and fail in strength, gradually growing paler and weaker, until they became chlorotic and bloodless. This can only be explained on the theory that the period in which nature was preparing the system for the purposes she had in view, caused a shock to the nervous system, which so disarranged the functions that the *sanguineous* system did not respond to the growth of the *generative* system.

Then there is another class of cases, where girls menstruate before they are old enough, and without their bodies showing any visible evidence of developed womanhood, who belong to the most obstinate cases for successful treatment.

The relative diminution of the red blood cells to the healthy standard is in some cases truly alarming. In the average healthy blood, there are, in one thousand parts of blood, one hundred and thirty parts of red blood cells; this falls to sixty, and even forty parts in the thousand in the chlorotic patient.

It is one of the peculiarities of this disease, that while the muscular tissue wastes away, the fatty tissue is not only preserved, but it sometime increases, so that in a family of several girls, the chlorotic girl is considered the '*most fleshy*,' but as fat is not flesh, the appearance is deceptive.

When we stop to think a moment, that the *red blood corpuscles* are the messengers which absorb the oxygen in the lungs during the respiratory movements, and carry it to the different organs and tissues of the body, without which all tissue change would cease. And that the same red blood cells must return again to the lungs for exhaling the carbonic acid, one of the waste products of tissue growth, then the diminution of the red blood cells in the proportion above given, must affect the entire system very injuriously.

This is indeed the case; the natural respiratory movements are insufficient on the slightest exertion, so that patients tell us that when they walk a little fast, go up the stairs, or even sweep the room, they feel a shortness of breath.

There are other symptoms that point to carbonic acid poisoning, which it will be interesting to review. A great majority of these symptoms are to be found in every case of chlorosis. The muscles become weak at first, because their nutrition is interfered with, and they waste away, and secondly they become irritable from the poisonous presence of the carbonic acid, and so are often very painful. The patients are easily tired out; some, indeed, feel tired all the time, getting up in the morning as worn out as when they retired at night.

The nervous system suffers as much, because the principal nerve food is oxygen, and if there is no blood, there can be no oxygen; a starved nerve is a painful nerve. We find neuralgias, affecting the different parts of the body, the rule; when these are located in the external muscles, they are easily recognized, but when located in the deep organs, as the ovaries or the womb, they are generally mistaken for something else. The nerves of these individuals being in such an irritable state, it is natural to infer, that hysteria is often to be found as one of the complications, so that habitual sadness, and abnormal longings after chalk, lead pencils, and other indigestible articles are prominent symptoms.

The circulatory system suffers derangements that are characteristic of chlorosis. Palpitation of the heart is a prominent symptom; this is partly due to the irritation of the carbonic acid on the cardiac nerves, and partly to sensitiveness of the patient, owing to a morbidly-increased sensibility of the whole body. Chlorotic patients blush up at times, only to be followed by a green paleness that is peculiar to the disease. Pain in the region of the heart, and disturbances of the digestion, are sometimes prominent symptoms. There is no feeling of hunger; eating is not so much from hunger, but more from a sense of duty to keep up the strength. A heavy or full feeling is often experienced after a meal, and a sourish eructation will give relief to the oppression, because the walls of the stomach are relaxed and in sympathy with the general debility.

But in all cases of chlorosis the sexual functions are the seat of the greatest disturbance; amenorrhœa or the suppression of the menses is the most prominent symptom. The ovaries no longer seem to expel ripened ova, for there are no indications that point to their activity, because there is not only an absence of the show, but also an absence of the other signs that were noted when we considered menstruation and ovulation.

There are a great many other diseases of which amenorrhœa is a prominent symptom; these will be referred to when separate diseases become the subject of special inquiry.

The treatment of amenorrhœa is, indeed, in the great majority of cases, the treatment of chlorosis, and that should be conducted on common-sense principles. If the child has vicious practices, they must be corrected, and everything else that has been mentioned as a cause must be abandoned. Children who were once robust and strong require electrical treatment, while those who were naturally weak require nourishing food and tonics. If there is in the entire pharmacopœa a remedy that deserves the name of a specific, it is to that one which I suggest in amenorrhœa due to chlorosis or anæmia. Iron preparations are very numerous; every physician has his favorite prescription; some are to be praised more for their elegance and flavor than for any virtue that they possess. If in these cases any positive and decided result is to follow the administration of iron, it must be given in such a mild form that it can be taken in great quantities without irritating the stomach or interfering with digestion. If the contents of the whole alimentary canal are saturated or impregnated with the ferruginous medicine, there will be astonishing curative effects.

I have often observed chlorotic cases who have made the rounds of the different iron springs, and who have taken the numerous and various fancy elixirs, without the slightest perceptible effect, bloom up, after being fed, so to speak, on some harmless iron preparation, which was astonishing to themselves and surprising to their friends. The following is my favorite prescription for chlorosis or anæmia:

NO. I.

Take:	Powd. Carb. of iron, sacch. (Germ.)	1 ounce
	Powd. Aloes.	20 grains
	Powd. Tragacanth.	20 grains

Mix with sufficient water to make into a hard mass and divide into one hundred and fifty pills, and roll in powdered cinnamon.

Take three pills three times a day and after three days increase to four pills at one dose three times a day, then after another three days increase to five pills as many times a day as before; if these doses are not at first borne, begin with less, and if there is no costiveness or tendency thereto, omit the aloes.

If there is reason to believe that the impoverishment of the blood is partly or wholly due to scorfulous taints, then it is advisable to take fresh, pure cod liver oil in conjunction with the iron pills; three boxes of pills are, as a rule, necessary to effect a cure.

It happens quite often in chlorosis or anæmia that there is a distressing dyspepsia or indigestion with loss of appetite. In these cases I would first advise to put the stomach in order; this is done by first avoiding all indigestible food, such as cakes, pies, and puddings, and taking the following medicine:

NO. II.

Take:	Bicarbonate of soda	2 drams
	Subcarbonate of bismuth	2 drams
	Tr. of nux vom.	2 drams
	Fluid ex. of rhubarb	3 drams
	Simple syrup	1 ounce
	Peppermint water sufficient to make	8 ounces

Take a tablespoonful three times a day, and if the bowels move freely take less.

Hygiene in the treatment of every disease is to be an important factor; all vicious habits must be abandoned.

DYSMENORRHŒA.

Difficult or painful menstruation is the definition of the above word; all painful menstrual disorders that take place either before or during the menstrual flow come under this designation.

The seat of the pain, when of a colicky nature, is in the uterus; when a continuously dull ache is in the small of the back, it is located in the nervous plexus in the small of the back. The pain is very often in the ovaries and in that portion of the peritoneal membrane which folds over all the pelvic organs and extends on the sides of the womb, constituting the broad ligaments; when the pain is confined to these structures, it is principally felt below the stomach and over the lower part of the bowels.

Painful menstruation is a prominent symptom of a great many diseases, and it often strains the ingenuity of the most clever specialist to trace the symptoms to their real cause.

Obstructive dysmenorrhœa, as its name implies, is due to some hindrance or obstacle to the escape of blood from the cavity of the womb. The obstruction may exist in the neck of the womb, at its mouth, or in the vagina. When the obstruction is in the neck of the womb, it may be congenital or date from birth. The constriction or narrowness may be due to an acquired inflammation of the lining membrane of the neck of the womb. Every inflammation causes a swelling of the tissues, and if the inflammation continues, the swelling becomes permanent and a *stricture* is the result.

Such strictures are often the result of the applications of strong *caustics* and meddlesome tampering by the ignorant specialist and abortionist. The application of the *electrical current* by means of the uterine electrode is the most modern and effectual method of treating these cases successfully.

Flexion of the womb is understood to be a condition in which the uterus is flexed or bent upon itself at a sharp angle, just as a rubber hose that is bent sharply on itself becomes compressed at the kink so as to shut off the flow, in this manner the flow of blood from the cavity of the womb is partly shut off, and the obstruction is the cause of the painful menstruation.

In some women who have flexion or a bent womb there is no obstruction, because the probe passes the canal freely; in these cases dysmenorrhœa must be traced to some other cause. If it is clearly established that flexion is the cause of the obstruction, the most successful treatment is the electrical current. I have often had cases where little mucous growths no larger than a small marble, grew in the canal and obstructed the free escape of blood; after these were removed, the dysmenorrhœa ceased at once.

Other obstructions may be due to a stricture of the vagina or some deformity of the hymen; a very slight surgical operation will permanently relieve both of these hindrances.

There is a much larger proportion of cases that suffer from painful menstruation in whom the uterine organs are perfectly healthy, but who are systematically injured by dishonest or hungry specialists, by being subjected to *local treatments*. I have had cases of this nature fall into my hands very often. They had made the rounds of the specialists and had been made the innocent prey of avaricious professional competition, so that it is of the greatest importance to distinguish this class of cases from those in which the pelvic organs are the seat of the difficulty.

Nervous and congestive dysmenorrhœas are particularly adapted for the hygiene of home treatment. Nervous or neuralgic dysmenorrhœa is very often overlooked, and treated as a local lesion of the womb.

The psychical exaggeration which many women experience at the approach of the menses is abnormally heightened in dysmenorrhœa. The pains in the back, in the hips, and in the lower part of the abdomen disturb the normal operations of the mind. The irritation of the nerves of the womb is often reflected to distant organs, and pain is felt in remote regions. Some women suffer only just a day or two preceding the flow, while others suffer severely during the entire period, so that they are forced to keep to their bed the greater part of the time.

Professor William Goodell, one of the most profound and original female specialists in America, has this to say in a recent publication: "I have learned to unlearn the idea— and that was the hardest task of all—that uterine symptoms are not always present in cases of uterine disease; or that, when present, they necessarily come from uterine disease. The nerves are mighty mimers, the greatest of mimics, and they cheat us by their realistic personations of organic disease and especially of uterine disease. Hence it is that even seemingly urgent uterine symptoms may be merely nerve counterfeits of uterine disease. I have, therefore, long since given up the belief, which, with many, amounts to a creed, that the womb is at the bottom of every female ailment.

"Nerve strain, or nerve exhaustion, comes largely from the frets, the griefs, the worries, the carks and cares of life. Yet although the imagination undoubtedly affects it, it is not a mere whim or imaginary disease, as all healthy women and physicians think; but it is the veriest of realities. When some flippant talker or some slipshod thinker scoffs at nervousness as a sham disorder, I say to him: 'Can the bribe of a principality keep you from blushing when you are ashamed, or from blanching when you are afraid?' Under the flitting sense of shame or of fear these vasomotor disturbances are momentarily beyond your control; and so they are in the nervous woman, whose vital organs are, as it were—not transiently but—perpetually blushing and blanching under deficient brain-control over the lower nerve centers.

"Strangely enough, the most common symptoms of nerve disorder in women are the very ones which tradition and dogmatic empiricism attribute to womb disease.

"They are, in the order of their frequency, great weariness and more or less of wakefulness and inability to walk any distance, a bearing-down feeling, headache, nape-ache and backache, scant, or *painful*, or delayed, or suppressed menstruation, cold feet, and irritable bladder, general spinal and pelvic soreness, and pain in one ovary, usually the left, or in both ovaries. The sense of exhaustion is a remarkable one; the woman is always tired, she passes the day tired, and she goes to bed tired, and she wakes up tired, often, indeed, more tired than when she fell asleep. She sighs a great deal, she has low spirits, and her arms and legs become numb so frequently that she fears palsy or paralysis.

"There are many other symptoms of nerve strain, but since they are not so distinctly uterine, and, therefore, not so misleading, I shall not enumerate them. Now, let a nervous woman with some of the foregoing group of symptoms recount them to a female friend, and she will be told that she has womb disease. Let her consult a physician and ten to one he will think the same thing and diligently hunt for some uterine lesion. If one be found, no matter how trifling, he will attach to it undue importance, and treat it heroically as the offending organ. If no visible disease of the external organs be discoverable, he will lay the blame to the invisible endometrium, or on the unseeable ovaries, and continue the local treatment. In any event, whatever the inlook or the outlook, a local treatment is bound to be the issue."

The nervous variety of painful menstruation is frequently due to impoverishment of the blood, which, as we have learned, is often the direct cause of irritable nerves. The same treatment as for chlorosis will give the desired relief: the treatment with iron pills. If the stomach is deranged from dyspeptic disorders, then my dyspeptic mixture, No. II, is to be given. But there are cases that are purely neuralgic without any apparently serious lesion of the blood; cases in which the neuralgia of the womb or ovaries is probably due to exposure to cold or some other indiscretion; here the following recipe will effect a cure in the course of several months:

NO. III.

Take:	Fluid ex. of black cohosh	½ ounce
	Fluid ex. of ergot	½ ounce
	Tr. of guaiacum ammoniated	3 ounces
	Glycerine	2 ounces

Mix. Take a teaspoonful in a tumblerful of milk three times a day, between meals.

Congestive dysmenorrhœa is oftener in the nature of an acute or sudden attack, except when it is due to a chronic inflammation of the lining membrane of the womb. It is often brought on by a sudden or inadvertent exposure, just at the time when the menses should make their regular appearance.

Persons of a plethoric habit and those who have been the subjects of inflammations either of the womb or in the tissues surrounding the womb, are more liable to this form of dysmenorrhœa than others. It will often be ushered in with a chill, followed soon with fever. There is headache, the skin becomes dry and hot, and often there is considerable irritability of the bladder, straining of the rectum and diarrhœa. Unless the pain is due to an obstinate displacement, it yields to proper treatment. For the straining and irritable bladder a hot sitz-bath should be employed for ten to fifteen minutes.

In the absence of a suitable vessel for a sitz-bath an ordinary bathtub can be used by filling it six or eight inches with water, at a temperature of 104°F., and while sitting in the bath allow the boiling water to run slowly into it, so as to keep the temperature up. These sitz-baths should be taken several times a day, and after each bath the patient should rub herself thoroughly dry and wear flannel next to the skin. The extremities and feet should also be kept warm by wearing woolen hose.

Towels wrung out of hot water should be carefully folded and applied to the lower region of the abdomen and then covered over with a thickly folded flannel cloth so as to retain the heat and moisture; when the towel has cooled off repeat the dipping in hot water.

The Femina vaginal capsules are of inestimable value in this class of diseases. They relieve congestion of the womb by allaying the irritation. The best time to use one is just before retiring, and after taking a sitz-bath, or a vaginal injection of hot water, or both. Persons who are of a costive habit should pay particular attention that, about the time their monthlies come around, their bowels act freely, and to accomplish this purpose the Femina laxative tablets should be taken, one each night for several nights before the courses are expected.

MENORRHAGIA AND METRORRHAGIA.

By *menorrhagia* is meant, as the composition of the term implies, an excessive flow of blood at the regular monthly period; by *metrorrhagia*, a flow of blood from the womb at any time irrespective of the regular menstrual periods. Neither of these forms can be called a disease, as they are solely the symptoms of several kinds of uterine affections. In the course of our investigations, we will find that one of the most prominent and common symptoms of different womb diseases is *hemorrhage* of the womb.

If the hemorrhage is the result of general debility from protracted nursing, the child must be weaned, and recipe No. I, with a nourishing diet, will effect a cure.

Hemorrhage may be due to the presence of a fungoid inflammation, tumors, or affections of the mouth or neck of the womb, or congestion of the ovaries.

It is very often due to a "bad getting up" from confinement, where the womb has never returned to its original size. Sometimes it is due to a portion of the afterbirth that was retained in the cavity of the womb. It is also a symptom of cancer. As I have already said, it may be the symptom of so many different diseases that the proper course to pursue is to find an *honest* and competent physician to make a thorough examination, for the purpose of deciphering the real cause, and when that is discovered, it is as a rule, an easy matter to remove it and thus afford the patient permanent relief.

There is no remedy which on the whole is so effectual in controlling hemorrhage, no matter from what cause, as:

NO. IV.

Take: Fluid ex. of ergot   1 ounce

Dose: a teaspoonful in a little water every four hours until the flow ceases, or until a physician is consulted to diagnose the case. In pregnancy, the administration of ergot is not admissible; cold water compresses are also useful in checking uterine hemorrhage, and the utmost quietude should be observed.

Nervous exhaustion from protracted confinement, or mental worry from the loss of a child or the death of a friend, may also cause uterine hemorrhage. The ergot is useful in these cases, with a change of air and scenery.

CHAPTER X
HISTOLOGY OF INFLAMMATION

Inflammations of the various tissues assume different forms as far as the gross appearances are concerned, but the underlying condition is precisely the same. The various types of inflammations that are produced by one and the same process are of considerable scientific interest, but to the practical and inquiring reader, whose principal object is to obtain sufficient information to be able to cure herself, it would be confusing were I to attempt a description of their differences.

There is no word that is so often employed as *inflammation*, as a designation of disease, and when we learn that there is only one kind of inflammatory process, whether of the brain, the lungs, liver, kidneys or bowels, the entire subject of inflammatory diseases at once becomes greatly simplified, because if you understand one you must understand all.

I will in the subsequent chapters speak only, or principally, of inflammatory affections of the different organs that come within the province of this specialty, and I am convinced that if the reader will bear with me, so that I may take sufficient time and space to explain the most advanced scientific views of inflammatory processes, she will be more than compensated, by a clearer understanding of what will be said in succeeding pages.

Inflammation comprises a series of phenomena, which partly take place in the vascular apparatus or blood vessels and partly in the tissues comprising the structure of the organ. Inasmuch as inflammation is not a single process, a definition of a few words is insufficient to convey to the mind its real meaning. If I were simply to describe the peculiarities of the circulation, that characterize the inflammatory process, we should only have an incomplete idea of the changes that were taking place.

Since the time of Galen, who lived two hundred years after Christ, *inflammation* was recognized by four cardinal symptoms, namely redness (Ruber), *swelling* (Tumor), *pain* (Dolor) and the increased temperature (Calor). To these modern pathologists have added a fifth symptom, which is lessened or diminished function (Functio Læsa).

The above five cardinal symptoms can be established in the majority of the acute stages of inflammation: in the chronic or subacute variety, one or the other symptom may be absent, or so obscured as to escape notice.

The nature and structure of the tissue materially modify some symptoms and exclude others, so that redness, pain and even perceptible swelling may be absent. Galen already in his time attributed the redness to an increased blood supply and the swelling to an exudation of lymph or serum, through the walls of the blood vessels: this was as near the truth as scientists arrived, until within our own time. The discoveries in this field of science have been greatly enriched in the last twenty years through the researches of the German school. Various theories have been advanced from time to time, as to the probable causes or processes that are going on in the tissues while inflammation is active. One observer believed that he had found the solution of the inquiry in a supposed spasmodic contraction of the capillary blood vessels, another in their paralysis, while still another adhered to the belief of a neurotic affection. Professor Virchow, the father of the modern school of pathological science, ascribed the conditions of the tissues to an irritable state of the inflammatory process, inducing an exaggerated cell growth; while his former pupil, Cohnheim, through an extended series of newly-devised experiments, has conclusively proved that none of the theories advanced are supported by demonstrable facts.

Our present thorough knowledge of the combined disturbances and phenomena, that play their part in the vessels and tissues, of the body during the inflammatory action in living tissue is due to the unremitting toil of Professor Cohnheim. He was the first to speak from facts, as they presented themselves to his eye under the microscope. It was he who had the genius that suggested the examination of the whole process of inflammation, in the living tissues under the microscope. This he accomplished by narcotizing a frog, and while alive, but insensible to pain, a portion of the peritoneum or mesentery, which is almost transparent, so that the circulation may be plainly seen, was fastened with pins upon an ingeniously-devised rack or stage. The inflammation is now excited by etching the membrane with a little acid and a sharp needle, and then the object is placed under the microscope. If the operator is careful, so as not to tear or crush the vessels or tissues, and preserves the moisture, by spraying with warm water from time to time, the circulation and the abnormal processes of inflammation that are going on, may be observed and studied with great exactness for several hours. I will now describe what may be seen in the field of the microscope.

The first change to be observed is in the vascular system and within the vessels themselves; this begins with a widening of the small arteries, then of the smaller capillaries and veins. This increases the current of blood with greater velocity through the widened vessels. Sooner or later this rapidity of the current lessens; there is a marked slowness to be observed in the stream. The single or separate blood cells, which in the beginning of the observation could not be distinguished, can now be distinctly seen, especially in the veins and small capillaries, in which, from the slowness of the current, the blood accumulates. In the veins there now appears at the periphery of the current a pellucid plasmatic layer, in which there are white blood cells, that have separated themselves from the main current; the white cells either float slowly along or adhere to the walls of the vessels. This phenomenon the Germans term "Randstellung der Farblosen Blut Körperchen," which means, bordering of white blood corpuscles. Not long after the "bordering" of white cells, a change takes place in the cells themselves, that is very interesting. The white cells become elongated and spear-shaped at one extremity, which pierces the wall of the vessel, and after a little while the sharp extremities will appear on the outer surface of the wall of the vessel, and a little later on, indeed, the entire protoplasmic cell will have emigrated into the tissue, outside of the vessel. Or, in other words, the colorless blood cells will have passed through the walls of the vein or capillary, and this constitutes an *extravasation*.

The first extravasated cells will soon be followed by others in great quantity, so that in six to eight hours veins and capillaries are surrounded with white corpuscles. In their normal destination these become organized into fibrous or granulation tissue; and for this reason, an organ that is the seat of chronic inflammation becomes immensely enlarged from this inflammatory accretion. We can now readily appreciate why the womb, liver or kidneys become augmented in size from inflammatory processes. Indeed, this applies to all growths and even to bone, and if a part is injured by a cut, accident or disease of some sort, precisely the same processes are at work to repair the lost tissue. It cannot fail to become apparent at once, that to understand the phenomena of inflammation is to possess the key that opens to our understanding the operations not only of most diseases, but of the healing processes of wounds and injuries. In the course of the experiment we see also red blood corpuscles transude, which are always accompanied with more or less fluid or plasma.

The above detailed account seems to explain in a clear manner the different cardinal symptoms that have become recognized features of inflammation since the time of Galen. The great vascular activity explains the redness, swelling and increased temperature. The pain can be traced to the pressure from the exudation, to which the delicate nerve filaments were exposed, while lessened function would be the natural result of nerves or tissues so compromised.

I made an attempt to initiate the reader into the science of inflammatory processes and if I have succeeded in making myself understood, then I am satisfied with having imparted a most useful lesson, because there is no process in the entire field of disease that is so general; it is almost safe to say that with the exception of functional diseases, there is perhaps no class of diseases with which an inflammatory process is not more or less associated. This is true of consumption, which is an inflammatory process excited by and around the bacilli or micro-organisms, and these inflammatory nodules are called tubercles. The growth of a cancerous tumor is associated with an inflammation. The development of a common boil is an illustration of an inflammation, breaking down or destroying part of the tissue which is inflamed. It is the same in inflammation of the lungs or pneumonia as it is in ordinary catarrh; the differences that are presented to the eye are only modifications of degree and peculiarities that are due to the difference of the tissues of which the organ or membrane is composed.

CHAPTER XI
URETHRITIS AND NEURALGIA
OF THE URETHRA

Inflammation of the canal by which the urine is conducted and discharged from the bladder is termed urethritis.

There is no organ of the female anatomy that is oftener the seat of local inflammation.

The acute and chronic inflammations that affect the male urethra, also affect that of the female, only perhaps to a more limited extent, owing to the comparative smaller mucous surface of the tube, it being only from an inch to an inch and a half in length.

Inflammation is oftener confined to this portion of the urinary apparatus than is generally supposed, because any derangements of these parts is at once attributed to the bladder, and it is an actual fact that many women have doctored uselessly for years, for the one, when it was the other that was diseased. Symptoms of urethral inflammations are so very similar to inflammations of the bladder that the points of distinction are easily overlooked.

The trouble begins with frequent desire to void urine and a continual bearing down or straining sensation, which may be accompanied with a sense of heat suggesting to the minds of the most chaste and pure women, sexual desire, which the gratification of that indulgence does not relieve nor satiate, but, on the contrary, the sexual passion becomes only exaggerated. It is only the strongest force of character and Christian fortitude that keep some of these unfortunate women in the path of rectitude and virtue, and it is only the scientific specialist who can appreciate the real cause. In many instances women, truly noble in character, have fallen from their high estate, because uncontrollable impulses swept them into the maelstrom of licentiousness, which might have been averted, if they had known of whom to seek proper advice.

This irritation is often innocently and ignorantly acquired in early girlhood by fingering the parts, or practicing masturbation, which sets up an inflammatory condition of the urethra that becomes chronic, and in time may entail the terrible consequences to which I have already alluded. For that reason mothers should not be over-delicate; they should not only keep a watchful eye on their children when in seclusion, but should make it their holy duty to gradually initiate their children into a knowledge of physiology and of the diseases that may result from any violation of youthful virtue.

Why is it that many children who have been reared in an atmosphere of sanctity, children who have enjoyed from their earliest recollection moral and spiritual administration, have fallen into vice and depravity? The reader should stop to answer this question for herself, while I too will answer it for her.

It is because moral teachers overlook the fact that human beings are dual; that we are all animal, however spiritual, and that the functions of the animal nature must be understood in order that the spiritual nature can control them.

A false delicacy has entirely neglected this part of the education of our children, which I stamp as the height of stupidity and hypocrisy.

Among other causes of this malady is hot and acrid urine, or gravelly discharges from the bladder, cutting and irritating the mucous membrane in its passage; abrasions of this nature often lay the foundation for ulcers. When the urine is in that condition, it is probably due to a complication of diseases of the bladder, the kidneys and the liver. A chemical and microscopical examination of the urine will be the only means of settling these questions.

The urethra often takes on the inflammations of the neighboring tissue or organs; disease of the vulva or of the vagina will spread itself to the urinary canal. I have seen cases in which the whole trouble was traceable to a catarrh of the neck of the womb.

Gonorrhœal infection of the vagina will in the great majority of cases extend itself to the urethra as well as to the cavity of the womb and neighboring organs.

If treatment in these complicated cases is to be successful, it must be directed to the disease in all of its strongholds; this, of course, can only be done under the direction of a skillful specialist.

There is a predisposition on the part of the mucous surfaces to become infected by eruptions of the eruptive fevers, and the urethra is particularly liable to this invasion. Children who have had the measles and scarlet fever will often be troubled with frequent and smarting micturition and after convalescence from all the other symptoms of the respective fevers, they are still more or less annoyed for weeks or months with a urethritis. I have had cases of this nature that dated back years. If the early treatment is neglected and the case becomes chronic, it generally spreads to the bladder, which also becomes similarly affected.

Smallpox pustules are apt to break out in the urethra during the acute stage of the disease, and excite a very itching and painful urethritis. Dysentery in children may give rise to the disease. In adults I have noticed the affection in connection with typhoid fever, but this generally passes off with convalescence. Hemorrhoids or piles give rise to urethral inflammation which does not yield to treatment, but subsides at once after the removal of the piles. The application of a Spanish-fly blister to any part of the body may also cause a stranguary or a urethritis.

Mothers may become uneasy, as to the cause of the muco-purulent discharge from the urethra of their little girls. I have known them to entertain suspicion of some specific infection being introduced into the genitals, in some mysterious manner; a little inquiry into the history of every case, dispels these absurd delusions, and it will be found that pinworms have caused the inflammation. In adults, however, the subject should be made the object of particular inquiry. During delivery, the passage of the child's head exerts great pressure on the urethra, so that it may be crushed or torn across. Women may be troubled with derangement from this cause for a long time, or for their whole lives, if the real cause of their ailment is not recognized. Displacements of the womb in different directions, principally when it is tipped backwards so that its neck impinges on the urethra or neck of the bladder, compresses the canal, so that its caliber is diminished, and a painful obstruction and retention of urine ensue.

Papillated growths and mucous polypoids that were so small that they were hidden from external sight, but readily detected by scientific methods of examination of the urethra, by means of the urethral specula, were the exciting causes of some cases that came under my treatment. The unfortunate victims were under the impression that their kidneys or their bladders were diseased. The numerous quack medicines advertised for the cure of these maladies were copiously consumed, doing, of course, more mischief than good. The removal of the growths in each instance at once put a stop to any further inconvenience.

In pregnancy, after the third month, the womb rises out of the pelvis, so as to accommodate its increasing size. This naturally drags the bladder upwards, and so stretches the urethra that it becomes sore and extremely irritable. To relieve this distress until the parts have accommodated themselves to their new relations, the Femina vaginal capsules are of the greatest value, and without the slightest ill effect arising from their use.

Vaginal irrigations of hot water are also of decided benefit, especially before using a capsule.

Mix. A teaspoonful to be given to an adult every four hours till relieved.

The symptoms of inflammation of the urethra are always very pronounced, because the mucous membrane of the urethra is the most sensitive part of the bladder. In the healthy state the coloring of the lining membrane is of a pale red; when inflamed or catarrhal, it assumes a dark red, or a cherry color. The membrane is also considerably swelled and puffed, and feels hot to the touch, and imparts a burning sensation to the patient. The muco-purulent secretion excoriates or chafes the skin, so that the parts look angry and red in the neighborhood; this is oftener observed in children. The characteristic symptom of frequently urinating is never absent, while very little is passed at a time, yet the straining to pass water continues, after the last drop is voided.

The treatment is cleanliness to begin with. In grown people, the entire vulva and vagina must be rinsed out with a warm borax solution, in the proportion of one teaspoonful of the powdered borax dissolved in a quart of water. In little children the same object, that of cleanliness, is to be accomplished with a small ear syringe.

After the external parts and the vagina are thoroughly cleansed, then, by means of a hard rubber syringe, No. 1, three or four syringefuls of clean borax water are injected into the urethra for the purpose of cleaning that too. To relieve the straining and frequent desire to micturate, which is accompanied with more or less pain, I give:—

NO. V.

Take: Fluid ex. of gelseminum   1 dram

Sweet spirits of nitre   7 drams

Mix. A teaspoonful in a wineglassful of water three or four times a day for an adult; children in proportion.

The patient must confine herself to a bland liquid diet, principally of milk, raw eggs beaten up in bouillon or broth. Vegetables may be eaten, but they are not to be seasoned with anything but salt; and alcoholic liquors, wine or beer must also be suspended for the time being.

NEURALGIA OF THE URETHRA.

The female urethra is sometimes the seat of simple neuralgia, by which is meant a painful condition in which there is no apparent disease or inflammation of the tissues.

This pain assumes often a spasmodic character; that there is a cause for this is certain, but it is as a rule remote from the sensation which attracts attention. It is often found to be the symptom of some of the diseases to which I have already referred. These are ulcerations, displacements, or inflammation and congestion of the neighboring organs. Abnormal growths or tissues will often be painfully reflected on the nerves of the urethra. I remember a case of internal hemorrhoids, which was never suspected by the patient because there were no painful symptoms pointing to the rectum, but in which the urethra was very painful in its entire extent. The suffering from this urethral neuralgia had lasted for years, but disappeared at once, on the removal of the piles. I have called attention to a catarrhal inflammation of the urethra, from stretching occasioned by the ascending womb after the third month of pregnancy; there is a similar pathological process after the seventh month of gestation, when the pregnant womb begins to descend again into the pelvic cavity, and this is particularly marked in the pregnancy with the first child, when the pain is often very severe.

If in a first pregnancy there is no abnormal disproportion between the dimensions of the child's head and the maternal pelvis, or if there be no abnormal position of the child, then there is an obstetric rule that the womb, or rather the child's head, begins to descend into the pelvis after the seventh month of gestation, so that it can accommodate or conform itself to the maternal parts. This occasions a drag on the urethra downwards and backwards, which is painfully annoying, and there is a constant inclination to pass water.

There are two mechanical methods of relieving this distressing symptom; one is to obtain as much rest as possible in the recumbent position, and the other is to wear an abdominal supporter or bandage around the lower abdominal region, so as to take the weight off the urethra. The internal medication consists of an occasional dose of a mild laxative medicine.

In the newly married, the urethra becomes sometimes the seat of a painful spasmodic contraction; this is due to a tense hymen, which should be slightly nicked with a pair of scissors. Exposures to colds will also cause neuralgia. Fresh beer and sour wine make the urine irritating, and also occasion painful symptoms.

A thorough examination of the mucous membrane of the urethra which does not reveal any inflammatory condition or abnormal growth, establishes its neuralgic character. The next step will naturally be to make such a careful examination of all the surrounding tissues and organs, for the purpose of ferreting out the real cause. When the cause is removed or cured, it will also relieve the urethral pain. In the absence of a clear comprehension of the true nature of the malady, the treatment must be palliative. The sitz-bath is always one of the most palliative measures for all sorts of pelvic pains and aches. Vaginal injections of hot water, not too hot, from 105 degrees to 108 degrees, are another sort of general panacea,—the quantity of fluid should be large, from half to one gallon, in which a teaspoonful of pulverized borax has been dissolved. If the pain is very severe, then a Femina vaginal capsule should be used every night before retiring, and immediately after having used the vaginal irrigation. The bed should always be previously warmed with a hot bottle, unless it is very warm weather.

If the urine is irritating, a cupful of buchu tea three or four times a day, or German chamomile tea, should be drunk between meals. If these measures do not give relief, then consult an honest, competent physician, in whose integrity you can rely.

CHAPTER XII
INFLAMMATION, CATARRH, AND OTHER DISORDERS OF THE BLADDER

The female bladder is easier approached than that of the male. This is clearly illustrated in the anatomical Plate II, which should be thoroughly studied before this chapter is read.

The bladder lies directly behind the symphysis pubis, above or in front of the vagina. On account of the comparative shortness of the female urethra, to that of the male, the cavity of the bladder is also much more accessible through this channel, and if access through this communication does not suffice, then the interior of the female bladder may be exposed by an incision through the anterior wall of the vagina, but this resource becomes rarely necessary. Formerly we had to content ourselves with external appearances, that were confined to the external anatomy of the urinary canal on the anterior vaginal wall, aided only by a delicate sense of touch. Valuable as these means of examination sometimes were, they were far from satisfactory to either physician or patient. Now we are able to examine with the finger, aided with the eyes, almost the entire lining of the bladder.

Professor Simon, of Heidelberg, was the inventive genius of this improved method of examination, by means of a series of graded specula or hard rubber bougies, which are known by his name. The specula are simply small, smooth, pin-shaped, hard rubber bougies, about three inches in length, beginning with a size that is three-tenths of an inch in diameter, to the largest, which is eight-tenths of an inch in thickness. These are carefully introduced into the urethra, commencing with the smallest size, which is retained for a few minutes and then withdrawn, and the next size inserted, and this continued until the largest one has been inserted, or the required dilatation accomplished, either for the purpose of introducing the finger into the bladder, or exposing its lining membrane for inspection. While this procedure does not fall into the sphere of home treatment, it is of sufficient interest to women in general that they should know what can actually be accomplished by the expert specialist. Were I to review the malformations, or dislocations, of the bladder, or the history of stones in the bladder, or other foreign bodies, that the female specialist is very seldom called upon to treat, I should only worry the patience of the reader with things that she would not readily understand. The same is true of growths and tumors of the bladder, which have principally a scientific interest for the practitioner of medicine, but for the casual reader they are too profound in their details for a clear understanding.

INFLAMMATION.

Inflammation of the bladder is in medical language termed cystitis. It presents itself under two varieties or subdivisions, *acute* and chronic, depending on the duration, whether recent or protracted.

The disease begins in the mucous membrane, and the acute inflammation comes on suddenly. It rarely occupies the entire mucous surface of the bladder, but usually occurs in irregular spots. Some spots are as large as the palm of the hand, while others are only the size of a ten-cent piece. The parts that are most frequently affected, are the neck of the bladder and its posterior wall, although no portion of its lining membrane is exempt from inflammation.

It rarely happens that the inflammation spreads over the entire extent of the bladder, or that it invades the muscular tissue; if it should complicate the latter, it would involve the peritoneum; this would add a very serious complication, namely, a peritonitis. Cystitis may be due to an extension of gonorrhœal infection from the vagina and urethra, or from other purulent affections. Women who are unable to pass water after confinement, may be liable to the disease from retained urine, decomposing in the bladder and causing inflammation. On the other hand, a filthy catheter used by a midwife or doctor who is careless or ignorant of the necessary antiseptic precautions, and who fails to brush and boil out the catheters, and uses one catheter on different patients, without the precaution of even thoroughly rinsing it, may give rise to dangerous cystitis. The most serious case that I ever have seen was directly traceable to this cause. If impure air gets into the bladder this will also excite cystitis; to prevent that, is to close with the finger the outlet of the catheter that is used for drawing off the urine, when withdrawing the instrument, a precaution seldom observed.

Newly-brewed malt liquors, alcoholic stimulants taken in excess, diuretics of spirits of turpentine and cantharis, or highly-seasoned and rich food, are among the exciting causes; irritating injections into the bladder or vagina, and even cold-water injections into the vagina, must be added as exciting causes of this painful affection. Venereal excesses operate in exciting visceral inflammation, and when the slightest symptoms are felt, prudence and good common sense dictate continence. The first feeling that manifests itself is a dull, heavy, aching sensation, immediately after urinating, and an involuntary inclination to further relieve or empty the bladder by pressing or bearing down. Soon after the first indication to void urine, there is another desire to empty the bladder, and the same symptoms repeat themselves, only in a more aggravated form. The distress of micturition gradually becomes continuous so that during the short intervals between the times that urine is voided, and as the disease progresses, the pain becomes sharper. This is accompanied by a kind of gnawing uneasiness in the region of the whole bladder, which has intermissions, but is greatly increased when the desire to make water is felt. If the disease progresses, the pain is now felt in the neighboring organs and a general constitutional disturbance manifests itself. The patient will now generally have a severe chill; this is followed with heat and thirst and an increase in the pulse. The desire to void urine at shorter intervals becomes more prominent and only drop by drop, accompanied with distressing spasm and a burning sensation along the urinary canal.

The region of the bladder becomes in the advanced stages of inflammation extremely sensitive and tender, and if the peritoneum is involved, even the weight of the bedclothes becomes intolerable. The limbs are drawn up and the body is inclined forward to relieve the tension of the abdominal muscles and their pressure on the bladder.

The neighboring organs begin to sympathize with the advanced state of the inflammation at this stage; cutting pains are felt in the rectum, while darts of pain shoot from the bladder towards the groins and ovaries.

Owing to the spasmodic action of the urethra, the bladder is never completely emptied so that the urine gradually accumulates in abnormal proportions; the retained urea rapidly decomposes into ammonia and the urine becomes very hot and irritating, thus greatly augmenting the suffering. Under these circumstances, the bladder may become greatly distended and feel as a sensitive globular tumor above the pubis. The retention of the urine may be complete, owing to a partial paralysis of the bladder and now complicated with spasmodic stricture. Nausea and vomiting are rarely absent in this stage, the tongue becomes coated and dry, while the expression is anxious and the fever very high.

In the commencement of the disease there is some difference in the symptoms of inflammation of the bladder which arises from the nature and seat of the inflammatory process.

If the neck of the bladder is mainly affected, the spasmodic desire to urinate is more pronounced, and the pain is felt low down in the vagina and anus, while the symptoms are higher up in the rectum, with constant inclination to go to stool, if the base or posterior wall of the organ is principally involved.

Acute cystitis runs its course in six or eight days; under favorable circumstances and appropriate treatment all painful symptoms will in that time have subsided, and the patient will have entered upon a course of permanent recovery.

If through a constitutional habit, or through neglect or improper treatment, the disease is not curbed, the result will be quite different; the inflammation may pass into a suppurative stage or assume the chronic form.

The treatment in the acute stage will resolve itself into two different measures of relief; these are first to subdue the spasmodic pain and nervous excitement, and secondly, to quiet the local irritation. The pain is best controlled by morphine powders, one-fourth of a grain each, given every four hours. Warm teas of German chamomile or flaxseed, so as to dilute the urine, may be freely given. Hot vaginal injections of borax water have a remarkably soothing influence; the hot sitz-bath is another useful adjuvant. It has been customary in this country and England, to apply hot water compresses or hot poultices over the *hypogastrium*, which is that part of the lower abdomen corresponding to the region of a distended bladder.

After eight years of extended experience in this country, and a thorough trial of hot fomentations for inflammatory affections of the abdomen, I became convinced that the German method of cold-water compresses gives more relief and is more in the nature of an *abortive*, hence curative.

I recommend to my patients, instead of the hot-water applications, a rubber bag, filled with broken pieces of ice, and applied over the region of the bladder.

The bowels should be freely moved with castor oil or a dose of salts and senna, or by an enema of warm soapsuds.

The food should be bland and of a fluid nature as nearly as possible, broths with an egg, milk gruels or bread and milk.

CHRONIC CYSTITIS.

If the acute attack of cystitis in the course of eight or ten days becomes modified, but convalescence is not established, then it is quite probable that the disease is drifting into a *chronic* stage.

The mucus or slime that formerly accompanied the urinary discharge is now assuming the character of matter or has become muco-purulent. While this is a very rare symptom of the acute variety of cystitis and usually of brief duration, in chronic inflammation it is one of the characteristics of the malady, and often lasts for a long time; the muco-purulent fluid is occasionally remarkably profuse.

The pus is not always furnished by the free surface of the mucous membrane, but may be traced to small abscesses, situated in the tissue between the mucous membrane and the muscular wall of the bladder. The locality for the formation of these abscesses is principally at the neck of the organ, although there is no part of the organ that is entirely exempt from them. Fortunately, the abscesses generally point inwards or towards the cavity of the bladder, but it not infrequently happens that they break through and empty into the vagina or even into the adjacent bowel or abdominal cavity.

The occurrence of pus or suppuration is by itself so grave a process that it is always accompanied with certain well marked and stereotyped symptoms, which are cold chills, alternating with flushes of heat, increase of heat or fever, anxiety and restlessness. The pain now becomes dull and throbbing in character, and the burning or stinging is only felt when the patient urinates. When there are abscesses, the nervous derangement may be so great as to cause the mind to wander in delirium. Before the appeerence of pus in the urine, nothing but a skillful examination can establish the existence of an abscess.

The treatment for suppuration of the bladder, when limited to the surface of the mucous membrane, is always curable with intelligently-directed treatment, which is the same as that for chronic catarrh of the bladder, to be detailed further on.

ULCERATION OF THE BLADDER.

This is perhaps seldom a condition by itself, but rather a complication of the preceding disease. The ulcers occupy the place of what were formerly little abscesses, that have broken into the cavity of the organ. Foreign bodies in the bladder by their direct pressure on the delicate tissues of the membrane have been the cause of ulcerations, that gave rise to dangerous hemorrhage. Earthy concretions or stones will naturally form in the bladder, and the end of a gum catheter has also been found in the bladder broken off in the bungling act of drawing off the urine, or, what is more likely, by boring and poking within the cavity of the bladder, with a catheter or bougie, by persons ignorant of pelvic anatomy or in the belief that the bougie was in the cavity of the womb, for the purpose of inducing an abortion.

Ulcerations will always be accompanied with more or less inflammation or visceral catarrh, so that the symptoms will fall under that head which has already been considered.

CATARRH OR SUBACUTE INFLAMMATION.

The mucous membrane of the bladder, like that of the nose, mouth or bronchial tubes, has its natural secretion of healthy mucous. When any of these membranes become irritated or congested from any cause, this natural secretion becomes so increased as to make a perceptible *flow* of the secretion of mucus, and this is what the term *catarrh* signifies. Catarrhs always presuppose the existence of inflammation, which in its nature is subdued or mild, so that it has been qualified as subacute, which is intended to convey the idea that the tissue need not be red nor hot and swollen as is always the case in the acute form of inflammation.

Chronic catarrh of the bladder is traceable to any or all the causes that have been enumerated in the acute processes, because every acute inflammation of the bladder may terminate in a chronic form. It occurs at any period of life, but it is most common in elderly subjects; it is always an attendant of ulceration of the bladder or some abnormal growth in the bladder. If the disease is once established and is due to a complication, it is liable to become aggravated or re-established after a brief subsidence by exposure to cold, excesses in diet and drink, or diseases of the vagina, uterus or rectum.

The secretion of catarrh is white and glairy and resembles the discharge of leucorrhœa or whites. When disassociated with acute inflammation of the bladder, it comes on gradually, or in a slow, insidious manner; for this reason the term subacute inflammation is sometimes employed by authors, because there are no fiery symptoms at the onset of the affection.

The urine is always more or less altered in character, because the inflamed mucous membrane predisposes the urine to speedy decomposition. There is frequent and difficult micturition, and the entire region, but in particular the affected organ, is more or less sensitive and sore.

The quantity of mucus which passes off with the urine varies greatly at different periods and in different cases. In the early stages it may entirely escape notice, being so small that if the urine is not saved in a vessel and accumulated for the twenty-four hours the mucus can hardly be detected; thus, the entire quantity of the above period may often not exceed two teaspoonfuls. When the disease becomes more advanced, the quantity of mucus may be equal to the quantity of urine that passes. The secretion is very thick and sticky, and settles to the bottom of the vessel or adheres to its surface. If there is pus mixed with the mucous secretion, it becomes a more serious question, and it may then be inferred that other organs are involved, the conductors of urine from the kidneys to the bladder, for instance, or the kidneys themselves. If the disease is confined to the bladder, the prospects for a cure are very favorable; only when diseases of other organs in the neighborhood are the exciting causes of the malady are the chances for a cure correspondingly limited.

The success of any treatment will depend in a great measure upon the nature of the exciting causes. These require to be removed, if within the possibility of medical skill, before the catarrh can be made to subside.

Should the mucous or muco-purulent secretion be very abundant, the bladder must be thoroughly rinsed out; first once every twenty-four hours, and afterwards every other day, so that the mucous membrane will be cleansed from all foreign irritating elements. I am employing for this purpose Thiersche's Boro-Salicylic solution. This of course can only be carried out by a skillful physician.

When the disease is in its incipient stage it is amenable to intelligently-directed home treatment.

The most perfect rest of mind and body is one of the essentials to success, the entire suspension of stimulating drinks of an alcoholic nature, of which beer is the most irritating, and tea or coffee must be discarded. A milk and vegetable diet is the most beneficial to subsist on, and all condiments, even salt, must be dispensed with.

If the bowels are costive they must be regulated either by means of enemas of warm water, or what may prove of greater and more lasting benefit is the use of Femina laxative tablets. One tablet should be taken every night at bedtime, and if one operates too much, then one every other night may be all that is required.

Demulcent drinks of flaxseed tea, or slippery-elm water, should be drunk freely, and for the catarrh of the bladder there is no prescription that ever gave me the same satisfactory results as this one:— —

NO. VI.

Take:		
	Borate of soda	2 drams
	Fluid ex. of gelseminum	1 dram
	Fluid ex. of belladonna	x drops
	Fluid ex. of buchu	1½ ounces
	Fluid ex. of senna	1½ ounces
	Distilled water	2 ounces
	Syrup of orange peel sufficient to make	8 ounces

Mix, and take a tablespoonful or less three times a day.

Wear flannel drawers and woolen hose, so as to guard against sudden changes of the weather.

NEURALGIA AND NERVOUS IRRITABILITY.

The bladder is often the seat of functional derangements that are characterized by a morbid sensibility and pain.

The principal symptom of this disease is a frequent desire to urinate. A careful examination of the urine reveals nothing abnormal in the fluid that would point to the slightest affection of the bladder, nor are any of the symptoms that characterize inflammation present. There is no mucous sediment, but in a large proportion of cases there is an abnormal deposit of the phosphates that would point to nerve waste. There is often a similar irritability in the vaginal canal, in fact, there is such a mutual sympathy between the two, which can hardly be located in any one particular organ.

Hemorrhoids and constipation are sometimes found to be the cause.

In women of a nervous temperament the bladder often becomes the seat of a steady neuralgic pain. Sometimes this pain is periodical, recurring every day and about the same hour and lasting the same period. This pain is of a lancinating character, and radiates from the bladder to the neighboring organs. I have noticed these symptoms, particularly in women who had lived in malarial districts, and whose blood had become impoverished by malarial fevers, or from excessive hemorrhages due to some uterine trouble.

Sexual excesses and other abuses that lower the tone of the nervous system will also develop a neuralgic condition of these parts. Persons who seek relief from this distressing complaint must first abandon their vices before they can expect alleviation from any treatment. This affection is not in itself dangerous, but the frequent recurrence of paroxysms of pain render life miserable. If the general system requires toning up, I would recommend the iron pills after Formula I, with a good liberal diet of eggs and milk. For immediate relief of the painful spasms, the sitz-bath and hot vaginal injections are of great value. And for the irritable bladder I can recommend:— —

NO. VII.

Take:		
	Bromide of sodium	3 drams
	Fluid ex. of gelseminum	1 dram
	Water sufficient to make	8 ounces

Mix, and take a tablespoonful three times a day.

The gouty and rheumatic bladder is so very rare that a detailed description is hardly necessary. But it might be well to remind the reader that if she is of a gouty or rheumatic disposition and has also bladder trouble, it may be due to the bladder being compromised or influenced by gout or rheumatism. In that case, appropriate treatment directed to the rheumatic diathesis will also cure the bladder.

PARALYSIS.

The female bladder becomes paralyzed from various causes; some of these are located in the organ itself, while others are due to disease of the brain or spinal cord. An obstruction to the flow of urine through the urethra causes the bladder to become overdistended with urine and induces paralysis. A prolonged pressure from the child's head during delivery is oftener the cause of transient paralysis than any other. It happens that lying-in women cannot pass their urine for several days after confinement. Violence from without, as a blow or a kick, may have a similar effect. This results from the pressure to which the bladder was subjected. Operations on the rectum, vagina, or any of the pelvic organs, are frequently followed by a partial or complete paralysis. In all these cases, there is only one precaution to observe, and that is to draw off the urine at regular intervals so as to avoid an enormous accumulation of fluid.

The paralysis becomes dangerous and obstinate to treatment, in proportion as the bladder becomes abnormally distended, and the length of time that the muscular tissues are under the excessive strain.

In those cases where the paralysis is due to spinal or brain disease, there is little prospect of a cure. In other cases, as for instance after confinement or an operation on the rectum for piles or fistula, it generally passes off in a few days.

Great care and cleanliness must be exercised in using the catheter, so that the bladder is not infected from filth or virus from another patient. A catheter that has been employed on a patient who had her urine drawn off while she suffered from purulent catarrh or puerperal fever, will inoculate a healthy person with the same disease, and in this manner diseases are often communicated. The bladder is exceedingly liable to infection.

HEMORRHAGE.

A discharge of blood from the bladder is not of frequent occurrence, but it occurs often enough to make it noteworthy, and women should at least know that there is such a thing. It oftener takes place in men than in women, as a symptom of some grave or serious disease, or it may be only a trivial disorder. Hemorrhage of the mucous membrane takes place very readily, owing to the delicacy of the tissues and the great vascularity of the submucous layer, and there is a much greater tendency to hemorrhage in some persons than in others.

Persons who are weak and debilitated bleed much easier than strong, vigorous ones, because the blood may become so thin or poor in fibrin that it greatly loses its property of coagulating. Some diseases bring this particular diathesis about, such as scurvy, also measles, scarlatina or smallpox. Worms have been found to make their way from the rectum into the cavity of the bladder, and caused profuse and even fatal hemorrhage. A violent fall of the body, rupturing an artery in the bladder, severe horseback riding, and venereal excesses, have all caused almost fatal hemorrhages, to which must be added ulceration of the mucous membrane. The most profuse hemorrhage of the bladder that I was ever called upon to witness, followed drinking a strong decoction of wormwood; irritating diuretics, like spirits of turpentine or tincture of cantharides, are also liable to cause bleeding. Hemorrhage is always accompanied with frequent desire to pass urine and spasmodic pains at the neck of the bladder. The blood may also coagulate in the bladder, causing an obstruction. The treatment consists principally in keeping the patient very quiet, and a rubber ice bag should be applied over the region of the bladder; nothing but bland liquid food is advisable, but no hot drinks are permissible. If the urine does not pass, a soft rubber catheter should be employed for the purpose of drawing it off.

Hemorrhages of the mucous membrane, whether of the bladder, the bowels or lungs, generally yield to the following mixture:— —

NO. VIII.

Take:	Gallic acid	4 scruples
	Tr. of digitalis	½ ounce
	Fluid ex. of ergot	1 ounce
	Simple syrup	½ ounce

Mix, and give a teaspoonful in a little water every four hours; children in proportion.

URINARY FISTULA.

By this is meant a permanent unnatural opening into the bladder from without, through which urine escapes.

The situation of the female bladder, just in front and over the vagina, and also its attachment to a portion of the cervix or neck of the womb, exposes it to injuries, especially from pressure of the child's head during delivery. By referring to Plate II, it will be seen at a glance how easily an accident can take place from this cause. It was at one time supposed that delivery by forceps was the most fruitful cause of this lesion. That this is likely to happen only where the instrument is in incompetent or bungling hands, there is no reasonable doubt. A thorough acquaintance with the entire subject has proved that there are other causes that are the mainspring of this, sometimes very serious accident.

Indeed, the opposite view is now entertained by the profession; that is, that prompt delivery by forceps will prevent the parts from being injured, when the soft parts, and particularly the bladder, is under severe and prolonged pressure by the child's head. There is no question that there is greater peril to the mother and child, in undecisive delay, provided the attendant has the requisite judgment and experience to act intelligently.

The hypothesis upon which this is based is the restorative property that living tissue possesses, to regain its vitality, after it has been subjected to severe and inordinate pressure. This we may observe in our daily experience; when, for instance, we jamb or crush our finger, or a child has its fingers momentarily crushed between a closing door, the fingers are sometimes crushed flat, but upon being released, they rapidly regain their shape and vitality. If the pressure were continued for any length of time, the blood in the tissues would have become congealed, and the circulation permanently shut off, so that recuperation would have been impossible, and the tissues would have sloughed or mortified.

If the bladder, under the direct pressure of the child's head against the pubic bone, be subjected too long, the same results would naturally follow: the tissues could not regain their vitality, and they would either tear or subsequently slough or mortify, which causes the *fistula*.

The vagina and bladder, like every other tissue of the body, except that of the brain or nerves, will suffer a great deal of contusion for a short time, but if protracted beyond a reasonable length of time, it will be permanently destroyed or injured.

A urinary fistula is always a serious malady, since it exercises a deleterious influence upon the patient's health. If the opening is only small, a spontaneous cure may take place, but if it reaches considerable dimensions, it requires to be accurately adapted and stitched together. The best time for the repair of the injury, is six to eight weeks after the receipt of the injury.

Rupture of the female bladder is comparatively rare, for the reason that women are not exposed to the same serious accidents as men; but if women will persist in doing everything that men ought to do for them, the statistics may be reversed. When the bladder is distended and violence is brought to bear on the abdominal walls, corresponding to the region of the filled bladder, a rupture is likely to result. Surgical measures should at once be resorted to, so that the injury can be repaired before inflammation of the peritoneum sets in.

CHAPTER XIII
ACUTE AND CHRONIC INFLAMMATION
OF THE VAGINA

When speaking of inflammation of the vagina, reference is had to its mucous lining alone. It undoubtedly happens that structures or tissues beneath the mucous covering become involved in the inflammatory action, but this occurs so seldom that it is not of sufficient moment to make it the subject of an inquiry in a practical work.

The mucous membrane of the vagina, like all other mucous surfaces, has its natural secretion for the purpose of lubricating and keeping its surface moist. In a perfectly healthy state, the color of the vaginal mucous membrane is a pale red, this becomes scarlet red upon irritation. In girls who are not irritated or women who have not been abused by sexual excesses nor infected by disease, the normal secretion is just sufficient to preserve the moisture of its surfaces, but not in such an excess as to be noticed as a secretion or discharge outside of the vaginal canal. There is a physiological exception to this normal rule, a few days before and after the menstrual period, when the mucous membrane of the vagina sympathizes with the general congestion of the pelvic organs. The mucous secretion becomes then greatly increased, amounting to a catarrh or flow, this, however, is only transient and subsides with the cessation of the menses. This might with propriety be termed a natural or physiological catarrh.

For convenience of description and corresponding with the anatomical changes and the sources of their origin, inflammation of the mucous membrane of the vagina may be *acute* or *chronic*, simple or specific.

Acute inflammation in this instance is no different in its characteristic symptoms from inflammations elsewhere; it develops suddenly, and there is congestive swelling and pain. There is considerable heat in the parts, increased redness, and the canal is very sensitive. In the beginning the mucous membrane is dry and contracted, but after a few hours or a day, relaxation and moisture supersede. The secretion is very scant at first, but becomes more abundant as the disease progresses, its character also changes from a white, glairy mucus to a creamy, muco-purulent or yellowish discharge. The urethra may also become involved, and then the symptoms that were detailed in connection with urethritis are also present.

Acute vaginitis may arise from a great variety of causes, but the worst case that ever came under my notice was the scalding effect of a hot-water injection, given under the advice of a physician who had ordered the patient to use the water "as hot as she could stand it," and also told her "the hotter the better." This *profoundly wise* suggestion was carried out by the patient with a vengeance, for she used nearly boiling hot water, which she had tested by putting in her finger and quickly withdrawing it. The steaming fluid so scalded the vagina that a most pronounced acute inflammation of the vagina was the immediate result. I have had other cases of the chronic form come under my notice that were aggravated by similar advice, so that a word of warning against the thoughtless and indiscriminate use of hot-water injections will not be without value.

The vaginal irrigations of hot water, as a general stimulant to the mucous surfaces, or as an alterative to stimulate the absorbents to increased activity in removing old pelvic exudations, deserve a recognized place as a useful therapeutic measure, often of the greatest value, but too hot or "as hot as the patient can bear it," is superlative nonsense and absolutely injurious.

No water injections into the vagina that are kept up any length of time should be warmer than 110 degrees Fahr. and never should vaginal injections be employed without using a thermometer to gauge the heat. When the solution is medicated, 103 degrees should be the average temperature, but it should never exceed 107 degrees Fahr. Exposure to cold and moisture especially during the menses is prominent among the causes of acute vaginitis; injury from pessaries or coition, retained putrefying secretions in the vagina, or the application of chemical preparations, or injury during confinement, will all induce this disease. Prolonged nursing causes anæmia, which predisposes the system to catarrhs. During the child-bearing period catarrhs of the vagina are quite common, and excessive coition excites a very painful inflammation of the vaginal mucous membrane.

Gonorrhœal infection arising from a specific contagion gives rise to a very painful and dangerous vaginitis. The character and nature of the specific virus admits of no particular description, because its infectious quality of a specific nature does not at all depend upon the physical appearance of the infectious discharge from the male. Whether it is yellow or greenish, muco-purulent or a glairy mucous discharge, establishes no criterion, but the presence of microbes, the *gonococcus* of Neisser; this, of course, a careful microscopic examination can alone establish. This much is true, that careful researches in Europe, by competent and reliable authorities, have established the fact, from carefully-prepared statistics, that this is a far more fruitful source of uterine diseases than was formerly dreamed of.

A specific vaginitis has a greater tendency to spread itself along the mucous tract of the genital organs of the female than a simple non-specific catarrh. In the former the womb and Fallopian tubes become successively affected, as we shall learn more definitely when we have occasion to inquire into the diseases peculiar to these organs.

Acute inflammation of the vagina has pronounced symptoms, and when any one of them is felt by the patient, she should lose no time in resorting to treatment.

The first symptom that is generally perceived by the patient is a sense of heat and burning in the vaginal canal; this is also reflected in the neck of the bladder during micturition. As the disease develops, there is a constant desire to pass water frequently, and this becomes sometimes a prominent sign. A dull aching weight is felt between the vagina and rectum. After these have lasted for some days, an offensive discharge from the vagina ushers in the second stage, excoriating the skin around the vulva, and if the disease should spread itself to the neighboring organs, there is a violent throbbing pain in the whole pelvis.

Women who are suffering with acute painful vaginitis should take to bed; all pelvic diseases of any acuteness at all are treated at a great disadvantage when the patient is running around and on her feet. The disturbance in the circulation, the exposure to cold from cold floors or damp sidewalks, and the impossibility of preserving an equable temperature of the body, when out of bed, only aggravate the malady.

The vagina is to be douched several times a day with half gallon of warm water, in which a half teaspoonful or one tablet of Femina antiseptic uterine lotion has been dissolved, and when the canal is rinsed, a Femina vaginal capsule should be introduced, but only once a day, and that is preferable at bedtime. The feet and extremities should be kept warm, and in married women total continence should be observed while the slightest irritation and soreness exists. By the non-observance of this precaution, the best directed efforts will often be frustrated and many female diseases which are readily curable in the beginning become chronic, and a moment's reflection ought to make this clear to any person of ordinary intelligence.

If there is the slightest suspicion that the disease is of a specific nature, the treatment must be antiseptic in its nature. Your physician should be reminded of the possible nature of the disease, for doctors as a rule are ignorant of the dangers that ordinarily accompany gonorrhœal infection.

Oppenheimer in Germany made experiments for testing the germicidal properties of various drugs on the specific germs of gonorrhœa, and he proved that a corrosive sublimate solution of 1 part to 20,000 will kill the gonococci. Corrosive sublimate is the corrosive chloride of mercury, one of the most powerful of the mineral poisons, and while it is perfectly safe in the dilutions that it is employed in, the greatest precaution must be constantly exercised to keep the drug isolated and out of the reach of children, especially the "antiseptic tablets," of which mention will be made below, because little children and adults also might at first sight believe that they were candy.

I am accustomed to employ the *corrosive sublimate* much stronger than the Oppenheimer experiments demand, a practice which I base upon practical observations, while in the Berlin clinics, and that is in the proportion of 1 to 2,000. John Wyeth & Bro., of Philadelphia, and other manufacturing chemists, make compressed tablets or wafers, which are very convenient and easily handled by any person of average understanding. These are sold by the druggists in little wide-mouth bottles, properly labeled, so that the required strength, 1 to 2,000, is obtained by dissolving one or two according to their strength in a half gallon of warm water. Whenever gonorrhœa is suspected, the vagina should be thoroughly rinsed out several times a day with the corrosive solution. If the patient fears mercurial poisoning, the antiseptic irrigation can be followed by plain warm-water rinsings as a safe precaution against mercurial absorption.

CHRONIC CATARRH, LEUCORRHŒA OR WHITES.

An acute inflammation of the mucous membrane of any organ may drift into the chronic or subacute form, so that any of the causes which give rise to the acute variety are among those that are to be looked for in chronic catarrh. The general characteristics of catarrh are the same, whether acute or chronic or whether located in the nose, throat, bronchial tubes or vagina. This fact greatly simplifies the whole subject of catarrhal inflammations, so that the general reader will find no difficulty in acquiring the necessary information for successful home treatment of this very common class of diseases.

Chronic vaginal catarrh has been divided into two varieties, *vaginal and uterine*. The distinction depends upon its origin or complication. Vaginal catarrh has its origin in and is limited to the vaginal canal. I have already called attention to a purely physiological catarrh that accompanies the menstrual flow and which subsides with the cessation of the menses; in addition to this, there is probably no woman who goes through life without at some time during her natural existence having this disease or symptom.

Often the discharge is so scant that it entirely escapes her notice, and not until it becomes annoying by its constancy and abundance do women seek assistance.

In ancient times and until quite recently, it was considered as a distinct disease, attributed to constitutional debility or an indication of impure blood; these theories are now entirely discarded. The modern school of Gynecology has given it quite a different interpretation, and considers leucorrhœa rather a symptom of some local disease than a disease itself. Experience, and careful research in, the sick chamber fully corroborate the correctness of this view, so that a simple local chronic catarrh is the exception to the rule. The exception applies oftener to children than to adults. We find it in young babies or little girls of all ages as a result of diarrhœal discharges which are acrid and filter themselves into the vagina and by their sharp, irritating action on the mucous membrane, excite at first an acute, and afterwards a chronic catarrh of these parts. Eruptive fevers have induced a similar effect upon the mucous membrane of the child's vagina and also upon that of the bladder; obstinate catarrhs are frequently traced to these fevers. I have known pinworms to make their way from the rectum into the vagina and by their irritating presence excite in the little child a very distressing vaginal catarrh.

The irritation or itching which the inflammation and decomposed secretion cause, makes the child involuntarily dig or scratch her vulva, which of course only aggravates the disease, and which has already been mistaken for precocious masturbation, and will undoubtedly often be so considered again by superficial observers. In later years a subacute inflammation of these parts will undoubtedly develop this pernicious practice, and I have known several cases myself where young girls became physical wrecks from a combination of chronic vaginal catarrh and self-abuse, no one ever dreaming of the real morbid condition, but attributing their decline to everything else but the right cause.

There is another complication that may arise from catarrhal inflammation in little children, and that is an adhesive inflammation of the vaginal walls; that means that the sides of the vagina may partly or completely grow together, and thus change the normal diameter of the vaginal canal. In after years this may entail frightful suffering, either by mechanically obstructing the escape of the menstrual blood or otherwise interfering with the normal function of the canal. There are many diseases from which we suffer in adult life for which the foundation was laid when we were young, through the ignorance of our parents.

The stormy symptoms that usher in the acute form are absent in the development of the subacute or chronic variety. This disease begins sometimes so insidiously that the patient may not be aware of its existence for quite a while. The secretion may not be at first changed in its character, save that it is noticed in greater abundance. In the course of time, the nature of the secretion will be greatly changed, from a white glairy discharge into a grayish opaque secretion; this will be tinged greenish some days and be of a muco-purulent aspect. In the great majority of cases it is a whitish cheesy discharge from which the names *leucorrhœa* or *whites* have been derived.

The color of the vaginal mucous membrane in chronic catarrh is of a bluish red tint, and its surface presents in places granulated patches, that bleed easily when they are touched. The vaginal walls are relaxed, so that women often complain that they have a sensation of "feeling open;" this is indeed the real state of affairs; the walls of the vagina may become so relaxed as to constitute a prolapse of the anterior portion or wall of the vagina, dragging the bladder and womb down with it.

A great many of the so-called *"falling of the womb cases"* are no falling of the womb at all but simply a relaxed vagina, in which the wearing of pessaries or any other mechanical uterine supporter will actually do a great deal of harm.

The treatment of vaginal catarrh is principally local, when there are no constitutional complications. Of course there are rules of conduct that apply to all catarrhal patients, whether the catarrh is of the genitalia, of the nose or throat or of the bronchial tubes; these rules constitute the hygiene of catarrh, a subject which is discussed in a separate chapter in this work to which the intelligent reader is referred.

The main feature of the treatment consists in thorough cleanliness of the vaginal canal and in the use of a soothing lotion. This object is best accomplished by the use of the Femina antiseptic lotion and in the following manner: Dissolve one tablet or half a teaspoonful in a cupful of hot water and then add this to a half gallon of warm water of a temperature of 103° F., and by means of an elastic bulb syringe, use the entire quantity at one time. If the discharge is profuse, or if any offensive odor is perceptible, then the vaginal injection should be made several times a day.

In case there is soreness and pain in the pelvis, and there generally is, a Femina vaginal capsule should be introduced into the vagina, just before retiring.

When the patient feels a dragging sensation, or such symptoms as would indicate a prolapse (falling down) of the vaginal walls from weakness or relaxation of the columns and muscular tissue which give them support, then the Femina antiseptic uterine lotion should be used, as before described, with this difference, that double the quantity should be dissolved in the cupful of hot water, and then added to the half gallon of warm water of the same temperature and used in the same manner. When the Femina antiseptic uterine lotion is used in its double strength, the remedy loses nothing in its healing effect but becomes more astringent, strengthening, and disinfectant.

Be sure that the nozzle of the syringe sweeps the entire vaginal cavity, and if the above quantity of fluid should not be sufficient to thoroughly cleanse the vagina, then use double the quantity of fluid.

With this prescription I have cured cases of leucorrhœa of twenty years' standing which had gone through the ordeal of all the different treatments that they were capable of undergoing.

I would recommend to those patients who feel their wombs dragged down, the *knee-chest posture*, that means, to kneel down on the floor with the hips elevated as high as possible and the chest close down to the floor. This position rolls the abdominal organs upwards and forwards, and thus naturally draws the womb and vagina into their normal positions, much better than any mechanical appliance or operator can possibly accomplish it. It simply allows the relaxed organs, through the natural law of gravitation, to gravitate where they belong. It is necessary to retain this kneeling position for only ten or fifteen minutes, repeated twice a day, say night and morning, and the curative effect is truly wonderful.

When I speak of the curative measures of displacements in general and of falling of the womb downwards and backwards in particular, I will give a detailed description of the knee-chest position.

There should be a choice in selecting a vaginal syringe or a syringe for vaginal bathing. The "fountain syringe" has several objections that are insurmountable. In the first place, the quantity of fluid that is to be used is limited by the capacity of the reservoir, or in order to replenish it, the even tenor of the rinsing is disturbed. Another objection is, that the convenient peg upon which to hang it is not always present, or a shelf upon which to rest it not high enough; then there is not the control over the stream that is desirable, so that considerable confusion arises at times from the fluid wetting things that had better be kept dry. For these reasons I prefer a bulb syringe.

CHAPTER XIV
HYGIENIC MEASURES FOR CATARRHAL DISEASES OF THE FEMALE ORGANS

No treatment for catarrhal inflammations in general and of the pelvic organs in particular is certain and complete without special attention being given to certain laws or rules that are laid down for the preservation and attainment of health, and these comprise one of the collateral departments of medical science which is termed *hygiene*.

What the skin or integument is to the exterior of the body, the mucous membrane which lines the respiratory passages and other organs is to the interior of the body.

The mucous membrane is only a modification of the skin, and while it differs in its glandular composition in the different organs that it lines, in the main, it retains the common characteristics of the skin or outer covering of the body.

The *corium* or fibrous layer of the mucous membrane is analogous to the *derma* of the skin; and it is in fact a continuation of it at the orifices of the body.

The corium of the mucous membrane supports an epithelial layer of cells that are of various forms, differing in the different organs that it lines.

Underneath the corium of the mucous membrane there is the fibrovascular layer, which contains the blood vessels, lymphatics and nerves and embedded in the epithelial cells supported by the corium are the numerous mucous glands or follicles. In some portions of the mucous tract and projecting out of it are little elevations called villi or papillæ, analogous to the papillæ of the skin.

These glands and papillæ exist only at certain parts and are modified according to the function that the organ performs. The mucous glands of the stomach differ from those of the intestines, and those of the mouth from those of the bronchial tubes. The mucous membrane of the womb differs from all the rest, by having no submucous or fibrovascular layer; the mucous glands of the womb are imbedded and extend directly into the muscular tissue of the organ. The secreting glands, which form a special feature of mucous membranes, are abundantly supplied by small capillary blood vessels and nerves, so that any disturbance of the general or systemic circulation or a derangement of the nervous system will at once greatly influence the healthy or normal secretion of the membrane, just exactly as the skin is affected by cold or fright.

In order to appreciate all the causes that operate for either good or evil, we must pause for a moment and consider the sympathy with and the close relation of the mucous membrane to the circulation of the blood and the nervous system. The mucous membrane of the different organs is often made the safety valve through which obnoxious materials or morbid conditions of the blood are eliminated from the system, and for that reason I have long ago discarded the usual harsh measures in the treatment of sudden or acute catarrhs. I have found that, by carefully watching and giving close attention to the details of certain rules of health, catarrhs speedily disappear of their own accord: on the other hand, if irritating local remedies are constantly used, catarrhs continue to grow worse.

This demonstrated fact so very often repeated, impressed upon my mind the importance of hygienic measures for the successful treatment of catarrhal inflammations, whether they are of the respiratory organs or of the female pelvic organs. The most prominent and efficacious measures are to be found in intelligent precautions for preventing colds and inuring the system to changes of temperature by appropriate outdoor exercise.

By far the greater proportion of female complaints are catarrhal inflammations, and these fasten themselves upon all the pelvic organs—on the bladder, vagina, womb and Fallopian tubes.

We generally know how we contract a bronchial catarrh or bronchitis, a nasal catarrh or sore throat; in precisely the same manner do women contract most of their pelvic catarrhs, that is, from a common cold or sudden chilling of the body or part of the body.

Dr. Thomas F. Rumbold, in his work on the "Hygiene and Treatment of Catarrh," says: "The history of every case of chronic catarrh attests that the complaint commenced with colds in the head and that the disease grew upon the patient almost imperceptibly, the first colds being so trivial in character as to attract but little attention."

This statement is as true of the great majority of cases of vaginal and uterine catarrh as it is of catarrhs of the air passages, and for this reason the measures and precautions for the prevention of colds must be one of the features in the successful treatment of female complaints.

The particulars of the causation of colds and the hygienic precautions for their prevention are hardly ever given the attention which their importance demands in the treatment for catarrhal complaints of women, so that a great deal of suffering is left unrelieved and a great deal of expensive and useless doctoring is endured. Altogether too much reliance is placed upon a wash or some local application made by the doctor to the affected parts, and, indeed, the mainspring of the catarrhal affection is entirely overlooked or neglected, which is, the susceptibility to the recurrence of fresh colds.

The injurious effects of taking cold or chilling the body or any part of it, have been the subject of special inquiry in Germany. The mucous membrane and the skin seem the most sensitive to sudden changes from a warm to a colder atmosphere, but observations have already proven that besides the usual catarrhal inflammations, there are other inflammatory conditions that are developed. The kidneys, lungs, and liver have been found to be the seat of inflammations in a series of experiments that were made with rabbits that were removed from a warm to a much colder apartment, and from this may be inferred that these conditions originate similarly in the human subject.

The logical conclusions of these researches have been, that the chilled or cooled blood becomes chemically altered and acts as a direct irritant in the small capillary vessels, and by that means all the phenomena of inflammation of the tissues are excited, and these of course develop wherever the cold may strike or locate.

When we speak of a slight or a bad cold, we cannot form the least idea of the remote effects that the cold may bring about. It may lay the foundation of a nephritis or Bright's disease of the kidneys, or some other lesion, and that it often gives rise to vaginal and uterine catarrh is as certain as that it gives rise to nasal catarrh or a cold in the head.

An aptitude to take cold grows with each repetition of the attack and the prolonged duration of the acute catarrhal symptoms. And for that reason persons grow into the habit of taking cold upon the slightest exposure or change of temperature. At this stage of catarrh there is an abnormal sensitiveness of the mucous membrane and skin, in which the slightest draught of air or even passing from one room to another occasions an attack of sneezing or a chill and other symptoms that will indispose the patient for several days.

The great majority of individuals have a natural predisposition to certain diseases.

In anatomy the body has been divided into systems. A system is an assemblage of organs composed of the same tissues and intended for similar functions, as the circulatory system, the nervous system, the muscular system, the cutaneous system, etc.; these systems are all liable to particular diseases. In one person the mucous membrane of the respiratory system is the most sensitive part of the body, while in another, and especially in women, it is the mucous membrane of the genito-urinary system. In other words, one person will take a cold and it will settle in the head or on the bronchial tubes, while another from the same exposure will get a catarrhal inflammation of the bladder or womb; this is only explained on the theory of natural predispositions, and, perhaps, hereditary taints.

If a person once knows the weak or vulnerable points, he can outgrow them, by employing such rules of hygiene as experience has taught to be useful. There is much more benefit to be derived in an educational treatment directed to the prevention of disease, for this is also in the nature of a cure, than in a blind obedient faith in the treatment or remedy of a physician who may be ignorant, and generally is, of the laws of health or the science of hygiene.

To promote health and to antagonize disease is greatly within one's own power, because there is no doubt that most diseases are the result of imprudence that cannot be attributed to ignorance, because persons commit these errors with a full knowledge of their evil effects.

A healthy habitation, that has all the advantages of pure air and sunshine, is an essential feature in regaining health and encouraging a cure. There are hundreds of persons who have been sick and miserable for years, and who have made the rounds of all the doctors they ever heard of, without the least benefit to themselves, because they were never told how to live, and their living rooms are dark and sunless and poorly ventilated.

The even and equable temperature of all the rooms of a house should be kept in constant view, so that sudden and extreme changes of temperature are avoided.

Warming a dwelling artificially should be one of the important features in the construction of a completely-furnished residence. This subject has been neglected, owing to the temperate climate of California, yet the moisture of the air, and the closeness with which dwellings are built in cities, exclude the rays of the sun and make houses too cold for health and comfort. In our climate we become more sensitive to the cold air than those who live in drier regions.

In shaded houses and rooms, especially in damp weather, we need artificial heating as much as they do in colder climates, so that architects should make it a study to introduce a system of heating that will insure an equable temperature throughout the entire building, at a minimum of expense.

The fireplace or open hearth, which has become so popular with us as the pleasantest and healthiest mode of heating and also insuring ventilation, should be discarded for something much better. The fact that the fire is directly beneath the chimney flue explains the fact that eighty-seven per cent of the total heat yielded by coal or coke and ninety-four per cent of that yielded by wood escapes through the chimney. This enormous loss of temperature arises from the current of air necessary for combustion, carrying with it a large quantity of the heat produced which is lost in the atmosphere. This of course is a means of *ventilation*, but a little reflection will convince almost anyone that it cannot be the most practical, and in this State where coal is very high it is equally expensive. The smoke, soot, and ashes that are inseparable from the open fireplace make it troublesome and dirty, not to say anything of the coal gas, which poisons the atmosphere of a room, and I have often noticed its noxious influence on infants.

There are objections against warming one or two rooms of a house and leaving the others cold. A warm sitting room, while the halls and bedrooms remain cold and chilly, is a very fruitful source of cold and catarrhs.

There is a vast difference between heating for health, and heating to have warm rooms; in the former, the warm rooms would be incidental to health and comfort, while in the latter you might sacrifice health for warm rooms.

Heating by hot air has serious objections that may be briefly stated as follows: Fresh air passing through or around red hot furnaces, becomes so rarefied that it no longer contains sufficient oxygen for healthful breathing purposes.

The expansion and contraction of the furnace allows the escape of the noxious gases of combustion which become unavoidably mixed with the hot air that is to heat the dwelling, and thus vitiate the air that is to be breathed, and should there be any malaria from defective sewerage in the basement that, too, would be circulated with the heated air.

It seems also to be impossible to distribute hot air equally to all the rooms of a house through long flues, for the hot air is choked off at the registers by the counter currents of cold air from the rooms on the side of the house exposed to the winds, while the protected side is always overheated.

I have practically demonstrated, in my own residence, that hot water is the most simple and efficient means of heating a dwelling for both health and comfort, and for several reasons: There is no danger of overheating, and there is no possibility of vitiating the air, because the temperature of the hot water is always lower than even the boiling point.

With a proper distribution of the heated water through pipes, and radiators of sufficient heating surface, all rooms can be warmed to an equal temperature. Another consideration is the economy in fuel when properly constructed heaters are used, for the water readily absorbs the heat and retains it for hours after the fire has ceased to burn. Unlike steam heating, a moderate fire will warm the house in moderate weather. Hot water heating does not exclude a practical scientific system of ventilation. There is no danger from explosion, nor from fire, the plant is absolutely odorless and noiseless, and requires neither mechanical skill nor close attention to run it. There is no doubt of the durability of a hot water system, for if properly constructed it should last as long as the building, and the cost is less than a number of mantels with the necessary flues.

The most comfortable average temperature for living rooms is from 65 to 70 degrees Fahr., for hospitals and sick rooms a higher temperature is generally required, say from 75 to 80 degrees Fahr.

Dr. Horace Dobell, of London, in his work entitled "Winter Cough," makes some very practical and useful remarks, when he says: "But before leaving the subject of sudden changes of temperature, I must not forget to speak of sleeping rooms. It is quite astonishing what follies are committed with regard to the temperature of sleeping rooms. On what possible ground people justify the sudden transition from the hot sitting room to a wretched cold bedroom, which may not have had a fire in it for weeks or months, it is impossible to say, but it is quite certain that the absurd neglect of properly warming bedrooms, is a fruitful source of all forms of catarrh. We cannot too much impress this upon our patients."

There is another source of danger in artificial heating, and that is, in having the air of the house always much warmer than the most favored temperature of the open air. This is a great mistake because it is under these circumstances almost impossible to go from an overheated house or apartment into the open fresh air without catching cold, and for this reason the thermometer should be found in every well-regulated household. Women who are under treatment for female disease should never get into a cold bed, even if there has been fire in the sleeping room during the day. In damp and cold weather there should be greater precaution in this respect. The best bed warmer is one or more earthenware jugs, like the German seltzer water jugs, filled with hot water. Earthenware radiates the heat better and retains the warmth longer than glass, while there is no danger of the heat cracking the jug, as it will glass bottles. One or two of these jugs filled with hot water and put into a bed an hour or so before retiring will bring the temperature up to an agreeable warmth.

Proper clothing is perhaps from a sanitary standpoint of equal importance with that of artificial heating and ventilation. With appropriate clothing, the body can be protected against the inclemency of the weather and the sudden changes of the atmosphere so that no ill effects are experienced from the great changes of temperature to which we are exposed. Women are dressed less warmly than men, although they do not possess the bodily strength to resist cold in the same degree as men. Their garments are not only made of lighter material, but the loose, fluttering manner in which they hang around the limbs does not protect their bodies in the same thorough manner that similar material made after the style of men's clothing protects men.

This does not imply that women should don men's clothing, because the present costume or outside apparel of women of civilized countries, is both graceful and modest. A reform, however, in her *underclothing* is not only desirable but in many cases absolutely necessary to insure permanent relief from catarrhal affections.

All women who are suffering from uterine or pelvic diseases, and who are still wedded to the injurious costume of open drawers and skirts, have an important lesson to learn.

A warm and complete covering for the lower extremities and pelvic organs is paramount to any medicine or treatment that can be given.

It is during the menstrual period that the pelvic organs are more susceptible to congestion and inflammation from exposures than at any other time, and from the manner in which women dress, it is surprising that there is not more sickness among them than there really is. Wide and open cotton drawers, and skirts hanging loosely around their limbs, with cotton hose, are no protection against drafts and sudden changes, so that it often happens that the extremities are chilled and cold, which is in itself sufficient to cause uterine diseases. When this exposure continues, with some already existing disease, it will neutralize the best-directed efforts to accomplish a cure.

It is said of the celebrated Boerhave, that among his effects there was a carefully-sealed prescription, which contained the secret for preserving health and vigor to a ripe old age. In his last will and testament it was provided that the prescription should be sold to the highest bidder at public auction. A physician who was anxious to procure the recipe of this renowned Dutch doctor, bought it for a very high price. On breaking the seal and anxiously unfolding the paper, he found these words: "Keep the head cool, the extremities warm, and the abdomen free." The buyer was greatly chagrined at the simplicity of the supposed panacea, but, if the profession and the public only appreciated the real worth of the advice, there would be much less sickness.

This strikes at most of the evils in dress that pave the way for diseases of women. It comprises the evil effects of tight lacing and compressing the abdominal organs by improper support for the skirts. A corset should never be worn so tight that the hand cannot be passed through the waist line. In the absence of a waist or shoulder straps for the support of the skirts from the shoulders, shoulder straps should be fastened directly to the corset, so as to relieve the hips and abdomen from the weight of the clothing.

The corset waist is not only a perfect substitute for a corset, in supporting the bosom and preserving the form so as to give a handsome figure, but it supports the skirts without restricting the circulation and respiration, or compressing the abdominal organs. In buying or making a waist or bodice, particular attention must be paid to the shoulder bands, so that these bands are short enough to give the waist or bodice support from the shoulders. If, then, the skirts are buttoned to the waist, the weight is taken from the hips, where it injuriously depresses the abdominal organs, and falls on the shoulders, where it cannot do any harm. There is a good deal of humbuggery about these new devices, and those who make it a business to sell them, never take the pains, or are incompetent, to properly fit the waist. If one only bears in mind that, if the waist does not support the skirts from the shoulders, there is nothing gained over wearing an old-style corset, imposition is impossible.

The dressing for the feet should be warm and comfortable. Women who go to balls and parties should always wear overshoes in going to and coming from an entertainment. Thin and light shoes must be avoided in cold and damp weather; in fact, there is nothing that women should be more careful about than too light and low shoes which do not keep the feet warm. For comfort and keeping the feet warm, there is nothing like a loosely-fitting leather shoe, with wide and thick soles, and a low, flat, English heel. It is also the best "corn remedy" I know of.

When the weather is wet and cold, rubber overshoes should be worn, and these should be removed when entering the house. Women who have a tendency to cold feet, will find the cork or felt soles worn inside of the shoes, a great source of warmth and comfort. The coldest stratum of air is invariably on the floor of the room, and there is, perhaps, no easier or more unsuspected way to take a cold than to exchange a pair of high, warm shoes that fit closely around the ankles, for a pair of light, low slippers. If you desire to rest your feet in a pair of light slippers, then add a pair of heavy woolen socks over the stockings, this will greatly lessen the chances of taking cold.

Women who are suffering from pelvic or womb diseases, and who are anxious to get well, and those who are troubled with painful menstruation, and menstrual irregularities, should wear woolen hose. Thin cotton, silk-mixed, or silk hose are not sufficiently warm, nor do they retain the natural heat of the body like woolen stockings.

Those who have once accustomed themselves to woolen hose, should not discard them in the summer months for cotton, linen or silk goods, and this is to be particularly observed on this coast, but the hose should be exchanged for thinner and lighter goods of the same material, corresponding to the demands of the season. It would not be wise or prudent to wear the same quality and amount of clothing in warm weather as in cold; otherwise the excessive clothing in the summer months will induce perspiration on the slightest exertion, and thus the system becomes most susceptible to cold when the weather changes or becomes cooler.

Elastic garters to maintain the tops of the stockings in position should be avoided. Rubber bands make a continuous compression on the vessels and nerves, although almost every woman claims that she does not wear her garters tight, yet at night when she removes the elastics there are deep furrows marking the constriction of the garters. The spring-wire garters are just as injurious, for they also exert a continuous pressure.

The veins of the legs are, for the most part, superficial, and this steady and gradual compression is very injurious to the venous circulation, so that the blood is prevented from returning from the limbs as readily as it should; this induces cold feet, and when the circulation is already weak, it often imparts a feeling of heaviness to the limbs, for which women doctor but without getting any relief. The only proper support for the hose is elastic straps that are supported from the waist; they are now so well known and for sale in every dry goods store that a description of them is unnecessary.

To keep the legs and body warm is not a question of quality or quantity of skirts or wraps. If the limbs under them are not separately enveloped and are only covered with thin cotton or silk hose and open cotton drawers, women are continuously exposed to the cold, damp emanations from the ground and to the drafts caused by the motion of the skirts, and blasts of wind.

The most intelligent suggestions for Dress Reform are those that are directed towards reducing the weight or displacing the heavy, stiff, and unwieldy skirts and clothing the extremities of the female in divided garments, so that they are no longer exposed to the dangers of cold and drafts. The divided skirt is in the direct line of a modest and desirable improvement of woman's dress, and it is growing in popularity among the most intelligent of reading and thinking women. If the specialists of female diseases were to study the interests of their patients with the same ardor that they study the methods how best to fill their offices with patients, on whom they perform useless and dangerous operations, they would be of some actual benefit to our wives, mothers, and sisters, and our women could be dressed as gracefully as at present with less than half the underclothes to pack around with them.

I am decidedly opposed to anything approaching in style or shape the bloomer costume; the present style of outside dress cannot possibly be improved for a comely garment, but it is underneath this that an entire change should be speedily effected. The divided skirt is cut like drawers that have a width of thirty to forty inches of goods in each leg. I believe that the width of each leg should not be more than twenty-five to thirty inches; this makes the skirt warmer and lighter. This is not attached to a band to fasten around the waist, but to a yoke, which should be buttoned to the bodice waist, suspending the skirt from the shoulders. The material will be a matter of individual taste; the two qualities that should be always looked for are softness and warmth, and for that reason Jersey flannel and ladies' cloth are the most suitable material; in summer or warm climates, pongee or wash silks may be substituted.

The skirt is cut on the bias to fit the hips, where it is fulled in and attached to a yoke instead of a band and in the back it laps about two or three inches. The advantage of the divided skirt is that it protects the limbs and body against drafts and cold emanations, and takes the place of *all underskirts and petticoats*. This skirt alone, however, would be insufficient to accomplish all that is desired by way of guarding against exposures; for this reason there is also a so-called *Union suit* worn under the divided skirt to complete the covering of the limbs.

Union suits, as the name implies, unite a pair of closely-fitting drawers with an undershirt. There is no particular advantage in uniting the underdrawers with the undershirt, but there is certainly no disadvantage. The principal object that is to be attained is not in unionizing drawers and shirts, but wearing such *closely fitting undergarments* that the *extremities* are permanently protected, and in having them so lapped or closed that the *abdomen and pelvic organs* are securely protected against cold.

Equestrian tights are made on the same principle and for a similar purpose as union suits, namely, to properly and surely cover the limbs and in a measure displace the great load of petticoats that women usually wear. They come in drawers and also in combination suits with the undershirts; a choice may be left to individual taste. There are different *brands* of these goods on sale in all the dry goods stores of our large cities, the prices being regulated by material and quality of the goods from which they are made. The woolen goods are preferable for practical purposes.

Women who do not like the woven closely-fitting drawers can take their choice between the latter and home-made flannel drawers, the French flannel for the lighter and the English bully for heavier and warmer clothing will be found to be the most serviceable materials; patterns for making up closed or button drawers may be had at the leading pattern stores of any city.

Women who cannot grow up to an appreciation of the divided skirt should by all means wear equestrian tights or buttoned flannel drawers, under cotton or linen ones; this will enable them to throw off one or two petticoats or skirts because the drawers will safely substitute the skirts and be much lighter. Some women dread the absence of skirts on account of appearing too scant; a little extra fullness and drapery to the dress make the absence of skirts not noticeable. If this were not quite so, there appears no satisfactory reason why a woman should feel embarrassed to modestly display the contour of her form any less than a man.

CHAPTER XV
METRITIS OR INFLAMMATION OF THE WOMB

This is an inflammation of the entire substance of the womb, which, like all inflammatory processes, is *acute* or *chronic*.

Inflammation does not always affect the whole body of the womb, but it is quite oftener limited to one or the other layer or membrane that enters into its architectural whole. Then, again, there is the anatomical division of the organ into a body or *corpus*, and a neck or cervix; of these either one may be affected, without the other, so that inflammation of the cervix should be the subject of a separate inquiry.

Most of the diseases of the womb are due to inflammation. This was the opinion of J. H. Bennett, of London, as long ago as 1845, in which year the first edition of his work on "Inflammation of the Uterus" was published. Up to that time, the subject had never been practically pursued to the same logical conclusions, so that the opinions of the leading professional minds were far from unanimous on this question. But the vigor and energy with which the young author defended his views, forced attention and conviction upon the greater part of the profession, in this country and Europe.

He started out with a view to prove: "1. That inflammation is the *primum mobile* in uterine affections, and that from it follow, as results, displacements, ulcerations and affections of the appendages. 2. That menstrual troubles and leucorrhœa are merely symptoms of this morbid state. 3. That in the vast majority of cases, inflammatory action will be found to confine itself to the cervical canal and not to affect the cavity of the body."

Since the appearance of the first edition of Dr. Bennett's work, which is now forty-six years ago, there have been many careful and clever observers in this field of pathology, but there is yet to appear a successful contradiction of the truth of his inflammatory doctrine. Twenty-six years after Dr. Bennett wrote the above book, he read a paper before the British Medical Association on the same subject, in which there is no modification of his first conclusions on the importance of inflammatory lesions. He says: "1. Uterine displacements are by many too much studied *per se* (by themselves) independently of the inflammatory diseases that complicate and often occasion them. 2. That the examinations made to ascertain the existence of inflammatory complications are often not made with sufficient care and minuteness, as evidenced by the fact that I constantly see in practice cases in which inflammatory processes have been entirely neglected, and the secondary displacements alone treated. 3. That inflammatory lesions are often the principal cause of the uterine displacements through the enlargement and increased weight of the womb, or a portion of its tissues, which they occasion. 4. That when such inflammatory conditions exist, as a rule they should be treated and cured and then time given to nature to absorb morbid enlargements before mechanical and surgical measures are resorted to."

If these propositions could be engrossed and a copy sent to every doctor in the land, as a safe and sure guide in his treatment of diseases of women, it would prove a great boon to the suffering women of this country. One of the notorious abuses of the profession, is the penchant for the employment of mechanical means, either by means of instruments or the surgeon's knife. Women are wantonly subjected to painful and tedious treatments which in many cases only aggravate their original suffering, while a few simple rules of hygienic treatment would not only restore them to health and vigor, but would save them the privation of paying fees to incompetent, unscrupulous or avaricious doctors, who have only one ambition, that is, to get the patient's money. I have known an instance where this barbarous course under the guise of scientific treatment, broke up the home of a once happy and prosperous couple, and finally when the resources were so low that the expense incident to housekeeping and a nurse could no longer be defrayed, the household effects were disposed of, and, as a last resort, the overdoctored woman was taken to a hospital, where her last hopes were lulled into an artificial sleep, while the surgeons performed an operation from which her depleted body and squandered vitality could never recover. She died.

I am convinced from observations in large female clinics in Berlin, and from my own studies in the pathological laboratory while a student abroad, that Dr. Bennett's conclusions are corroborated by actual facts. The freedom with which dangerous operations are undertaken for comparatively trivial complaints is degenerating into a license that is criminal and which in some cases is nothing less than murder. In the absence of a high moral sentiment which should control the profession, but does not, the State must step in and say who shall practice medicine and surgery, and by limiting competition, the evil propensity to make the most of one's opportunities will not be elevated into a fine art, and men, although unscrupulous, may be at least indifferent honest.

Acute metritis comes on suddenly, and this occurs quite often during the menstrual period. Women as a rule are altogether too careless during menstruation; they seem to forget that at this time the womb is congested and swollen, and that if the natural flow of the blood is interfered with, this congestion will turn into an inflammation. Exposure to cold, or getting the feet damp, or inordinate exercise that overheats the system, will bring this about. Sometimes there may be a tumor or swelling in the womb which occludes the cervical canal, so that the menstrual fluid cannot escape; this will also cause inflammation. A stricture of the cervical canal, occasioned by the womb being flexed, will interfere with the egress of the menstrual flow, and this also may give rise to inflammation. Vaginal injections either too hot or too cold, and particularly immediately after copulation, when the pelvic organs are still in a high state of congestion, is quite liable to excite metritis. Gonorrhœal infection is another source of inflammation, but this is invariably preceded by an *endometritis*, which I will consider separately.

Large, ill-fitting pessaries worn in the vagina for a supposed retroflected or prolapsed uterus, or a stem pessary, are fruitful causes of metritis.

Other causes are criminal abortion, complicated with blood poisoning from the unclean probes or instruments, that the abortionist has employed on previous operations without thoroughly cleansing and disinfecting them; the application of strong caustics to the cervix of the womb, as well as injections into the cavity of the uterus. Meddlesome doctoring by means of the unskillful and unnecessary use of instruments, like the probing of the womb without proper antiseptic precautions, or the scraping, stretching or operating on the womb without the essential antiseptic precautions which a scientific comprehension of the subject demands, has frequently caused this affection.

It occurs very often as a part of the general inflammation produced by the absorption of putrid or septic matter during the childbed period. This indicates a lack of cleanliness on the part of the attendants during confinement; inflammations of this nature constitute one of the types of *puerperal* or childbed fever.

The most prominent symptom is pain. This is greatly aggravated on the slightest pressure, or on moving or turning in bed. Upon a digital examination, the womb is found enlarged or swollen, and when the organ is tilted up on the examiner's finger, there is a sharp lancinating pain radiating from it in all directions.

The first symptoms of pain are always accompanied with fever, and this may have been ushered in or alternated with a chill. The pain may be first felt rather deeply in the pelvis, and this is increased by a frequent desire to pass urine and a straining of the rectum. It may further become complicated with a looseness of the bowels, or an obstinate constipation. Nausea and vomiting is a frequent symptom during the course of the disease, and if the metritis is developed during menstruation, the flow may suddenly stop, but, on the other hand, the hemorrhage may become alarmingly profuse. Standing, walking, coughing and straining at stool excite the most excruciating pain, so that a recumbent quiet position is the only comfortable way for the patient to maintain herself, with the head as low as possible to insure the most easy recumbency.

The treatment for acute metritis depends somewhat on the cause in each individual case. There are, however, two indications that require to be met, and these are common to all inflammations, namely, to relieve the pain and check the inflammatory process.

The former is quickly relieved by introducing into the vagina a Femina vaginal capsule in the usual manner; repeating every six to eight hours, until the pain is sufficiently alleviated to occasion no suffering; then one capsule should be employed every night until cured or until restlessness requires that something must be done to calm the patient.

If the metritis is due to suppressed or checked menstruation from cold or exposure, then, and only then, are hot fomentations over the entire abdomen the most appropriate application, and if the patient is plethoric, I advise a half-dozen leeches to the inguinal region of one or both sides to be of unequaled value for checking the disease.

Until my experience and observation in German hospitals, I was in the habit of employing hot applications for all acute inflammations of the abdominal organs. These were either in the form of hot-water fomentations or flaxseed poultices. Hot applications undoubtedly give relief, but I doubt whether they ever cut short or abridge the inflammatory process in any case. I am inclined to believe that in a great many instances hot fomentations have the tendency to encourage suppuration, and that an abscess is often the result of their use. I have seen decidedly better results from *cold applications*, and the colder the better, so that I now employ them universally in all acute inflammations of the pelvic organs except in the noted exception in which the inflammation is due to a sudden check of the menses from exposure. As a preventive of inflammations, after delicate operations on the uterus, I apply the *rubber* ice bag with invariable success.

The most suitable rubber bag for this purpose is a size of six by twelve inches; it should be filled with broken pieces, and then securely tied. I prefer to envelop the bag in a thin layer of flannel, so as to take off the cold, clammy sensation which the rubber imparts to the skin. There should be two of these bags, in case of accidentally tearing one, and so that the reserved one may be in readiness when the other is removed. The cold does not only check and control the inflammation, but it also benumbs the nerves, so that it greatly relieves pain. I keep these ice bags applied over the region of the womb, until all the acute symptoms disappear. The vagina, however, should be irrigated with medium hot borax water, once a day, so as to remove any irritating discharge from the uterine cavity.

The digestive derangements that so often accompany acute metritis; the nausea and vomiting of this and kindred diseases, are alleviated by this formula: —

NO. IX.

Take:		
	Subcarbonate of bismuth	2 drams
	Bicarbonate of sodium	2 drams
	Tr. of opium, deodorized	2 drams
	Tr. of nux vomica	1 dram
	Simple syrup	1 ounce
	Peppermint water, sufficient to make	6 ounces

Mix, and take a tablespoonful every one or two hours, until relieved; to allay the thirst and dryness, take small pieces of ice. Constipation of the bowels should be relieved by taking a Femina laxative tablet every six hours until the stools are freely moved; after that one should be taken every night or perhaps every other night, so as to keep the system regulated.

Some persons suffer from costiveness because they do not drink enough water, and when taking medicines to correct this disorder it is always well to drink a large tumblerful of water at the same time, and especially at bedtime, three or more hours after supper, and early in the morning is another good time for drinking water and taking a laxative.

CHAPTER XVI
CHRONIC METRITIS OR CHRONIC INFLAMMATION OF THE WOMB

When from neglected or improper treatment, the acute inflammation is not checked, so as to restore the organ to its normal condition, the inflammatory process assumes a chronic character. As inflammation is an *abnormal vital activity*, which results in the proliferation or building up of fibrous tissue, it must be naturally inferred that if the inflammatory process is active in an organ for a considerable length of time, the tissues of this organ must grow or increase, so as to augment its size and weight. This is indeed so, hence the other names that have been given to this disease to distinguish it from the acute or transient form, all imply *tissue growth*, as hypergenesis of the connective tissue, engorgement or inflammatory hypertrophy of the uterus.

The entire organ may be thus affected, or it may be limited to either one or the other anatomical divisions of the uterus, namely, the body or the neck.

Of all the different varieties of chronic inflammation of the womb, that of the neck or cervix is the most frequently met. This is due to the fact that in married women and those who have born children the cervix of the womb is exposed to mechanical injury from coition, friction against the vaginal walls in walking and from lacerations during delivery.

The body of the womb is further removed from all these mechanical agencies to which the cervix is exposed, for the body is within the abdomen of the female, and for that reason it is less liable to be injuriously affected by influences that cause inflammatory enlargement. But notwithstanding all this, it is a common disease.

A great many cases of womb complaint that do not yield to ordinary treatment are really of this nature, but owing to carelessness or incompetency are never recognized. The symptoms of this disease, which are obstinate leucorrhœa, falling of the womb or displacements, are mistaken and treated for the disease itself. Women who suffer with this complaint are extremely liable to go on for quite a while feeling comparatively well and in hopes that they are recovering, when some extra exertion or exposure to cold brings on a relapse, which lights up an acute inflammatory process. This passes into the old troublesome disease and this resumes its chronic form. After a repetition of the general routine treatment, the patient may again live under the delusion that she is going to get well only to have her hopes blasted by a sudden reappearance of the former painful symptoms, that are alike discouraging to herself and a puzzle to her friends.

The cause of inflammatory enlargement of the uterus is usually connected with *parturition* or *abortion*.

There never can be either the one or the other without more or less *vascular activity*, which is essential to the repair of the womb and its restoration to its physiological or healthy condition. All the uterine tissues are at this time in a high state of irritability, and if there is a natural predisposition to inflammatory diseases, then the slightest obstacle to an uninterrupted recovery will kindle an inflammatory action, that will fasten itself on the uterus. In the very nature of things this results in a deposition of inflammatory material, with a consequent increase of intermuscular fibrous tissue which increases the size and weight of the uterus.

What our mothers termed in former days "a bad getting up," that is, when women get up from their confinement weakly and with more or less pain and dragging in the pelvis on walking or the slightest exertion, is generally owing to the above-described condition. This disease is now almost as common as ever. I can always trace these cases to a confinement or an abortion.

It is very rare that it is due to a depreciation of vital forces from improper food, over-exertion, a prolonged nervous depression or a constitutional tendency to tubercle, scrofula or some other hereditary diathesis, although these undoubtedly predispose the patient to the disease.

Abortions stand at the head of all the causes that excite this affection. When the uterus is pregnant and its natural growth is abruptly checked by the destruction of the embryo, then the organ becomes at once the seat of a congestion and great vascular activity, for the purpose of repairing the injury that the premature expulsion of the embryo or fetus inflicted.

If this congestion is delayed from improper care or treatment which fails to recognize the important fact that an abortion or interruption of pregnancy is a much greater shock to the system than a delivery at full term, it must result in arrested *involution* or permanent inflammatory enlargement. This most persons fail to appreciate, and, as a result, they do not take the same precautions that they would after the delivery of a living or fully-developed child.

I am well aware that criminal abortionists are in the habit of deceiving their patrons by assuring them that there is no danger or bad results to be feared from their criminal operations. This is a vicious falsehood, and, coupled with the statement that there is as yet no living being in the womb, the crime of manslaughter is added to that of malpractice. In every case of abortion, whether accidental or criminal, the same care and attention must be given to the woman as during any natural lying-in period.

There is a class of chronic inflammations that I have noticed in women who have always suffered from painful menstruations or from excessive or prolonged hemorrhage at the regular monthly period. This is complicated with some ovarian disease, which yields, however, to appropriate treatment.

There is quite a series of symptoms that denote the existence of chronic metritis; these are not all present in each particular case but quite enough of them to diagnose the disease. Some of these symptoms are in the nature of complications, which in themselves may be mistaken for an individual disease, but upon a careful inquiry they can be traced directly to a chronic metritis, which if removed disposes of all the lesser ailments.

The following are the most noted signs of this affection: painful copulation, and pain on defecation; a dull, heavy, dragging pain through the pelvis, much increased by walking; during menstruation the mammæ are sensitive or painful; several days before the approach of the menses there is a dull pain, which lasts during the menstrual flow; around the nipples, there is pigmentation or darkening; sometimes nausea and vomiting, and dyspepsia, headache, and languor; pressure on the rectum with tenesmus and hemorrhoids; leucorrhœa from catarrh of the womb; pressure on the bladder with tenesmus or straining.

This disease may continue for years uninterruptedly, and, if there is not a cure accomplished, or successful measures for its relief are not employed, it will continue until the menopause, or change of life, which may effect a spontaneous cure.

The enlargement is most noticeable in the cervix or neck. This is sometimes so great as to extend one or two inches into the vagina, and this condition is often mistaken for falling of the womb or prolapse, which is far from a correct diagnosis. A growing of the womb from chronic inflammation is the proper explanation.

The hygienic suggestions given in a former chapter, form an important auxiliary in the treatment of this complaint, and for that reason it should be carefully studied.

The treatment of chronic metritis has been, up to within a very recent period, anything but satisfactory in its results. This was owing to an inadequate knowledge of the real nature of the disease, which was marked by so many symptoms that were in themselves obscure and hard to separate as such, from the main affection.

This confusion of the true nature of the pathological process, resulted in a great many vague therapeutical resources, so that the treatment is even yet far from uniform and thorough. Many of the recognized resources laid down in the text-books, on diseases of women, are not only useless, but absolutely injurious, and, in order to save the reader time and money, I will make a brief mention of the most prominent of them.

Depletion, or the abstraction of blood in chronic metritis, effects no permanent benefit in the inflammatory process. I am convinced that, in the long run, the patients grow worse, because this treatment lowers the vitality and reduces the recuperative forces, which are so important, in the treatment of all chronic complaints.

Scarifications or puncturing the cervix with a sharp lance or pointed knife, will not sufficiently impress the morbid process, so as to stimulate it into a healthy action.

Some authors speak very highly of cauterizations and blisters upon the neck or lips of the womb; this I have repeatedly tried, and in not a single instance was it of the slightest use, but it aggravated the symptoms, and in one case it excited a severe, acute metritis that proved almost fatal.

Specialists, as a rule, fall into routine practice, and exercise neither originality or intelligence in practice, outside of the text-book on their shelf. They inject strong fluids or caustics into the cavity of the womb with a view of checking the inflammation in that manner. This treatment is dangerous and delusive. If the patient endures the treatment, she may be stimulated for a time with the idea that something very curative is being done, but my experience has been that the disease only becomes worse, because the womb is too delicate and sensitive an organ to improve under these repeated irritating assaults.

There is a *home treatment* for mild cases which I recommend to my patients, with satisfactory results. It consists principally of dissolving one teaspoonful of the Femina uterine lotion in a cupful of boiling hot water, after which this should be added to a gallon of warm water of a temperature of 105 degrees F.; these irrigations are to be taken every night, and if the water can be borne hotter the temperature may be gradually increased to 107 degrees F. A napkin should be worn and the bed warmed with a hot water bag before retiring. Ten to fifteen minutes later a Femina vaginal capsule is to be introduced high up into the vagina, by first quickly dipping the capsule into warm water.

In obstinate cases I have used electricity with the greatest success. This is administered by means of a broad dispersing electrode applied on the abdomen, and another electrode, covered with a sponge, is carried up the vagina, to the womb. In this manner I employ an intensity of sixty to one hundred and fifty milliampères, for ten to fifteen minutes. This is repeated several times a week, and from three to six weeks, and with other hygienic treatment the patient recovers.

When women are in moderate circumstances, and can spare neither time nor money to visit the office, for the length of time that is required for the electrical treatment, I follow the plan of the Berlin clinic, which originated in Vienna, with Prof. Carl Braun, and is strongly recommended and practiced by Dr. Martin, in Berlin. This consists in an *amputation of the cervix*, or, in other words, the abnormally elongated and enlarged uterus is trimmed down, and the diseased membrane is scraped out. While the cervix is recovering from the operation, there is also a diminution in the size of the body of the organ, and the chronic inflammation subsides with it. This operation is not dangerous to life, and in my experience I have as yet never had a bad symptom to interrupt the recovery. In obstinate cases, it is, perhaps, one of the most useful surgical measures that was ever devised, and we owe it to the genius of Professor Braun, that all obstinate cases of this nature are amenable to successful treatment.

CHAPTER XVII
ENDOMETRITIS OR CATARRHAL
INFLAMMATION OF THE WOMB

Endo means within, and metritis signifies *womb* and *inflammation*, and when all are combined, the compound term denotes inflammation of the lining membrane of the womb, which is the affection that I am now to consider.

It would be impossible to find a single person of middle age who has not experienced sometime during life the discomforts of a catarrh or cold of some part of the respiratory passages, whether in the head or bronchial tubes.

The mucous membranes are especially sensitive to noxious influences, and sound a timely note of warning by an *acute catarrh*, which, if heeded, will in many instances save the person from a dangerous, if not fatal sickness.

The adage, "Prevention is better than cure," is one of the most truthful sayings in the English language, and, if persons would profit from the admonitions of a *"slight cold,"* many a fatal pneumonia or bronchitis could be averted.

What is true of the mucous membrane that is common to both sexes is true of that which is peculiar to the female organs alone.

There is no mucous membrane that is more liable to catarrhal inflammations than that lining the uterus. There never was a woman who was not some time in her life afflicted with a transient uterine catarrh. It may have been of so mild a form that the symptoms which it occasioned were hardly noticed, or, perhaps, ascribed to some other ailment.

There are several varieties of endometritis; some of these are based upon the length of time that the affection has lasted, while others owe their classification to the anatomical division of the uterus into body and cervix. Those that relate to the duration of the disease are either acute or chronic.

Acute endometritis is the most common form; it has also been described under the names of acute uterine leucorrhœa, acute uterine catarrh, and acute internal metritis. It usually runs a rapid course, ending in recovery or in the chronic form. It undoubtedly passes unrecognized in many instances, and in this way many cases of painful menstruation or suppressed menstruation are explainable.

It can be said that at each and every menstrual period there is a *physiological catarrh,* which belongs to the natural process of the menstrual function. During each menstruation there is a hyperæmia, or congestion of the mucous membrane, so that the turgent blood vessels rupture, and this constitutes the menstrual flow. Before this congestion reaches the point of bursting the capillaries, and about the time that the sanguineous flow ceases, there is an increased and altered mucous secretion of the mucous membrane. If this secretion is prolonged beyond the normal period that constitutes healthy menstruation, or if it continues to be present at any time between the menstrual periods, it constitutes a disease or a catarrh. Now when we consider the close relation that the normal functions of the womb have to those that are *abnormal,* and that the one may be the stepping-stone to the other, we need not be surprised that endometritis, or catarrh of the womb, is one of the most common affections to which women are liable.

Chronic endometritis is where the disease has lasted for a long time; some authorities consider it a rare affection, but this is a great error. Any disease so frequent as acute endometritis must, in the very nature of inflammatory processes, become chronic, in a large proportion of cases.

Endometritis of the body of the womb, in contra-distinction to a partial inflammation, located and confined to the mucous membrane of the neck or cervix of the womb, forms another or third variety of this affection. This disease has been described under the names of chronic corporeal endometritis, uterine catarrh, uterine leucorrhœa, and internal metritis, and the seat of it is confined to the lining membrane of the cavity of the womb, without complicating the cavity of the cervix; but there is no doubt that when either the one or the other is the seat of a stubborn catarrh, the remaining portion of the uterus must become sooner or later more or less compromised in the diseased process.

Chronic cervical endometritis is where the inflammation affects the membrane of the neck; this has been described under the names of cervical catarrh, cervical leucorrhœa, and endocervicitis. These terms are all derived in composition from the Latin word *cervix,* neck.

The uterus is really divided into two cavities that run into each other; one of these is the cavity of the body, while the other is the cavity of the cervix, a fusiform canal, measuring about one inch and a quarter in length. The cervix partly projects into the vagina, and, as a result, is liable to injury and irritation, to which the other portion of the organ is not exposed.

Friction and other influences aggravate the inflammatory process, so that erosions, granular and cystic degenerations, follicular ulcers and chronic enlargements, become complications of the catarrhal inflammation of the cervix.

To return again to a consideration of the general aspect of catarrh of the womb, for it is one and the same pathological process that underlies the different forms. There is a simplicity in the relation of cause and effect, that will strike the casual student as one of the most instructive lessons that it is possible to learn, because it also suggests the simplicity of the measures of which persons can avail themselves for the prevention or cure of this affection.

From the physiological reasons that were mentioned as a cause of endometritis, it follows, as a natural consequence, that the predisposition to catarrh of the womb, varies greatly with the age of persons, so that before the age of puberty, at a time when there are no periodical congestions of the womb from the menses, it occurs very rarely, while from the period of pubescence, and during the functional activity of the pelvic organs, it is very prevalent, but at the approach of the menopause and sexual decadence the predisposition is again lost.

As far as the character and nature of uterine catarrh is concerned, that which in technical language is termed the *pathological anatomy* is no different from what it is in catarrhal inflammations in other organs, so that the remarks that were made on similar affections of other organs, apply with equal correctness to catarrh of the uterus.

There is, however, one exception of which I desire to remind the reader, and that is a hemorrhagic or granular variety of inflammation. In this form of the disease the mucous glands, and the blood vessels that are distributed between these glandular tubules, increase or multiply enormously, so that I have seen the mucous membrane in some places a quarter of an inch in thickness. This is the most obstinate variety to yield to ordinary remedies, and as it occasions excessive and at times dangerous hemorrhage from the womb, it should not be treated as conservatively as the other varieties of which I have spoken.

There is only one sure method of cure that proved in my hands a success, and that consists in the entire removal of the diseased mucous surface.

Dr. Düvelius of Berlin made the discovery and demonstrated the fact that the mucous glands of the uterus project into the muscular tissue of the organ, and that if the diseased mucous membrane is removed or scraped off, down to the muscular layer, a healthy membrane is regenerated from the terminal glandular ends that remain imbedded in the muscular tissue. This seems to have been proved by experience, for I have performed this operation in several obstinate cases of uterine catarrh, and in several instances the woman became subsequently pregnant, which proves at least that the regenerated mucous membrane is capable of performing its physiological function, as though it never had been interfered with. With proper antiseptic precautions and in skillful hands, there is absolutely no danger in this operation, but the technique should be thoroughly understood by the operator.

The etiology or causation of uterine catarrh resolves itself into predisposing and exciting causes. Predispositions are defined as that constitution or condition of the body which disposes it to the action of disease under the application of an exciting cause. Persons who possess a thoroughly healthy constitution may be exposed to exciting causes without the slightest danger of contracting diseases, to which others who are predisposed fall victims. The predisposing causes of endometritis are a naturally enfeebled constitution; the existence of a scrofulous or tuberculous habit; impoverishment of the blood from chlorosis; prolonged mental depression; improper and insufficient food; prolonged lactation; frequent parturition under unfavorable surroundings; any indiscretion after delivery which interferes with the regeneration of the womb; styles of dress that depress the uterus; want of fresh air and wholesome exercise.

Professor T. G. Thomas, in his work on Diseases of Women, asks the question why most of these influences should produce this affection more than others. His answer is that "they do not do so." "Sometimes they cause chronic pneumonia; at other times granular lids, and again at other times chronic endometritis."

The exciting causes laid down by the same eminent authority are "displacement of the womb; excessive or intemperate coition; the use of intra-uterine pessaries; puerperal endometritis; exposure or fatigue after confinement; efforts at production of abortion and prevention of conception; vaginitis either simple or due to gonorrhœal infection; painful obstructive menstruation; exposure during menstruation; sudden checking of the menstrual flow; and tumors in the uterine cavity or walls." Some of the causes here enumerated are much more fruitful of the disease than others. A woman whose constitution has been weakened, and whose digestion is deranged, by habits of indolence and luxury, whose style of dress so depresses the abdominal viscera that her uterus is pressed down into the vagina, is particularly liable to develop a catarrhal inflammation from connubial approaches. When these are not without pain, then there is some predisposition that should be inquired into and righted.

Uncleanliness is not spoken of by authorities as among the causes of uterine catarrh, yet it is a very frequent one. I have succeeded in curing so many catarrhal affections of the vagina and uterus by simply advising the use of vaginal irrigations with *borated* warm water, that I am convinced that a lack of personal cleanliness is a very prolific cause of this affection. The accessible generative organs, both of the female and male, should be the object of thorough rinsings so as to reduce the possibility of infection to the least degree. All mucous membranes have their natural secretions, and these are on light provocations abnormally increased. The vagina is always the seat of more or less bacterial fermentation or decomposition, and if this is retained for any length of time, it becomes not only putrid and offensive, but also a direct source of infection to the mucous membrane of the womb. This is more so in a married woman, who is exposed to the carelessness of her male consort, who has not been apprised of the dangers of septic infection, that may be innocently communicated to the wife by negligence of his own person. The wife is exposed to all and every impurity that the male has on his person, and thus she is in constant danger of having her internal organs infected, from the outer organs of the male.

There is no doubt that many women become infected from this source, and that obscure and stubborn catarrhs of the vagina and womb are strictly traceable to personal uncleanliness of the male. From the researches of Dr. Noeggerath of New York, it would seem that in a great many cases of pelvic diseases in women, the affections can be traced to a *latent gonorrhœa* in the male. This phrase means a gonorrhœa in the male apparently cured, which even two years after the supposed cure infects a healthy vagina, causing a discharge and a complication of the uterine mucous membrane. I have seen some cases that fully corroborate the views of Noeggerath, so that before we put the blame of uterine disease solely on the shoulders of the wife, let us find out how much the husband is to blame.

Specialists in particular, but doctors in general, often forget that a woman has other organs besides a womb and ovaries; there is a relation of cause and effect between valvular lesions of the heart or diseases of the lungs, that obstruct the return of the venous systemic circulation to the right cavity of the heart, and catarrhal diseases of the pelvic organs.

Biliousness or an affection of the liver, that interferes with the portal circulation, or the pressure of tumors or swellings on the uterine veins, are also among the causes, while the accumulation of feces or habitual constipation is often overlooked as too trivial to deserve professional notice, and yet its removal is often the only successful means to cure the patient.

The various eruptive and infectious diseases, like smallpox, scarlatina, measles or typhoid fever, may excite in their course a uterine catarrh, that will remain behind as a chronic complaint, after the acute affection has subsided.

The acute variety of endometritis is much more prevalent as a disease than is commonly supposed, but, owing to an absence of specific or definite signs, pointing directly to the mucous membrane, which the woman herself can recognize, it is generally mistaken for something else.

The disease begins with signs of an active congestion in the pelvic organs; such as drawing pains in the small of the back and in the groins, and a feeling of fullness and weight at the bottom of the pelvic floor. The urine is voided with pain and there is a sensation of heat in some parts of the urethra. Pressure on the lower abdominal region is painful, and the sensitiveness diminishes from the middle towards one or the other side. In mild cases these symptoms are not accompanied with fever, headache or a disturbance of the nervous system; there may be diarrhœa due to reflex irritation of the rectum, and the stools are accompanied with bearing-down pain. After three or four days there is usually a discharge of a viscid liquid, which in eight or ten days becomes creamy, purulent and often tinged with blood. The fluids that are discharged from the vagina sometimes become so acrid and irritating that, when they come in contact with the skin of the vulva, abdomen or thighs, it becomes irritated and inflamed, which leads to excoriations and an itching, that may spread over the entire body. The reaction of this discharge is either acid or alkaline, depending upon whether the discharge of the uterus or that of the vagina predominates; as the discharge from the uterus is always alkaline and that from the vagina always acid, there is nothing of a practical diagnostic value in ascertaining the chemical reaction of the secretion. The vagina will generally be found to be hot and more or less swollen as in ordinary vaginitis. The womb itself, however, will be enlarged and sensitive, while the cervix is gaping or open. Through the speculum, it is seen to be red and congested, and from the gaping mouth there issues a clear, albuminous-looking fluid or a muco-pus.

In the subacute or chronic form the symptoms are by no means always so prominent as to indicate the existence of the affection, or they are so marked, by some of the numerous complications, which are in the nature of cause or effect, that its recognition will become extremely difficult. The effect which the disease has on the general organism varies greatly in different individuals. Some women of robust appearance have an aggravated form of uterine catarrh without any immediate ill effects on their nutrition or general health. Other women lose flesh early and become weak and worn; they become pale, and the face assumes a yellowish ashen hue with dark rings under the eyes. Through reflex irritation from the nerves of the uterus other nerve centers become involved, so that a general neurasthenia becomes developed with its characteristic concomitants of neuralgia, muscular spasms, uterine colic and hysteria.

With a third class the inflammation spreads from the lining membrane to the substance of the womb itself, causing an enlargement of the uterus, which induces displacements and a dragging sensation in walking, pain in coitus and painful defecation. The inflammation does not limit itself to the womb, but an ichorous discharge creates distressing symptoms of vaginitis, inflammation of the bladder, and pruritus vulvæ.

When the uterine cavity is the seat of an abnormal vascular activity, there often exist symptoms of pregnancy that may mislead the patient or physician. Nausea and vomiting are sometimes present, the darkening of the skin around the nipples, and an enlargement and sensitiveness of the breasts, meteorism, or a swelling of the abdomen, caused by the accumulation of air in the intestinal canal from reflex nervous irritation, and when this symptom is added to the irregularity of menstruation, it is easy to fall into the error of diagnosing pregnancy.

Sterility on the one hand, and habitual abortion on the other, should direct attention to the probable existence of endometritis. Very often barrenness has led to an investigation of the condition of the uterus which disclosed the existence of the disease. A woman who conceives, and then loses her child in the first months of pregnancy, is afflicted, in all probability, with a chronic endometritis. In these cases, where conception takes place, it is to be presumed that the sensitiveness and irritability of the inflamed mucous membrane is not suitable for the permanent fixation of the ovum, so that the slightest shock will open the flood gates of a congested uterus, and thus the embryo is separated from its attachment, and lost.

The cervix is sometimes the seat of a special feature of uterine catarrh, that is due to the chronic inflammation of the cervical mucous membrane, stimulating a growth or proliferation of its own tissue or structure. This growth causes an enlargement and elongation of the entire cervix, and a spreading of the lining membrane of the cervical canal to the vaginal surface of the cervix. This encroachment of the cervical lining on the vaginal lining is the displacement of the pavement epithelial cells of the vaginal portion by the cylindrical or columnar epithelial cells of the cervical canal, and this gives rise to *erosions* and follicular ulcers.

These erosions have a glandular arrangement, and are often mistaken for cancerous or malignant growths. There is no doubt in my mind, that most of the so-called successful cures of cancer were nothing but cures of erosions.

The microscopists, whose lively imaginations make them see things that do not exist, would make us believe that they can take a small section of the suspected growth, and establish the existence of cancer by microscopical examination; this is utterly impossible, because the cancer cell is no different from normal cells, and in erosions we often find the follicles so close to each other, and their cells so closely packed, one on the other, that no candid mind can say whether it is a malignant or an innocent growth.

The claim that "nests of epithelium cells," as the stereotyped phrase goes, constitute scientific evidence of cancer, is utterly absurd. Such eminent authority as Professor Arnold, of Heidelberg, makes the assertion that positive diagnosis of cancer, from a small section or scraping, is impossible. I am myself fully convinced of the truth of this assertion, for while I was making microscopical studies in Germany, I had abundant evidence of the truth of this statement. It is indeed very unfortunate, both for science and suffering humanity, that as yet there is no absolute means of diagnosing cancer positively, and for that reason the quacks, and those who are not quacks, will continue to fleece their victims for supposed cancer.

I believe that the cause of cancer is either due to a *ptomaine* or organic poison that is generated in the body, or to a specific germ or bacillus. If it be due to the latter, and the germ theory of disease makes that highly probable, there is no doubt that a method of staining will soon be discovered, that will make the specific microbe recognizable in the field of the microscope, but as yet most cancer diagnoses by microscopy are only surmises.

TREATMENT.

Continence in sexual intercourse is one of the prerequisites to the successful treatment of all uterine diseases. This is so often overlooked by those giving advice in such matters, that their otherwise appropriate suggestions for treatment are frustrated. The women who are suffering, appreciate the value of this interdiction without further argument, but the average man does not appear to have the common sense to readily comprehend that the mechanical irritation incident to the sexual act, and the accompanying physiological congestion, will surely aggravate an inflammatory process, no matter of what nature. Men, whose animal instincts dominate their entire being, so that reason, if they ever had any, is dethroned, should stop to consider their immoderate conduct, which perpetuates the suffering of their wives from ailments which men themselves have often inflicted, and for which women are innocent martyrs.

The acute variety of uterine catarrh is to be treated like all other acute inflammatory diseases.

The patient should at once take to bed, so that she may keep herself warm and quiet.

If the inflammation is due to cold or exposure during menstruation, and the menstrual flow has been suddenly checked, then three or four leeches, applied to the inguinal regions on both sides, will be of decided advantage. Over the lower abdominal regions hot compresses should be applied; these are made by wringing cloths or a large folded towel out of hot water, over which a piece of oiled silk, rubber, or oilcloth is laid to retain the heat and moisture. At other times, that is, when the inflammation is not due to cold and a sudden stoppage of the menses, the application of ice bags is preferable to the hot compresses, in the manner elsewhere described.

The pains which are felt in different parts of the pelvis are relieved by using the Femina vaginal capsules; say one every six to eight hours, after a hot vaginal injection of plain water, or a hot sitz-bath. If there is nausea or vomiting that too is often relieved from the soothing influence of the capsule which allays the nervous irritability.

Should the stomach not be in a condition to take nourishment from biliousness or other causes, prescription No. II should be taken in tablespoonful doses every four hours until the stomach is settled and the system regulated; if any food is taken it should be between times and of a liquid nature.

If there is straining or diarrhœa, I prefer to employ an *enema* of one pint of warm German chamomile tea, to which half a teaspoonful of McMunn's elixir of opium or laudanum is added. If the pain and straining are very severe, one teaspoonful of either is not too much; by requesting the patient to retain the enema for ten or fifteen minutes, the medicine is directly absorbed, and the effect is both soothing and healing. This may be repeated several times a day, if the pain does not subside after the first injection.

The bowels are sometimes found to be in an opposite state, namely, constipated; this must be relieved at once. An enema of warm soapsuds answers the purpose, or a half-tablespoonful of warm water, in which a half-tablespoonful of glycerine is dissolved, makes an excellent injection for constipation.

Hot vaginal irrigations should be at once commenced, and repeated as often as twice or three times a day. I always dissolve a teaspoonful of powdered borax in the hot water, of which no less than half a gallon is used at one time; this is antiseptic and healing. After six or eight days, once a day will be sufficient.

Chronic uterine catarrh or uterine leucorrhœa does not require the active treatment which was recommended for the acute form. It depends quite often on causes, whose removal is absolutely necessary to the intelligent and successful treatment of the affection.

The causes that have been enumerated must be carefully and repeatedly reviewed, so that each individual case can be traced to its source. Those causes that are improbable must be eliminated from those that are probable, so that by a gradual process of exclusion we narrow the number down to those that actually exist. This simplifies the treatment to actual conditions that can be intelligently met.

Vaginal irrigations constitute in the chronic form of the disease an accepted and most useful therapeutic resource. There is nothing that will ever contraindicate a thorough cleansing of the vaginal canal, so that the organ may not be bathed in its own morbid and irritating secretion. It is a wholesome auxiliary to any course of treatment that may be adopted. It avoids *self-infection* and places the pelvic organs in the best possible condition for the healing powers of nature to work out a cure.

If the uterine catarrh is the result of a venous obstruction due to a congested liver and a general derangement of the digestive apparatus, then any local treatment will be of no avail without first removing the hepatic derangement.

Costiveness or constipation is a very common complaint with women and a very painful cause of womb disease, but it is so simple and ordinary in its nature that the wise will not deign stoop to notice such trifles, but if it required for its removal a surgical operation, for which a handsome fee is the inspiring motive, then we should hear of it as often as we do of lacerations or flexions of the cervix as a cause of uterine catarrh, and its removal would then indeed become absolutely necessary for effecting a permanent cure.

Why is it that the treatment of uterine disease has degenerated into "professional faking" that is alike disgraceful to the profession and a daylight robbery of the patient. A woman, for instance, is suffering from what she supposes to be *womb disease*. She consults a doctor, or what is still worse, a time-serving specialist, who examines her and sees at once signs of uterine catarrh.

He at once applies a little tincture of iodine or carbolic acid diluted with glycerine or a solution of nitrate of silver to the cervical canal. The woman is now informed that this application must be repeated two or three times a week, for which she must call at the office that number of times every week, for an indefinite period. At each visit she is subjected to the same routine humbuggery for local medication, but does she get any better? In my early professional experience I innocently and ignorantly tried these methods myself, and I say no! But, as a matter of fact, this constant irritation and poking around and into the womb will inflame any healthy uterus, and much more one that is already slightly irritated, so that patients lose their hope and become convinced themselves that they are no better, but feel worse than when they first commenced treatment.

This inefficient treatment, like the examination, is conjectural and mechanical and therefore incomplete and unscientific. The cause of her entire trouble is never approached. The woman suffers for years from constipation, which also inclines her to piles, because the pressure of the hardened feces on the hemorrhoidal veins obstructs the flow of venous blood and the same pressure on the uterine veins congests the mucous membrane of that organ and gives rise to the symptoms of endometritis. All these conditions should be inquired into, and many others, before local treatment is decided on; simply running to the doctor's office and having these medical applications made to the cervix or canal of the womb amount to nothing; this, as a general rule, does only harm, and is as superfluous as if one were to take a nasal douche of salt water or some other catarrh remedy, whenever he feels a little cold in the head.

The proper course to pursue in this and similar cases is to prescribe an appropriate diet, and regulate the bowels. It is precisely in this way that women who have made the rounds of the doctors, happen to take some patent laxative or nostrum that relieves their constipation, and accomplishes the *wonderful cures* of which we often hear and that were no doubt Godsends to the sufferers that were cured, after all the *first-class* doctors failed. By far the greatest proportion of cases of uterine catarrh are of a simple and transient nature and are only intensified by probing and local treatment.

When I first began the practice of medicine, I made the same mistake in following the advice of books and those who should have known better, for they have had ample opportunity to be convinced of the *fallacy* of these local measures in the great majority of cases, but some minds are incompetent to learn from experience, for that requires close observation, and logical reasoning.

I soon discovered that the catarrhal inflammations got worse, in proportion to the trouble and pains I took to treat them locally, so that I became ashamed of my ill success and abandoned the local treatment entirely, and this I shortly discovered was the means of curing them. Instead, I simply directed patients to rinse themselves with quite warm salt water, that is, a tablespoonful of ordinary cooking salt dissolved in a gallon of water. Now I prefer Femina antiseptic lotion to the same quantity of water, which has greater healing properties than either pulverized borax or common salt. I particularly advised them to keep their feet and lower extremities warm, regulating their diet and keeping their bowels open. I noticed that the patients began to improve, and that the improvement continued until they were fully restored to health and vigor. This method of treatment would not keep an office overcrowded with deluded patients, but it proved far more satisfactory to all concerned than meddlesome measures, and illustrated one of the most common abuses to which suffering women are liable.

In taking a *laxative* patients must feel their way as to the proper dose to take in their own individual case; constitutions differ very much in this respect, so that it is impossible to lay down one and the same rule for different persons. It is not good practice to give medicines three or four times a day in cases of habitual constipation, for it is liable to derange the digestion and interfere with the appetite. The proper method is one dose at bedtime and this should be increased or diminished until the suitable dose of the remedy has been ascertained; when this is accomplished, the dose of the remedy should be gradually lessened, a few drops every day, till it can be entirely dispensed with. If the ordinary dose fails to relieve the bowels, an additional treatment of glycerine enema at or about the time that the stool is to take place is to be employed. One or two teaspoonfuls of glycerine should be diluted with an equal quantity of water, and by means of a hard rubber piston syringe thrown into the rectum. The stimulating effect of glycerine on the nerves and mucous membrane, materially assists in relieving the torpor of the rectum, which has become insensitive to the irritation of its natural contents.

Patients who are costive must get into regular habits of relieving themselves, that is, have a regular hour every day when to go to stool, then the medicine will in time cure the most obstinate cases of constipation, otherwise it is impossible to cure it. It takes a constant amount of *effort to get well*, so that those who are too indolent or think it too troublesome to exert themselves, cannot hope to recover.

If there is great debility and impoverishment of the blood, then I would advise prescription No. 1, which are the *iron pills*, of which three pills should be taken three times a day. The moderate use of wine, either claret or

Riesling, with the food, instead of tea or coffee, is very beneficial, between meals a glass of Porter to relieve the *gone-in* feeling, until the system has recovered sufficient strength to do without it, that is when ordinary exertions are no longer a burden.

The small percentage of cases that do not yield to the above treatment, become legitimate subjects for an honest specialist, for there may be extensive lacerations of the cervix that require surgical treatment, or an elongated cervix that should be amputated, or a granulated hypertrophied membrane of the uterine cavity that should be scraped out; all these operations are without danger if the operator has thoroughly *mastered the details* of antiseptic surgery and has the manual skill to do the work properly.

CHAPTER XVIII
THE NATURAL POSITION OF THE UTERUS AND HOW IT IS SUPPORTED

The uterus is not a stationary fixture in the female pelvis, but enjoys a mobility within physiological bounds, which in itself explains the great diversity of opinions which may and do arise respecting the normal or abnormal position of the womb in any given case.

When the surrounding organs and tissues of the womb are in a healthy condition, and the abdominal walls are not compressed by the weight and pressure of skirts, nor the liver or diaphragm forced down towards the pelvis by a tight-fitting corset, the organ is movable in every direction, without the slightest pain or suffering.

The uterus is not tied down by any ligaments, as one might imagine from a description of the several ligaments that constitute only in a small degree its support, for it changes its position in retching, coughing, breathing, singing, walking and all other violent movements.

The question now naturally arises: What is the normal position of the uterus, and what constitutes its natural supports? To answer this interrogation is to controvert one of the most baneful fallacies in gynecological practice, for the amount of torturing and useless doctoring to which women are constantly subjected, owing to some fancied displacement of the womb, illustrates the force of precedent or of accepted opinions, that were fortified by years of erroneous teaching.

It was supposed until quite recently that when the body of the womb was inclined horizontally forwards, this was unnatural or a sign of disease, until Prof. B. S. Schultze, director of the gynecological clinic of Jana, successfully controverted this doctrine. In his work *"Die Pathologie und Therapie der Lageverænderungen der Gebærmutter,"* which is the most classical work extant on displacements of the uterus, says: "From the *post-mortem* findings it was inferred that the uterus occupied in the *living* woman the same position as in the cadaver; such an assumption did not take into account the actions of the muscles on the position of the uterus in the living subject nor the intra-abdominal pressure which is entirely absent after death, so that the dead organ naturally gravitated backward after the remains had lain for several days on the back." Another observer, Dr. Hach, found in a number of cases that he had examined during life, the uteri bent forward or antiflexed; twenty-four hours after death he discovered the same uteri in an opposite direction or retroflexed.

This and similar subsequent researches have demonstrated the fact that when the body of the womb rests on the bladder it is not in an abnormal position as formerly supposed and called *anteversion* or anteflexion, but that it is natural for it to be so, and when the body is elevated and its axis forms an obtuse angle with the horizon, the inclination is a *post-mortem* condition.

With these precursory remarks I am now able to answer the first clause of our query, and would say that the uterus is in its normal position when its long axis is nearly parallel to the horizon or at right angles with the perpendicular or long axis of the body. The normal position of the uterus is modified when the bladder is full or distended, for this lifts the body of the uterus upwards, thus temporarily making an acute angle with the vertical axis of the body, which was formerly considered to be the permanent and natural pose of the organ.

In referring to the bony pelvis, Plate I, it will be observed that the same is in the nature of a canal, for the passage of the child into the world. At other times than during the child-bearing process, this canal must be effectually closed to perfectly retain its contents. To accomplish this purpose it is provided with a bottom or floor, which is to give this necessary support, not only to the organs that the pelvic cavity contains but also to the abdominal viscera that are superimposed upon them. In order to accomplish this, its outlet must be as effectually closed as the bottom of a box or barrel in which material things are stored for the purpose of carrying them from place to place. In the human subject this bottom is called the pelvic floor, because it serves the purpose of a bottom or floor to the pelvic canal.

The *pelvic floor* is not a simple structure but a complicated arrangement of organs and tissues. If we begin to examine it from below upwards, we first have its outer covering in the skin; then, the superficial and deep fascias, the triangular ligament of the bladder and a group of interlacing muscles. The organs that enter into the composition of the pelvic floor and interwoven with the preceding structures, are the bladder, the vaginal walls, the rectum and connective tissue. Examine Plate II.

Through this floor there are several openings, which are guarded by a special set of constrictor muscles that are termed *sphincters*. These are sufficiently strong in the bladder and rectum but in the vagina they would be entirely insufficient to close this canal effectually.

The vagina, or, for our purpose, it will be clearer if we say "*vaginal canal*," divides the pelvic floor into an anterior and posterior segment, and it is by means of this division that the whole structure of the pelvic floor is weakened; this will be perceived at a moment's reflection, when we compare it with the pelvic floor of the *male*, who has no vagina; and for this reason men are never troubled with the *prolapses* to which women are liable. Nature, however, has made an attempt to compensate this physical defect in a manner that reduces the weakness occasioned by the vaginal canal to its minimum. The vaginal canal does not enter the pelvic cavity in a directly upward or perpendicular course, but obliquely upwards and backwards, as may be seen by referring to Plate II. The result is that the intra-abdominal pressure falls on the vaginal walls from above, and thus compresses and approximates the anterior and posterior walls of the vagina to each other, so that it constitutes a self-closing valve, but, notwithstanding all these provisions, this slit or opening through the pelvic floor still remains the weakest point of the inclosure for the pelvic and abdominal viscera. When the causes are sought that underlie the various displacements of the uterus, they are generally to be found in an impairment of the pelvic floor, through some changes or accidents that are peculiar to pregnancy and delivery.

As we are also to inquire in the succeeding chapter into the displacements to which the womb is liable, it would greatly assist our understanding if we first got an idea of what constitutes the natural supports of the uterus? The word ligament is defined as anything that ties or unites one thing or part to another; a bandage; a bond. This is the *idea* in the popular mind, so that when the terms broad and round ligaments of the womb are employed it is supposed that they are for the same purpose for which ligaments are usually intended. This is, unfortunately for a clear understanding of the subject, a great mistake, because these ligaments are an exception to the generally accepted meaning of the term, for they neither tie nor support the uterus in its natural position. One may readily imagine that this erroneous conception would lead to a mistaken course in the treatment of most cases of displacements, because too much importance is bestowed upon structures that have no physiological bearing on the disease.

Drs. Hart and Barbour, of Edinburgh, in their "Manual of Gynecology," which is the most scientific and practical work that has lately appeared in the English language, have this to say in speaking of the support of the uterus: "The question of the support of the uterus is still disputed. The broad and round ligaments have nothing to do with its support, they are only useful as giving fixed points for the contracting uterine muscles during parturition. The chief support is the compact unbroken pelvic floor, on which the uterus rests just as one sits on a chair. It is the whole pelvic floor that supports the uterus and viscera, not the perineum alone." The perineum (see anatomical Plate II) is only a small though strong part of the pelvic floor. If the reader will now patiently review the organs that, together with the other tissues, constitute this floor, and this can be most profitably done by studying Plate II, there can be no confusion of ideas whatever. In the following pages I have occasion to refer to what is understood by the term pelvic floor.

CHAPTER XIX
PROLAPSUS OR FALLING OF THE WOMB

If one desires to familiarize himself with a thorough understanding of this subject, it is absolutely necessary to bear in mind what was said of the natural support of the uterus, for unless one has a full knowledge of the foundation of a structure, how can he comprehend its defects and remedy them when the structure falls? The workman who potters on a building that has shifted from its foundation without first devising means for a new and solid basis for it to rest upon, would be considered a fool. The term "falling of the womb" has no longer the significance that it once had, for it is only a symptom that something is wrong, and in the present state of our knowledge it is misleading and a misnomer, inasmuch as it conveys the impression that it is due to an affection of the uterus, when as a matter of fact it is not due to any disease of the womb at all. If the prolapsed uterus has become involved in a morbid process, it is the result of the abnormal conditions that have brought the prolapsus about, and in which the uterus was in no way concerned.

Professor Schroeder, of Berlin, takes a similar view of these cases, and he groups into one chapter three distinct varieties, yet, because one is depending on the other, he considers them all as one disease. These affections are: prolapse or falling of the womb; prolapse or falling of the vagina, and an inflammatory elongation or *hypertrophy* of the cervix or neck of the womb. He says "that the displacement of the womb is very seldom a primary affection, but that it is oftener the consequence of a prolapse or falling of the vagina, and a giving way of other structures, or of the pelvic floor, and, as such, 'falling of the womb' cannot be properly separated into an individual affection of the womb."

Falling of the vagina is principally due to a widening of the vaginal canal, a relaxation of its walls, and injuries or lacerations of the pelvic floor. Lacerations of the perineum generally occur during confinement, in which the vagina tears through the vaginal orifice backwards towards, or into, the rectum. This so weakens the pelvic floor that it becomes inadequate to support the pelvic organs and tissues, and this predisposes to all the varieties of *prolapsus* that have been enumerated above. It is during the period of gestation that the vagina grows considerably longer and wider.

In the latter months of pregnancy the womb ascends and its body inclines greatly forwards, which naturally tilts the cervix high up in the pelvis, and also draws that portion of the vagina to which the cervix is attached with it, but notwithstanding this upward dragging of the vagina, the lower portion of the vaginal canal has so augmented its proportions that it often protrudes between the lips of the vulva during the last period of gestation. The normal relation of the vagina to the neighboring organs is more or less disturbed, that is, its attachment to the bladder and rectum is stretched and loosened, so that under the most favorable circumstances the mucous membrane of the lower portion of the vagina falls out of the vulva or prolapses, of course in the majority of cases only in such a degree that it neither inconveniences nor is it noticeable by the pregnant woman.

Immediately after confinement, in a healthy state of affairs, nature should rectify these abnormal proportions, that were only designed by her to serve a temporary purpose, namely, to accommodate the child and provide for its safe passage into the world. Medical writers have invented a special term to designate this process of regeneration, namely, *involution*. This means to infold or grow less so as to assume the former natural proportions of organs. Unfortunately, nature is often contravened in her wholesome regenerative purpose, by adventitious circumstances that completely frustrate her intentions, and the reparative process being thus balked, the organs and tissues remain in their abnormal proportions, which constitutes now a disease, and this uncompleted effort to repair is termed *subinvolution*.

It takes at least from six weeks to three months after delivery for the reparative process or involution of the organs and tissues to be completed. And women cannot exercise too much care after confinement to avoid any possible check to the regenerative process. If the involution has been arrested, the vagina retains its large, flabby proportions, so that its relaxed walls naturally protrude or prolapse, and that entails all the other consequences.

Intra-abdominal pressure should be explained in connection with this subject, for it constantly encourages prolapsus of the organs under consideration. By that is meant the pressure which the contents of the abdominal cavity exert on its walls, and this is greatest at its most dependent part, which is the pelvic floor. This pressure is continuous on the organs of the pelvic floor while the woman is standing, and greatest at the point of least resistance, which is the relaxed and enlarged vagina, so that it bulges out at the vaginal orifice. When the patient resumes a recumbent position, this point is greatly relieved from pressure, and the vagina may regain its normal relations, but whenever the woman is in the upright position, the intra-abdominal pressure will again force the weakened pelvic floor and vaginal walls downwards. After a time the prolapse no longer subsides after the pressure is reduced, for the tissues have lost their recuperative power, and the prolapse becomes permanent. When the intra-abdominal pressure is supplemented by the action of the diaphragm and the contraction of the abdominal muscles, as occurs in a long paroxysm of coughing, repeated vomiting, and inordinate and prolonged bearing down at stool, a prolapse may take place quite suddenly, precisely as in a rupture or hernia, and for these reasons some authorities (Drs. Hart and Barbour, of Edinburgh) have described prolapsus of the womb as a *sacro-pubic* hernia.

A permanent distension of the bladder or an accumulation of feces in the rectum facilitates the development of a prolapse of the vagina, because the former pushes the anterior wall of the vagina downwards, while the latter depresses the vaginal wall.

A large or subinvoluted uterus is by some considered as a fruitful cause of prolapse; this Professor Schroeder denies, and I am convinced from experience that he is right. A uterus that is simply enlarged is not inclined to prolapse, because the enlarged pregnant uterus never prolapses if the pelvic floor is in a normal condition. But a chronic endometritis or uterine catarrh may in time involve the vagina in a vaginal catarrh and this may induce a prolapse. A chronic vaginal catarrh or leucorrhœa can so relax the vaginal walls that its lower folds protrude from the vaginal orifice.

Women who are beyond the change of life and in whom the lost elasticity of the tissues and a general absorption of fatty and connective tissue has destroyed the natural support which retains the vaginal walls, may be annoyed with partial prolapses of the vagina.

The most aggravated types of prolapses are found among the working classes, who cannot avail themselves of the comforts and hygiene of the lying-in chamber that are so essential for a complete and permanent recovery.

Elongation or hypertrophy of the cervix of the uterus is the third variety of prolapses that Professor Schroeder includes in the group. This form is consequent upon a falling or prolapse of the vagina, and it occurs in the following manner. The body of the uterus being retained by its natural supports or by adhesion of a former inflammatory process in the pelvic cavity, remains stationary where it naturally belongs, while the upper end of the vaginal canal being attached to and surrounding the cervix or neck of the womb, gradually draws or stretches the cervix out, so that it grows one or two inches longer than it is natural for it to be. The cervix of the womb projects under these circumstances down into the vagina, and in some cases it may be seen between the lips of the vulva. This condition is mistaken for falling of the womb, when in reality it is a falling of the vagina with an incidental lengthening of the cervix of the womb. To recognize and make these distinctions is of the greatest practical importance, for thus alone can the measures adopted for the relief of these distressing complaints be successful.

The symptoms of prolapsus grow principally out of the changed relations of the uterus to the surrounding organs and tissues. The mechanical interference and pressure of the womb on neighboring parts, and the changes that are induced in the organ itself by the altered circulation in its tissues, cause the inflammatory enlargement or hypertrophy that is characteristic of one variety of the affection.

In some persons the development of the disease is so gradual that it has progressed for years without any serious inconvenience and the symptoms that did exist were generally attributed to other causes. In the course of time there is such a combination of morbid processes, like painful menstruation, inflammatory enlargement of the womb and erosions of the cervix with profuse leucorrhœa, as to render the parts painful and sensitive to pressure and friction. These symptoms excite in the end suspicion, so that the sufferer may seek advice that will reveal to her the real condition of her case.

Other signs of these affections are a dragging down or a feeling as though a weight pulled the pelvic organs downwards; there is also traction on the bladder, making this viscus exceedingly irritable, so that there is a frequent desire to micturate; the rectum suffers also from similar traction. There is another sign that is very often present, and particularly in the early stages, and this is a feeling as if the vagina was open; this is due to the relaxation of the vaginal walls. Walking for any distance becomes burdensome and causes great fatigue; pain in the back and loins is hardly ever absent. There is an inability to lift weights, because the pelvic floor cannot endure the extra strain that is superimposed on the intra-abdominal pressure; ascending or descending stairs aggravates the symptoms much more than walking on the level floor.

TREATMENT.

This must be directed to the accomplishment of two ends, without which no relief, much less a cure, is possible, and these are, *first*, to return the displaced organ to its normal position, and, *secondly*, to retain it there. The course first indicated is, as a rule, not difficult to follow out; in fact, if the patient is placed in a favorable position, the uterus replaces itself through the natural forces of traction and gravitation, unless it has become so enlarged that it is a physical impossibility.

The *"knee-chest"* or *"knee-elbow posture"* is the term that has been given to this position, and it is assumed in the following manner.

The woman gets down on her knees, the thighs being kept in an upright or vertical line; the object of this is to keep the pelvis as high as possible, while the chest is bent or inclined forwards until the head rests on the floor; the shoulders must be as low to the floor as it is possible for the patient to endure.

This position at once reduces the intra-abdominal pressure on the pelvic floor to the least degree, and besides this, the abdominal viscera gravitating towards the diaphragm, the prolapsed uterus and surrounding tissues are drawn upwards and forwards with it. If the prolapse was complete or nearly so, so that the organ almost protruded through the vulva, then the patient should retain this posture for ten or fifteen minutes before an attempt is made to replace the organ; for the intense congestion should be first allowed to subside.

No sudden or violent force should be employed, but a gentle, steady pressure. In cases where the organ has simply descended into the vagina, the knee-chest posture alone will replace the uterus. Those displacements that are due to a chronic catarrh of the vagina are particularly suitable for home treatment, because the patient can surely cure her vaginal catarrh, and combining with this the knee-chest posture, which should be practiced night and morning, for at least ten minutes, and until the catarrhal inflammation has entirely subsided, she has at her command the most useful and beneficial resource to accomplish a cure.

If the reader will refer to and note carefully what was said in this connection, she will learn that the phrase *falling of the womb* is sometimes nothing more or less than a relaxation of the vaginal walls that is due to a chronic catarrh of the vagina. It is quite natural that it should be so, for if the structures that make up the pelvic floor lose their tonicity and strength, the womb must naturally descend. If we now succeed in temporarily replacing the organ by assuming the knee-chest position, and in the meantime cure the catarrh and inflammation the patient must get well. The reader is again referred to the chapter on vaginal catarrh.

The fatigue or lassitude which makes every physical effort of some patients a great hardship, can be greatly relieved, if not cured, by this formula.

Take:	Tincture of nux vomica	2 drams
	Fluid extract of ergot	4 drams
	Fluid extract of golden seal	1 ounce
	Compound elixir of calisaya sufficient to make	8 ounces

Directions: A tablespoonful three times a day, between meals.

When the prolapse is due to some of the structural defects that were enumerated in the causation of displacements, and that were traced to the accidents of childbirth, then no permanent relief can be hoped for, until these defects are remedied.

Pessaries or rings that are introduced into the vagina for the purpose of stretching or spreading out the relaxed folds of the vagina, that they cannot prolapse or fall down, and thus indirectly support the uterus, were suggested by the ancient fathers of medicine. In view of the fact that they were wholly ignorant of the causes that were responsible for prolapses, the remedy was quite practical and ingenious, but to-day, when we are acquainted with the causes that operate in bringing the prolapse about, they are, to my mind, a very unsatisfactory *makeshift*, and afford only a temporary amelioration.

A woman who is compelled to wear a ring or pessary is certainly not well, and if she has any hard work to do or must be on her feet a great deal, the pessary will sooner or later so irritate the vagina that it must be removed. Besides this, I always contended that, in the long run, this extra strain on the vaginal walls would only relax them more, and, instead of ever being able to dispense with the use of a pessary, she must increase the size after a while.

There are a great many devices in the form of pessaries; some of them are absurdly ridiculous, and more in the nature of instruments of torture than of remedial expedients. Since I learned to know better, I no longer recommend them, and those who desire a radical cure for a prolapse of any kind, will surely be disappointed if they pin their faith to them.

I am convinced that they are a great source of evil, and a sure index of ignorance on the part of those who habitually recommend them. The German school of gynecologists have of late years greatly perfected the plastic operations of the vagina, in fact, it is almost a sub-specialty in itself, to which they have given the term *prolapse operations*. A specialist, who is competent in the details of these prolapse operations, can hold out the very best possible chance for a radical and permanent cure, and while the operation requires a certain degree of skill and special training, which should be obtained by practicing these operations on the cadaver, in order to save time, and not bungle the operation on the living subject, as too often, unfortunately, happens. In skillful hands, the operation is entirely without danger, and under proper antiseptic precautions, the results are very satisfactory.

The question is simply this: If the knee-chest treatment, and the remedies that have been suggested, do not give permanent relief, then there must be some such defect in the pelvic floor as I have heretofore described.

If the vagina is too wide, it should and can be narrowed to its normal dimensions, by removing the excessive tissue; if the vagina is torn into the perineum, this too must be united. Should the cervix of the uterus be abnormally elongated, so that it makes it physically impossible to return it to its natural position, it should be shortened or amputated, and if all these three complications coexist, then an operation combining and remedying all these defects, should be performed at one sitting. This method alone will restore the patient to health and usefulness.

CHAPTER XX
VERSIONS AND FLEXIONS OF THE UTERUS

Version, in the nomenclature of diseases of the womb, means that the entire organ without any deflection in its normal axis turns, inclines or leans either forwards, backwards or sidewards.

The prefix *ante* is used in the sense of forwards and in composition with *version* we have the word *anteversion*, which in conjunction with the term uterus, signifies that the organ is inclined forwards. The prefix *retro*, signifies backwards, and in composition with the word *version* and in connection with the word uterus, it implies that the womb is turned backwards.

The word *flexion* differs from *version*, inasmuch as it signifies a bending or bowing, which breaks the normal axis of the womb. The neck or cervix of the uterus may retain its normal position, while its *body* is abnormally deflected or bent in any direction. The prefixes *ante* and *retro* are also used in composition with the word *flexion* as they are with *version*. These distinctions should be remembered.

ANTEVERSION OF THE UTERUS.

In anteversion the uterus has so far changed its normal shape that the cervix of the organ is stretched out or extended in a line with the axis of the body. This occurs when the uterus is unusually swollen from inflammatory enlargement. The normal location of the body does not materially change in these cases. It is a little more depressed on the fundus of the bladder and the cervix is correspondingly elevated, so that the latter stands considerably higher than in health. If the bladder is empty, and the patient bears down or does anything that increases the intra-abdominal pressure, the body of the womb is forced down, upon the anterior vaginal wall, which prolapses into the vagina, while the cervix is raised, so as to point upwards and backwards. When the bladder is full, the body of the uterus is naturally raised, and the cervix correspondingly depressed. And this is attributable to a rigidity or stiffness about the organ, that is characteristic of a chronic inflammatory enlargement of the uterus. Sometimes the organ is permanently fixed by inflammatory adhesions, that lessen or prohibit these movements.

The symptoms of anteversion are what may be expected from an enlarged congested organ. This enlargement is due either to a subinvolution of the uterus or to an inflammation of the intermuscular substance, a chronic metritis. One of the most annoying symptoms of the anteverted uterus is the feeling of looseness in the pelvic cavity. This is partly due to the relaxed state of the surrounding tissue, and partly to the abnormal size of the womb. The patient feels the organ roll from side to side, as she changes her position. This causes unnatural sensations and mental suffering that disturbs the nervous system and induces hysterical complications. And the patient complains about something moving in her abdomen.

The inflammatory adhesions that sometimes tie down the organ in an anteverted position, compromise the normal expansion of the bladder; this induces an irritation, which causes a frequent desire to urinate.

The treatment must be directed to the removal of the cause. This disease is really only a symptom or condition of chronic corporeal metritis or subinvolution, and as such, it is only amenable to the measures that will cure this disease. The employment of rings and pessaries to remedy this evil is contrary to good sense and of no permanent value.

The intelligent employment of electricity, so as to stimulate the absorption of the hypertrophic enlargement of the uterus and cause the absorption of the inflammatory adhesions, will often give permanent and positive results.

ANTEFLEXION OF THE UTERUS.

This was considered at one time the most frequent of all uterine displacements, not because it existed formerly oftener than at present, but because the natural or normal position of the womb was confounded with that which was supposed to be abnormal.

The discovery that in the living subject the body of the uterus naturally inclines forward, so as to rest on the bladder, and that the body makes quite an angle with its cervix, altered the conception of things very materially. To-day an actual aggravated anteflexion, that occasions no impediment to the menstrual discharge, is not a proper ground for treatment, although this is as yet by no means familiar to physicians in general, for many of them have not learned to make the distinction.

The reader should carefully study Plate II, which diagramatically illustrates how the body bows over the bladder so as to show its natural anteflexion. If the angle between the body and neck of the womb becomes too sharp or acute, so that the canal of the uterus becomes compressed at the point of flexion, in a degree that obstructs the escape of the natural secretions of the uterine cavity, then the anteflexion becomes a source of disease. This degree of flexion is happily very rare, and we find it in about equal proportions due to a congenital defect, that springs into prominence when the girl arrives at puberty, for then the obstruction to the menstrual flow is first realized.

The other class acquire the affection in adult life, after a once healthy or natural menstruation has been established. Of this class there are two species, which must be separately analyzed, so as to avoid a confusion of ideas, that often makes this subject, *which is the most simple,* one of the most intricate, in the text books in gynecological practice.

One variety of the acquired affection can be described, in common with the congenital form, to which I first referred: because the anteflexions in both cases are due to precisely the same pathological conditions, namely, a loss of muscular tone in the uterine walls, so that the organ becomes flabby and weak, like a green wilted stalk, allowing the body of the uterus to topple forwards.

The relaxation of the uterine walls is usually more pronounced at that portion which is distinguished as the *isthmus* of the uterus, and corresponds to that part of the organ where the cervix goes over into the body, forming a sort of natural hinge joint between body and neck.

If the bladder is empty, the body of the womb will naturally drop, not necessarily forwards, for it may fall backwards, but in the majority of cases it drops forwards, because the womb is already inclined forwards in its natural position, so all that is necessary to induce an excessive anteflexion, is for the body of the uterus to sink lower than it is natural for it to be. A kink or sharp bend will cause in any canal an occlusion. Take a small rubber tube, for instance, and bend it sharply at right angles; the result will be at the corner of the deflection, that the tube will be flattened, and its walls will come together. In the case of the uterine canal, where there is an abnormal flexion, there is precisely the same condition, and as a result an obstruction not only to the menstrual fluid, but to the mucous secretions, which are pent up in the uterine cavity. The retained fluids decompose and irritate the mucous lining; and this entails a complication of inflammatory diseases, which can never be cured, unless the flexion is remedied.

The other variety of the acquired flexion is due to a pelvic cellulitis. This is an inflammatory process, entirely outside of the uterus.

The womb is surrounded by a great deal of loose cellular tissue, that fills out the interspaces between the different ligaments and pelvic organs. This tissue often becomes the seat of an inflammation. The exudation from the inflammation may be of such a nature that it forms strands of *fibrous tissue*, running from the isthmus of the uterus backwards to the sacrum. These strands contract or shrink in the course of time, and this draws the isthmus of the uterus backwards, and fixes or attaches it to the posterior pelvic wall. By this contraction of the fibrous tissue the cervix is constricted and the body falls unnaturally forwards.

The prominent symptoms of anteflexion are painful menstruation and sterility. Dysmenorrhœa or painful menstruation is the first sign of the existence of anteflexion at the age of puberty. It happens that young girls are thus tortured for days with violent uterine colic, that is occasioned by spasmodic efforts of the uterus to force through the constricted canal the pent-up secretion. This lasts until the menstrual fluid has sufficiently dilated the cervical constriction to allow its escape. These painful paroxysms of uterine colic repeat themselves at each recurring menstrual period, and through these repetitions of pain and suffering, the general health becomes greatly deranged. The nervous system becomes the seat of functional disturbances, and hysterical disorders are not uncommon.

The organ becomes involved in chronic inflammatory processes that make the uterus exceedingly sensitive, so that the colicky pains become aggravated and prolonged far beyond the cessation of the menses. Some of these patients suffer for several weeks, from the time the courses ought to begin, so that they are actually sick half the time.

Sterility is not an absolute certainty in all these cases, but it is traced so often to an aggravated flexion, that it may be accepted as one of its most prominent signs. Conception has taken place in extreme flexions, because the spermatozoa can gain admittance into the uterine cavity for several days after the uterine colic and menstrual fluid have forced the canal open. And if the uterus has not become involved in inflammatory processes, then conception is the means by which nature effects a cure through her own resources.

During the menstrual period, the anteflected uterus becomes greatly congested and swollen, and, having already grown considerably larger from the chronic inflammatory conditions which the anteflexion has induced, it impinges on the bladder, so as to interfere with its free expansion. This occasions a frequent desire to void urine, and this becomes a very distressing symptom in a certain proportion of cases.

Treatment for this affection is not within the sphere of the original purpose of this work, for the efforts at home treatment must be aided by mechanical methods of the physician. From what we are taught of the physical cause of this affection, the fact seems self-evident that the acute or sharp flexion must be modified to give permanent relief. The employment of rings, pessaries, sponges or medical applications are nonsensical, and the method of introducing a stem in the uterine cavity, for the patient to wear for an indefinite length of time, is not without great danger. Even though a woman cannot give herself all the proper treatment, it must be a great satisfaction to her to be informed of the proper methods that should be adopted.

The vagina should be thoroughly rinsed before each and every treatment of the uterus, so as to guard against the possibility of infecting the cavity of the uterus.

If the manipulations that are required for the purpose of carrying out some of the mechanical or surgical treatments of uterine diseases, were always preceded with thorough cleanliness, which implies *asepsis*, or without putrescence, then all these operations would be shorn of their greatest danger, namely, that of exciting inflammation and suppuration.

If a probe of the usual curve can be readily introduced into the supposed anteflected uterine cavity, then there cannot be sufficient flexion to constitute an obstruction, hence the flexion is not the cause of the disease. In genuine anteflexion, the cervix and body of the uterus are doubled up on each other, often like the letter V, the cervix representing one line of the V, and the body the other; bi-mammal palpation in the hands of an expert clearly establishes this conformation.

When the diagnosis is established, the treatment should be as follows: The patient is inclined on a table, either on her back or side, a Sims' speculum is introduced into the vagina and the cervix exposed. The posterior lip of the cervix is now seized by means of a tenaculum forceps, and gently drawn downwards and backwards, which greatly reduces or obliterates the angle or flexion between the cervix and the body of the womb, this greatly facilitates the introduction of a uterine electrode. After two or three treatments, the forceps are no longer required because the electrode can then be readily introduced into the uterine cavity without them. The other electrode is spread on the abdomen. (See this illustrated on Plate V.) A current of electricity is now passed through the uterine tissues for ten minutes; this is gauged all the way from sixty to one hundred *milliampères*. The operation is repeated only once a week, and the cure is effected in six weeks to three months. Great care must be exercised during the treatment, to avoid exposure and undue exercise.

Those forms that are due to inflammatory deposits and strands outside of the organ, should be preceded with an electrical treatment twice a week, somewhat modified from the preceding course. This is done by employing a *vaginal electrode*, properly protected and gently pressed against the adhesions. The other *electrode* is applied to the small of the back. A current some fifty *milliampères* stronger is passed directly through the adhesions; when these are absorbed, the intra-uterine electrode is employed, as in cases that are not complicated with them.

RETROVERSION OF THE UTERUS.

This consists in a posterior inclination of the uterus, so that the body of the womb approaches the posterior walls of the pelvis, while the cervix of the womb is raised against the base of the bladder.

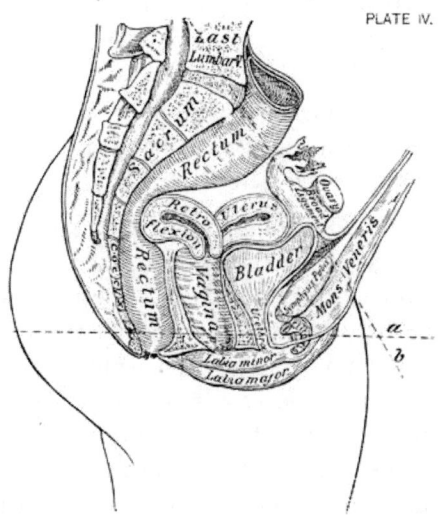

PLATE IV.

Retroflexion of the Uterus, or the Womb, bent backward.

This plate elucidates the womb bent or turned backward and pressing on the rectum. This condition is generally traceable to the vicious custom of lying on the back after confinement or during childbed. The natural position of the organ, inclined forward and resting on the bladder, is also shown.

As a permanent pathological lesion, this form of displacement is very rare, but as a forerunner of retroflexion it is of frequent occurrence. The length of time that elapses for a version to take on a flexion depends on the degree of induration or stiffness of the uterine walls.

The chronic inflammatory enlargement of the uterus predisposes the organ to posterior displacement, and the displacement favors the development of flexion. This takes place in the following order: After the uterus is displaced backwards, and its cervix has become fixed by inflammatory adhesions, the body of the womb gradually glides down on the posterior pelvic wall, from gravitation and intra-abdominal pressure. And in this very simple manner a retroversion is converted into a retroflexion. The causes, symptoms, and complications that characterize this variety of displacement, with its subsequent modification into flexion, are the same as those of retroflexion, to which the reader is referred.

RETROFLEXION OF THE UTERUS.

This form of uterine displacement exists when the body of the womb is bent towards the posterior wall of the pelvis, which is in an opposite direction to that where it naturally belongs. I have already pointed out, in speaking of the normal position of the uterus, that the body is directed forwards and rests on the bladder, while its cervix points downwards into the pelvic cavity. I now refer you to Plate IV, in which I plainly show the uterus in a directly opposite position to that in health, namely, turned back, resting on and depressing the rectum.

In retroflexion the cervix of the uterus continues to point downwards, into the pelvic cavity, in almost the same direction as in the natural position, while the body is directed backwards, or backwards and downwards. We seldom, if ever, find this condition as a congenital affection, but as an acquired displacement it is undoubtedly more frequently met with in gynecological practice than all other displacements combined. The round ligaments of the uterus were at one time, and are even yet by some, supposed to be the means that retain the womb in its normal anteflected position. Upon this theory a new surgical operation sprung into prominence for the relief of this class of cases. It was reasoned, that if the round ligaments actually tied the uterus down, and retained it in its natural anteflected position, that to shorten these ligaments by opening the inguinal canal in the groin, and drawing them out, would remedy a displacement of the womb, whether a prolapsus or a retroflexion. This operation was performed, it was claimed successfully, and if the view that the round ligaments retain and support the uterus were a correct one, it must be admitted that the operation would have been *ideal*. I convinced myself, however, of the utter fallacy of this position, in dissections on the cadaver, where in several instances the round ligaments could not be reached without opening the abdominal cavity, and even then it was impossible to trace them. These views were expressed in an article in the *American Journal of Obstetrics and Diseases of Women and Children*, and as the operation fell shortly afterwards into merited disrepute, I partly claim the credit of having been instrumental in bringing that about. I said:

"That this ligament has nothing to do in fixing the uterus in its normal anteverted position, is proven from many facts which occur in daily practice. The insertion or origin, whichever one chooses to call it, of these cords at the groin, is somewhat irregular and sometimes so rudimentary that it cannot be found upon a most careful and tedious dissection. It may be found divided into a number of processes, one being connected with Poupart's ligament in the inguinal canal, the other being lost in the labia majora, and another may be traced to the sheath of the rectus muscle.

"If these cords were so important as the advocates of the Alexander-Adams operation try to make us believe, in binding the uterus forward, and, as we are recently informed, have a strength equal to support four and one-half pounds weight, a great deal of uneasiness, if not actual pain, would be felt and located along the inguinal canal, following this structure to its points of insertion, in sudden dislocations of the uterus backwards. This is, however, not the case; when sudden painful symptoms arise, they are invariably referred to the sacral region. In sudden retroversions or flexions, as in the pregnant uterus, occurring accidentally or those retroverted or flexed uteri which are so often met with in a state of subinvolution after confinements, there are no symptoms pointing to a tension of these cords at all, but all symptoms point to uterine pressure on the posterior pelvic wall, which can be precisely located. And these pains disappear as soon as the offending member is put right."

There is no doubt that the uterus retains its abnormal retroflected position by the same forces that keep it in a normal or anteflected state; these are (1) intra-abdominal pressure, and (2) the force of gravitation of its own weight.

In some women there are certain predispositions to the occurrence of a retroflexion. If the walls of the uterus are weak and relaxed, especially that portion where the cervix unites with the body of the womb, then the body may fall in any direction, and, as the bladder is liable to be distended, and thus raise the body of the uterus upwards, folds of intestine are likely to intervene, so that the organ is inclined backwards, and the abdominal pressure, now falling on the anterior surface of the body, presses the womb backwards and downwards into a flexion.

A fall backwards or a violent push or jump may cause retroflexion any time during life. Retroflexions of this nature are not as a rule injurious, and if the circulation is not compromised, nor the uterine canal obstructed, women may go through life without feeling any the worse because their womb occupies an abnormal position. It is only when the organ is congested and swollen, so that its own tissue is painfully sensitive, and the surrounding tissues are compressed by the foreign body, that it requires measures for relief.

In those women who have borne children, and those who have gone through a miscarriage, retroflexion is frequently met. A little reflection will make this clear, for when we remember how the pregnant uterus at any time from conception to final delivery becomes congested and the seat of a corresponding growth of its own tissue to accommodate the growing fetus, we at once perceive that either after an abortion or on delivery at full term, the enlarged and congested uterus is in the best possible condition, to lose its normal place and sink backwards. The pernicious custom in vogue in most countries, of keeping a woman on the flat of her back after delivery, has never been as vehemently opposed by the intelligent members of the profession, as the gravity of the subject demands. Some women have an idea that the longer and quieter they remain on their backs, the surer they are to make an excellent recovery from the lying-in chamber. American and English practitioners are inclined to recommend this as the most proper way to lie, but there is no doubt that this not only favors the occurrence of retroflexion, but that it actually causes it.

The woman who rests on her back gives to the heavy body of the womb an opportunity to sink backwards, after the distended bladder has pushed the organ high enough up so that its own weight may throw it over, until it finds resistance on the posterior wall of the pelvic cavity. Many nurses insist on the dorsal position for days, and never permit the patient the privilege of lying upon one or the other side. Aside from the injurious effect that this has on the position of the uterus, it is exceedingly tiresome to be compelled to remain for several days in one position. Women should be allowed to lie on all sides, after delivery, and no longer on one side than on another. And to insure against a retroversion or flexion, she must also lie on the abdomen a certain length of time during each twenty-four hours.

Tight bandaging after delivery, for "preserving the figure," greatly aggravates the displacement; the binder should be so applied that it feels comfortable but not too tight, its purpose being to offer a gentle support to the suddenly relaxed abdominal muscles, and thus stimulate them to contract to their normal form.

The symptoms of retroflexion are greatly varied by the pathological conditions that affect the uterus, or by the complications that may have caused the flexion.

It is indisputable that the uterus may be retroflected for an indefinite length of time without causing any inconvenience. From this it may be inferred that the retroflection itself does not constitute the disease, but the inflammatory processes, in which the organ is involved, or the relaxation of the adjacent structures, as we find them immediately after confinement, constitute the actual diseased conditions.

One of the most constant symptoms is pain in the back, and this is severe in proportion to the swelling and sensitiveness of the organ, when it presses on the sacral nerves and rectum.

As a result of the flexion, the circulation in the organ is interfered with, so that the congested uterus feels heavy, and there is a sensation of fullness and bearing down, that greatly hinders walking. Uterine catarrh and hyperæmia place the organ in such an irritable state that prolonged and excessive menstruation is the rule. This may last for fourteen days, so that the patients become anæmic and greatly debilitated from the excessive loss of blood. The menstruation is always more painful, especially at the beginning of the flow; this pain may be interrupted or spasmodic, so that it assumes the form of a uterine colic; the lower abdominal region becomes painful and the pain radiates towards the groins. The degree of suffering is very seldom as great as that which characterizes anteflexion, because the obstruction in the latter flexions are much greater than in retroflexions.

Those women who have borne children suffer less pain during menstruation than those who have never been pregnant. It may be presumed that, in the latter class, the flexion was congenital or acquired in early childhood, which makes the obstruction or constriction more complete and obstinate, and for that reason it induces sterility. With those who have once borne and afterwards acquired the flexion, the possibility of conception is much greater.

When the enlarged and swollen body of the uterus is pushed backwards and downwards, it presses on the sacral plexus of nerves; this is a bundle of nerves that supplies branches to the legs, and from this pressure the lower extremities become lame or paralyzed either on one or both sides. The paralysis subsides after the removal of the offending body. There is quite a number of other neurotic affections that can often be traced to a retroflected uterus. These are all of a functional nature, and appear in the form of hysteria, epilepsy, St. Vitus' dance and neuralgias of almost any part of the body. Dr. Chrobak, of Vienna, reported a case of asthma that had resisted all the treatments that could be suggested, until it was finally traced to a retroflected uterus; that being rectified, the asthma subsided.

Irritability of the bladder is not so frequent a symptom of this variety of displacement as of others; should there be inflammation complicating the bladder, then, of course, there would be considerable annoyance from this source.

Habitual constipation is often very prominent and in some of the cases it is the only sign that leads to an examination, which reveals the retroflexion. Hemorrhoids or piles, due to a compression of the veins of the rectum, are another complication included in the signs of this displacement.

TREATMENT.

There is a small proportion of cases in which the system has become accustomed to the retroflected position of the womb, and if the abnormal condition is rectified, a great many painful symptoms spring into prominence, that are attributable to the interference. This is particularly the case in women who are in those years that we term "change of life," and for this reason they should be let severely alone.

Excluding the above class of cases, the question arises in other cases whether the uterus can be replaced without violence, or whether it is fixed or grown to its surroundings by inflammatory adhesions. It is not always an easy matter to dispose of this question at once, because the enlarged and congested body is often so firmly wedged down between the posterior pelvic wall and the vagina, that any attempt to dislodge it is accompanied with such acute pain that one feels constrained to desist for a time. When there is great pain or sensitiveness, the patient should take to bed, so as to give the pelvic organs every chance to get rid of the inflammatory irritability. Hot-water compresses should be applied to the lower abdominal or pelvic region, and hot vaginal irrigations thrown into the vagina; these should be copious, no less than a gallon of water at once, at a temperature of 107 to 110° Fahr., repeated twice daily. The bowels should be kept loose, say several operations each day, for three or four days; after that once a day will be sufficient.

In the course of several weeks the congestion will have subsided, so that, in the great majority of cases, reposition can be readily accomplished. If the resistance of the womb still persists, then it is reasonable to infer that the organ is tied down by old inflammatory adhesions; these, then, should be treated with galvanism, after the manner described for removing adhesions in anteflexions.

The statistics show that, out of every five women who are suffering from female diseases, one has a posterior displacement, either a retroflexion or retroversion. The greatest number of these are traceable to their last confinement. All these displacements, as well as those that are accidental or induced by a fall, jumps or the like, should be replaced as soon as possible, otherwise inflammatory adhesions may complicate and greatly obstruct the replacement.

The reposition or replacement of the womb may be accomplished through natural agencies, that can be employed by the patient herself. These are, in a great measure, the same forces to which the womb's posterior displacements are to be attributed, namely, intra-abdominal pressure and gravitation. To employ these for the purpose of remedying the evil, the so-called knee-chest position must be assumed by the patient. The first step towards assuming this position is to get down on the bended knee, the thighs in a vertical position, then the body is gradually inclined forwards until one or the other shoulder touches the floor or level of the knee. If this position is retained for ten minutes it will alone replace the organ forwards, sometimes suddenly, at other times gradually, provided the organ is moveable and not squeezed into the pelvis or adhered by inflammatory exudation.

Dr. Henry F. Campbell, of Georgia, introduced this natural therapeutic agent into the profession, but it appears to be very little known or understood by the profession, perhaps because it is so very simple. Dr. Mundé, in an article on "Uterine Displacement and Its Curability," in the *American Journal of Obstetrics*, indorses the knee-chest or knee-shoulder position in the following language: "A moment's thought will demonstrate the utility of this combined *vis a fronte* (gravitation of the abdominal viscera towards the diaphragm) and *vis a tergo* (air suction into the vagina and pressure against the vaginal roof). This position is to be assumed several times daily, and maintained each time as long as the patient can bear it, continued for months, if necessary; the best time is at night at retiring, when the lateral position is to be taken for the night."

In a certain proportion of cases the knee-chest position alone will not dislodge the retroflected uterus, so that manual aid is required to effect that purpose. There is a number of methods that have been suggested from time to time, but none are so good as that in which the knee-chest position is combined with the manipulation of the operator. Reposition may occur spontaneously, and it undoubtedly does in a large proportion of cases, in which the retroflected organ becomes pregnant. When the retroflected organ occasions symptoms of retention of urine, the bladder should first be emptied with a soft No. 8 catheter, then the patient is directed to kneel on both of her knees, her thighs remaining perpendicular, while her body inclines forward until one or the other shoulder touches the floor or level of her knees. The operator may then gradually lift the womb and elevate the body sufficiently so that it will fall forward into its natural place. When there is no bladder trouble from compression, and the womb resists even mild force to replace it, I have accomplished gradual reposition by keeping the woman in bed for three or four weeks, with the instructions that she resume the knee-shoulder position two or three times a day, and from five to ten minutes, also that she shall lie on her side and chest and never on her back. In this manner I have accomplished in time and without force what could not have been accomplished with forcible attempts without inducing an abortion.

It curiously happens that there are cases of retroflection which are never suspected nor recognized until the patient has become pregnant. After the woman is about three months gone, the growth of the pregnant uterus can no longer be accommodated in the pelvis, because the direction of its growth is in the direction of the retroflected organ, namely, backwards and downwards (see Plate IV) which makes it a physical impossibility to escape from or grow out of the bony pelvis. The symptoms are retention of urine or a constant dribbling of urine and a straining at stool or pain in the rectum or pelvis, and, of course, the absence of the menses since the commencement of pregnancy. Retroflection may be also acquired during the first three or four months of normal pregnancy, from a jump or fall on the back, in which all the symptoms that indicate this condition are suddenly manifested.

In pregnancy, the course that is to be pursued, in order to rectify the displacement, must be obviously different from that pursued when the woman is not pregnant. The pregnant uterus is a "touch me not;" it permits of no tampering without running the fearful risk of inducing an abortion, and no one but a tyro or an ignoramus will ever meddle with the pregnant womb.

The replacement of the retroflected uterus, that is positively not pregnant, and there must be no question about it either, will admit of introducing a sound into its cavity. This sound is used as a lever upon which the organ may be lifted out of its abnormal position and inclined over the bladder in an anteflected position, which is its natural one. The sound which I employ, and which is my own invention, for replacing the uterus is screwed into a thimble, and from two and one-half to three inches long. The object of this is to artificially elongate the finger so that it can be introduced into the womb. The force which one employs by using this instrument is keenly appreciated by the operator, hence there can be no undue strain, that otherwise might be exerted on adhesions which are too strong to be safely lacerated or even stretched, while slight and recent adhesions might be torn without any bad results. Truax, of Chicago, manufactures my repositor.

Before introducing any sound into the uterine cavity, it is absolutely necessary that the vagina should be thoroughly cleansed with borax water.

The inflammatory enlargements of the womb, subinvolutions, uterine catarrhs, and any of the complications that may exist at the time that the organ is replaced, should be treated on the same principles that have been laid down in the respective chapters on these diseases; in fact, these complications constitute part of the after treatment for retroversion or flexion. The other treatment is to be directed toward retaining the womb where it naturally belongs. The daily exercise in the knee-chest position should never be neglected, and in cases in which this is insufficient, it is very probable that the pelvic floor or natural support of the uterus has been injured or lacerated during confinement, and this may require a plastic operation as a preliminary to a cure. In obstinate cases there is no cure so effectual as pregnancy and a full-time delivery, provided precautions are taken so that the mother will not acquire a new retroflexion during her lying-in period, from the cause that has been already detailed. The patient must accustom herself to sleep either on the chest with face turned to one or the other side, or in a semi-prone position on either the right or left side. Perseverance in sleeping in this manner for a few weeks cultivates the habit that gives more refreshing sleep than lying on the back, which most persons are inclined to do.

CHAPTER XXI
DISEASES OF THE FALLOPIAN TUBES

The Fallopian tubes are the ovi ducts, along which the spermatozoids pass from the womb to fertilize the ovum, and along which the fertilized or non-fertilized ovum, as the case may be, is carried to the cavity of the uterus.

They are two small canals, between three and a half and four inches in length, and constitute the only means of communication between the womb and ovaries; their caliber is exceedingly small and lined with a delicate mucous membrane.

The diseases which affect the Fallopian tubes are inflammation, stricture, distention and displacements.

The inflammation is distinguished as salpingitis, from *salpinx*, Fallopian tube, and *itis*, in composition, inflammation; this consists of a catarrhal inflammation of the lining membrane of the tubes, which rarely if ever originates in the tubes themselves, but is secondary to an inflammatory process in the neighboring organs.

Chronic endometritis or catarrh of the womb is undoubtedly the most fruitful cause of salpingitis, although this is not absolutely the rule, for there are some women who have had uterine catarrh for years without its affecting the tubes in the least. But there is a type of uterine catarrh that has a special tendency to spread from the womb to the lining membrane of the tubes, and this is the infectious endometritis. An infectious inflammation of the womb may be due to many different sources of infection; the retained products of conception after an abortion may become putrescent and furnish one source; carrying putrefactive germs into the uterine cavity from the vaginal canal by means of probes or instruments, that are in themselves defiled by not having been thoroughly cleansed and purified since their last employment, is another source of infection; the latter is perhaps the commoner cause of blood poisoning in criminal abortions by the abortionists. Gonorrhœal infection seems to have a greater tendency than any other to spread itself from the uterus to the tubes; this has been the subject of special inquiry, and has been thoroughly confirmed, and this may arise many months after the infected male has imagined himself entirely cured.

The diseases of the tubes that I have enumerated are in the relation of cause and effect; a catarrhal inflammation is quite likely to induce a stricture or an occlusion, and this causes a distention from retention of the secretions, whether the secretions are a natural or an inflammatory product. If the inflammation has an infectious origin, then the retained secretion becomes purulent, or it may be a muco-pus secretion from the commencement. The dilated tube may also contain blood or serum; the latter constitutes tubal dropsy; or it may contain a fertilized ovum; this gives rise to tubal pregnancy.

Tubal dropsy may be a distention of the tubes when both ends are sealed by inflammatory adhesions; these distentions vary in size from the thickness of a finger to a large ovarian tumor, from which it is not an easy matter to distinguish it.

The most dangerous form of tubal obstruction and distention is where the contents are pus or purulent matter; this is liable to be poured into the peritoneal cavity from ulceration or rupture of the sac, and excites fatal peritonitis.

Salpingitis can only be viewed as a complication of some prior inflammatory process in some of the adjacent organs and tissues; these are the uterus and ovaries and the pelvic peritoneum and pelvic cellular tissue.

The symptoms of inflammation of the tubes are not so clearly defined as to indicate the nature of the affection, because it is hardly ever limited to the tubes alone, the surrounding tissue being always more or less involved. These patients are so seldom free from pain that their lives are a constant suffering. If the pain subsides, it is only for a few days, and the slightest exertion brings about a relapse, so that walking or standing must be avoided. During menstruation the pain always increases, and the menses may be excessive at one period and scant at another; these harassing pains make powerful inroads on the patient's strength; she becomes pale and debilitated, while her emaciated form and careworn expression give us a picture of the typical invalid. Fortunately, this complication is not as frequent as one might expect from the intimate relation of the tubes to the womb and ovaries, but the possibility of the Fallopian tubes becoming inflamed should admonish women against taking any chances by neglecting the rules of hygiene, that I have laid down in another chapter, for the old saying that "prevention is better than cure" is only too true of this malady.

TREATMENT.

The curative measures for inflammatory diseases or abscesses of the tubes have not been, on the whole, until within a comparatively recent period, very satisfactory.

When this affection complicates uterine or vaginal catarrh, then the treatment that is recommended elsewhere for the relief of these complaints should be adopted; quietude is of paramount importance, and total continence must be practiced by the sufferer. Hot sitz baths and warm fomentations are important auxiliaries in the treatment. Vaginal irrigations of hot water, night and morning, relieve the congestion and stimulate the absorbents of the pelvic glands. Femina vaginal capsules are a great assistance towards accomplishing the same end; one capsule introduced into the vagina at bedtime should be combined with the other treatment.

If these measures fail to accomplish a cure, then a surgical operation may be required as a last resort, which consists in extirpating the diseased tubes and ovaries.

This operation has given some brilliant results, but it has also hurried a great many to an untimely grave. Fool-hardy surgeons or operators are the rule; doctors of only mediocre talent worm themselves into positions that give them prestige in the community. Where nature refuses a capacity for the acquirement of solid wisdom, she seems to compensate her creatures by endowing them with faculties for cunning and intrigue, that galvanize the spurious into the apparently genuine. They have charge of hospitals and are professors in colleges, and are ambitious to imitate the operations of the European masters. On the other hand are the statistics of able surgeons, who seem to have an inborn genius for a special line of operations; such a one is Lawson Tait, of Birmingham, and Martin, of Berlin. Tait has had phenomenal success in cutting open the abdomen and removing diseased tubes and ovaries. He possesses the faculty and skill to select only those cases that are especially suited for an operation, and those that are not adapted for the knife are excluded. In the exercise of this judgment the danger of the operation is reduced to a, minimum. The tubes and ovaries are often so matted and tied down with inflammatory adhesions, that their removal means sure death, and does the average surgeon know this? To have the genius of a Tait is to be one in ten thousand, and for this reason his statistics should be neither a guide nor an excuse for the other nine thousand nine hundred and ninety-nine, to attempt to do as he does. To assume that they can, is as absurd as to admit that our indigenous colonels of the State militia can plan or execute the campaigns of Napoleon.

Galvanism or electricity has come to the rescue of this class of cases, as a safe and reliable method of treatment; of course it takes more time and patience. Should not this outweigh the selfish ambition of the unscrupulous surgeon who desires to boast of the number of times he has opened the abdomen, with little compunction of the confiding lives that he has sacrificed?

I have myself had abundant experience to be convinced of the usefulness of electricity as a curative agent in this class of diseases, but I prefer to illustrate the treatment by quoting from a paper on "The Value of Electricity as a Substitute for Laparotomy," by Augustin H. Goelet, M. D., in the New York *Medical Journal*. He says:—

"Mrs. T., aged twenty-six. Severe pelvic pain referred to left side; profuse leucorrhœa; prolonged and painful menstruation. Diagnosis: Pyosalpinx (or pus) in the left tube. Laparotomy (opening the abdomen) advised at Woman's Hospital. Treatment: Tube emptied into the uterus by applications of positive galvanism to the left horn of the cavity of the uterus. Intravaginal applications afterwards, completed the cure. Duration of treatment, four months Complete relief of pain followed the removal of the pus from the tube. At the end of the treatment she had completely regained her health. Menstruation was normal, and symptoms relieved."

CHAPTER XXII
DISEASES OF THE OVARIES

There is an analogy in the reproductive apparatus, running through the whole animal and vegetable kingdoms. The bulb at the lower extremity of the pistil of a flower is called the ovary, and it contains the seed, which in the course of development becomes the fruit.

In the human female, the ovary contains the seed, or germ, which, becoming fertilized, develops into the human embryo, or the fruit of conception.

The seeds of the ovaries are termed ova, or eggs, and the organ or gland in which the germs, or eggs, are prepared is the ovary.

In the human female the ovaries are two follicular glands, about the shape and size of small almonds, situated on each side of the uterus. The follicles, or small sacs, of which the ovaries are composed, are cemented together by delicate fibrillar connective tissue, which is known as the *stroma* of the ovary, while the follicle is termed Graafian vesicle, after the name of its discoverer. Professor Barry, another investigator, gave the follicles the much better and more appropriate designation of ovisacs, because each of these capsules or follicles contains a single ovule, or little egg.

It is carefully estimated that there are 30,000 Graafian follicles or ovisacs in each ovary, of which only an insignificant number develop and rupture at each menstrual period. It appears, from the researches of Valentine and Pflueger, that the Graafian follicles are formed at a very early period of embryonic life, from a series of minute tubules, that gradually become constricted from surrounding stroma, at regular intervals; the ova are subsequently developed in the interior of the follicles.

Ovarian cysts or tumors cannot be considered in a work for home treatment, but a desire must be awakened in the minds of thoughtful readers, to learn the origin of these growths, and it seems to me quite appropriate at this juncture of the subject, to state that Professor Waldeyer, of Berlin, has discovered that ovarian tumors are developed from the remnants of the little tubules from which the Graafian follicles originate, so that the cause or source of these tumors is already laid before the patient is born; hence cannot be attributed to any fault on the part of the afflicted person. From the earliest period of intra-uterine development up to the age of puberty, the growth of the ovaries is entirely passive, but after that a continuous change takes place in the substance of the ovaries; the contents of the ovaries become active from the period of puberty, from which dates the commencing aptitude for procreation, until the menopause, or final cessation of the menses, which, in popular language, is termed "change of life," when the aptitude for conception ceases with the proliferation of the ova.

The period of fruitfulness is characterized by the persistence of the menses, and this terminates, on the average, in the forty-fifth year; during all of this time the little ova, or eggs, continually ripen, and at their maturity the ovisacs, or Graafian vesicles, rupture from an increased secretion into their cavities. This ripening of an egg and rupture of a follicle corresponds with the monthly flow. The human ovum is very small; the largest does not measure above 1-120th of an inch in diameter, and very often it measures only half that size.

The situation of the ovary is not fixed in the pelvic cavity with any absolute degree of certainty, but it enjoys a degree of mobility that is even greater than that of the womb itself, to which it is attached by means of the ovarian ligament. Its usual place is about an inch from the uterus and a little backwards. It is partly surrounded by folds of peritoneum, and partly by the tissue that pads out the interspaces between the pelvic organs. If we remember the physiological fact, that at every monthly discharge of blood from the uterus, which is called menstruation, an ovum or egg ripens and an ovisac bursts, we cannot fail to appreciate the importance of the intimate relations that these functions must have, to the health of the individual and the perpetuation of the species.

This process of ovulation has the peculiarity of the first stages of an inflammatory action, because the ovaries become congested whenever an ovisac ruptures.

Through the nervous sympathy existing between the ovaries and uterus, this too becomes congested, so that the network of uterine vessels becomes so engorged that the capillary blood vessels of the mucous membrane of the womb rupture, and the hemorrhage that is the result constitutes the menstrual flow.

There are three physiological processes concerned in the menstrual phenomena: first, irritation and congestion of the ovary, rupturing the ovisac; second, congestion of the Fallopian tubes and uterus; third, consequent rupture of the blood vessels of the mucous membrane of the uterus and probably of the Fallopian tubes.

There may be one or more supernumerary ovaries without disturbing the normal functions; one or both ovaries may be congenitally absent. The entire absence of both ovaries is generally accompanied by deformities of so serious a nature that the newly-born infant is incapable of living.

If the defect is principally limited to congenital absence of the ovaries, then there is an absence of the changes in which puberty is recognized; the mammary glands remain flat; there is not the roundness and fullness of the girl's figure that signalizes budding maidenhood. The apparently undeveloped form and girlish characteristics are prolonged into the years of adult age, and she remains weakly and small.

In an incomplete or rudimentary development, from an arrested or imperfect evolution of the ovaries, there is often a condition that resembles the above very much; neither are these cases nearly so infrequent as those whose organs are entirely absent. The ovaries may persist in their fetal state, or their growth may be arrested at any time before the expected period of puberty. The diagnosis of this pathological condition must be inferred from the undeveloped state of the different organs and from the absence of those signs which the approach of the menses communicate.

Displacements of the ovaries are often the cause of suffering and disease, that may excite symptoms quite remote from the seat of trouble. I remember the case of a young woman, who had suffered from obstinate dyspepsia, which subsided at once after the removal of the prolapsed ovary. It has been already alluded to, that these glands are naturally very movable. Anything which increases their weight, whether inflammatory enlargement or a dragging in connection with some inflammatory adhesion to a neighboring organ, may cause their displacement in various directions. It happens that the ovary may form the contents of a hernia or rupture. A prolapse or descent is the most common form of an ovarian displacement. We often find one or the other ovary resting in the pouch between the uterus and rectum, and if the patient should be troubled with constipation, the hardened feces may give rise to painful symptoms in the ovaries, and pain in the rectum, while it also is one of the causes of painful sexual relations. The irritation to which the dislocated ovary is exposed gives rise to inflammatory affections, that may be the cause of continual suffering.

INFLAMMATION OF THE OVARIES, OR ACUTE OVARITIS.

What inflammation is elsewhere, it is again here in these glandular structures.

I endeavored to point out in the beginning of these articles, that the difference of inflammatory diseases was not due to any difference in the inflammatory processes, these are identical, but the modification of the processes are due to the nature of the structure of the tissues that are involved.

If the intelligent reader will bear this in mind, she will form a clear idea of all the inflammatory diseases that come under consideration.

Pathological microscopists have recognized two forms of *ovaritis*, the follicular or parenchymatous, in which the Graafian follicles or ovisacs are the seat of the inflammatory process, and the *interstitial*, in which the intervening or interstitial connective tissue, the *stroma*, between the follicles is inflamed. This distinction has only a scientific interest because it is impossible to distinguish one variety from the other in the living subject; this can only be done with the aid of a powerful microscope after the suspected ovary is removed from the body. Whether the inflammation is follicular or interstitial or both combined, it is liable to destroy all the follicles or ovisacs which contain the ova, that are essential to procreation, and the consequence will be sterility.

The great functional activity to which the ovaries are subjected at each menstrual period, make them extremely liable to an inflammatory process, so that women cannot be too careful of themselves at this precarious period. It is during menstruation that the ovaries become periodically congested, and this alone offers an excellent predisposition for inflammation. As a complication of other inflammatory diseases, ovaritis is very common; it seems hardly probable that there can be an inflammation of a pelvic peritoneal fold or of the pelvic cellular tissue in close proximity to or surrounded by it, without involving the corresponding ovary. There cannot be a serious inflammation of the womb or of the Fallopian tubes without being communicated to the ovaries, and this is always true of the infectious catarrhs, especially the gonorrhœal form.

There is a great tendency in inflammation of the ovaries to suppurate and change the entire tissue of the ovary into an abscess. Ovarian abscesses are not much different in their behavior from abscesses in the Fallopian tubes or cellular tissue. It is claimed that they have a greater tendency to break into the bladder than other pelvic abscesses; this may be due to a displacement of the ovary, which locates the gland near or between the bladder and uterus, before the advent of the inflammation. There are no infallible signs that point to the existence of acute inflammation of the ovaries, owing to the complication of other inflammatory processes in the majority of cases. The characteristic pain of an inflamed ovary is of a throbbing or pulsating nature.

I cannot imagine an ovaritis without at least a circumscribed peritonitis, and one can hardly suppose a pelvic peritonitis to exist without in a certain degree compromising the ovary.

If the ovary has once become inflamed, whether alone or as a complication of other diseases, then the most important question to decide is the existence of an abscess. This can only be recognized by an experienced and careful specialist, who has trained his sense of touch, so that he can feel the abscess between the fingers of one hand in the vagina, and the other making counter pressure on the abdomen. The history of each case must in a measure decide the nature of the fluctuating tumor, whether it may not be an ovarian cyst instead of an abscess, although an abscess may have been a small cyst.

The development and course of different cases, present various aspects for consideration. The enlargement may become obstinate to the ordinary methods of treatment and assume the chronic form of subacute inflammation. The inflammation may spread from the ovary to the peritoneal membrane that partly covers it; these are the broad ligaments of the uterus. This may be the means through which the organ may grow to the surrounding tissue and adjacent organs, so that it becomes utterly impossible to move it or even successfully extirpate it from its intimate attachments.

In other cases the ovary remains entirely free from attachments or complications, and while it can be generally felt lower down pressing perhaps on the rectum, it is readily movable or replaced. In the majority of cases only one ovary is involved, but in these cases there is a predisposition which in a large proportion sooner or later compromises also the other ovary in a similar diseased process.

TREATMENT.

The treatment of this affection is greatly modified or influenced by a knowledge of the causation of the inflammation. In every case, however, the patient should take to her bed. If there is a profuse vaginal secretion it should be ascertained if the disease is of infectious origin, and where this is suspected, the vaginal canal should be thoroughly rinsed with an antiseptic solution of corrosive chloride of mercury in the proportion of one grain of the sublimate to two thousand grains or parts of water, or about fifteen grains to the half gallon of water. There are tablets to be had at the drug stores which contain the requisite amount of corrosive when added to a given quantity of water; these are preferable and more convenient than the crude drug, and as they are a *deadly poison* they should be kept under lock and key. There is nothing to equal the corrosive for an offensive vaginal discharge, for it is the most reliable disinfectant there is in the entire pharmacopœa. Half a gallon of this solution should be used at a time, and after the vaginal canal has been thoroughly disinfected, about a pint of the same solution must be passed through the uterine cavity by means of a double catheter, that has a reverse flow and is especially made for the purpose. To insure against mercurial poisoning I am in the habit of following mercurial irrigations with warm water, that was previously sterilized by boiling. One pint of the simple water is generally sufficient to displace all the mercurial water that might have remained in the uterine or vaginal cavities. These medicated irrigations should have an average temperature of 105 degrees Fahr. and be repeated daily for about a week.

If the vaginal secretion is not of a specific nature, then the Femina antiseptic uterine lotion is a safer remedy.

Ice bags applied over the regions of the painful ovaries check the acute inflammation from going into suppuration and forming an abscess. Should the latter be found to exist, it should be opened by means of a trocar or aspirator. The bowels should be kept free by taking a daily dose of Femina laxative tablets.

CHRONIC OVARITIS.

If an acute inflammation does not terminate in prompt recovery or an abscess it may lose its fiery nature and tone down into a low grade of prolonged congestion which does not go on to the production of suppuration. This would constitute the chronic form of inflammation.

It does not follow that all chronic inflammations are preceded by the acute form, for there are inflammations that are subacute from the beginning, that is, that there is not the heat nor feverishness in the tissues which is one of the principal features of the acute process.

Chronic inflammation of the ovaries is much more frequent as an original or individual affection, than the preceding form. A peculiar feature of this affection is a gradual growth or enlargement of the ovary, all the way from a moderate swelling to a good-sized orange. There has been some discussion as to the particular tissue of the ovaries that is involved in the inflammatory process, whether it is the interfollicular structure or the follicules or ovisacs themselves; practically the solution of this question has no bearing on the treatment, although it may have an influence on the function of the organ, which may be more injuriously affected by the latter than the former variety. The disease occurs almost exclusively after the age of puberty and during the period of sexual activity. It is not as often met in the unmarried as in the married, and with the latter it is more prevalent in the first years of married life. Inordinate sexual indulgence is a frequent exciting cause, and when this is coupled with pernicious means that are employed for preventing conception, it becomes still more frequent.

Chronic inflammation of the vagina, womb, and of the Fallopian tubes is often transferred to the ovaries.

The infectious catarrh to which the genital tract of the female is more or less exposed from a lack of proper cleanliness of her own person, or a gonorrhœal infection from her male companion, show a peculiar tendency to gradually spread the inflammatory processes to the ovaries. Some careful observation has established the fact that an apparently cured gonorrhœal infection in the male may, after a year or two, excite a gonorrhœal catarrh in the genitals of the female; a great many diseases of the ovaries have been traced to this source of infection.

As gonorrhœa is not an uncommon affection among the male portion of the community, it is not sufficient for the intelligent members of the medical profession to know of these dangers of infection, but every man and woman should be apprised of the great danger there is of infecting the marital chamber with the pollution of the brothel.

The symptoms of chronic ovaritis are more or less dependent on the causation of each individual case.

Sometimes it is traced to the fiery stage of the acute affection, while in other instances it can be laid to some indiscretion during the menstrual flow, then, again, it may have developed itself so stealthily that the greatest acumen and skill are required to detect its origin. The most important and constant sign is a steady pain in one or both ovaries. When this pain is violent, it shoots toward the back and rectum and down the thighs. The pain becomes heightened from an accumulation of feces in the rectum, which a habitual constipation entails. Marital excesses near the approach of the menstrual period or shortly after the disappearance of the menses are quite likely to precipitate the painful symptoms. The bladder sympathizes in a certain proportion of cases, so that there is a frequent desire to pass water. In the course of time the distressful symptoms that have been enumerated derange the digestive apparatus; the patients lose their appetite and decline into a debilitated and nervous state, so that one or the other hysterical phenomenon become more or less prominent in persons of a nervous temperament.

Sterility is a rule with this class of women, even if there is only one ovary affected; this would indicate that the apparently healthy one sympathizes with the other, or an accompanying catarrh of the uterus or tubes may prevent the passage of the fertilizing germ. If both ovaries are inflamed, then it is quite natural to suppose that the delicate follicles and their contents, the ova, become destroyed or so altered that they no longer answer the purpose of reproduction. It is seldom that one meets a chronic ovaritis without a uterine catarrh, and how much this contributes to the sterility is not easy to tell.

TREATMENT.

The course of this affection in the majority of cases is favorable. If the treatment is intelligently administered, the pain and congestion gradually subside, and as this class of patients have generally learned from sad experience that negligence or indiscretion on their part will excite a relapse, they soon learn to avoid these, so that they enjoy comparative immunity from suffering for a considerable length of time.

There is a smaller proportion of cases whose unfortunate surroundings or lack of intelligence makes remedial measures of no avail. These poor women have neither respite from physical labor nor freedom from the animal passions of their husbands, and thus living in constant pain they become drooped in spirit and reduced in vigor, so that they fall an easy victim to any intercurrent affection that may attack them.

In proportion as the patients can give their diseased ovaries freedom from irritating influences are the chances for their complete recovery increased.

To accomplish this object, quietude in the recumbent posture, sexual abstinence and a free daily stool form the basis for recovery. If there is much pelvic pain, this is best controlled by means of the ice bag, 4x6 inches in size, of which one on each side, wrapped in one thickness of flannel, should be applied to the groin or region of the ovaries; cold-water compresses, thoroughly wrung, so as not to drip, and covered with flannel so as to keep the bed covering dry, are also advisable, but only a poor substitute for the ice.

Iodoform suppositories greatly stimulate the absorption of the inflammatory exudation; one of these should be introduced into the vaginal canal each day. If the patient can get up without any painful symptoms, she should take the hot sitz bath for ten or fifteen minutes daily, and as a general tonic, this is a useful prescription.

NO. XI.

Take:	Bromide of sodium	2 drams
	Iodide of potassium	1 dram
	Comp. tinct. of gentian	2 ounces
	Water, sufficient to make	8 ounces

Mix. A tablespoonful three times a day.

There is no affection in the entire category of diseases of women, in which the confidence of women has been more abused by specialists, than by meddlesome surgical invasions, for the extirpation of one or both ovaries, to cure real or imaginary diseases of these glands. There is a veritable mania among surgeons for this operation, but the conservative portion of the profession are awakening to a conviction that this is entirely wrong, and a presumption on professional license that is altogether unpardonable.

If these castrations were confined to the removal of ovaries that are unmistakably degenerated or diseased, and that had resisted intelligent treatment for some time, there would not be the same objection, but when ovaries are removed that are apparently healthy, but through ignorance or incompetency are supposed to be the offending members, then, I say, that is an outrage.

There are a great many women who have been subjected to the dangers of a so-called normal ovariotomy, without being in the least benefited by the operation. The symptoms which the extirpation of their ovaries was to relieve, persisted as before, and they discovered, when it was too late, that spaying is not a panacea for the ills that suffering women are heir to.

The ovaries are in delicate sympathy with all the other pelvic organs, and when these are affected there may be more or less pain in one or both of these glands. They may be even the seat of a neuralgic affection without any structural change in the organ or in the neighboring organs. This would be simply a reflex sign of a general debilitated condition, and to mistake all these for ovarian disease and to make it an excuse for their removal, is not warranted by careful observation. Electricity is now coming to the front as one of the most valuable remedies for just this class of affections, and I will give a detailed account of the nature of this remedy and the requirements for its successful application, which persons who speak lightly of its virtue, never acquire nor take the pains to possess.

CHAPTER XXIII
PERIMETRITIS AND PELVIC PERITONITIS

The peritoneum is a delicate, thin, serous membrane, that lines the whole internal surface of the abdomen and envelopes more or less completely all the abdominal organs, so that the viscera glide smoothly against each other with the least possible friction. The peritoneum dips down almost midway into the true pelvis, and its boundaries constitute also the limit of the abdominal cavity. That portion of the general peritoneum, which partly invests all the pelvic organs, is distinguished from the other by the term *pelvic peritoneum*. When the entire membrane becomes the seat of inflammation, the affection is a general *peritonitis*, but when the inflammation is limited to the organ that it infolds, the prefix *peri*, signifying *around*, is compounded with the name of the organ, and the suffix *itis* is added, which indicates that the peritoneal covering of such an organ is inflamed, hence, the term *peri-metra-itis* means inflammation of the peritoneum around the womb.

Pelvic peritonitis means that the peritoneum of the entire pelvic cavity is involved in the inflammatory process. This may include the peritoneal covering of all the other pelvic organs besides that of the womb as well as the peritoneal folds, that enter into the formation of the broad and other ligaments of the pelvic organs.

Perimetritis is rarely an independent uncomplicated disease, but oftener a complication of inflammation of the womb, the Fallopian tubes, ovaries, or of the cellular tissue that surrounds the organs and in which they are imbedded. The pelvic peritoneum and the cellular tissue are so intimately connected with each other by means of their vessels, nerves and lymphatics, that an inflammation easily runs from one tissue to another.

If we now inquire into the causes which induce this disease, we shall find that there is not a single inflammatory disease of any of the pelvic organs that may not lead to its inauguration. Metritis after an abortion or a confinement is a fruitful source, so are all the other causes that operate in exciting metritis indirectly concerned in this affection. Since etiology or the causation of diseases has been made a special study in connection with this subject, some startling discoveries have been made in regard to the origin of pelvic peritonitis.

Dr. Noeggerath, of New York, has found in the majority of cases that came under his observation, that pelvic peritonitis, either acute or chronic, is due to gonorrhœal infection. He claims that gonorrhœa in the male is in the majority of instances incurable; although it may be apparently cured, it continues as a latent affection which regularly infects his female companion. This shows itself at first as a slight vaginal catarrh, which gradually and stealthily spreads to the cavity of the womb, thence to the Fallopian tubes and ovaries and afterwards involving the pelvic peritoneum, for it must be remembered that the Fallopian tubes open directly into the peritoneal cavity.

Dr. Noeggerath has collected statistics that agree with those of the celebrated French physician, Ricord, which show that on an average 80 per cent of the male population have had gonorrhœa, and, believing themselves cured, when not, enter into married relations, and unwittingly infect their wives. He says that "it has come to pass that young ladies dread to marry, because all their friends become invalids soon after the nuptial rites." The late Professor Schroeder, of the Berlin Gynecological clinic, says that "the assertions of Noeggerath are extravagant, but that he must particularly emphasize that chronic inflammatory conditions of the internal female genitals, like catarrh of the vagina and uterus, metritis and perimetritis, are extraordinarily frequent results of gonorrhœal infection."

I am inclined to think, from my own experience, that the more conservative view of Professor Schroeder is perfectly safe and true, but if Dr. Noeggerath made due allowance for the number of invalids among newly-married people whose uterine diseases, especially pelvic peritonitis, were traceable to criminal abortions and monthly probing of their uterine cavities to induce the menstrual flow, his views would about coincide with those of the distinguished Berlin authority. These catarrhal affections cause sterility, and if conception supervenes, then there is a likelihood of a miscarriage or a premature birth, or a perimetritis during pregnancy or confinement.

Menstrual disorders in which the flow is either obstructed or suppressed may also give rise to perimetritis.

Blood poisoning from criminal operations contributes its share in the causation. Traumatic agencies, like blows, falls, lacerations, and other injuries during labor, may result in pelvic peritonitis.

Either too hot or too cold vaginal irrigations have given rise to this affection, and injections into the cavity of the womb for medicinal purposes, in which some of the fluid escaped through the Fallopian tube into the peritoneal cavity, has caused, in several instances, fatal peritonitis.

The inflammation of the womb after childbirth invariably involves the peritoneum. The course and duration of this disease is by no means uniform.

The disease under consideration is an example of an acute inflammation affecting a serous membrane.

I have taken pains to inform the reader that the phenomena of inflammation are always the same, but that the results are modified by the peculiarity of the structure of which the tissues are composed.

A serous membrane differs completely from a mucous membrane, inasmuch as it contains neither mucous glands nor mucous cells, and for that reason can never be the seat of catarrh; instead of this, it possesses the power to secrete or transude the serous portion of the blood, hence its name. The serous membrane in a healthy condition has only a sufficient quantity of secretion to moisten the membrane, but not to furnish any appreciable quantity of fluid. If the secretion takes place as a result of congestion, especially when this congestion is due to an obstruction to the return of blood from heart or liver disease, it is secreted in such large quantities that it constitutes dropsy.

Under the stimulating influence of the inflammatory process, a similar secretion is the result, only that it contains also *fibrin*, which renders the secretion or exudation spontaneously coagulable, and, further, possesses the capability of passing into the condition of an organized tissue, either fibrous or granular, and thus forming false membranes on inflamed surfaces, or solidifying into tumors or swellings.

These inflammations have their various degrees of severity, from a temporary reddening of the membrane with barely enough effusion of inflammatory material to cause a thin layer of deposit, to extensive and violent attacks, that pour out enormous quantities of effusion or exudation, so as to fill the entire pelvic cavity with a solid mass. The nature of the inflammatory material may be purulent from the beginning, because its origin was of an infectious or septic nature.

Suppuration may develop slowly and lead to an abscess; this may open or break into the peritoneal cavity, causing general septic peritonitis, which will cause death in a few hours or days. The abscess may also suppurate and break into some of the adjacent organs or tunnel its way in different circuitous routes, being guided in its course by the pelvic and muscular fasciæ, so that it may perforate at the groin, show itself at the inside of the thighs, or in the lumbar region near the kidneys. It ruptures most frequently into the rectum, next in frequency into the vagina and into the bladder. I had a case, that came under my treatment, in which both rectum and vagina were perforated, and purulent matter discharged from both fistulæ; under appropriate treatment the patient recovered completely.

If the inflammation is not of infectious origin, the exudation gradually becomes absorbed, and each day grows less, until finally nothing but a few fibrous bands can be felt, and these too may disappear in time.

The symptoms of perimetritis depend in a great measure on the nature and severity of the attack.

There are three distinct stages of this disease, and each has its characteristic symptoms. The first stage is that of inflammatory congestion, which is generally ushered in with a distinct chill or a chilly feeling, which is speedily followed by a high fever and a rapid pulse. The lower abdominal region becomes exceedingly sensitive and very painful on pressure; the abdomen becomes tympanitic or bloated, and it is a relief for the patient to draw her limbs up, so as to relax the abdominal walls. A vaginal examination in this stage gives only negative results; there is nothing but a painful sensitiveness, great heat, and the vaginal walls are puffed or swollen; there is as yet no inflammatory exudation that can be felt by the finger.

After the affection has lasted one or more days, the second stage of the disease is recognized, this is the effusion or exudation. The characteristic physical signs of effusion are the only absolute proof of the existence of this disease. These signs are (1st) an immovable fixed state of the womb, which is quite the contrary to its natural healthy state, that permits of a mobility in all directions; (2d) a hard, non-bulging condition of the tissues that surround the womb, so that the impression which one receives gives the idea of all the pelvic organs being cast or set in wax, because everything is glued down and immovable; (3d) an indistinct fullness is felt by the patient, high up in the pelvis; this is the free exudation of the inflammatory material, which has now become solidified and has some characteristics of a tumor. This may push the organ forward or to either side or surround the womb on all sides.

The third stage is that of absorption or the gradual disappearance of the exudation; this is usually a slow process, and may take from three to six months. I have known residues of the exudation, in the form of fibrous bands or adhesions or solid lumps to remain for years in the pelvic or peritoneal cavity. These bands may tie or fix the uterus to the rectum or to the pelvic walls, so that it will resist all ordinary efforts to replace it. Pelvic hematocele, or an effusion of blood into the pelvic peritoneum, inclosed either by anatomical structures or previously-existing inflammations, greatly resembles the sero-fibrinous exudation of perimetritis. The pallor of the countenance aided by other signs of hemorrhage must assist in distinguishing the affections.

Chronic perimetritis is developed in numerous affections of the womb that exert a continuous irritation of its peritoneal covering. These are fibroid and malignant tumors, painful and difficult menstruation, as well as enlargement of the tubes and ovaries. Inflammation of the uterus and a discharge of blood or matter through the tubes and into the peritoneal cavity, may bring about a chronic pelvic peritonitis from the beginning.

Chronic perimetritis or chronic pelvic peritonitis, for the terms are often interchangeable, is most abrupt in its development, because it is not heralded by fiery, acute febrile symptoms, but a close inquiry will usually recall to the minds of patients the commencement of the trouble. The fact that the peritoneum is also reflected on the bladder, causes an irritability of this organ, to be the first and only symptom, for quite a while. There is nothing stereotyped in the development of any disease, so that the symptoms may or may not be painful from the beginning. The pains in the pelvis are more or less continual, there is an incapacity for bodily exertion, the bowels are out of order, either there is constipation or a chronic diarrhœa; these morbid conditions destroy the appetite and the patient becomes lean and weakly. From time to time all these abnormal signs become aggravated, so that the sufferer may be forced to take to her bed.

Some women have great powers of resistance and endure suffering with great fortitude, so that they are comparatively free from harassing pain, although their pelvic organs are tied down by inflammatory adhesions, and unless they lift or make other unusual muscular efforts, that increase the intra-abdominal pressure, so as to drag on the adhesions, they suffer little or no pain. Another sign of chronic perimetritis is painful intercourse, which jars the adhesions, and this is particularly the case if the womb comes down quite low. The danger to be apprehended is that no one knows at what moment some indiscretion will light up an acute attack with all its serious consequences.

In view of the possibility of any local or circumscribed peritonitis becoming general, and as such may prove fatal, the importance of recognizing it in its first stage, or early, becomes readily apparent.

Preventive measures of circumscribed or local peritonitis are to be found in avoiding the causes that have been referred to as inducing the affection under consideration, among which, criminal abortions are the most fruitful. It seems to me that if women were cognizant of the dangers that threaten them, they would not only be more careful in observing the ordinary rules of health, but they would voluntarily shrink from committing crimes that not only stain their souls with the blood of their own kindred, but also entail disease and death, that unexpectedly waft their spirits into the presence of their Creator, whose laws they have outraged. How often have I been told by women who lay prostrated on their death bed, "O doctor, I did not know that the induction of an abortion was a crime and dangerous, because the person who performed the operation told me that it was neither dangerous nor criminal." Alas! poor woman, there is no greater crime, and nothing more pernicious to your health and life; would that others would only learn and profit from the inexorable fate into which your delusions enticed you.

TREATMENT.

The treatment in this affection, when prompt and intelligently administered, offers every chance of success. In the acute stage of pelvic peritonitis, we must resort to remedies that promptly counteract the inflammatory action. The internal administration of opium or some morphine preparation is invariably demanded, not only to relieve the pain, but also to completely check or constipate the bowels, so that their peristaltic action is entirely suspended, for their motion would irritate the peritoneum. Dr. McMunn's elixir of opium in one-half to one teaspoonful doses should be given every four hours, until the pain is relieved and the bowels controlled.

Rubber ice bags should be applied to the lower abdominal region. This course of treatment will generally limit and check the inflammatory process in a few days; then the bowels should be gently moved every day, with an enema of warm water impregnated with a little soap; after which, complete quietude in bed for another week or two, will complete the cure.

Chronic perimetritis must be treated according to its complications; should there be a gonorrhœal infection, then what was said of the treatment of this complaint elsewhere, applies with equal force to these cases. The patient's strength must now be an object of jealous solicitude. The diet must be of the most nourishing nature, and milk or egg punch should be the principal food, at regular intervals of four hours, alternating with strong soups or beef teas, to which a raw egg thoroughly beaten should first be added.

Vaginal and uterine catarrhs, if they exist, require the attention that is recommended in the preceding pages.

Warm compresses or fomentations and daily hot sitz baths are of great value in chronic perimetritis, for they stimulate the healing process and the absorption. The bowels must now be daily moved, and here I prefer the patient to employ simply warm water enema in tolerably large quantities slowly injected, until a quart or more of the fluid has been thrown into the rectum; these enemas will not only move the bowels, but also stimulate the healing process. If the patient lies on the left side while these injections are taken or given, the enema flows higher up, and it should be retained for a reasonable length of time. These enemas should only be taken every other day, and between days a suitable dose of purgative elixir. Tincture of iodine can be applied to the groins every second day, or iodoform suppositories introduced into the vagina. Mud baths are also very beneficial in removing old inflammatory adhesions.

If the exudation suppurates and an abscess forms, it should be freely opened as soon as possible. This can generally be best accomplished through the vagina, but if there be a tendency of the abscess to point towards the groin, then this situation would be preferable, although I prefer, in even these cases, to make a counter opening in the vagina, for this precludes the possibility of the abscess sacking or burrowing further into the tissue. The cavity of the abscess should be thoroughly rinsed out with a 2 per cent carbolic acid or a 1 to 2,000 corrosive sublimate solution, and if there is a tendency in the abscess to close before its cavity is healed out, a rubber drainage tube should be inserted, so as to give the pus all the possible facility to escape. If the abscess breaks into the bladder or into the rectum, then a counter opening into the vagina will greatly insure and expedite recovery.

Sometimes the ovaries and tubes become diseased as a result of the perimetritic inflammation; this, then, becomes a subject of special inquiry and treatment. It should hardly be necessary to remind the reader that sexual relations are to be suspended while there is the least sign of the affection to be discerned. Although old adhesions and displacements, the result of old chronic pelvic peritonitis, are often naturally and permanently removed through a supervening pregnancy, the intelligent use of the galvanic current will also accomplish that end.

CHAPTER XXIV
PELVIC CELLULITIS OR PARAMETRITIS

The term *cellular* was given to this tissue, because under the microscope it shows large meshes or cell-like cavities, that are also termed areolæ, hence, the tissue is often called areolar tissue; it is also called connective tissue, because it combines all the different organs and structures of the body together. It is very elastic and contractile, and by the fluid which it contains in its areolæ, motion of parts on each other is facilitated.

Professor Virchow has applied to it, in the region of the womb or pelvis, the term *parametric* tissue, from the Greek prefix *para*, beside, and the Latin *metra*, the womb, signifying the tissue near and around the womb, from which the Germans derive *parametritis*, instead of the English, who employ *pelvic-cellulitis*, each meaning one and the same thing, namely, inflammation of the cellular or connective tissue in the pelvis or around the womb.

The female pelvic organs have interspaces between the bladder, vagina and uterus in front, and the uterus, vagina and rectum behind, also on both sides, between the womb, ovaries, and the folds of the broad ligaments, and lastly, between these organs and the walls of the pelvic cavity are interspaces. These interspaces are filled in or padded out by loose cellular tissue. M. Nonat, a celebrated French authority, has described this in a beautiful figure, by saying that "the organs of reproduction float in an atmosphere of cellular tissue." This is indeed so, and a consideration of an inflammatory condition of this structure, is to conclude the inquiry into the inflammatory diseases peculiar to women.

Pelvic cellulitis is one of those diseases for the comprehension of which we are particularly indebted to the researches of modern pathologists, who have discovered that infectious germs are the cause of numerous diseases; pelvic cellulitis is one of these, because it originates as a secondary result of septic absorption.

The bacteria or putrefactive germs belong to Protophytes—the smallest and simplest of all plants, some of them are so small that it requires the highest powers of the microscope to make them visible. Their growth and multiplication have been experimentally demonstrated by artificial cultivation, and this now constitutes one of the most interesting studies of modern pathology.

Pasteur, Lister, Nægle and others, regard the decomposition in the tissues as a direct result of the vegetation of the bacteria. "Decomposition and fungus are inseparable; the one ceases when the other is removed. Processes of this nature set up by bacteria are best distinguished as *fermentations.*" Professor Ziegler, of the University of Tuebingen, says: "The healthy organism is always beset with a multitude of *non-infectious bacteria.* They occupy the natural cavities accessible from without, and especially the alimentary canal. They feed on the substances lying in their neighborhood, whether brought into the body or secreted by the tissues. In so doing they set up chemical changes in these tissues. While the organs are acting normally, these fungi work no mischief to the tissues in which they lie, or to the system generally. The products of decomposition set up by such non-specific micro-organisms are either harmless or are conveyed out of the body before they begin to be active.

"Settlements of this kind may, however, become of importance, if the bacteria proceed to develop to any unusual extent. This happens when the contents of the natural cavities in question remains unchanged for any great length of time, or when (as in catarrh) the normal secretion undergoes some alteration. The products of bacterial fermentation may then accumulate to an excessive amount, and products may be found which do not normally occur. Highly poisonous substances are formed in many of the bacterial decompositions. One of the most speedily fatal diseases, septicæmia, is due to blood-poisoning of the system with the products of bacterial putrefaction, or sepsis.

"Putrid or septic poison may be absorbed by wounds as well as by mucous surfaces. Septicæmia, which has just been cited as an instance of septic poisoning, is generally due to wound infection. It is due to the absorption of products of bacterial decomposition formed in a wound contaminated by bacteria.

"*Infectious bacteria* have the power of settling, not merely in the ingesta and secretions or in dead tissue, but also in living tissue. This happens chiefly in the mucous membrane of the lungs. The uninjured skin is protected against invasion by the horny epidermis. Many bacteria can settle in perfectly healthy mucous membrane. In the case of others we must imagine that they do not find a proper soil for their development, unless the mucous membrane is injured or altered. Of course, injury or alteration of this kind may serve to make the outer skin or any other accessible tissue, the starting-point of a bacterial invasion (wound infection). All that is necessary is that a bacterium should reach a spot that affords the conditions for its development. If this occurs, it multiplies and forms colonies or swarms. These may, according to the species of the fungus and the nature of the soil, remain in aggregation, forming heaps or masses, or may spread through the tissues. In general terms we may say that local settlements of bacteria will sooner or later bring about degeneration and necrosis of the affected tissue. When this may occur, and how widely it may spread, are circumstances depending on the nature of the bacteria and of the tissue.

"The inflammatory processes set up by bacterial action may be of very different intensity and extent in different cases. It may be slight or transient, or may be severe and issue in suppuration and an abscess."

The above quotation is perhaps as concise and complete an explanation as the space in this article will permit, and if thoughtfully considered, it will be the means of understanding what is to be said of the disease under consideration.

Pelvic cellulitis is oftener found in childbirth, premature labor and abortion, for the reason that it is a wound infection, and the female organism, is always more or less wounded under these circumstances. In confinement the cervix is always more or less torn, and septic matter deposited there often speedily spreads along the lymphatics and veins to the pelvic cellular tissue, in fact, the entire uterine surface forms a suitable soil for bacterial growth. The vagina is also more or less injured or bruised through parturient efforts; this may be in the nature of a laceration or an abrasion of its mucous surface.

Outside of the above causes, the infection may be of traumatic origin, the most common causes being operative measures on the vagina or womb of a cutting, scraping or stitching nature, that were not carried out under strictly antiseptic precautions, guaranteeing the exclusion of septic germs. Dilation of the cervix with sponge tents or with instruments or probes that were not perfectly cleansed, causes infection and a decomposition of the retained secretions, which, becoming absorbed, leads to pelvic cellulitis. In surgical operations and puerperal conditions in which infection has been positively excluded, by careful antiseptic measures, pelvic cellulitis is impossible.

The inflammation in this disease is excited by the irritating influences of products of septic decomposition; these may have been introduced into the system at the time of confinement or of an operation, or they may have been in the vaginal tract before the operations were commenced. This teaches an important lesson, which few seem to have learned; it is this, that *the strictest antiseptic regulations in a confinement or operation are of no avail, if the patient herself is not first thoroughly disinfected before the operation begins.*

In the German Empire there is a legal provision giving full instructions for the necessary disinfection of the lying-in woman and her attendant; if there were such a wise provision in this country, we would not hear of so many deaths of women in childbed, from blood poisoning. At the Copenhagen International Medical Congress (1884), Professor Esmarch, one of the most celebrated of German surgeons, said that "humanity demands antiseptic treatment of wounds and wounded." I believe that the time will soon come that antiseptic regulations in the treatment of diseases will not only be compulsory, but that a neglect of the same, causing death by blood poisoning, will make the attendant liable for exemplary damages.

Pelvic cellulitis generally develops itself in an acute form, and the symptoms are very similar to those of pelvic peritonitis, and, like the latter affection, there is always an exudation of inflammatory material in these cases, so that the meshes of the tissues become soaked like a sponge with water. The invasion of the infection is usually signalized by a distinct chill or rigors followed by an increased bodily temperature and a correspondingly rapid pulse. The commencement of a parametritis is not often without distinct symptoms that affect the nervous system. The patient feels uncomfortably depressed, a tired, worn-out feeling overcomes her, she loses her appetite, and there is pain in the pelvic cavity. This pain is partly due to an accompanying peritoneal irritation, or in some cases to a circumscribed inflammation of the peritoneum. Often the pain runs down the groin, along the course of the great vessels and nerves; this is occasioned from the exudation pressing on the trunks of these structures in the pelvis. Pain in the small of the back, and painful defecation, with an irritable bladder, are due to the same cause.

Phlegmasia alba dolens, or what was called before the dawn of modern pathological science, *milk leg*, is only another form or a complication of pelvic cellulitis. This occurs where the infectious inflammatory process runs along the cellular or connective tissue of the large vessels and nerves, to the connective tissue of the thighs; this is a very easy matter, because the vessels and nerves are imbedded in cellular tissue, and as the vessels leave the pelvis at the groin, this tissue is continuous with that of the extremities. When the inflammation gets into the thighs, it invades either the subcutaneous cellular tissue, that is, the connective tissue under the skin, or it runs along the trunks of the nerves and vessels; the affected limb becomes then edematous or swollen, hence the vague term of milk leg, because the milk has never anything to do with it. One time it was supposed that this affection is only possible after confinement, but this is an error, because phlegmasia alba may develop at any time from purulent infection, originating from any cause.

The so-called puerperal or childbed fever is also nothing more nor less than an infection of purulent secretion.

The extent of the exudation varies greatly, both in the pelvis and in the limbs. In the pelvis it is sometimes only a little swelling on each side of the womb, and between the folds of the broad ligaments, small nodules the size of walnuts can only be felt, while in other cases the entire pelvic roof is covered and soaked with the inflammatory effusion. The consistence of these swellings or tissues feels at first doughy or soft, but after the absorption has been going on for a while, it becomes as hard as a board. If the exudation begins to suppurate and an abscess forms, then the surrounding tissue becomes soft again, so that the fluctuation of an elastic tumor becomes recognizable.

In the majority of cases the inflammatory process becomes circumscribed in the pelvis, the fever subsides, and the pain and sensitiveness in the pelvis disappear. The exudation has also a circumscribed limit, becoming harder and smaller, until it finally has become entirely absorbed. In another class of cases, the swelling remains stationary for a long time and a solid tumor remains in the pelvic cavity, that may be mistaken for an ovarian or fibroid growth, but in the course of a long time, it may gradually become absorbed. In a certain proportion of cases the course of the disease becomes protracted or chronic, because the effusion is very slow to disappear. In these cases there is danger of general septic infection or septicæmia, and of a spreading of the cellular inflammation to the general peritoneal membrane, which would prove, quite likely, fatal. If the inflammation is violent and the infection intense, suppuration and abscesses will destroy the cellular tissue, and if the lower extremities become involved, the circulation in the affected limb may become permanently injured. The cellular tissue around the veins, or even the veins themselves, become more or less affected by the inflammatory process, so that the veins become compressed or constricted from the cicatrization around them, or their caliber may become obliterated from inflammation of the walls of the veins, thus offering a permanent impediment to the return of the blood to the heart; the affected limb now remains swollen, and the swelling may entirely subside in the recumbent posture at night, but during the day it returns again, to make the leg thick and clumsy.

TREATMENT.

Prevention in these affections is much better than cure. The treatment of a recent case of pelvic cellulitis must be energetically antiseptic. The seat of the infection must be discovered; the vagina or cavity of the uterus, as the case may be, must be thoroughly washed out with a 1 to 2,000 corrosive sublimate solution. After a thorough disinfection, the inflammation and pain can be checked or controlled by the application of ice bags; this is the remedy *par excellence* to check acute inflammatory processes. These bags are preferably of rubber, about 4x6 inches in size, and when filled with ice and before applied it is more comfortable to the patient to envelop the bag in a thin layer of flannel, which takes off the clammy coldness. The patient should be kept perfectly quiet and the bowels daily moved by a mild purgative. After the sensitiveness and the fever have subsided, the absorption of the hardened inflammatory remnants is promoted by the daily employment of hot sitz baths and the application of tincture of iodine to the inguinal regions, as well as the use of iodoform suppositories.

The employment of blistering fluids or plasters is of no particular value either to check the inflammation or promote the absorption.

If there are symptoms of suppuration forming abscesses, these should be freely opened into the vagina and their cavities thoroughly rinsed out with a disinfecting solution.

In the case of phlegmasia dolens alba I have used cold water compresses fortified by ice bags with brilliant results, but only after all the other treatments that are laid down in different treatises had been tried, and failed to give the slightest relief. Among these were hot fomentations, large repeated doses of morphine, and liniments of everything that is usually prescribed to relieve pain; for the pain in phlegmasia is sometimes excruciating.

My experience of the beneficial effects of ice bags and cold-water compresses in the acute stages of pelvic cellulitis and perimetritis, led me to believe that the same measures would be useful when the cellulitis was in the cellular tissue of the extremities, which constitutes phlegmasia dolens, ignorantly termed milk leg. This appeared to be heroic treatment to the patient, who dreaded the shock and feared bad consequences, but she finally consented.

The following was my method: an ordinary large towel was dipped into iced water, wrung out and clapped around the affected limb, a heavy flannel roller bandage was then applied from the toes upward to the groin; flannel is preferable, because it does not get hard when moist and remains softer under similar conditions than cotton material. On the most painful parts, like the inner aspects of the thighs, the back of the flexure of the knee, or popletial region, and the calf of the leg, I laid rubber bags filled with ice in addition to the cold-water compresses; these were kept in place by a circular binder independent and outside of the roller bandage.

The patient is naturally a little shocked when the cold towel is first applied, but the unpleasantness is only momentary, and then the reaction brings ease and comfort, so that she desires the ice bags to be renewed quite often at first, for the patient has now found a remedy that relieves the pain as nothing else has ever done before. When the towels become dry and hot, the painful symptoms return, so that they should be dipped four to six times in the twenty-four hours. If the sensitiveness on pressure and other indications denote that the acute inflammatory process is checked, then the compresses and ice may be discontinued. This treatment avoids suppuration and the formation of abscesses, while hot applications encourage them.

A mild stimulating diet of milk and egg punch with ten to fifteen grains of quinine each day should be given in all infectious inflammations.

CHAPTER XXV
ELECTRICITY AS A REMEDY

In a brief reference to the medical virtues of electricity in the treatment of diseases of women, only an outline of its physics can be given, so as to give the reader an approximate idea of its origin and phenomena.

The use that is being made of electricity in the arts has convinced everybody that it is a most powerful agent, which manifests itself in so many different phenomena that it is as mysterious to-day as it was centuries before Christ, when the Greeks first observed it in amber when rubbed with silk, and from which the term has been derived.

Electricity is developed in bodies from a variety of causes, among which are friction, pressure, chemical action, heat, and magnetism. We are acquainted with it only through the peculiarity of its action, and it behaves as a subtile, imponderable fluid of a compound nature, possessing opposite polarity when excited, giving rise to positive and negative electricities, but when at rest these forces seem to neutralize each other, and as such pervade all matter.

Chemical action is usually the most convenient for obtaining electricity for medicinal purposes, and the arrangement through which this is accomplished is called a cell or battery.

A battery in its simplest construction is made of a plate of zinc and a plate of copper partially immersed in dilute sulphuric acid. A disturbance of the neutral electricity now ensues, and by means of a delicate instrument, it may be observed that the zinc plate possesses a feeble charge of negative and the copper a feeble charge of positive electricity; at the same time there is a slight escape of hydrogen from the surface of the zinc. If now the plates are connected by means of a metallic wire, the chemical action increases and the hydrogen gas is now discharged from the surface of the copper. The wire is now traversed by an electric or voltaic current, which imparts to the connecting wire, thermal, magnetic and other properties.

PLATE V.

Apostoli's method of employing intense galvanic currents without discomfort or injury to the patient.

The internal electrode, which he calls the excitateur intrauterin is held in the hand of the operator. The dispersing electrode covers the abdomen.

The electricity does not, however, correspond to that which was peculiar to the metallic plates before they were connected by the wire, but the opposite electrical conditions discharge themselves from the wire: the direction of the current in the fluid, being from the positive or copper plate to the zinc or negative plate, and vice versa, so that the wire of the zinc plate is now positive, while that of the copper is negative.

Poles and electrodes. The wires or terminals are called the poles of the battery; instead of the term *poles*, the word *electrode* is now generally used. From what was said of the origin and direction of the current in the fluid, it is important to remember that the positive electrode or wire is connected to the negative plate, while the negative electrode is connected with the positive plate.

According to the extent of surface of both zinc and copper plates, exposed to the chemical action of the diluted sulphuric acid, or to the number of cells that are employed, by connecting the copper plate of one cell to the zinc plate of the next, the force and quantity of the electric current is correspondingly increased.

Batteries which consist of one solution and two metals rapidly lose their intensity, partly from the decrease in the chemical action owing to the neutralization of the sulphuric acid by its combination with the zinc, and partly from secondary currents, depositing a layer of hydrogen and metallic zinc on the copper plate, which destroys the dissimilarity of the metals, so that the electrical action ceases or the plates become polarized.

For this reason these single fluid batteries have almost entirely gone out of use, and batteries with two liquids have taken their place.

Electrolysis means to dissolve or decompose, by means of electricity, an organic or inorganic substance into its original elements. If, for instance, a current of electricity of four or five Bunsen's cells is conducted to two inverted glass tubes, filled with water slightly acidulated to increase its conductivity, gas bubbles rise from the surface of each pole, and upon examination it is found that hydrogen is liberated at the negative pole and oxygen at the positive pole; and as the volume of hydrogen liberated is about twice that of oxygen, the experiment gives at once the qualitative and quantitative analysis of water.

Professor Bartholow, in his treatise on Medical Electricity says: "As animal tissues are composed of substances amenable to electrolytic decomposition, it is obvious that they must yield up their component elements in accordance with the laws of electrolysis. Albumen is coagulated, salts are separated into acids and bases, and water is resolved into oxygen and hydrogen. When the salts contained in the animal tissues—soda, potassa, lime—and water, are decomposed, the acids and oxygen appear at the positive pole, and the alkalies and hydrogen at the negative. It follows that if the positive electrode be composed of metal, it will be corroded by the action of chlorine and the acids, and the negative will remain unacted on and smooth. The tissues in the vicinity of each electrode are necessarily affected by the elements brought to them in accordance with chemical laws. About the positive the mineral acids and chlorine form combinations, and hence do not attack the tissues with the same energy as those about the negative pole. If, however, the positive electrode is composed of zinc, for example, the chlorine attacking it will form chloride of zinc, a very corrosive material. This principle has been utilized to produce caustic effects at the positive pole. Although the negative electrode remains smooth, much more than at the positive are seen these destructive effects from the action of the free alkali liberated in its neighborhood. When an ordinary electrode of carbon covered with soft sponge is made to conduct a strong galvanic current, the skin speedily becomes reddened, and may be made to ulcerate if the contact is sufficiently prolonged. If the carbon is applied directly, an intense burning is produced and the tissues are destroyed, leaving a slough, which is slowly detached and the ulcer remaining is difficult to heal. The caustic action is due chiefly to the soda, potash, and lime. Some effect must also be allowed to the disassociation of the tissues, to their transference from point to point and at the negative pole to the mechanical action of the liberated hydrogen."

Interpolar regions. The reader must have been impressed with the peculiarity of each pole in possessing affinity or attraction for certain elements that constitute the animal tissue. Oxygen and acids accumulate around the positive pole, while alkalies are attracted to the negative pole; thus it must be an absolute fact that an actual transfer of particles in both directions to each pole must traverse the tissue lying between the two poles; this accounts in a great measure for the difference of the local effect on the tissues around the poles, one being in the nature of an acid the other of a caustic alkali. This naturally gave rise to an inquiry as to the effect that the galvanic current has on the structure between the two poles.

Dr. G. Betton Massey, author of "Electricity in the Diseases of Women," asks and answers this question in the following manner: "What can be therapeutically accomplished when the seat of the disease is necessarily situated beyond the direct reach of the electrode? An answer drawn from both neurological and gynecological experience is that much can be accomplished; and this is doubtless due, in the first place, to the influence upon nutrition of the chemical changes that occur throughout the circuit, in the onward progress of the particles that appear free finally at the poles to the influence upon nutrition of the circulatory changes that result from vasomotor stimulation, and to the contractions produced in unstriated muscular tissue by heavy currents even at a distance. These results of quiet current transmission are governed in magnitude at a given spot by the *density* of the current at the situation and by the *duration* of the application. To accomplish much in the more distant parts of this region considerable strength must be employed, hence a delicate judgment is demanded in the selection of the size of the active pole to avoid cauterization on the one hand, and too great a diffusion on the other."

To within a comparatively recent period, the methods of applying the electric current for the removal of abnormal growths have been somewhat crude if not dangerous. It appears that formerly altogether too much stress or weight was laid on the chemical or electrolytic effects that the electrodes wrought in the tissues, and very little or no credit was given to the *passive* current of galvanism as it traversed the tissues from pole to pole. Dr. Ephraim Cutter, of New York, advocated the so-called electro-puncture, and in the galvanic treatment of fibroid tumors of the uterus, these punctures were made through the abdominal walls. The electrodes for this purpose were stiletto shaped, with blades five inches long and three-eighths of an inch at their widest part; these were inserted into the tumor from opposite points. Wounds that were thus inflicted, necessarily involved more or less danger, and, although Dr. Cutter reported a great number of cures, the percentage of mishaps was too great to make electrical treatment popular among the profession.

It was not until Apostoli, a French physician, greatly modified the methods of employing electricity in the treatment of fibroid tumors, and sheared it in a great measure, not only of its dangers, but also of pain, that the medical profession took the question of electrical treatment in real earnest. The practice of Apostoli and his results were published in a monograph by Carlet, entitled, *Du traitement electrique des tumeurs fibreuses de l'uterus, Paris, 1884*. Apostoli evidently started out with a view to modify the most objectionable features of the electrical treatment. This consisted in reducing the number and size of the punctures and to lessen the painful sensation of the electric current to its minimum, so that the main points of difference are the shape and size of electrodes, and the site that is chosen for the puncture. In the first place he uses only one piercing or needle electrode, which is much smaller than that of Cutter, this may be attached to either the positive or negative cord of the battery, according to the accompanying symptoms. When hemorrhage is a symptom, the positive pole is used internally or carries the needle on account of its anti-hemorrhagic property, otherwise the negative pole carries the piercing electrode. This electrode is always used internally to puncture through the vagina or through the cervical tissue into the tumor; this is not nearly so painful as piercing the abdominal walls, nor does it wound the peritoneum.

The other electrode is called the *dispersing* electrode, because its purpose is to so disperse or scatter the current of this pole that it is hardly felt by the patient, much less produces any electrolytic or chemical effect on the skin. This electrode is made from a sheet of lead or copper nine by ten inches and covered with a layer of wet absorbent cotton; it is applied over the abdomen. This method is much safer than that formerly advocated by Dr. Cutter, and the results are much better. Dr. Engelman, who has accepted this method, says: "In electrolysis an intensity of 50 to 250 milliampères may be used for from three to eight minutes. All possible precautions must be taken in the first sitting in order to discover any idiosyncrasy of the patient, and a current of 50 milliampères will suffice, attained by slow increase.

The patient should lie down quietly for several hours after the application. If an intensity as high as 100 milliampères is used at the first sitting, it is preferable that she remain in bed for the first twenty-four hours, and that a cold compress or an ice bag be placed upon the abdomen, to overcome any tendency to inflammatory reaction which may occur; hence the attention to details which is necessary, and the precautions desirable in a first puncture, until the sufferance of the individual patient is tested. The application is repeated, according to the demands of the case and the severity of the treatment, once or twice a week."

The milliampere meter is a galvanometer to measure the quantity of electricity that is applied, and as a chemical battery will of necessity change, a meter is the only means of judging the intensity of the current; so that without one there is danger of applying the current too strong, or an injustice may be done to the patient, and reproach cast on the treatment by not using it strong enough.

At the annual meeting of the American Medical Association, at Chicago, in 1887, Dr. Martin read a paper, in which he reported three cases that were treated with the most satisfactory results without puncture. The positive or external electrode was applied over the abdomen after the manner of Apostoli, and the negative electrode was placed in the rectum, vagina or uterus, in such a way as to cause the current to traverse the largest diameter of the tumor; this method is to my mind the *ideal* of an electrical treatment, it is galvanism without corrosion or electrolysis.

The number of eminent authorities that I have quoted, can hardly fail to convince the reader that electrical therapeutics in the treatment of fibroid tumors are not only efficacious, but in the infancy of experimental growth, so that every day will add new proofs and improved methods to the history of this most interesting subject. But this treatment is not limited in its usefulness to the removal of abnormal growths, for it has proven itself equally as effectual in the treatment of chronic inflammatory conditions of the pelvic organs. I have myself attained great success in curing certain forms of these diseases since the publication of "A New Treatment of Chronic Metritis," by the same indefatigable author, Georges Apostoli, of Paris.

The value of electricity is now so firmly established that a physician who, ignorant of its virtues, and laboring under this self-imposed ignorance, brushes aside any reference to or desire for electrical treatment with a supercilious air, claiming "that there is nothing in it," advertises himself as incompetent or insincere.

It must be apparent to anyone who has followed this brief outline from the beginning, that this subject requires a special and individual devotion, so as to become familiar, not only with the elementary principles of the physics of electricity, but with the *technique* of applying the treatment in each individual case. This, few persons have the honesty or ambition to acquire, and if they own a battery, it is more for show than for use. I am convinced that there are great possibilities in store for the curative value of the galvanic current, but it also requires a high order of intelligence to employ it, in order that those hopes may be realized.

"*The positive pole* is anodyne, sedative, anti-congestive, and anti-hemorrhagic. It combats and prevents the tendency to excessive vascularization, and consequently relieves congestion and inflammation and the pain depending upon these conditions. Its local or polar action, when used within the uterus, is hemostatic or styptic, and caustic, with high intensities of current.

"*The negative pole* is stimulating and has a marked electrolytic action. It tends to produce congestion, and a derivative effect which favors absorption of tumors, inflammatory deposits and adhesions. But great care must be observed in using it in some conditions, lest a new inflammation be rekindled."

I have the record of a case where the womb was retroflexed and tied down by old inflammatory adhesions for nine years; the retroflexion dated back to a miscarriage. This woman had been an invalid since that time; her appetite was poor, and her digestion poorer, she was excessively constipated, suffered from pain during menstruation, but at other times there was a constant pain in the small of her back, which ran down the right thigh, the bladder was irritable, and there were neuralgic pains shooting from the ovaries down the groins. All these symptoms became more or less aggravated every few weeks or months. The womb was so firmly fixed or glued down on the lower portion of the spine, that it could not be moved an iota. This woman had tried all the remedies that I could suggest, except galvanism. This I concluded to try, by placing a large dispersing electrode on the small of her back, and the other electrode, properly prepared, so that it did not burn or cauterize, was introduced into the vagina, against the posterior aspect of the uterus. A current strength of from 90 to 120 milliampères was applied every other day for ten minutes; in six weeks the organ was quite movable, and in five months all adhesions had melted away, and the womb occupied its normal position, and the patient was in every way restored to health.

The diseases that are curable by galvanism are the different forms of subacute or chronic inflammation of the ovaries, and the consequent enlargement of these organs, small cysts or fibro-cysts of the ovaries are also amenable to the galvanic puncture.

Catarrhal inflammation of the Fallopian tubes, or when either or both ends are agglutinated with inflammatory exudation, so as to pen up their contents, which may be mucous, water, pus or blood, these fluids should be first aspirated or drawn off, and then, by means of appropriate galvanism, the normal conditions of the tubes may be restored.

Chronic catarrhs of the womb are especially suited for galvanic treatment, and when the inflammation invades the muscular structure of the uterus, giving rise to what was described as chronic metritis, there is no remedy that will yield the same positive and satisfactory result as electricity. Plate V gives a practical illustration of the employment of electricity for chronic inflammation of the uterus; the internal or negative pole is introduced into the uterine cavity and held there by the operator, the external or dispersing pole spreads over and rests on the abdomen.

Subinvolution of the uterus. I have already referred to this affection as an arrested involution of the womb after confinement at the end of the natural term, and after abortion. The womb in this condition remains permanently and preternaturally enlarged, and its entire tissue becomes the seat of a subacute or chronic inflammatory process. The vagina is also more or less relaxed, so that the heavy uterus sinks down into the pelvis, imparting to the patient a dragging or bearing-down sensation, which makes walking or any other exertion exceedingly difficult. In subinvolution an extra uterine electrode is not required, but only a vaginal electrode, so employed that a current of high intensity is passed through the uterus; this varies from 50 to 150 milliampères. The duration of each galvanization is from eight to ten minutes, and should be repeated every third or sixth day. I succeed as a rule in six to eight weeks in restoring the organ to its normal size, which I ascertain through comparative measurement at the beginning and end of the treatment.

If the subinvolution is complicated with *retroflexion*, then intra-uterine galvanization after the organ is replaced is the most effective treatment. Old pelvic adhesions and exudations as a result of pelvic cellulitis or peritonitis are amenable to galvanization after hot douches, sitz baths, and other discussives have failed to excite absorption.

Hemorrhoids and prolapse of the rectum; the former is a frequent concomitant of constipation, and the latter may be the result of an imperfect involution after confinement. I have employed galvanism for either with the most brilliant results.

It would be interesting for the reader were I to continue to cite different diseases in which electricity has been successfully employed, but that would require a systematic arrangement of the subject, which would be incompatible with the original purpose of this book. I simply desire to awaken an interest in a comparatively new remedial agent, in its present field of employment. There may be a great many ways to get relief, but that course which offers the least risk to *life* and the least suffering to the *living* is the one that should recommend itself to the sufferer. What patients need is not brilliant surgical exploits to make the reputation of an ambitious operator, but the conscientious aid of the conservative physician who is content to labor in the less pretentious capacity of an assistant to nature's curative energy.

CHAPTER XXVI
SIGNS AND SYMPTOMS OF PREGNANCY

Pregnancy is the condition in which the female has within her an impregnated, *fecundated* germ, which gradually becomes developed in or out of the womb. In a perfectly normal state of things, the impregnated ovum becomes attached to the inner surface of the womb by virtue of a preordained vital force by which the ovum becomes animated at the moment of conception. It obtains its nutrition from a plexus of blood vessels, by means of which the ovum is attached to the inner side of the walls of the uterus, and this complex of vessels grows with the development of the fetus, and constitutes the *placenta*, which, together with the membranes and the umbilical cord, is called the afterbirth.

The growth of the embryo, which is the predestined child in the mother's womb, occupies a period of ten lunar months, or two hundred and eighty days—this is the average term of pregnancy, although the duration of pregnancy is prolonged in a large proportion of cases to three hundred days, and even longer, while in a small proportion of pregnant women the period of gestation falls naturally shorter than two hundred and eighty days.

In a small number of pregnancies the impregnated ovum is arrested at the ovary, or on its passage from the latter through the Fallopian tubes; it then does not arrive in the cavity of the uterus. This state of things is unnatural, hence termed *preternatural,* because the growth of the fetus takes place out of the uterus, and this is also called *extrauterine* pregnancy, which may take place in the ovary, Fallopian tubes, or cavity of the abdomen. False pregnancy implies that there was no pregnancy at all, or in other words, that there was no fetus, and that the enlargement was due to something else.

In pregnancy the female experiences signs and symptoms resulting from changes in the condition of her organs and functions. The suppression of the courses or menstrual discharges is considered in the popular mind an unerring proof of pregnancy, yet, as a matter of fact, this is far from the truth. I have known of two women who menstruated regularly during the entire period of their pregnancies, and there are a number of reliable cases recorded of women who menstruated during pregnancy and at no other time.

It is a rule, that the menses cease during pregnancy, but it is equally certain that the menstrual function becomes suspended from other causes, and these are quite numerous, so that taken by itself, the sign is of little importance. Young married women not infrequently have a slight menstruation for two or three periods after their first conception, and on the other hand, newly married women will have their menses occasionally arrested, and this may continue for two or three months and indeed no pregnancy exist.

Nausea and vomiting is also presumptive evidence of gestation. Some women are affected with sick stomach almost from the moment of conception, and from actual experience they are so certain of their condition, that they can calculate with certainty the day of their confinement from the time when they had their first feeling of nausea. Experience seems to teach that a certain amount of nausea, *the morning sickness*, and the vomiting which accompanies or follows it, is to be met in women who go through a natural or healthy pregnancy, so that many eminent authorities have looked upon this symptom as a physiological accompaniment, and one of the most constant and reliable symptoms. The vomiting and nausea of pregnancy is different from that which is an indication of general ill health; in pregnancy the vomiting is followed with a sense of relief, and the patient is for the time being quite easy. The length of time that women feel this gastric irritability varies in different individuals; ordinarily it will cease about the fourth month, sometimes sooner, and it may return again during the last two or three months of gestation. It is supposed to be due to a reflex action of the spinal cord from the uterus to the stomach. It must be remembered, however, that a disease of the uterus, a fibroid or ovarian tumor, and a suppression of the menses from other causes than pregnancy will occasion nausea and vomiting.

A capricious appetite is another of the peculiarities of pregnancy, a longing for unnatural food, so that some women will enjoy eating such things as chalk, slate pencils, and similar indigestible stuff; this I have always considered a form of hysteria, that is, a functional derangement of the nervous system, for which I gave ten grains of bromide of sodium three times a day, with the best results; others again became passionately fond of sour salads, or strong condiments like mustard, Worcestershire sauce, and salt fish, while others again long for fruits.

Salivation of the mouth is another very unpleasant symptom which annoys some women when they are pregnant, for they will secrete such enormous quantities of saliva, that they cannot help drooling from the mouth when they speak. In salivation of pregnancy the gums do not become sore as in the salivation from mercury; in the former the irritation is confined to the salivary glands alone. The wonderful sympathy that exists between remotely situated organs of the body is here strikingly illustrated between the sexual organs and the salivary glands in both sexes. In mumps also, which is an inflammation of the salivary gland, it is not unusual for the testes in the male and the mammæ in the female to become swollen and painful, and as soon as this swelling takes place, the inflammation of the salivary gland disappears.

The breasts become enlarged and otherwise altered in pregnancy, the enlargement is accompanied with more or less sharply shooting pain, they also become harder and are more movable than otherwise. The nipple becomes more prominent and painfully sensitive, the veins that run from the breast become distended so that they can be readily traced by the eye. The presence of milk in the mammæ is another sign, but that, too, is only presumptive, because the secretion of milk takes place in other conditions than that of pregnancy; even the newly-born infant has sometimes milk in its breasts, and milk has been recognized in the breasts of some males and not infrequently in those of young virgins.

Pigmentation or the deposit of coloring matter in pregnancy has long been observed as a prominent symptom and when taken together with other signs it is worthy of careful consideration, but here, too, we encounter the obstacle to anything of a positive nature, for discoloration is also met with in females who are suffering from pelvic diseases and who are not pregnant. Areola is the technical name of that peculiar circle which immediately surrounds the nipple. In a healthy virgin this circle is characterized by a beautiful rose-tinted blush, but under the influence of disease, even in the virgin the circle becomes more or less discolored. When pregnancy has occurred the areola around the nipple becomes darker and darker; other parts of the body become similarly discolored, this occurs on the abdomen and perineum.

The womb descends during the first two months of pregnancy, this constitutes a kind of physiological falling of the womb and indeed the accompanying symptoms of a pregnant woman are often similar or identical to that diseased and permanent condition of physical suffering, namely, falling of the womb. Perhaps the most common symptoms of the descent of the uterus will be more or less frequent desire to pass water, because of the dragging of the womb on the neck of the bladder; sometimes there is also a straining or inclination to go to stool, owing to pressure on the rectum from the same cause.

The umbilicus or navel becomes painful and even depressed from traction of the superior ligament of the bladder, which is attached to the umbilicus, thus illustrating the operation of cause and effect, namely, as the bladder is depressed by the descended uterus, the bladder in turn pulls on the umbilicus to which its ligament is attached. The pregnant uterus remains only the first few months in this depressed state; at the third month, as a result of its continual growth and that of the fetus, the uterus ascends out of the pelvis and as a natural consequence the symptoms of the bladder and rectum subside. Towards the end of the ninth month the womb again descends into the pelvis and with this there may be a return of the irritation of the bladder and a feeling of bearing down or tenesmus of the rectum. The descent of the uterus toward the close of pregnancy diminishes the prominence of the abdomen, and as the diaphragm has freer play, the respiration becomes easier; if there was any cough that, too, disappears, and on the whole the woman feels herself more comfortable and in happy spirits. This may even arouse suspicion in her own mind as to her condition, because she does not know the cause of the change; it may portend to her that something is not right, that she is not pregnant or that her child may be dead. In women who have borne one or more children in a natural manner, the descent of the womb is of no particular moment in the last months of gestation, because the abdominal walls having been stretched by previous pregnancies the body or fundus of the womb may fall forward and give the lungs and other organs relief from pressure, but in the first pregnancy this is never the case, because the abdominal walls are too tense to allow this normal anteversion.

The German school of midwifery has laid down an important rule as a consequence of this observation, and I have never known an exception to occur in my experience. The rule is that when the uterus does not descend into the pelvis toward the close of the first pregnancy, it is because there is a disproportion between the child's head and the maternal pelvis, or in other words that either the child's head is too large for a natural or unaided delivery to take place, or that the pelvis of the mother is too small for a natural delivery to take place, and this is true, and knowing this to be true at the outset or commencement of a confinement it would be only torture and a valuable loss of time to wait at the bedside of a woman suffering with the pangs of childbirth in the vain hope that she might deliver herself— when in truth and as a fact that cannot be done without the aid of scientific assistance.

The vagina and external organs are more or less modified in pregnancy. The vagina becomes wider and shorter and as there is an increase of spongy tissue, it presents a swollen appearance. The mucous glands become larger and secrete a greater abundance of mucus. The internal surface of the vagina becomes discolored in consequence of pregnancy and I believe that it is one of the most reliable presumptive signs; the mucous membrane presents a sort of bluish tint, a French authority calls it a violet hue, not unlike the lees of wine.

Quickening is a term that is employed to designate the particular length of time that pregnancy has existed, and at the same time to furnish evidence to the mother through the movements of the fetus that she carries within her womb a living being. In a former chapter I have already detailed the theory of the ancients upon this subject, which was as absurd as it was fanciful. The late Professor Bedford defines "quickening as nothing more than the ordinary result of progressive increase when the physical organization of the fetus has reached a state of development which imbues it with the power of movement—a movement dependent upon muscular contraction." The period of quickening is usually about the fourth and a half month or the middle term of pregnancy.

Pulsation of the fetal heart, when heard, is no longer presumptive but absolutely positive evidence that pregnancy exists. That the heart of the child can be distinctly heard to beat in its mother's womb was one of the greatest discoveries in midwifery. The pulsations of the fetal heart are much faster than those of the mother's heart, hence there is no danger of getting them mixed; while the child's heart averages from one hundred and ten to one hundred and sixty per minute, the heart of the mother averages from seventy-five to eighty beats. There are cases where the mystery of a pregnancy can be solved beyond a possibility of a doubt, through the recognition of the pulsations of the fetal heart, and yet a woman may be pregnant in whom it will be impossible to distinguish the action of the child's heart, at the termination of her period of gestation she will bring forth a healthy child.

The question whether a female is pregnant will, from the very nature of the symptoms always remain debatable in a certain proportion of cases, or, in other words, there is no sign or symptom that is reliable and if reliable it is not uniformly present. From a medico-legal standpoint the question will always be of great importance, as it frequently involves the guilt or innocence of the accused; the social standing of one, or the merited punishment of the other, and it does seem like a travesty on both science and justice that at certain stages and in certain conditions no signs or symptoms are absolutely reliable. The unfortunate creatures whose illness may imitate or simulate the symptoms of pregnancy must always receive the benefit of the doubt, this would avoid the possibility of wrecking innocent lives. Professor Bedford reports a case in his work on obstetrics which is as sad as it is instructive, he says: "I was requested to visit a lady who was residing in the State of New Jersey, about thirty miles distant from New York. On my arrival I was received by her father, a venerable and accomplished gentleman. He seemed broken in spirit, and it was evident that grief had taken a deep hold of his frame. On being introduced into his daughter's room, my sympathies were at once awakened in beholding the wreck of beauty which was presented to my view. My presence did not seem to occasion the slightest disturbance; she greeted me with these words: 'Well, doctor, I am glad to see you on my beloved father's account, for he will not believe that I cannot yet be restored to health. Life, however, has lost all its charms for me, and I impatiently long for the repose of the grave.' These words were spoken with extraordinary gentleness, but yet with an emphasis which at once gave me an insight into the character of this lovely woman.

"Her father was a clergyman of high standing in the English Church, and had a pastoral charge in England, in which he continued until circumstances rendered it necessary for him to leave that country, and seek a residence in America. At a very early age, this young lady had lost her mother, and had almost been entirely educated by her father, whose talents, attainments, and moral excellence admirably fitted him for this important duty. When she had attained her eighteenth year, an attachment was formed between her and a young barrister of great promise and respectability. This attachment soon resulted in a matrimonial engagement. Shortly after the engagement she began unaccountably to decline in health; there was a manifest change in her habits; she was no longer fond of society; its pleasures ceased to allure and prove attractive; the friends whom she had caressed with all the warmth of a sister's love, now became objects of indifference; in a word she was a changed being—her personal appearance exhibited alterations evident to the most superficial observer; her abdomen enlarged, the breasts fuller than usual, the face pale and careworn, and the appetite capricious, with much gastric derangement. Many were the efforts made to account for this change in the conduct and appearance of the young lady in question. Speculation was at work, and numerous were the surmises of her friends. The rumor soon spread that she was the victim of seduction, and her altered appearance the result of pregnancy.

"The barrister to whom she was affianced heard of these reports, and instead of being the first to stand forth as her protector, and draw nearer to his heart this lovely and injured girl thus measurably assuaging the intensity of grief with which she was overwhelmed, addressed a letter to her father requesting to be released from his engagement. This was, of course, assented to without hesitation. The daughter, conscious of her own innocence, knowing better than anyone else, her own immaculate character, and relying on heaven to guide her in this her hour of tribulation, requested that a physician should be sent for, in order that the nature of her case might be clearly ascertained. A medical man visited her, and after an investigation of her symptoms, informed the father that she was undoubtedly pregnant, and suggested that means should be taken to keep the unpleasant matter secret. The father, indignant at this cruel imputation against the honor of his child, requested an additional consultation. This resulted (as usual) in a confirmation of the opinion previously expressed, and the feelings of that parent can be better appreciated than portrayed.

"That good man resigned his pastoral living to proceed with his daughter to America. On her passage to this country, the daughter became extremely ill, and the advice of the physician on board the vessel was requested; he too told the father that there was danger of premature delivery, for he simply took appearances as his guide, and at once concluded that she was pregnant.

"This is about the substance of what I learned of this interesting and extraordinary woman. I proceeded with great caution in the investigation of her case, and after a faithful and critical survey, most minutely made in reference to every point, I stated in broad and unequivocal language that she was not pregnant. The only reply the gentle creature made on hearing my opinion, was—'Doctor, you are right.' The father was soon made acquainted with the result of my examination, but he indicated not the slightest emotion. He asked me whether something could not be done to restore her to health, and I thought that the old man's heart would break when I told him that his daughter was in the last stages of consumption.

"It was the misfortune of this young lady to labor under an affection of the womb, which simulated, in several important particulars, the condition of pregnancy, and which the world in its ignorance and undying thirst for scandal, might have readily supposed did in fact exist; yet, there was no excuse for the physician, guided as he should have been by the lights of science, and governed by the principles of sound morality. The result of my investigation impressed me with the conviction beyond any shade of doubt, that the entire train of symptoms indicating pregnancy was due to the presence of a large *fibrous tumor* occupying the cavity of the uterus. About four weeks from this time I received a note announcing her death and asking that I would hasten to the house for the purpose of an examination. Dr. Ostrom, now practicing in Goshen, assisted me in the autopsy. As the father stood before me he was not unlike the stricken oak in the forest, which, though stripped of its branches, was yet upright and majestic. The moment I removed the tumor from the womb he seized it convulsively, and exclaimed, 'This is my trophy; I will return with it to England, and it shall confound the traducers of my child!'

"Here, you perceive, both character and life were sacrificed by error of judgment on the part of those whose counsel had been invoked. Without a due responsibility, heedless of the distressing consequences, the medical gentlemen rashly pronounced an opinion which consigned to an early grave a pure and lovely being, and broke the very heart strings of a devoted and confiding parent."

CHAPTER XXVII
PRECAUTIONS AND SUGGESTIONS
TO PREGNANT WOMEN

There is a hygiene of pregnancy which the enceinte female should observe, for by so doing, she will not only make the period of her gestation less onerous to herself, but she will be able to materially contribute toward the accomplishment of a natural childbirth. Although pregnancy is a physiological process, the conditions in the female economy, under which this is carried on, are at variance with those which are to be found in the unimpregnated state, and as a consequence it rationally follows that the pregnant female should endeavor to conform to the demands which the altered relations require.

If the pregnant woman is properly clothed to begin with, she will greatly mitigate some of the symptoms which very often mar her well-being. The clothing should neither be too heavy in summer, nor too light in winter, she must dress so as to conform to the season and feel comfortable; but by all means the chest and abdomen should be kept free from pressure, the skirts must be supported from the shoulders, and the corset also, should be dispensed with, and a waist worn instead, one that partly answers the purpose of a corset, and to which the skirts can be fastened or buttoned at the same time. I have no respect nor patience for those women who desire to conceal by tight lacing, the appearance of their pregnancy. Motherhood, whether active or prospective, is a divine function, and as creatures are the instruments of the Creator, there is nothing to be ashamed of by those who have complied with the usages of civilized peoples, and wherever an exhibition of pregnancy becomes indelicate, a person who hopes or expects to be a mother should not be. If a woman has the true characteristics to make a good mother, she cannot, nor will she trifle with her own health or that of her child; in truth, mothers cannot begin too soon to consider the welfare of their offspring.

To guard against taking cold is one of the maxims, that the pregnant woman should heed, especially during the last half of gestation when the prominence of the abdomen shortens the skirts in front and removes them off from the limbs. Flannel drawers properly adapted to the limbs and worn underneath the muslin ones affords the best protection that can be adopted, and it replaces cumbersome skirts. Sudden extreme variations of temperature should also be avoided, like going from an overheated apartment into the cold outside air, or into another cold chilly room. In making these changes, one should gradually cool off, and then by putting on additional clothing, wraps or shawls, the danger of taking cold may be removed. Hot coffee or tea or hot alcoholic beverages are equally as dangerous as overheated apartments, for anything which stimulates the circulation of the blood in an inordinate degree is liable to produce a congestion of the placenta, and thus incite an abortion; hence fevers of all kinds are known to have brought about an expulsion of the fetus. On the whole, either very hot or very cold temperatures are to be avoided, for instance, prolonged staying in cold weather or lengthened exposure to the rays of the sun should be prudently guarded against by the pregnant female. Of course this is not to be construed as meaning, that she should not partake of exercise in the open fresh air—far from it, but the exercise shall not be forced or driven, it shall at all times be voluntary and passive, so that when a tired feeling comes on, she can rest and refresh herself. The best time for these little walks is in the morning and evening in the summer season and in the middle of the day in cold weather. A rough, uneven walk should be avoided because she may stumble; jolting in either street cars or wagon is equally pernicious. A great deal of stair climbing is injurious, and when it becomes necessary it must be done slowly; running the sewing machine has caused many miscarriages. Avoid running, jumping, riding on horseback, and lifting heavy weights, hanging laundried clothes on lines, in fact everything that can strain the muscles, bear down, increase the intra-abdominal pressure and excite the nervous system.

The prospective mother must resign her amusements at evening entertainments in crowded halls or theaters, in which the air becomes foul and overheated from large congregations of persons. Here she is also threatened to be jostled and jammed, and perhaps injured in other ways. Her sleeping apartments should be thoroughly ventilated through the day, and coition, if not entirely suspended, at least restrained and only passively exercised, for any excess of this nature is not only injurious to the child, but may cause a miscarriage. It is not expected that the pregnant woman should sit in the arm chair during the period of gestation, far from it, but it is even greatly desired that she continue her usual vocation. Exercise of a passive nature is always wholesome, and for this reason it will be conducive to good health if enough work is done over every day to keep the system in gentle activity; the domestic duties of a household will or should always furnish that. All good women take a pride in their household affairs, if they do not they are not good; and those who boast that they never put their hands to anything in the house, have mistaken their vocation as women, and are either indolent or worthless, and often both. No one should boast of idleness, rather be ashamed of it. Employment makes character; it gives buoyancy to the spirit and tranquillity of mind. The influence that an equable temperament exercises over the nervous development of the unborn child may eventually be demonstrated by its resistance to the shock of diseases which superinduce convulsions and death. It is not advisable to sleep during the day, it is better to retire early after a light supper, so as to rest a few hours before midnight. This makes one fresh and spry in the morning, being on hand early in the morning, it gives ample time to dispose of domestic duties, and thus avoid confusion and rushing during the day.

Cleanliness is one of the cardinal virtues of the pregnant woman— as pregnancy will be followed with childbirth, and as cleanliness is but another name for *antiseptic*, and that will guard against childbed fever, the importance of *cleanliness* springs at once into unusual prominence. No person can be filthy and slovenly during the entire period of gestation, and then at the moment of confinement become clean, even if in the last moment the person becomes bathed and brushed, everything else around and about her is soiled and dirty, unless she be taken to a lying-in home. Cleanliness must be cultivated, and finally it becomes second nature. The daily ablution of the external genitals should not be neglected, and general bathing in water not altogether too warm, say 90 to 94 degrees F., twice a week will prove beneficial in many ways. The linen that is worn, and that which is in the bed should be kept sweet and clean, and cleaner than ever on the day of confinement.

The mammæ of the pregnant woman are sometimes very painful; as pregnancy advances they enlarge, the lacteal glands become congested and swollen. To relieve this I recommend the application of a liniment of equal parts camphorated oil, laudanum, and tincture of belladonna gently applied several times a day. The breasts should always be extra well covered with flannel so as not to take cold in them, otherwise an abscess may form in them long before the child is born. If the nipples are sensitive it is advisable to begin to harden them during the last few months of gestation. Tannate of glycerine is perhaps the best thing to apply for this purpose; it is best done by means of a small camel's hair brush. If the nipples are sunken into the breast, and too short for subsequent use for the baby, it is well to draw them out by means of a breast pump, the bowl of a new clay pipe, or by employing a bottle from which the air has been replaced by filling it with hot water and then pouring it out; the mouth of the hot bottle is applied over the depressed nipple, and as it cools off, the vacuum thus formed draws the nipple out.

Nausea and vomiting in pregnancy is often so annoying and weakening that the strength of the patient becomes seriously threatened, and hence some measures must be employed to counteract it. A great variety of agents have been suggested for this purpose. Tincture of nux vomica in two or three drop doses every three or four hours is a useful remedy; the oxalate of cerium is another valuable agent for this purpose, in five to ten grain doses three times a day, but a more valuable remedy than any other that I know, is the Femina vaginal capsule, to be used every night at bedtime, and in severe cases, also in the morning.

Salivation is not constantly an attendant upon pregnancy, but when it does occur it is weakening and debilitating. There are many remedies for this disorder, but one of the most effectual ones is an occasional dose of Epsom salts, say a teaspoonful in a half tumbler of water every other morning, so as to produce free discharges from the bowels; when salts are found objectionable, the Femina laxative syrup taken in doses that have a similar effect will be a most excellent substitute.

Constipation is one of the most common derangements of the pregnant woman; it is the rule in which the exceptions are few and far between. I do not include those cases of costiveness which are habitual, and which are to be attributed to carelessness in not responding to nature's call when there is an inclination, but to those in which constipation is contemporaneous with pregnancy. We have already seen the sympathy between the stomach and other organs in pregnancy, and that a similar derangement should exist between the uterus and rectum is not at all unreasonable, and, indeed, it can be explained in that way. In the early months of pregnancy, the torpor of the bowels may be due to the general derangement which follows digestive disturbances; in the latter months, the enlarged uterus presses against the large intestines, so as to obstruct more or less the descent of the feces into the rectum. This torpor of the bowels should not be allowed to be unrelieved, for if permitted to continue it may not only induce a miscarriage, but it is apt to cause fever, headache and loss of appetite. Harsh cathartics must not be employed; and if a simple enema of warm water early every morning does not give the desired relief, I would recommend a daily dose of Femina laxative syrup. If it is found that in attempting to administer an enema, the fluid is immediately returned, then it will probably be owing to lumps of fecal matter which clog up the rectum; this will likely give rise to more or less straining or bearing down in the back passage, and to pains in the pelvis and lower limbs, all of which is not without danger of exciting premature labor pains; the fecal lumps must be removed even if it becomes necessary to use the finger.

Diarrhea is the opposite condition of things, namely a looseness of the bowels. This may be occasioned by improper food, cold or any other cause capable of producing diarrhea when pregnancy does not exist. Habitual costiveness is often followed by diarrhea from the irritation which the hardened feces excite. A dose of castor oil is sometimes an efficient remedy for this variety of diarrhea, but when the disease becomes obstinate and painful, the following remedy can always be depended upon for relief:—

Take: Tr. of catechu.

Tr. of kino, of each   4 drams

Paregoric   1 ounce

Chalk mixture   2 ounces

Mix and take a tablespoonful every four hours until relieved.

Bladder trouble is not infrequent in the early and last stages of pregnancy; the causes of this were pointed out when the symptoms of pregnancy were inquired into. Recipe No. V is sometimes very useful to relieve this irritability, or a Femina vaginal capsule introduced into the vagina every night at bedtime, is sure to give the desired relief.

The kidneys of pregnant women should not be neglected. On this question Dumas, an eminent French authority, says: "Physiological pregnancy, by modifying the quality and quantity of the blood is a predisposing general cause of albuminuria or Bright's disease. But to produce the last a cause must be added, and this may be due to a true pathological state of the blood, a morbid condition of the kidney, an accidental cause or mechanical pressure exerted by the uterus, where it has acquired a sufficient size." If the pregnant woman notices that her urine becomes thick and foamy, that her head aches and her limbs swell, she should pay particular attention to keep her bowels free, and besides drink a cupful of buchu tea every night at bedtime.

Palpitation of the heart is a source of great annoyance to some women in the earlier months of pregnancy. Women of a nervous temperament and those who are of a full plethoric habit are most likely to suffer from distressing palpitation. Nervous women should take ten grains of bromide of sodium in half tumbler of water at bedtime, and only a very light supper, while those who are full blooded should keep their bowels freely opened and remove all pressure from the chest and abdomen by wearing the clothing loose.

Pain in the abdomen walls from the sixth to the ninth month is particularly apt to occur in the first pregnancy. The abdominal walls offer a firm resistance to the growth of the uterus, and being thus put on the stretch by the combined development of the child and the womb, the muscles and skin become excessively tender and painful. I have recommended for this complaint:—

Take: Tr. of opium (laudanum).

Glycerine, of each   1 ounce

Mix and apply by means of gentle friction every night at bedtime or night and morning.

Itching of the external organs will sometimes make the life of the pregnant woman miserable. I have seen it in so aggravated a form that the constant scratching to which the patient had recourse in the hope of being relieved, lacerated the parts so that they became ulcerated. The causes of this condition are numerous, the patient from motives of delicacy conceals her suffering until she can endure it no longer. It also happens that pregnancy has nothing at all to do with the itching for it may be due to diabetes, inattention to personal cleanliness, the presence of small parasitic insects, acrid discharges from the vagina, or from pinworms in the rectum.

If owing to parasites, mercurial ointment will cure the disease, if from vaginal discharges warm vaginal douches in which the Femina antiseptic tablets are dissolved will be the efficient remedy, and after a thorough ablution, the application by means of a camel's hair brush of a solution of cocaine will relieve the itching.

Hemorrhoids, or piles, frequently torment the pregnant female beyond reasonable endurance. Piles may be either external or internal, in either case they are exceedingly apt to be very painful. When they occur in pregnancy they are due, in the first place, to an obstruction to the free return of blood to the heart by the enlarged uterus pressing on the large venous trunks and secondly, to constipation, which as we have learned is so frequently an attendant upon pregnancy. If the piles bleed it may give temporary relief, but if the bleeding occurs too frequently, the patient becomes pale and weak from the loss of blood. I know of no painful and troublesome malady in which the application of a little common sense has greater brilliant results than in piles, yet of all maladies, with perhaps the exception of catarrh of the nose, it is the most abused by senseless and meddlesome doctoring. The first step to engage the attention of the patient is to regulate the bowels and overcome the constipation; the passages must be kept soft and soluble, unless this is accomplished all the other efforts fail. The constipation must be partly relieved by proper dieting, and partly by suitable remedies. A simple bland diet, for a short time at least, is very useful; bread and milk, thin milk gruel, fruits and vegetables are to be preferred; abstain from solids, from meat and eggs and everything of the nature of beer and wine or alcohol, even coffee is irritating; while the disease is at its height eat sparingly of everything, but drink plenty of water, warm or cold, but not iced cold. The bowels should be regulated by taking a mild, efficient laxative, none being better than the Femina laxative syrup. Another precaution, very essential to success, is that after each stool the parts are gently bathed and washed with tepid or cool water by means of a soft sponge; gentle pressure can be exerted at the same time so as to assist the piles to return into the rectum. If they cannot be returned in this manner, the patient must learn to use her index finger and with it oiled with a little sweet oil or vaseline the piles are gradually shoved back into the rectum which alone relieves the suffering, because it relieves the strangulation and swelling which the sphincter muscle of the rectum causes. The pushing back after each stool and even between times is one of the essential features of a successful home treatment for piles, and it must be kept up for years, if necessary, to insure comfort and to guard against a relapse. Better than plain oil or vaseline is the nutgall ointment to be had at any drug store, but if the pain and distress continue use the following recipe:—

Take:	Cocaine.	
Ex. Belladonna, of each	10 grains
Vaseline	4 drams

Mix and make into an ointment; apply to the piles at bedtime or whenever they come down and have to be returned; a few days in bed will materially aid in the recovery.

The diet of the pregnant female should be made a special study for upon the regimen of food not only depends her immediate comfort, but its ultimate effect on the process of parturition is equally marked. I do not agree with the opinion, laid down by some of the highest authorities, that "as far as eating and drinking is concerned, the pregnant woman may continue her accustomed diet." I believe that there is a diet peculiarly adapted to the pregnant woman and very beneficial to her if she lives up to it. Stimulants of every kind are not good; wine, beer, whisky and even strong coffee and tea, as well as highly seasoned food, salty or sour salads should not be eaten.

How very often does it happen that a very strong, muscular, robust, healthy young woman, who, during her entire period of gestation, was in the best of health and spirits, and from whom, from all appearances one may predict that she will have an "easy time" in her confinement, quite the opposite occurs. And why as a matter of fact and experience is this not so, is indeed an interesting inquiry. I believe that the answer to this question can be made so plain and reasonable, that a mere statement of a few simple facts will make it apparent.

The process of delivery, presupposes the contraction of the uterus and the descent of the child down into the pelvic canal and its further passage through the floor of the pelvis.

The pelvic floor forms the bottom of the pelvic canal through which the child must be forced. The vagina is the opening through this floor, and this is composed of the muscles and membranes of the vagina, the skin, two layers of fascea, the triangular ligaments of the bladder and a group of interlacing muscles. In the birth of the child all these tissues are forced to relax to such an extent, that the vaginal canal (or the vagina) will be sufficiently widened or dilated to allow the child to pass through into the world. A moment's reflection will at once make clear, that in a strong muscular person, the resistance to the necessary dilatation will become correspondingly great, because the muscles are so strong and tense. I have attended some women where the muscles under the excitement of labor pains felt as tense and hard, as though they were made of strong india rubber. It is apparent that the muscular resistance that is offered by these strong, tense muscles, clearly obstructs and delays the passage or birth of the child and it makes the strongest labor pains of no avail. And experience teaches, that the progress of labor is slow and the delivery generally prolonged until the pains and physical suffering of many hours, exhaust and relax the muscular resistance so that the child is allowed to pass. If the above truths were generally understood and generally recognized they might be guarded against by a proper dietetic regulation, and thus an infinite amount of suffering could be avoided.

Painless childbirth is only relative, and in the absolute meaning of the term it is not true, and for this reason, that severe contractions of the womb are always painful, and extreme tension of tissues and muscles such as the passage of the child will occasion in its passage through the soft parts is also more or less painful and there is no natural childbirth possible without both these factors being present. Painless childbirth in its absolute sense, as a scientific fact, is not true, but to assure a comparatively painless childbirth in accordance with scientific facts which are capable of demonstration is not only reasonable but absolutely true.

The term "food" is understood to be all those substances, solid and liquid, which are used for the process of nutrition. For our present purpose foods may be divided into three classes: *carbo-hydrates, albuminoids,* and *phosphates.*

The carbo-hydrates furnish fat and warmth, as an example we have starch, sugar, and fats. Persons who are fed principally upon this class become warm and fat, but will lack muscle and nerve.

The albuminoids are also termed nitrogenous substances, and constitute the muscle making material. They are derived both from animal and vegetable sources, and in their most concentrated form we find them in eggs, milk or cheese, and in meats also in certain meals; wheat, for instance, contains fourteen per cent of nitrate or muscle-making material.

Phosphates are generally taken into the system as phosphate of lime contained in certain foods we eat, as fish, lobster, beef, Southern corn, peas and beans, barley, sweet potatoes and oats.

It is obvious from what was said of painful and prolonged childbirth, that the pregnant woman should avoid as much as possible nitrogenous or muscle-making food; she must starve her muscular system as much as it is possible for her to do, and the result will be that her muscles will become soft and relaxable and that means a comparatively easy or painless childbirth. In Europe, the peasantry who eat meat sparingly or very seldom, have comparatively little pain, because vegetables enter largely into their daily diet; the same is true in Asiatic countries where the staple is rice, the throes of labor are very light. The squaws of our Indian tribes are remarkable for the little pain they suffer in childbirth and for the shortness of its duration, and the recuperation is also a speedy one, for an Indian woman will travel or be about in a few days after her confinement with her pappoose on her back.

I would recommend to the pregnant woman to live as much as it is possible for her to do on a fruit and vegetable diet. Her meals must be taken at regular intervals, otherwise derangement of the stomach is sure to follow. Excess in eating even the plainest kind of food must be studiously avoided, and all food must be eaten slowly and thoroughly masticated. Wheaten bread or rice and milk diluted with water should form the main diet. Thoroughly cooked garden vegetables and fresh, ripe fruit like apples, grapes, peaches, plums, etc., should be used in summer, and some of the same fruits canned in winter, or dried fruits slowly simmered until they are soft; it is always better to soak dried fruit for several hours or overnight before it is put over to boil.

CHAPTER XXVIII
WHILE IN CHILDBED

By childbed is usually meant the period of delivery, but I mean to include the lying-in period, from the moment the mother has the first signs of her approaching delivery, to the time when she is supposed to have fully recovered and is able to be out of her bed and about.

If the suggestions that were thrown out in a former chapter are complied with, there will be little reason for uneasiness for the prospective mother, but it will be conducive to her welfare if she be buoyant in spirit and hopeful of the best possible result.

The nurse should be a quiet, orderly woman, and neither too young or too old; she should have had experience in nursing during confinements and taking care of newborn babies; with all this she should not be set in her ways, but should be accommodating and active, so that she will carry out conscientiously the instructions of the attending physician.

The choice of a physician should not be delayed until the last moment, but it should be made several months before the expectation of delivery, and a woman should never engage a doctor for her confinement, unless she knows that he has had practical experience in at least ten cases of confinement, for some of our leading medical colleges and all of the poor ones, graduate hundreds of doctors each year who never attended a single case of confinement, and some have, even, never seen one; yet the newly fledged doctors are turned loose upon the unsophisticated communities to attend women in the most trying period of their lives, and at a time when both the experience and science of her physician should be her sheet anchor of hope. A physician who is not always sober, of good moral character, and cleanly in his habits and appearance, should never be allowed in the lying-in chamber, nor one who is prating of the many severe confinements he has attended, or who boastingly speaks of the number of times it was necessary for him to use instruments, for it is quite likely, that the many severe confinements of which he spoke, were either fictitious or due to his ignorance of the subject, and the frequency with which he used instruments was owing to a lack of patience on his part or to a desire to be meddlesome and make himself officious. There are a great many medical gentlemen who are not charlatans in disguise, and these should be singled out. The pregnant female should have herself thoroughly washed and bathed just before confinement, and the vagina should be thoroughly rinsed out with half a gallon of warm water in which a tablespoonful of pulverized borax has been dissolved; this precaution will wash out any infectious germs that may cause inflammation.

The bed in which the confinement is to take place should be scrupulously clean, and in order to insure this, it should be made a rule that the bedstead be taken apart, and taken out-of-doors where it is thoroughly washed and afterwards exposed to the purifying influence of the sun and air. The mattress must also be taken out for a similar dusting and cleaning, and kept for a time exposed to sun and air. The confinement chamber should go through the same renovating ordeal; the carpet of this particular chamber should be taken up, the floor thoroughly scrubbed and the walls and ceiling washed off and whitened. It will be better if a few clean mats or rugs can be substituted, and the old carpet not relaid until after the confinement, when the woman is up and around again. These precautions will guard against the possibility of infection and the dangers of childbed fever, and the many different phases of inflammation which are the result of carelessness in the details of cleanliness. Of course, the nurse and attending physician must be equally anxious of their own personal cleanliness. If he or she leave any of the infectious diseases, like scarlet fever, measles, typhoid fever, erysipelas and puerperal fever, either of them is quite sure to communicate the contagion to the innocently ignorant lying-in woman, and entail upon her endless suffering and death. In France and Germany, stringent precautions for nurse and physician against the dangers of infections are mandatory under the laws, but in free America such legal injunctions would be considered as curtailing our liberty; in the meantime, innocent lives are sacrificed, through lack of systematized regulations, at the cost of liberty degenerating into license.

On the day of confinement the bed is held in readiness for the occasion, by spreading over the mattress a large piece of oiled cloth, or what is preferable, rubber cloth; this must reach up high enough so as to afford proper protection and lap over the side of mattress and bedstead. Beside the bed an extra mat should be laid, to catch any fluid that may run down the rubber cloth on the floor.

The preliminary signs of labor pains that make themselves felt by the pregnant female, are of considerable interest to her and I believe, that if she will familiarize herself with their character she will have less anxiety and more confidence in a happy termination of her condition. For some days, and occasionally for two or three weeks prior to the commencement of actual labor, a sense of uneasiness about the uterus will be felt by the female; this uneasiness will be observed several times during the day and night. When the patient complains of this local disturbance, she may feel, by placing her hands over the region of the womb, that the organ becomes hard for the time being, and as soon as the sense of uneasiness passes away, the womb becomes soft again. These symptoms are called the "independent contractions of the uterus" and in the first pregnancy they are felt earlier than afterwards. This is simply a muscular irritability of the womb and is not accompanied by "bearing down" which is the true characteristic of labor. These preliminary skirmishes must not be mistaken for the commencement of labor, otherwise great mischief may be done by harassing the case into a premature delivery which might sacrifice the child. The pregnant female will often become very anxious when she first experiences these independent pains and she may imagine that something is wrong; for this apprehension there is no reason, because experience has taught that the greater this local disturbance before the beginning of labor, the more favorable the progress of labor will be when true labor pains set in.

"The righting of the organ" will be observed for some days previous to the confinement, by a change of the position of the pregnant womb. The womb places itself, as it were, in readiness for the expulsion of the child, which is shortly to begin. This is done by the body of the uterus inclining forwards and sinking downwards, and correspondingly relieving from pressure the organs of the chest; this makes breathing easier, and in proportion as the body of the womb comes down, so will the lower portion of the organ descend, and this may give rise to irritation of the bladder and frequent desire to pass water; sometimes the passage of urine may be entirely obstructed, so that the water must be drawn off by means of a catheter. Some women become very nervous just before the commencement of labor; this is generally due to fear or anxiety, for which there is no reason, and agreeable companionship will generally dispel all evil forebodings and restore her to self-confidence.

Labor pains are divided into *true* and *false*, and this distinction is entirely based upon their different sources. True labor pains are due to the contractions of the muscles of the uterus, and at the beginning they are slight. They commence in the back and run on down to the thighs; one feature about them is that they are intermittent, that is, that they are not continuous; there is always an interval, especially at the beginning of labor, in which there is no pain at all. When labor sets in, the pains are grinding or cutting, but as soon as the mouth of the uterus is fairly opened or dilated, the character of the pain changes to a bearing down or forcing out nature. If the hand is applied over the region of the womb, during the presence of a pain, the organ can be felt hardened and swollen; this subsides with the pain, and in the interval, the organ relaxes. This is a wise provision of nature, for it gives the woman an opportunity to recover and regain fresh strength for each succeeding effort. False labor pain has no connection with the process of child-bearing, but is only an incidental complication. It may be caused by gas in the intestines, indigestion, diarrhea, constipation, disease of the kidney, neuralgia, or rheumatism of the muscles of the abdomen or bowels, and by the passage of gallstones; where the false pains have been traced to their origin they can be properly dealt with.

A muco-sanguineous discharge from the vagina is another sign that labor has begun, but it will sometimes happen that it is absent, and this constitutes a *dry labor*. The mucous discharge which is thus observed, subserves a very important object in lubricating the parts and relaxing the neck of the womb and the vagina. There is often a slight tinge of blood, due, perhaps, to a rupture of small blood vessels in the mouth of the womb; this is called a show, which some women have for several days before labor commences.

"Stages of labor" are arbitrary divisions, so as to simplify the explanation of the entire process of labor from the time the womb begins to act, up to the last act of parturition, which is the expulsion of the afterbirth, and these have usually been divided into three stages. The first stage is the dilation or opening of the mouth of the womb, including also the breaking of the membraneous sac which holds the fluid in which the child floats, so as to protect it from pressure that the walls of the uterus would be continually exercising, which would prevent its proper development. In this stage the woman should not exert herself by bearing down; this will only waste her strength which she should preserve for the second stage, when the mouth of the womb has opened and the progress of the child into the world has commenced; during this stage, the female should make an attempt to relieve her bladder, and if she has had no stool for several hours before, it will be a good thing to use an enema of warm water, and empty the bowels.

The second stage of labor begins when the bag of water has broken and the waters escape; the contractions of the womb increase now in violence and become decidedly of a bearing down character. At this period the patient should be furnished with something that she may grasp with her hands; a sheet attached to the post of the bed is the best for this purpose, and with her feet steadily braced, holding her breath she bears down whenever a pain comes on; bearing down between pains, only exhausts the patient and does no good. During this stage of labor, the pain in the patient's back will sometimes become intense, she exclaims: Oh, dear, doctor, my poor back feels like breaking! what shall I do? The greatest relief that can be given at this time is to support the back with the flat surface of the hand, or by folding a towel and placing it under the back, the two ends being held by assistants.

As the birth of the child progresses and it approaches the vulva, the patient will feel an urgent inclination to go to stool; upon this she must not insist, for at this advanced period of labor she may injure herself and child. The desire is caused by the pressure of the child's head against the rectum; any fecal matter that is thus pressed out should be at once removed by the nurse.

The third stage of labor consists in the expulsion of the placenta or afterbirth.

There is a natural detachment of the placenta and a natural expulsion, but one must have the patience to wait. What presumption of the officious doctor or midwife to suppose that nature was so derelict as to require some meddlesome assistant, immediately after the birth of the child, to drag or pull on the placenta: no, more than that, carry the hand up into the cavity of the womb and detach the placenta with the fingers and bring it down and out. When I first started out to practice I was foolish enough to believe and do the same thing, and afterwards I congratulated myself how wonderfully skilled I was, but now I am convinced that this procedure was due to ignorance of the laws of nature. The truth of the matter is, that the sooner and the more one pulls and feels on the placenta, the more irritable the womb becomes, and the more will the uterus contract, as though it protested against interference.

I have had it happen, and others must have had the same experience, that the womb closes and contracts firmly in ten to twenty minutes after delivery, the afterbirth becoming tightly inclosed so that one not experienced would be frightened into the belief, Oh! here the placenta has grown to the womb. This is a delusion which may lead to an interference that may entail dangerous consequences to the mother. The condition is simply this, that as the afterbirth was not completely detached at the birth of the child, the uterus contracted immediately upon and around the retained placenta, and for two physiological reasons: (1) to accomplish the very object which was imagined was not accomplished, namely, by contracting, the uterus naturally peels itself off from the placental attachment, and (2) were it not for this immediate contraction of the uterus after the expulsion of the child, the mother would likely *flood* from the uterine vessels of the partly detached placenta. Of late years I never experienced a single case in which the placenta did not detach itself, and if I had known twenty years ago as I do now, I never would have had one.

After the delivery of the child, the woman should be made as comfortable as possible for the time being, and by the time the child is washed and dressed, the placenta will generally present itself in the vulva. If the afterbirth has not come away at once there is no need to become alarmed. I have waited for six to eight hours for that event to take place, and if there is delay over an hour, two teaspoonfuls of fluid extract of ergot will so excite contractions of the womb that its contents will be expelled.

Whether the afterbirth comes away immediately after the birth of the child, or is delayed, it must not interfere with putting the mother in a warm, dry, comfortable condition. Everything that is damp from perspiration or wet from the waters, both dress and bed linen must be removed and replaced with warmed, dry, clean linen; this insures against taking cold. To me it looks like a crime against science and nature to allow a woman to remain in the wet and soiled bed after her confinement for twelve or more hours, and the doctor or nurse who permits this, is ignorant and negligent of his duties.

After the placenta is removed, the binder or bandage is applied; this is simply a piece of unbleached muslin about eighteen inches wide and long enough to reach one and a half times around the body; it should be brought down to cover the hips and then fastened with strong safety pins. The object of the binder is to give support to the flabby and relaxed abdominal muscles, which is a great comfort and aid to restore the muscles to their former shape.

How a woman should lie after confinement is of much greater importance than how she should lie during childbirth; in fact it does not matter much how she lies during labor so long as she feels comfortable, but after confinement and during her convalescence, her position in bed has an important bearing on her recovery; to avoid repetition I refer the reader to of this work. Vaginal douches of hot water, of a temperature of 104 degrees F. serve a very useful purpose in washing out the secretions that will naturally accumulate in the vagina, and after a short time undergo septic decomposition; these rinsings also assist nature to repair and heal the tissues. The quantity of fluid that should be used at once is half a gallon of water in which a tablespoonful of powdered borax has been dissolved. Great care should be exercised by the nurse, lest the bed and linen of the patient get wet, and through this she become liable to take cold. The second day after the delivery is about the right time to begin using the douche, and about this time the mother should also get a mild laxative, either of castor oil or of Femina laxative syrup, which is very palatable and suitable for the occasion.

The last throes of labor which usher the child into the world constitute the climax of the parturient effort and as there is little or no interval between the pains, the pains at this period have been appropriately termed *double labor pains*. There is more or less excitement and apprehension on the part of the lying-in female and the experienced practitioner or nurse will concentrate his effort to calm and encourage the sufferer in the last minutes of her travail.

It is best to wait a few minutes after the child is born before tying the cord, so as to give the circulation time to equalize itself; especially is this desirable when the cord was wound around the child's neck or when it is otherwise compressed. The cord is tied about an inch above the navel, and half an inch higher the cord is cut with a pair of sharp scissors. In the meantime, the nurse, if properly instructed, will have in readiness on the side of the bed a warm flannel or blanket which is to receive the little stranger. There is a proper way to pick up a newborn babe, so that it will not roll or slip from the hands, which I have known to happen. The little baby must be taken hold off with the same gentle firmness as an older child. To prevent any accident, place the posterior surface of the child's neck in the space bounded by the thumb and index finger of one hand, and with the other hand gently seize the thighs and in this manner place it into the blanket, to be conveyed to a warm place of safety,—the newborn child must be kept warm, for its very life may depend upon it. After the mother has had her temporary wants satisfied, the nurse prepares for the *first toilet* of the child.

The care of the baby is differently understood by different persons, and as a result of this difference of opinion I have observed a great many unfortunate consequences. There is no reason why the care of the baby should be resigned to custom and habit for both are often extremely hazardous to the life of the child, and this I will illustrate in the course of my remarks.

How often are newly born infants taken into a cold room in which, from the arrangement of the doors, a draft sweeps through whenever a person goes out or comes in? How the child is laid bare in readiness for the ordeal of a thorough cleaning! The child is generally first rubbed with oil and afterwards put into a bath tub or some other vessel of sufficient capacity to drown several babies at once. It is now treated to a soaping process, after which, by means of a cloth indifferently selected, the child is scrubbed with an ambition which would have been laudable if applied to the nurse's own person, but why this little innocent should be the object of such abuse has been a standing wonder to me from the time I witnessed the first outrage.

By the time the nurse gets through bathing the child, it is shivering and blue from cold. I had not been practicing medicine very long before I became appalled by this barbarous procedure, nor had I practiced very long before I was called upon to sign a number of death certificates of infants who contracted colds that resulted in bronchitis, pneumonia and congestion of the lungs, which caused their death.

There is no sense in this dousing and soaping of a newborn child, and aside from its danger by undue exposure, it is absolutely useless. But habit is often so thoroughly intrenched that the good judgment which persons exercise in most of their duties may become entirely suspended, when this force of habit has established a custom that is well-nigh universal.

My method of directing the first toilet of the baby is without the possible dangers to which I have referred, for it has for its object not only to clean the child, but to dress it as quickly as possible and again wrap it in flannel. Warmth is the life of the newborn babe; it does not require much food, if any, the first twenty-four or forty-eight hours of its life, but it requires to be kept warm. The room in which the child is to be cleansed must be warm and free from draft, and if there is a fire in the chamber where the mother is, the toilet of the child had better be made here under her eyes and those of the physician. The nurse or person delegated to dress the baby provides herself with a vase or bowl of warm water and a saucerful of warm olive oil or vaseline and a few soft cloths. She then seats herself in a low chair, and by means of a small piece of flannel she applies the oil all over the baby's body, rubbing in an extra quantity in the armpits, groins and other places where the cheesy substance is thickest. When the oil has softened the sebaceous material, take a soft muslin cloth, provided for the purpose, and beginning on the head the oil is wiped off again; where there are blood stains left, wash these off with a soft flannel cloth; at the same time the eyes are to be bathed and the mouth washed out. I have not mentioned the use of soap, for the reason that it is not at all necessary and very often injurious. The oil removes all the caseous matter and what oil remains is rather an advantage than otherwise; it preserves the warmth of the child and protects its skin. If the soap comes in contact with the eyes of the infant it often becomes a fruitful source of that annoying and often dangerous disease of the eyes that is technically termed *purulent ophthalmia*.

Never apply oil or any other greasy substance to the cord before it comes off, for this will prevent its drying and delay its falling off. When the cord has come off, you simply keep the navel clean by washing it daily with a little warm borax water and afterwards apply a small compress on which has been smeared a little zinc ointment. Always see to it that the baby is lying dry and use dusting powder freely; the *precipitated chalk* is the best and cheapest infant powder that can be used. The child that is nursed on its mother's breasts has little to fear from overfeeding, yet it should not be allowed to hang on the nipple too long or sleep with the nipple in its mouth. Nurse the child every two hours during the day and awaken it if it should sleep to give it its nourishment, but at night allow it to sleep as long as it wants to; this will cultivate regular habits in the child and it will thrive much better. If the baby cries and is restless between times do not imagine that it is always hungry, but rather colicky, for which there is nothing better than the old German domestic remedy, *fennel seed tea*; of this give the baby all it will drink every day and until it is a year old.

Sore nipples are a great annoyance to a mother and often very obstinate to treatment. The skin covering the nipple is made exceedingly tender by the sucking of the child's mouth and in a few days it cracks and becomes fissured. Sometimes, the pain that the mother endures whenever the infant nurses is excruciating, for every time the child is put to the breasts the cracks open anew. The most fruitful cause of this condition is to allow the child to hold the nipple in its mouth when it does not nurse or perhaps to allow it to retain the nipple in its mouth while it sleeps.

This practice must be at once discontinued, and the child must be at once removed from the breast as soon as it is satisfied. The nipples should be washed with borax water, and then a salve should be made by mixing the yellow of one egg with half an ounce of Peruvian balsam. This is to be applied by means of a camel's hair brush to the sore nipple every time after the child is through nursing. Should the nipple be too sensitive and the suction of the child too painful, then a breast pump had better be used for a few days and the child not applied until the teat has sufficiently improved.

Abscess of the breast constitutes a distressing complication of the puerperal condition, inflicting upon the patient intense suffering, and very often leading to a long delay in recovery. It may be due to cold, and in one case it developed from this cause two months before confinement, but this is an exception. Sore nipples are a fruitful cause, for the soreness of nursing makes the mother reluctant to have the child draw all the milk out, hence, the breast cakes and hardens with the above result. It also is due to neglect in not having the nipple properly drawn out; or to a foolish custom, derived from remote ancestry not to allow the infant to be put to the breast for two or three days after its birth. In this way the milk ducts become greatly distended, inflammation sets in, which, if not properly arrested will terminate in an abscess. If gentle friction of camphorated oil and hot, moist compresses or poultices do not enable the child to draw out the secretion, a young pup should be obtained, for he draws with a gentleness and activity which surpasses the most perfect machine. The patient must drink sparingly of fluids and properly support the breasts by means of handkerchiefs placed under them and made to cross the shoulders, and the bowels should be thoroughly opened. Should an abscess form it should be opened by a free incision, and the poultice discontinued, but instead a wad of absorbent cotton should be applied and the breast tightly bandaged with the handkerchief.

CHAPTER XXIX
DISEASES PECULIAR TO CHILDREN

The diseases of children that I propose to inquire into, are not those of so serious a nature as to require the skill of a physician, but rather those trivial ailments which are common among children of tender age and which neither good care nor healthy surroundings seem to be able to ward off. And for this reason, mothers and nurses should familiarize themselves with these ailments and their appropriate treatment, for trivial as they may seem to begin with, if permitted to go on uncontrolled, they often lead to more serious and perhaps fatal consequences.

A coated tongue in children is not always a sign of digestive disturbance, for most nurslings have a white coated tongue in the first three or four weeks of their lives. With the ancients, and even up to within a recent period, the tongue was considered the *mirror of the stomach*; this was a delusion because nothing definite or of great importance can be deciphered in any case from the appearance of the tongue alone, but this superstition became so deeply rooted in the minds of the public, that even now a medical examination is considered incomplete unless the physician says *put your tongue out*, for the purpose of a physical inspection.

When the child loses its appetite and the stomach and bowels become deranged, the tongue generally becomes coated. Children who are overfed and in whom the food is not digested, may have a thick fur over the tongue, but as a rule only on the back of the tongue there is a whitish coat. In diseases of the mouth that are purely local, the tongue is sometimes coated, quite independently of any disease of the stomach, as for instance in thrush, in catarrhal inflammation of the mouth, diphtheria, burns and other injuries.

(*a*) Catarrh of the mouth is an inflammation of the mucous membrane and is recognized by redness and increased secretion. It is most intense on the tongue, which presents the appearance as though it were coated with raspberry syrup. Sometimes the redness is most on the inside of the cheeks and soft palate, while the tongue is covered with soft fur. The inflammation of the mucous membrane of the mouth, extends in aggravated cases to the throat and nasal passages and along the Eustachian tube into the ear. There is many a baby suffering, no one knows from what, when it has an earache due to this cause. When the catarrh has existed for some time, clear, minute water-vesicles rise upon the tongue, gums and mucous membrane of the lips and cheeks. These burst and leave behind them small, flat ulcers, which in the first few days run together and present large, flat, ulcerated surfaces. The children become feverish and refuse to eat and drink for days, partly because to do so, pains them and partly from a loss of appetite.

The most common cause is the eruption of the teeth. Mothers of experience know that when the baby drools, it is teething, and if she examines a little closer she will discover the catarrhal condition described. Another cause is the old-fashioned sugar teat with its souring contents; so is the nursing food, when either too hot or too cold, and in older children irregular or improper food has the same effect, for instance, sour ripe fruit eaten in excess.

The treatment for catarrh of the mouth is simple and successful if directed to the removal of the causes that we have enumerated. The mouth should be cleansed every few hours with a little borax water, and the febrile symptoms generally subside with a dose of mild laxative.

(b) Putrid sore mouth is an aggravated stage of the above affection; it begins on the borders of the gums as inflamed patches coated with a thin layer of yellow mucus. The slightest touch of the ulcerated places causes bleeding, and the affection can be recognized at quite a distance from the mouth by the sense of smell. The disease is contagious and may be imparted from one child to another. Carious teeth are the predisposing agents; mercury or *calomel* in repeated and large doses produces a similar effect. A very simple and efficient remedy for this affection is a saturated solution of chlorate of potassa, in the proportion of a teaspoonful to a teacupful of boiling water; with this solution wash the mouth out every two hours, and allow a little to be swallowed at the same time; children under one year of age can swallow ten drops; under two years, twenty drops; under three, thirty drops, and larger ones can take a teaspoonful.

(c) Thrush, sprue, or soor is another type of sore mouth that falls to the lot of some children. It resembles catarrh of the mouth, but must be considered a different disease, inasmuch that it is proven to be due to a fungus growth. The disease begins with a change of color from the natural bright red, to a livid, dark red color; the entire mucous membrane of the mouth is uniformly discolored; the discoloration never occurs in spots, and the surface presents the appearance as if a thick coat of raspberry syrup had been smeared upon it. The mucous membrane becomes dry and sticky and the secretion of the mouth is acid. On inspecting the mouth the fungi can be seen, at first as small white points if only existing a few hours, but their growth is very rapid, and they soon form large white patches, which may run together and cover the entire mouth. The treatment is directed towards removing the cause in the first place; if the child has been using the sugar teat that must be discontinued, and even a milk diet should be suspended for a few days, on account of its containing sugar and cheesy matter, and instead the child should be fed with a little thickening of arrow root or wheaten flour. The mouth must be kept sweet and clean with a solution of borax applied with a small camel's hair brush; if the disease is obstinate, dissolve the borax in creosote water obtained from a druggist, and apply this every hour or two as above.

(*d*) Parotitis, or mumps, is an inflammation of the parotid or salivary gland. The disease shows itself as a swelling between the angle of the lower jaw and the ear. Several days before the swelling and pain begin, the children feel tired, ill-humored, feverish, lose their appetite, lounge around or voluntarily take to bed. Nervous children show brain symptoms; they complain of headache, are delirious and have convulsions. After two or three days they begin to feel pain behind the jaw, and when they open the mouth, masticate, or on slight pressure, the pain becomes aggravated. The swelling over the corresponding cheek extends to the lower eyelid and back to the neck. The skin over the swelling becomes inflamed and red. In males the swelling may suddenly move from the neck to the testes, while in the female it may strike on the mammæ.

The course of mumps is usually favorable, but there is a possibility of an abscess forming, and this may break directly outward, or burrow backwards and burst into the ear, perforating the ear drum, causing lifelong deafness. I have had one case in which the disease went to the brain; the little boy, a child of seven, died. The patient who has mumps must be kept warm; over the swelling apply hot poultices for three or four days, and besides wrap the entire head and neck in flannel. If the swelling is painful, and the child in robust health, a few leeches applied to the swelling will relieve the pain and have a good effect on the cause of the disease. Belladonna ointment is a valuable remedy for older children, but with babies it must be used with extreme care. The diet must be bland and light; bread and milk, or gruel, is the most appropriate. Give a little paregoric at night to soothe the restlessness, and open the bowels with the Femina laxative syrup.

(*e*) Tonsilitis or quinsy sore throat is often mistaken for the mumps, but to the experienced practitioner or nurse there is no resemblance, and to mistake one for the other is almost impossible. In tonsilitis the cheek never swells, the swelled tonsils being felt only behind the jaw and quite below the ear. Tonsilitis occurs oftener than mumps, and unlike the latter affection, when the patient has had one attack of quinsy he is likely to have a recurrence whenever he gets a fresh cold. The disease begins with difficult deglutition, pain, heat and dryness in the throat, and always more or less fever, from which some children become quite delirious. The affected tonsils become as large as pigeon eggs, and can be readily felt beneath the angle of the lower jaw. The swollen tonsils are red and dotted with yellowish spots, which is due to the suppuration of the follicles of which the gland is composed. If both swell at the same time so that they touch each other, symptoms of suffocation may ensue. The writer suffered from tonsilitis when he was a student, and the pain was indeed excruciating for a time. The pain is sometimes greater in swallowing fluids than solids. In examining the mouth a little skill is required. Some children are so well trained that they will respond at once, and then by means of a spoon handle the tongue is depressed, and the tonsils come into view. Others again have their own sweet will about these things, and simply will not voluntarily open their mouths. Then it takes two persons to manage them in the following manner: while one person holds the child in his lap, its back and head braced against his chest and the hands held down, the other person slides the handle of a teaspoon along the tongue until he touches the soft palate; this makes the child gag, and at that moment the tonsils are brought plainly into view.

The treatment for tonsilitis should be prompt and active; that is, when the disease is recognized, something should be done at once to relieve it. If the bowels are constipated give a laxative at once, and over the painful tonsils apply a flaxseed poultice, keeping the neck and head wrapped up well at the same time. For the fever give a dose of *antifebrine* in the forenoon and at bedtime; for a child one year old, one grain for a dose; at the age of three or four, give two grains at once, and at eight to twelve years, three grains can be given. Chlorate of potassa is the best remedy for a gargle, and for internal use also. Make a solution of chlorate of potassa by dissolving one teaspoonful in a teacupful of hot water, and when cooled off, have the child gargle every hour or two, and swallow a half to a teaspoonful of the solution at the same time.

(f) Diphtheria of the throat is eminently an epidemic disease and of a highly contagious and infectious nature. Of late years, the disease occurs in every season of the year, and independently of any epidemic or contagious influence, but it is presumed that the contagion or spores are cultivated in improper sanitary conditions arising from defective sewerage and filthy accumulations. The disease invariably begins with fever, a marked increase of the pulse, increase of the temperature of the skin, and general depression. There is first a difficulty of swallowing, a snuffling voice and stiffness in the neck; the first two signs are due to the swelling and diphtheritic coating of the tonsils, palate and nasal passages, while the last symptom is due to a swelling of the lymphatic glands of the neck which is never absent in genuine diphtheria. If the throat is examined in the early stage, the white membrane is first seen in the tonsils and as the disease progresses it spreads to the palate, the pharynx and the nasal passages. The color of the membrane also changes; after several days it passes into a yellowish-white or grayish-white tint. It has another peculiar feature that distinguishes this membrane from the exudation of ordinary tonsilitis, which the practical eye at once detects; the membrane of diphtheria makes the impression of having eaten into the tonsil or as though it was pressed into the tissue by the finger. And that is really so too, because as a scientific fact it is no membrane at all, but a death or slough of the mucous membrane which may extend down into the tissue beneath the membrane. To treat diphtheria successfully is simple enough but it requires great skill and experience, and I will outline what I consider the proper thing to do and which in my hands saved those lives that were intrusted to my care.

The treatment resolves itself into perfect cleanliness or disinfection, stimulating nourishment and internal medication.

Everything must be kept clean around the patient, and a vessel must be provided, containing a little chloride of lime into which he spits or hawks the phlegm from his throat. The membrane or slough in the throat or nose must be thoroughly disinfected and the only evidence that this has been successfully accomplished is when all offensive odor has disappeared. For this purpose as a local application I employ the following preparation: Solution of subsulphate of iron (Monsel's solution) 3 drams, glycerine 5 drams; mix and pour ten to twenty drops into a saucer and by means of a camel's hair brush apply to the diphtheritic membrane until the character and odor of it is destroyed; this application repeat every four hours. Should the nasal passages be also affected mix a teaspoonful of the preparation to a teacupful of warm water and by means of a syringe wash the nasal passages out several times a day. Give the patient internal medicine to disinfect the stomach and for its alterative action on the blood: for this purpose use tincture of iron 4 drams, simple syrup, add to make 4 ounces. To a child seven to ten years old give a teaspoonful, ten or fifteen minutes each time, after the brushing. Between the times of brushing and giving the medicine, that is two hours afterwards, give the nourishment and stimulant; this consists of milk punch. A child seven to ten years old should take no less than a tablespoonful of whisky, with or without a little sugar, in a half to a teacupful of milk beaten thoroughly together with an egg beater; this is to be taken for a meal and drank at once, and repeated every four hours. No other food or nourishment must be given for a number of days, and if the child is thirsty between times allow it to drink sweetened water and whisky. Sometimes the glands of the neck and the tonsils swell and become very painful; for this the Belladonna ointment applied with gentle friction night and morning and the neck enveloped in cotton batting are certain to give relief. The efficiency of this treatment depends upon the intelligence and faithfulness with which it is used.

(g) Croup is a term derived from the German Kropf the crop or craw of the bird; this disease is known by a great many different names, but on account of its shortness, *croup* has received the preference. The disease has to do with an affection of the organ of the voice, the *larynx,* which is the upper part of the air passage, and situated between the trachea and base of the tongue at the upper and front part of the neck where it forms a projection in the middle line which is prominent above and called the pomum Adami or Adam's apple. The larynx contains the vocal cords, running from before backwards on both sides; these form the narrow fissure or chink, the *rima glottidis,* through which we breathe. Like all other air passages this too is lined with mucous membrane. The symptoms that foreshadow croup are not particularly significant, for they simply indicate that the child has a cold. The children have a cough, they sneeze, and their appetite is capricious for a few days; they are not as lively as usual and are more or less feverish. In a certain proportion of cases there is nothing noticeable before the croup develops, for the children may go to bed perfectly well and sleep calmly the first few hours of the night, when suddenly they are awakened with a barking cough, which greatly frightens young children and they begin to cry. The cough may repeat itself at short intervals, the voice become hoarse and husky and lower and lower, so that in the morning a well marked croup is developed. The voice finally disappears so completely that it is not heard above a whisper, and the greatest pain and harassing symptoms of suffocation do not enable the child to utter a loud sound. The respiration becomes labored in proportion to the swelling of the vocal cords and other obstructions to the passage of air through the larynx. Croup has vagaries that cannot be foretold. One child may have symptoms of so threatening a nature that one believes it will suffocate at any moment, yet, with a few simple remedies, the symptoms will gradually lessen and it recovers in a few days, while another may be suffering comparatively little and from appearances one would imagine that there is little or no danger, but at once it will change and grow worse so rapidly that it will die in a few hours. For this simple reason no case of croup should be carelessly or lightly considered. When a child has croup it should be put at once into a warm room; a big fire should be kept up, and the child given hot drinks or a cupful of hot tea so as to make it sweat. The front part of the neck should be rubbed with equal parts of turpentine and sweet oil until it feels warm and the skin reddens. If the child has eaten a good supper, a teaspoonful of syrup of ipecac should be given every half hour until it vomits; otherwise vomiting should be omitted. The following mixture always gives relief and with other precautions is all that is usually required.

Take: Bicarbonate of potassa 2 drams

Water 1 ounce

Hive syrup,

Paregoric, of each ½ ounce

Mix and give half to one teaspoonful every two hours until relieved; then every four to six hours.

What we have considered thus far is also called spasmodic, catarrhal or *false* croup, to distinguish it from another variety that is described under the name of *membranous* or diphtheritic croup.

This form of croup as its name indicates is characterized by a membrane which forms upon the surface of the inflamed mucous membrane of the larynx as an exudation, and sometimes the croupous membrane extends down into the windpipe or trachea.

This variety of croup begins just like the simple or catarrhal form only as the disease progresses the symptoms gradually grow worse, and remain persistent. It is fortunately a very rare disease and almost always fatal when it does occur. An ordinary or catarrhal croup may, when neglected, run into the membranous form and for that reason children who are croupous, no matter how light it may appear, should be carefully nursed until the symptoms have passed off. The treatment for membranous croup has been on the whole very unsatisfactory; the membrane which forms in the larynx and windpipe is the cause of suffocating the child, and the question how to remove this has never as yet been answered. Of course a great many remedies have been suggested and used but at times all have disappointed. The successful case of membranous croup that I treated many years ago was cured by giving the little patient inhalations of lime water with a steam atomizer and besides giving whisky and milk as nourishment; how much of the success in this case was due to the child's vigorous constitution and how much to the treatment will always remain a mystery. In the commencement, the same treatment that was recommended for false croup is advisable; later on the skill of a good physician is required.

(*h*) Bronchitis or catarrh of the bronchial tubes is generally the cause of the ordinary cough due to exposure or taking cold. Its danger depends upon the severity of the bronchial inflammation and upon the age of the patient;

the younger the child the more dangerous the disease. In older children or adults there is no connection between a bronchitis and a pneumonia, but in infants or children under two years of age who are suffering from bronchitis the tendency toward a complication with pneumonia is ever present; in fact, in children of this age, pneumonia usually begins in that way.

Cough is the most prominent symptom and it is always present from the commencement of the affection, and apprehensive of this the parents seek medical assistance. The expectoration in young children is generally swallowed after each paroxysm of cough, hence the nature of it can rarely be seen. In the first part of the night the cough is always more severe than during the day, and the paroxysms may last from half to one minute, recurring several times in the hour. Some children are less disturbed in their sleep than others, for they sleep on, notwithstanding the cough, while others always awaken, become annoyed from the disturbance and cry. These interruptions in their night's rest reduce them in strength and flesh. Children who cough more when laid on one or the other side than when they lie on their back and who distort their face when coughing or, when old enough, complain of pain during or after coughing have something more than a simple bronchitis; they have a complication of pleurisy or a pneumonia. There is always fever and this may run very high, so that the child becomes delirious; even before the fever becomes very pronounced or the cough very annoying, their little hands and faces feel hot to the touch, indicating that they are not well.

Infants require good nursing when they are suffering from bronchitis, and it is not good to let them lie on their backs all of the time; when they have a coughing spell take them up quickly and lay them across the knees, with their faces downwards; this gives the mucus a chance to run out of the bronchial tubes and mouth which is better than swallowing it. The most important feature in the treatment of bronchitis is a warm room of even temperature night and day. If the temperature is allowed to go down during the night and the child inhales cold air into the lungs it will often bring on a relapse or aggravate the disease. When children have a cough and cold they must be kept warm in order to get well; this is no time for trying to harden them. A thermometer should be in every house and certainly in every bedchamber, so that the temperature of a room may be gauged to a certainty. In ordinary cases the temperature should not fall below seventy degrees Fahrenheit, and when the child coughs very much and the bronchitis is very bad it is best to keep the temperature of the room around eighty degrees night and day for several days, and as the patient improves, it is advisable to gradually drop to seventy.

The application of oil and spirits of turpentine is advisable in all cases of cold in the chest; it does good and one can hardly explain how and why. For the cough an infant can take with great advantage three or four drops of syrup of ipecac together with the same amount of paregoric, every four hours; older children take larger doses in proportion. When scrofula or tuberculosis is at the bottom of the bronchitis, a reliable preparation of cod liver oil emulsion should also be administered.

(i) Pneumonia is the technical term for inflammation of the lungs or *lung fever*. It consists of an inflammation, involving the air cells and smallest air tubules of the lungs; in other words, it is an inflammation of the substance or tissues of the lungs.

It is altogether a more serious affection than bronchitis, and in very small children exceedingly dangerous. The inflammation may affect either a small circumscribed portion of the lung, *lobular* pneumonia, or it may compromise an entire lobe or all the lobes of the lung, and is then called *lobar* pneumonia. Pneumonia is dangerous in proportion to the extent of lung tissue involved and the symptoms become correspondingly aggravated. The disease occurs extremely often in children, but it is altogether different from that which occurs in the adult. In children it is of a bronchial nature, that is, the ordinary bronchial catarrh has a tendency to extend to the very small bronchial tubes (capillary bronchitis), thence into the air cells of the lungs. In this variety of pneumonia the lungs do not become inflamed in their entirety, but here and there patches of lung tissue become the seat of lobular pneumonia. In the nursling, catarrhal pneumonia is an extremely frequent affection and I believe that it is principally due to the carelessness and promiscuous bathing of infants to which I have already referred. In foundling hospitals this disease destroys a great many children, and the chief cause has been attributed to their lying both night and day in a horizontal posture.

It has been statistically proven that many more children suffer from the disease in winter than in summer, and further, that in those parts of the lung that are inflamed the bronchial tubes which lead to them are also found to be inflamed. This relation of catarrhal pneumonia to bronchitis may be accounted for by the play of a mechanical force and thus illustrates the relation of cause and effect. The secretion of bronchitis not being expectorated, gravitates into the region in which the inflamed bronchial tubes terminate, namely, the air cells of the lungs, and by irritating and blocking or filling the air cells, a catarrhal pneumonia is developed.

The symptoms of pneumonia in children under two years of age are those of the catarrhal or lobular type; after they have passed through their first dentition they become subject to lobar pneumonia which differs in no particular from the disease which occurs in grown persons. Practice and experience make the discovery of catarrhal pneumonia possible in little children as soon as they are under observation for a little while. The most prominent sign is the rapidity of the respiration, which rises to sixty and eighty per minute instead of forty-four, the average normal respiration for the first year of infantile life.

The disease begins with a cough and more or less fever, and as it is always preceded with bronchitis, the symptoms that were enumerated when speaking of the latter disease are equally applicable to this one. Later on, when the transition of bronchial catarrh into pneumonia takes place, all the symptoms become at once aggravated. The breathing, for instance, becomes labored and increases and the nostrils dilate with each inspiration. The mouth is open, and its corners are drawn downward and outward, depicting distress and suffering, while the eyes roll anxiously about or become glassy and staring.

The treatment of pneumonia in its early stages would be the treatment of bronchitis, since every pneumonia in young children is preceded by a bronchial catarrh. The uniform temperature is of the first importance. The same remedy that was suggested for the cough in bronchitis is also here serviceable.

A systematic course of nourishment must form a part of every successful treatment for pneumonia; and as an old medical friend once told me in a consultation *"if the child is kept alive long enough with nourishment it is bound to get well."* In critical cases it is surprising the large amount of whisky a little infant consumes with avidity; its eyes begging and watchingly following the teaspoon from the cup to its mouth. I attended my own child once when only three months old and although there seemed no hope, for its tiny finger tips were blue and its lips livid from deficient aeration, yet it eagerly took its teaspoonful of whisky toddy every fifteen minutes through the longest part of the night, and towards morning it took a change for the better and its life was saved. I also believe that these babies must be kept in a constant sweat; this relieves the congestion of the lungs. The nourishment must be given at regular intervals of several hours just as you would give medicine, for indeed it is a medicine at this time.

Another valuable agent to which I attribute a number of recoveries is the application of a moist girdle suggested by Professor Alfred Vogel, of the University of Dorpat, Russia. In his work on "Diseases of Children" he says: "A diaper, or large white pocket handkerchief is folded up like a cravat; the bandage thus obtained should be three or four fingers wide, and the whole length of the handkerchief. This is now dipped in warm water, and wrung out so that the cloth does not drip, and then applied like a girdle around the chest of the child. A second cloth, double the size of the first, is folded up in the same manner like it, but which must be six to eight fingers broad, and then applied dry and warm over the first. It is very advisable to interpose a piece of gutta percha or oil silk between the dry and the wet girdle by which on the one hand, the moistness of the first cloth is preserved longer, while on the other, the second does not become wet. If the water with which the fomentations are made is not too cold, the child will tolerate them very well and in a short time, a slight retardation in frequency and improvement of the respiration are indicated by less motion of the nostrils. These warm compresses should be continued for from four to six days, and it is not at all necessary, during the entire time, to remove the bandage; the oil silk is raised up a little, and a few teaspoonfuls of water are poured upon the girdle or it is moistened with a sponge. The principal thing is not to allow a cooling of the skin by evaporation to take place. To secure this object, the dry cloth should properly overlap the moist one on all sides and as it is impossible to prevent the upper cloth from becoming wet, it should be changed several times during the day. I certainly have applied this girdle many hundreds of times, and have very often seen rapid improvement ensue; nevertheless, it cannot be denied that the half of these children perish notwithstanding. If cold compresses are applied the children cry of fright in consequence, and the symptoms become worse until the cold water has become warm." The application of blisters, cupping or leeching should not be tolerated.

CHAPTER XXX
DISEASES PECULIAR TO
CHILDREN—Continued

(*a*) Indigestion in very young children is generally accompanied with diarrhœa, because that portion of the child's food which is not thrown up or digested passes along the intestinal canal and acting as an irritant causes diarrhœa. An indigestion of only a short period of duration excites a catarrhal inflammation of the mucous membrane of the stomach, and this may be so slight that even a change or correction in the diet may be all that is required to relieve it. Children who are suffering from indigestion have stomach ache; this may be continuous or come on half an hour or an hour after nursing. The pain is due to the irritation caused by the nutriment or to the fermentation of the food and the consequent accumulation of gas within the stomach. The stomach becomes distended and sensitive to pressure. When the catarrh is severe the nutriment that the child takes into the stomach is immediately rejected or it may vomit glairy or greenish mucus from an empty stomach. At first the nutrition of the child may not be greatly interfered with, for some of the food is retained and digested in the small intestines, but in the course of time these too become irritated and then diarrhœa complicates the case and the child falls off and becomes rapidly emaciated. Children who are nourished from their mother's breasts rarely suffer from indigestion, but those who are fed on artificial foods become victims of stomach and bowel troubles. And for this reason it is natural to suppose that the chief reliance for a successful treatment is to regulate and study the diet of the sufferer; the chapter that is especially devoted to this subject should be consulted for further information.

(*b*) Diarrhœa is a derangement of the stools in which they loose their semi-solid, pap-like consistence and become watery liquid alone, or watery liquid in which indigested particles of food and fecal matter remain suspended. The quantity of alvine matter that is evacuated greatly exceeds that which passes in the normal state. The stools have an alkaline or acrid nature which irritates and often inflames the anus and the surrounding integument. "The normal form of the infantile feces in the first year of life is the pappy; the color is yellow like that of the yolk of egg; the smell is feebly acid, never putrid, and only in children who are fed upon a meat diet as repulsively pungent as in the adult; in later years they are no longer distinguished from the adult."

The passages of diarrhœa may be simply softer, but yellowish and increased in quantity, or they may be bright yellow and so watery as to squeeze out from the anus as from a syringe and soak through diapers and bedclothes, or the stools may be green, or bilious, and slimy. When children teethe they often have a diarrhœa for several days; this intestinal derangement has no connection with improper feeding, yet it requires to be watched lest it become serious and uncontrollable. There is still another kind of diarrhœa which is foamy and contains large quantities of mucus and little or no coloring matter. For the different varieties one and the same remedy will answer, and that which I here submit has never disappointed my expectation:—

Take:	Subnitrate of Bismuth	1 dram
	Powdered Kino	16 grains
	Rubbed thoroughly with Glycerine	1 dram
	Paregoric.	2 drams
	Chalk Mixture, sufficient to make	2 ounces

Shake the mixture thoroughly before using, and the dose can be regulated between ten drops for an infant to a teaspoonful for a child three or four years old.

(c) Dysentery or Flux is an inflammation of the mucous membrane of the large intestine, or colon, extending down to the rectum. Children under one year of age are not as liable to this affection as those who are older, and it is during their first dentition that the affection shows itself. In hot summer months, at the season of unripe fruits, the disease often becomes epidemic. The loss of strength and flesh is very rapid, and when children do not perish during the first few days of their sickness, they may succumb later when the disease has assumed a chronic form. Dysentery is extremely liable to become complicated with pneumonia, anæmia, pyæmia, perforations and strictures of the intestines, jaundice and abscess of the liver, and in proportion that these complications become developed life becomes seriously threatened. The symptoms of dysentery are striking and can hardly be mistaken for anything else. There is always pain over the abdomen, but on touching the abdomen near the navel and over the course of the colon the pain is greater than elsewhere.

Tenesmus is a characteristic symptom of dysentery. This is a straining sensation as if the bowels wanted to move, yet notwithstanding the violent bearing down, only a little mucus often streaked with pus or blood is discharged. The straining causes the lower folds of the rectum to protrude, and this portion of the bowel presents a livid red color; the sufferer is tormented a great deal by this fruitless bearing down, and the bowels should be anointed with pure zinc ointment and returned. The stools of the child are characteristic of this disease. Every passage contains glairy mucus formed into lumps resembling granules of boiled starch, streaked with blood and associated with a creamy looking substance which is purulent matter. If the disease has progressed to the formation of ulcers the evacuations become grayish red or assume a dirty ashen color, and the odor is putrescent. Portions of the mucous membrane slough off and large quantities of pus are discharged from the ulcerating surfaces so that the stools present sometimes nothing but purulent and bloody matter.

The treatment for this disease must be prompt and directed to the point; reliance must not be placed upon one single remedy, but a combination of expedients must be resorted to.

The greatest annoyance and source of pain is the straining and tenesmus, and to relieve this steps must at once be taken. There is hardly any use to give injections for this purpose for the irritable condition of the rectum makes it impossible for the child to retain them long enough to do any good. Use suppositories instead, and if need be, retain them by holding a soft compress of cloth over the anus, for ten to fifteen minutes until they are dissolved. For example, to a child one year old I employ the following suppository:—

Take:	Laudanum	1 drop
	Cocaine	$1/_{30}$ grain
	Bismuth Subnitrate	10 grains
	Cocoa Butter	10 grains

Make into one long suppository and roll in powdered bismuth, dip it first into oil or vaseline and insert into the rectum every three or four hours until the soreness and straining have subsided. If the child is not very sensitive nor very ill an injection of a teaspoonful of boiled liquid starch to which a few drops of laudanum have been added, may be used instead and as often as may be necessary. Cold drinks aggravate the pains, therefore give everything warm.

Cow's milk should be dispensed with in artificially fed children, and broths substituted to which a portion of a fresh egg is added, previously thoroughly beaten with an egg beater; in very young children the yolk alone should be used. A little whisky is always good for this class of patients, either in their broth, or given as a toddy in teaspoonful doses for the children are generally always thirsty and feverish. When children lose their appetites and refuse nourishment they must be coaxed and even forced to take food at regular intervals, otherwise they cannot rally and will perish from inanition. The medicine that I recommended for diarrhœa is also very useful for dysentery.

(d) Colic is the result of an abnormal accumulation of gas, *flatulency*, in the small intestine. There is always more or less gas in both stomach and bowels, but usually this passes off and there is no pain felt from it. It is when the quantity increases so as to distend the bowels that the walls of the intestines become the seat of pain. The pain comes on in paroxysms, or fits at short intervals, and increasing in violence. Children suffering from colic have the abdomen swollen or bloated, giving rise to that condition termed meteorismus or tympanites. Those who are under one year old are the most liable to colicky pains, for it is during this period of life that digestive disturbances are the most frequent, and these constitute the chief cause. Whenever the vermicular motion of the intestines becomes lessened or suspended, the gas is not expelled from the anus, and the accumulation causes the characteristic pains under consideration. In perfectly healthy digestion there is always more or less gas developed, and even then there may be colicky pains. The same pains originate with every diarrhœa that is due to improper food or feeding, and in dysentery too they are generally present. Infants who nurse at their mother's breasts are less liable, but not altogether exempt, for mothers' milk is very sensitive to impressions of purely physical exertions, or to emotions of fear or fright, thus her milk may become unhealthy for her child; or through her own digestion, suffering from temporary or permanent derangement, her milk may transmit a similar condition to her child; the mother may have eaten green fruit, or too much of a variety, or it may be too highly seasoned, or too fatty. Many mothers and nurses look upon the colic cry as a hunger cry, and hasten to feed the little one, and sometimes a few teaspoonfuls of milk or broth will relieve the cry for a few minutes, then the pain returns severer than ever, and the baby cries louder than ever. I have seen very nervous children thrown into convulsions from severe colicky pains.

My rule has been for years to nurse infants for the first two months not oftener than once in two hours; after that until they are six months old, every three hours, and from six to twelve months every four hours; between times the babies cry, of course, not because they are hungry, but because they have either pain or are thirsty. The old German household remedy for this is *fennel seed tea*; there is nothing as useful; it expels the gas and it quenches the thirst from which colicky children suffer, at least while they have the colic. This tea should be given regularly between times, and until they are twelve or fifteen months old; it is soothing, and what is of equal importance, it prevents overfeeding, which is the bane of artificially-fed children. The latter, bottle-fed babies, are all more or less colicky, and for these the fennel seed tea, between bottle time is indeed a balm. If the fennel seed tea does not relieve the child at once, or if the pain seems severe, then add a few drops of paregoric to the fennel seed tea, and give an injection of German chamomile tea, rubbing the bowels at the same time with a mixture of turpentine and sweet oil, and I believe that every case will be relieved. Permanent relief must be sought in ferreting out the cause and removing it. This may be due to improper food, or feeding, to indigestible contents in the stomach or bowels, and indeed, very often to constipation. When the stomach is overloaded, a dose of syrup of ipecac may give relief, and if due to constipation, the Femina laxative syrup is the most appropriate remedy.

(e) Convulsions, or spasms in children have long been well known to the laity, and from their frequent occurrence they make an important class of children's diseases. If there is one thing more frightful to behold than another, to the young and inexperienced mother, it is to see her baby's eyes unsteadily rolling, or turned up so as to show only the white of the eyeballs, or may be the eyes steadily fixed in a stare while the child becomes completely unconscious. A painful smile may play over its face, or an expression of fear or anger may distort the facial expression, while the muscles of the face twitch convulsively. The jaws are sometimes set, then again there is gnashing of the teeth, alternating with relaxation of muscles and ligaments. The child cannot swallow, and fluids poured into the mouth flow out again. The other muscles of the body also participate in the spasmodic contractions; those of the back contract and relax, and those of the extremities are involved in lively twitchings, or perform acts of thrashing, striking or twisting. The breathing becomes very irregular, and from the spasms of the muscles of the larynx or throat it may become entirely suspended, and if the spasm does not subside in two or three minutes the child may die. The skin becomes livid or congested and loses its sensibility so that blisters or irritants make no painful impression. Sometimes the child bleeds from the nose or mouth; the latter is generally due to the tongue having been caught between the teeth during the paroxysm. Frothy saliva wells up from the mouth and the urine and stools are involuntarily discharged.

All convulsive attacks have not every symptom above enumerated, some of them are usually absent and an attack may be quite mild, and last only a few moments; if convulsions last longer they are not only dangerous, but indicate serious disease, either of the brain or in which the brain or spinal cord is seriously complicated.

The period of the child's life at which convulsions are most frequent is from the time they are born up to the completion of the first dentition. Nervous children who had convulsions while they were teething are susceptible to violent attacks at the commencement of various diseases or during the developmental stage of the eruptive fevers. Perhaps the most frequent cause of convulsions in children is the eruption of teeth. The irritation which a growing tooth causes in the gums also irritates its nerve and this irritability is reflected on the brain, and this causes the spasm. An overloaded stomach, worms and digestive disturbances that accompany teething irritate the bowels and from this too convulsions ensue. The treatment for convulsions naturally resolves itself into first giving instant relief during the paroxysm, and secondly, finding out the cause of the attack. The latter is not always easy at first sight, and as the cause may be serious a competent physician should be sent for. But instructions that are serviceable while the convulsion is on are of the greatest importance to mother and child. The old and familiar remedy of giving the child a hot bath as soon as possible is certainly the best thing that can be done. The child should be undressed as quickly as possible so as to relieve it from all constriction and so that nothing can interfere with the respiration and circulation.

A towel wrung out of cold water should be placed over the child's head and its body immersed in hot water that is not so hot as to scald; the hands on which the child is supported while in the water must be well able to stand the heat. When the spasm has subsided, the child should be transferred to a previously warmed woolen blanket in which it is to be wrapped with its head softly elevated. If the bowels are constipated an enema of warm water and a little castile soap should be administered.

(f) Worms of different species infest the human organism; they get into the system from the outside world, with the food we eat and drink. Their abiding place seems to be the mucous membrane of the intestinal canal with the exception of the *trichinæ* which penetrate the mucous membrane and make their way to the different muscles throughout the body; the voluntary muscles seem to be their permanent dwelling place. These parasites are peculiar to the meat of the hog and as very young children do not eat this meat, they are so far totally exempt from them.

Tapeworms are rarely found in children under one year of age; it is when they get older and especially when they eat hog's meat, for this too is the home of the embryo tapeworm, that they become infected.

The roundworm, however, is peculiar to childhood. It is a yellowish or whitish worm resembling the earthworm, from one to twelve inches in length. The body is round, tapering toward each extremity. This worm inhabits the small intestine, but by acts of vomiting they are frequently ejected from the mouth or they may find their way into other cavities. On the Pacific slope these worms are not as frequently met with as on the other side of the Rockies. It is propagated by *ova* and taken into the system by means of drinking water containing them. The number varies greatly in different cases; sometimes there are only a few and again there may be dozens or hundreds coiled together so as to form balls or masses. They are most common between the ages of three and ten years. I do not believe that they ever exist in early infancy.

The symptoms denoting the presence of these parasites are on the whole obscure and depend somewhat on the temperament of the individual. A nervous child may be thrown into fits or convulsions from them. My first case of these worms in a child seven years old was rather exceptional and remarkable. The child was suddenly taken with a severe attack of spasmodic croup, for which I prescribed remedies without much relief. After the second day the child passed five large roundworms, the croup subsided, and while I claimed no credit that my remedies did not cure the croup it was generally conceded that they killed the worms.

The usual symptoms are colic pains, impaired appetite, diarrhœa, itching of the nose, swollen abdomen, puffy features, offensive odor of breath, dreaming sleep and grinding the teeth during sleep or twitching of the muscles.

The expulsion of the parasite is generally effected with simple remedies. Five to ten drops of spirits of turpentine in half to one tablespoonful of castor oil is a reliable remedy. The oil of wormseed is another convenient remedy in the same dose on a lump of sugar or mixed with oil; a cupful of tansy tea early three or four mornings on an empty stomach serves a useful purpose; pinkroot and senna administered as a tea has also a well-deserved popularity.

The thread, pin, spring or mawworm inhabits the large intestine and chiefly the rectum. It is a thin yellowish-white parasite from one-twelfth to one-third inch in length; the female has a straight, awl-like, pointed tail, the male has a strongly curved tail. It rarely, if ever, enters the small intestines. The worms occur chiefly in young children, but there is no period of life that is exempt from them. They cause pain and an itching sensation at the anus. This is particularly troublesome when the children lie in warm beds. The sexual organs are apt to become excited from the irritation and the habit of masturbation be thus formed. In girls the worms may travel into the vagina and leucorrhœa in children is often accounted for in this way; around the anus there may be pimply redness.

From the loss of appetite and sleep the general health of the child may become impaired; but the only possible evidence of the presence of worms is to examine the stools. If worms of the above description cannot be seen, yet the symptoms make their existence suspected, a dose of some of the remedies above suggested should be given and afterwards the stools again examined. Some children have a peculiar predisposition to pinworms, and although you seem to give them relief for the time being, in a short time afterwards the same symptoms return and the worms are as numerous as ever. In these cases a course of continual treatment becomes necessary to eradicate the morbid habit; for this course I recommend:

Take: Powdered wormseed,

Powdered chocolate,

Milk of sulphur, of each equal parts.

Mix and give half to one teaspoonful every night at bedtime.

(g) Constipation is the bane of artificially reared children and if the sagacity of mother or nurse does not correct the evil it often causes serious complications. Sometimes those who are nursed on the breast suffer from constipation, especially when the mothers or wet nurses are troubled with similar derangements. Children under one year of age should have two evacuations, and those from one to three years should have at least one passage a day; when this does not occur the feces become solid and constipation is the result. In most febrile affections constipation is caused by a loss of moisture through the skin and an increased urinary secretion. Certain foods constipate, especially the starchy or farinaceous variety, as soups containing corn starch, rice, sago, etc., and in older children certain dishes consisting of peas, beans, and wheaten bread. A great many medicines are constipating, for instance, most cough mixtures, for they contain opium in some form, also preparations of iron, lead, alum, bismuth, chalk, and vegetable remedies that contain astringents or tannin.

It must be laid down as a RULE never to be violated, that every child must have at least one passage a day from the day it is born, and it is the imperative duty of mother or nurse to see that it is accomplished. The infant of only a few days or weeks old may require only a few drops of olive oil, but if that delays in its effect it may become necessary to give relief at once, and for this purpose we have in a small warm water enema a most decided and effectual remedy. Soapsuds should never be used, except in very urgent cases, for I have known a diarrhoea to ensue from the irritation it caused which was very hard to control. If the feces are not very hard a soap suppository may be used with good advantage, and in the following manner: Take a piece of soap and pare it to a point the thickness of a lead pencil and about an inch long, moisten this and introduce carefully into the rectum; if the straining bring only the soap away it may be well to use the water enema afterward. If the constipation continues to be habitual a slight modification of the diet becomes necessary; starchy foods must not be given as often, and thinner than formerly; the milk too should be more diluted; broth or beef tea substituted once or twice each day will often have a good effect. When children are old enough to eat mixed food the diet can often be so regulated as to materially contribute towards opening the bowels. The children should be encouraged to drink a great deal of water; from the lack of that alone some children become constipated. Graham bread and boiled German prunes are especially to be recommended; so are ripe raw fruits, grapes, strawberries, apples, pears, etc. Children require fresh air and outdoor exercise to be well and robust; they run and jump more when in the open air, all of which gives tone and strength to the general system. If diet and outdoor exercise alone does not remedy the evil, then the Femina laxative syrup should be administered; it is efficient in its action, and pleasant to take, and unlike most laxative or aperient remedies, there is no danger of forming a habit of using purgatives.

(h) Whooping cough is the name of an affection deriving its significance from a characteristic which is peculiar to this cough. It commences like an ordinary bronchitis such as is the result of taking cold; there is the usual hoarseness, tickling in the throat, dry cough, sneezing, running from the nose; the eyes are red and watery, and there is more or less fever. Sometimes the cough is ordinary, but at other times it has a sharp metallic clang from the beginning. Owing to certain marked periods in the course of the affection it has been found convenient to divide it into three stages which may usually be distinguished, although in a certain proportion of cases the first stage (comprising some of the symptoms that have been enumerated above) may be submerged into the second or whooping stage. The first stage may last from four to five days to as many weeks. The second stage is when the peculiar sound or whoop begins; it consists of a great number of violent paroxysms, rapidly-recurring spasmodic coughs, until most of the air in the lungs is expired; there is then a sense of suffocation and the child becomes bluish red over the entire head and face, from which the German designation *blue cough* has originated. During this spell the face swells and the eyeballs become congested and bulge from their orbits and the nose often begins to bleed, while the urine and feces are often involuntarily ejected and the contents of the stomach thrown up from the violent contraction of the diaphragm. In a few moments the spell is broken by a protracted, whistling croupy inspiration, and this constitutes the whoop.

The whooping generally grows worse the first two or three weeks, after which time in favorable cases the cough gradually becomes milder, but this is not the rule by any means. I have had it in my own family to last, in two instances, six months, and in another eight months before the children had fully recovered.

Laughing or crying, swallowing dry, irritating morsels of food or cold and impure air will bring on a paroxysm of cough. When several children are affected together, the coughing of one will make the others cough.

The third stage is when the cough is wearing off and has lost its severity. The expectoration consists now of a yellowish or green-colored mucus; in otherwise healthy children this lasts only a few weeks, but in weakly or scrofulous ones it may last for several months. This disease is not as yet thoroughly understood. It is an epidemic, contagious bronchial catarrh, involving the nerves of respiration and attacks an individual but once. When complications arise the affection becomes exceedingly dangerous and the most common of these is pneumonia.

There is no specific cure for whooping cough; it has got to run its course, which may be either short or long. I have tried every agent so far known to scientific medicine, and there is none that will give prompt relief in every instance. Whooping cough being a bronchitis plus something else, it seems rational that the same precautions that are observed in a case of bronchitis should be followed here. Children with this affection must not be exposed to drafts or rough winds lest they get cold, which might seriously complicate matters. In summer when the weather is warm, outdoor life is beneficial in hastening recovery. Some children have the cough so light, that no extra precautions seem to be necessary; they have no fever, eat, feel and sleep well. But those who are feverish, who vomit freely, and whose appetite is capricious, require every attention. Their diet should be especially guarded, so that all dry, irritating nutriments are prohibited, and so that the diet consists principally of liquid nourishment. Warm drinks have a favorable influence on the disease; a plentiful supply of warm milk, first thoroughly beaten with an egg beater is the most suitable and convenient. The milk punch is often borne well, and the little whisky that enters into its composition is a needed stimulant to the sufferer; broths may be given for a change, and to these the yolk of an egg can be added with advantage. A great many remedies might be suggested, but the one which has served my purpose the best, is the following:

Take:	Deodorized tincture, of opium	½ dram
	Fluid extract, of belladonna	4 drops
	Fluid extract, of ipecac.	10 drops
	Simple syrup	2 ounces

For a child five years old, give a teaspoonful three or four times a day; older or younger children in proportion. If the cough is hard and dry, ten to twenty drops of syrup of ipecac alone should be given instead of the mixture, and when the cough is loosened, the mixture can be again administered. When in the course of the affection the breathing suddenly becomes labored, and the fever increases, it is fair to presume that the case is complicated with pneumonia.

(*i*) Eruptive fevers, as their name implies, are characterized by an eruption or exanthema. The most virulent of this class is smallpox. The eruption of this disease is of the nature of vesicles, or pustules, while that of measles, scarlatina, and rose rash is dry, and is properly called a *rash*. Chickenpox, however, has also vesicles and pustules, and for this reason it is very liable in times of an epidemic of smallpox to be mistaken for a mild form of the latter disease. For obvious reasons it is not proper to consider smallpox in this connection; its gravity and its management require experience, and further, it generally comes under special quarantine regulations of the proper constituted authorities.

The eruptive fevers are all divided into three stages, namely: a stage of invasion or development; a second stage when the eruption appears, and while it lasts; and a third stage, that of *desquamation*, when the eruption begins to fade or exfoliate in branny scales.

(*j*) Measles is generally a mild and not serious disease, and only attacks the individual but once in a lifetime; only through gross carelessness the disease becomes complicated, and then it may become a very dangerous affection. It begins with all the symptoms of a common cold. There is frequent sneezing, and an acrid muco-serous discharge from the nostrils. The eyes are irritable, reddened and watery, and there is more or less intolerance of light. The voice becomes hoarse and there is always a bronchitis present which is characterized by a dry, harsh cough. The patient is generally feverish, alternating with chilly sensations or shivering; the appetite is poor or absent and in some cases there is nausea and vomiting. The children feel drowsy; they complain of pain in the head and limbs and want to lounge around. The bowels may be constipated, but diarrhœa supervenes in a certain proportion of cases. In nervous children convulsions may occur; bleeding from the nose and false croup are not infrequently met with in the development of this disease. The duration of the first stage varies greatly in different individuals, and comprises a period extending from one to seven days. The eruption begins generally on the temples and forehead, whence it extends over the head and neck, thence down the back and over the entire body, occupying in its development from thirty-six to forty-eight hours. The eruption bears a resemblance to flea bites at first; it appears as minute red specks which gradually enlarge and become slightly elevated and arrange themselves in circular clusters. The portions of the skin that are free from the eruption retain their white appearance; the face is more or less swollen and the eyelids puffed. In some patients there is considerable annoyance from itching in the skin. The cough and bronchitis continue to be prominent symptoms, and the expectoration, consisting of yellowish sputa becomes abundant. In some children the fever runs very high in this stage and they become delirious and restless, but this is only temporary, for it generally diminishes with the eruption on the third or fourth day.

When the eruption begins to fade the third stage of the affection is inaugurated, and when there exist no complications, the patient may now be considered on the way to recovery which takes from four to eight days longer.

The treatment in measles should consist in good nursing, rather than in medication. Owing to the inflammation of the membranes of the eyes, the patient should be kept in a darkened chamber, and the eyes occasionally bathed with a solution of borax, by dissolving half a teaspoonful in a tumblerful of water. Good judgment forbids that the patient should be sweltered, but that he should be kept comfortably warm and never allowed to cool off suddenly is also very important. When the eruption is slow to develop a good sweat will often bring it out; so will undue exposure, to cold drafts and the transportation out of a warm bed into a cold one or drinking immoderately of cold drinks either delay the development of the eruption or drive it back, and from this undoubtedly dangerous complications arise, like pneumonia, diphtheritic croup, and convulsions. A mouthful of cold water now and then is harmless, but on the whole the drinks should be quite warm; the cough and bronchitis alone would require that.

Warm milk thoroughly beaten is the most suitable form of diet; broths and soups may be given for a change, so can a mixture of equal parts of weak hot tea and milk. The bowels should be moved with a mild laxative and if the fever runs very high, ten to fifteen drops of the sweet spirits of nitre, for a child five years old, in half wineglass of water every few hours will generally reduce the temperature. For the itching, the skin should be rubbed with equal parts of glycerine and warm water. The cough is generally the most troublesome feature, and the only symptom requiring regular medication; for this a good general cough mixture will serve every purpose, such as:

Take: Compound mixture of liquorice,

Syrup of wild cherry, of each   2 ounces

Mix and give to a child four years old a teaspoonful every four hours; older or younger children in proportion.

(*k*) Rose rash, sometimes called false or German measles is a comparatively trivial affection and of very little importance, for it never has any serious complications and lasts only twenty-four or forty-eight hours in the majority of cases. It is often mistaken for measles, and one attack affords no protection against recurrences. The eruption appears in small rose-colored spots or patches which are not elevated. It does not commence on the head, but appears on different parts of the body. The eruption may be preceded by headache, loss of appetite, occasionally vomiting, and more or less fever or chilly sensations.

The affection of the eyes and air passages, especially the bronchitis which is characteristic of measles, are wanting in rose rash, and when we hear of children having had measles several times it is reasonable to presume that it was rose rash instead. This eruption hardly calls for treatment, but a mild laxative and a regulated diet would fulfill all requirements.

(*l*) Scarlet fever or scarlatina has received its name from the color of its eruption. This affection presents itself differently in different cases. It may be so mild in its attack that it constitutes a trifling ailment and again it may be so severe that life is seriously threatened, and destroyed in a few days. This has formed the basis of dividing scarlatina into three varieties, namely: simple scarlatina, diphtheritic scarlatina and malignant scarlatina.

The fever, as a rule, is notably higher than in other eruptive fevers. The attack may begin with a chill, nausea and vomiting and headache. There is also bleeding from the nose in a certain proportion of cases. The most constant sign is redness and more or less swelling of the throat, either with or without a sense of soreness and pain in the act of swallowing. The stage of development lasts in the average twenty-four hours, although exceptionally it may appear in a few hours after the first symptoms of the disease have appeared. The eruption often begins on the back first, and from there rapidly spreads over the entire body in twenty-four hours. It greatly differs from the eruption in measles in not allowing any healthy or white skin to intervene between the red specks, but the entire skin has a reddish blush. This has given rise to the expression *boiled lobster* appearance in scarlatina, and indeed nothing could illustrate the color of the skin better than by comparing the one with the other. The eruption is sometimes accompanied with a great deal of itching and burning and reaches its fullest development on the third day after its first appearance; it lasts from four to six days.

The extent and redness of the eruption varies greatly in different individuals, in some it is very slight and transient while in others there is not a spot as large as a dime which is not covered. Yet a very light attack in one patient when communicated to another individual may develop in that one a most malignant form. One attack secures against a recurrence.

The throat affection seems to modify the eruption of the skin for in some instances in which the throat is very bad, the skin eruption is comparatively slight. There may be simply a little redness over the tonsils, extending more or less over the soft palate, or on the other hand, the disease in the throat may become in every respect equal to if not identical with the worst type of diphtheria. Some writers consider the sore throat of scarlatina and that of diphtheria identical, and from a practical point of view there is certainly no difference, and the very best results are obtained when all severe sore throats of scarlatina are treated precisely as if they were diphtheria; this has always been my practice.

The tongue is quite distinctive of the affection; early in the development of the disease it is generally furred, but later the coating peels off in patches, and these spots present the appearance of a ripe *strawberry*; sometimes the entire surface of the tongue looks as if cayenne pepper or red sand had been sprinkled on it.

The fever generally increases during the eruptive stage, and the skin becomes very dry and hot. The pulse may run up to 130 to 140 per minute, while the temperature runs up as high as 106° Fahrenheit; this state of affairs places the patient in imminent danger, he now may become restless and even delirious. In a certain proportion of cases the kidneys become involved and albuminuria is a result, but this usually passes off with the improvement and recovery of the patient.

In the third stage the cuticle begins to exfoliate in the form of branny scales. In the absence of serious complications this stage marks the beginning of convalescence; the fever subsides, the appetite returns, and the soreness and redness of the throat disappear.

The treatment of this affection always depends upon the nature of the case. Simple scarlatina requires no medical treatment; the precaution and intelligence which are comprised in good nursing supply everything that is required. There is not the same danger of the eruption striking in with scarlatina as there is with measles, and the patient need not be kept so warmly covered. When the fever runs very high, sponging the surface with cool water is very grateful and reduces the temperature. After the eruption has thoroughly developed, the water for sponging off may be very cold without the least danger, and this may be repeated as often as comfort or the high temperature demands. To relieve the burning and itching of the skin, the entire body should be rubbed over with glycerine night and morning; this relieves the system and makes the skin moist and supple. If the throat is only reddened, a teaspoonful of chlorate of potash dissolved in a cupful of hot water and when cold used as a gargle and a teaspoonful of the solution swallowed at the same time every two hours is all that is necessary. The diphtheritic scarlatina is treated precisely similar to and according to the instructions laid down for diphtheria in another part of this work. Move the bowels freely with the Femina laxative syrup.

(*m*) Chickenpox has neither distressing symptoms nor is it significant as regards danger. It is an eruptive fever which occasionally affects adults, but for the most part children. The eruption is generally preceded by a slight fever and nausea, and appears first on the body and afterwards on the scalp where it is usually more abundant. There always remains healthy white skin between the vesicles, which at first contain a transparent liquid, hence called by the Germans waterpox, which afterward becomes cloudy or opaline. The eruption begins to dry up from the fifth to the seventh day forming granular crusts that are sometimes followed by pitting. The disease is contagious and develops twelve to seventeen days after the exposure. Chickenpox claims no treatment; its only point of interest is its resemblance to varioloid, but as a successful vaccination guarantees against the latter, and as the vesicles of varioloid have a central depression while those of chickenpox have not, the individuality of the affection is readily established.

CHAPTER XXXI
EMERGENCY TREATMENT IN
SUDDEN ACCIDENTS

If the author reviews his experience of the last twenty years, he recalls to memory innumerable instances in which the lack of a little special knowledge, in cases of sudden accidents, did not only incur useless physical suffering, but cost lives which otherwise might have been saved. Knowledge of this nature is not intuitive, but must be acquired by study. He therefore offers for the guidance of the intelligent reader, common sense advice on the immediate management of accidents which are liable to occur at almost any moment.

If a child falls any considerable distance to the ground, the system receives a shock varying from the slightest functional disturbance to complete insensibility.

In the former case there may probably be only slight pallor of the countenance, the ideas become confused, there is a disposition to yawn and a feeling of nausea. Young children have a disposition to sleep, older ones rub their eyes, stare wildly around and even vomit, but after a short time they resume their accustomed employment: these symptoms illustrate a slight concussion of the brain.

When the injury is more serious all the above signs become aggravated and it may take several hours before the normal condition is restored.

The proper course to pursue in all these accidents is to lay the patient on a sofa or bed, with his head slightly elevated in a darkened chamber free from all noise and confusion and let him fall to sleep. In ordinary cases reaction takes place after a quiet slumber. If however the patient complains of pains in the head and there is irritability of temper, the advice of a competent physician becomes necessary.

(*a*) Broken bones or *fractures* are defined to be a destruction of the continuity of one or more of the bones of the body.

Fractures are divided into simple and compound; a simple fracture is one in which the bone alone is broken, and in which the skin or integument over the seat of the fracture remains perfectly intact. A compound fracture is one in which the skin and tissues over the fracture are lacerated or wounded so that the ends of the broken bones protrude or are exposed to view.

In a case of fracture, no matter of what variety, the first object to be accomplished is to carefully remove the patient to a place where he may be in a comfortable position. If the fracture is in the arm or leg it should be comfortably supported on a pillow so as to relieve the injured limb from all strain.

In compound fractures, the wound should be carefully covered with a soft clean compress which is kept thoroughly wetted with clean cold water until the surgeon arrives.

Sometimes the circumstances make it necessary to remove or transport a patient; then the injured limb must be properly supported so that it will remain motionless on the journey. In case the arm is fractured the above object is readily accomplished by placing it in a sling suspended from the neck. In the case of the lower extremities this object is more difficult. The leg should be wrapped in cotton first, or some other soft clean substance, after which a slat should be placed on the outside and inside of the limb, the same length as the limb; over and around these slats strips of muslin or a bandage is wound so as to keep them in place. This contrivance forms a temporary or improvised splint until the surgeon takes charge of the case.

(b) Wounds are defined as a recent sudden solution of continuity in the soft parts or flesh of the body. For the sake of convenience in description and for practical purposes, wounds are divided into incised, lacerated, contused, punctured, and poisoned wounds.

An incised wound is a clean smooth cut made by a sharp clean-cutting instrument.

A lacerated wound is one in which the parts have been torn asunder or in which the instrument was blunt or dull.

A contused wound is one the result of a bruise or blow inflicted with a blunt object or by a flat surface.

A punctured wound is one in which the flesh is pierced with a sharp-pointed instrument, like that made with a stiletto or bayonet.

Poisoned wounds are such as have become infected any time after the receipt of the injury, or which are the result of a bite or sting from a reptile or insect.

The danger of wounds depends on their extent and depth, and upon the locality or organ in which the wound is situated. The external wounds, that is those which admit of inspection, and situated on the head, trunk or extremities are of most frequent occurrence, and the most amenable to treatment.

The treatment of wounds has made wonderful progress since the antiseptic discoveries of the eminent surgeon, Sir Joseph Lister, and these sound principles have materially influenced almost every department of the healing art. It was he who first showed how dust-laden air affected injuriously the exposed tissues of the wounds; it was he who introduced all the precautions as to cleanliness of instruments; the disinfection of hands; the change of clothing; and the purification of sponges and dressings. The magnificent results of the practice of modern surgery are not owing to the superior skill of the surgeon of our time, but to the magnificent conception of the idea of *cleanliness* from which has grown the entire superstructure of antiseptic surgery, culminating in the grand triumphs of surgical art. To the question What to do with recent wounds? The answer now becomes self-evident; Keep them clean. The best dressing for any clean wound is its own secretion carefully protected from the outside world by a fold of clean soft cloth or absorbent cotton, wetted with pure cold water. This is to be kept in its proper place by means of a bandage, and when it is desirable to remove the compress, it must first be thoroughly soaked with water so as not to tear or irritate the wound.

Before Lister's great antiseptic discovery it was the generally accepted opinion that suppuration and pus were essential to the healing of wounds; this was an error and the opposite is now established to be the truth. Pus prevents or rather delays the wounds from healing, and suppuration in wounds is a fruitful source of blood poisoning.

If sand, earth, dust or dirt has gotten into or near the wound, it must be washed off with clean, fresh water, but never employ soiled or infected clothes for that purpose for these may poison the wound and do a great deal of mischief. After the wound is clean dress it in the manner described in a preceding paragraph.

Poisoned wounds are chiefly punctured. The danger of these wounds lies in the possibility that the poison is absorbed by the lymphatics and veins, and conveyed to the heart, whence the entire blood becomes infected. To prevent this a ligature should be tied above the wound, by means of a strip of muslin or preferably an elastic suspender, so as to check the free return of the blood by the veins and lymphatics. After which the poison should be sucked from the wound, or the wound should be cauterized, with carbolic or nitric acid by means of a sharp-pointed stick dipped into the acid and then applied to the wound, or *fired* with a red-hot iron, crochet or knitting needle. The poison of snakes and tarantulas is neutralized with an alkali;

the most efficient seems to be spirits of ammonia, but a strong solution of washing or even baking soda should be substituted when ammonia is not at hand. I would puncture and enlarge the wound of the sting with the point of a sharp knife or scissors, so that the alkali can come into immediate contact with the injected venom; the patient must be given frequent drinks of whisky, brandy or strong wine until a physician arrives to supervise further treatment.

Wounds inflicted by poisonous insects like the bumblebee, honeybee, wasp, hornet, yellow jacket and mosquitoes produce wounds which are instantly followed by a sharp, pungent, itching pain, and in a few moments after by a pale, circumscribed, inflammatory swelling. Some persons have a peculiarity in their constitution that the poison of an insect gives rise to exceedingly alarming symptoms, such as palpitation, nausea, dizziness, dimness of sight and an indescribable sense of suffocation. The sting is sometimes left in the skin; for this the wound should be carefully examined, and when present drawn out. The most prompt and useful application is water of ammonia, or strong salt water, or strong soapsuds. Turpentine is also a valuable application. If the insect has lodged in the throat, large quantities of warm salt water and mustard must be immediately administered until the patient has vomited freely, and if there is a sense of suffocation leeches and afterwards hot poultices should be applied to the neck. If the system has become poisoned, and some of the distressing symptoms that were above enumerated are present, the internal use of whisky or brandy is called for.

Hemorrhage is common to all wounds, and the loss of the blood depends upon the size and nature of the vessel that is injured.

The bleeding that takes place in ordinary superficial wounds oozes from minute vessels, the capillaries, and slight pressure temporarily applied controls it. When an artery is wounded, the blood flows in intermittent jets, or in a running pulsating stream from the vessel. The venous blood is dark red and flows in a continuous stream and not under the same pressure as that coming from the arteries, hence it is much easier controlled.

The clotted blood with which a wound may be filled, is nature's means of arresting the hemorrhage, and it must never be disturbed or washed off, lest this open the blood vessels again and thereby renew the bleeding.

The arrest of hemorrhage is accomplished by the application of cold or ice water, by hot water and by pressure upon the arteries. Persons fainting from the loss of blood should always be laid with their heads lower than the body; cold water should be dashed into their faces so as to restore them to consciousness. Moderate hemorrhage from the smallest vessels and from the veins generally ceases from slight pressure over the wounds or by drawing or pressing the edges of the wounds together. In a very short time the blood coagulates and forms a temporary plug until the vessels themselves become permanently sealed by a similar process. The pressure must often be continued for a considerable time until the object has been attained. A folded clean cloth or compress is laid over the wound which is the source of the hemorrhage, and this is retained by means of a properly adjusted bandage. If notwithstanding the pressure exerted by the bandage or with the hands, the scarlet blood saturates the cloth and continues to flow, it indicates that a very large vessel is wounded, and thus life may be seriously threatened and in proportion to the magnitude of the wounded vessel, a surgeon should now be summoned to make a further investigation. Hemorrhage from varicose veins of the legs may be checked by a compress fastened over the site of the wound by a bandage, but every constriction around the waist or above the knee by a garter must be loosened. If the patient's life is threatened from the bleeding, the limb must be elevated, and the pressure of the compress increased, or the pressure should be exerted on the trunk of the bleeding artery above the wound or injury.

(c) Burns and scalds are the most commonly fatal injuries which occur in modern life. The extended use of steam machinery, the universal employment of coal oil, the general use of the phosphorus and sulphur matches, and the flowing manner of woman's dress has materially increased the liability of this accident. Of all accidents, burns involve the victim in the most agonizing pain and protracted suffering. Burns are liable to serious complications; the obstinacy to the healing of vast ulcerated surfaces, or the lifelong mutilation to which they condemn the unhappy patient, the rapid draft they make on the patient's strength, and the danger of abscess and ulceration of internal vital organs which eventually destroy life.

These injuries have been classified into three divisions: First degree, superficial skin irritation. Second degree, cutaneous inflammation. Third degree, devitalization of the skin or deeper parts, or carbonization of a member, or the entire body. The first degree is only a superficial redness, fading without any definite edge into the natural skin. This may be produced by the sudden and momentary application of flame over a larger portion of the body, from an explosion of gas. The local injury is not dangerous, and the epidermis remains to protect the surface of the true skin until a new layer is produced, as the injured one peels off. This hardly calls for any other treatment but one or several applications of sweet oil. In the second degree, the local injury has penetrated a little deeper, and the sudden congestion of blood to the surface, raises the epidermis from the cutis in blisters filled with the serum of its vessels. Here there is a more serious condition, and indeed dangerous in proportion to the extent of surface that has become involved. Skirts draped largely with lace, and those made of cheese cloth, swiss, and other gauzy material are of a very inflammable nature, and when once ignited blaze into a flame that is almost sure to consume the material before it can be extinguished, so that it has been deemed advisable on the German stage, to first saturate these materials in a solution of sulphate of ammonia to make them non-inflammable; this does not interfere with ironing, nor with the texture or color of the fabric. Another source of scalds and burns is the wash boiler or tub on the floor, with hot or boiling water in it, so that little children stumble or reach into it. Vessels filled with hot water or other fluids standing on tables or on stoves within reach of little children, who innocently pull the vessel down, pouring its scalding contents over them, is another cause of numerous accidents.

The best course to pursue when skirts or clothing are on fire is to roll the victim, so as to smother the flames; but the patient herself has rarely enough presence of mind to do this. She will run for help, thus fanning the flames, the very worst thing she can do. Take the nearest blanket or quilt, or if that is not at hand, take an overcoat or wrap; wrap this around the burning person and throw her to the floor and roll her until the flames are smothered. Then get some cold water and pour it on the smoldering clothes until they are thoroughly saturated, for the hot charred clothing burns into the flesh. In scalding from hot water or steam the clothing should be cooled off in the same manner. Cold water must be poured over the hot and steaming clothes from head to foot, and thus the further action of the heat is suddenly checked. The patient should now be carefully removed to a warm room and laid in a blanket, on the table or floor. If he complains of thirst give a cupful of warm tea or a warm whisky toddy.

Visitors and strangers should now be requested to leave the room and the clothing should be removed from the body with the greatest care. The scissors or a sharp knife should be used to cut away the garments, so as to avoid all possible straining and dragging on the patient. The blisters must not be torn, and where they are very tense they can be pricked with a sharp needle, so as to allow the escape of the serum. The epidermis forms the best protection for the cutis, and where the skin is stuck to the linen do not tear this off, but allow it to remain and cut with a sharp scissors around it. The application of cold water generally increases the suffering, but sweet oil, lard oil, vaseline, castor and china nut oil will answer for the emergency or until a more suitable dressing can be obtained, after which the surface should be covered with cotton batting to exclude the air. A very useful application is a mixture of equal parts of lime water and sweet oil or linseed oil. Carbolized sweet oil is another useful dressing and superior to lime water liniment; it is made in proportion of half an ounce of carbolic acid to one pint of sweet oil; either of the above preparations can be poured over the burned surface and then it should be covered with cotton batting, or small pieces of soft linen cloth can be dipped and saturated in the oil and then applied over the burns. The advice of a physician should be sought in view of the dangerous complications that may occur from extensive burns.

(d) Frostbite is the result of exposure to cold, and in certain regions during the winter months a considerable number are liable to this accident. But extreme cold weather is not alone responsible for frostbite; very often this accident occurs in moderately cold weather, for instance, if persons exhausted from hunger or fatigued from long travels or stupefied by alcoholic drink lay themselves down and fall asleep, and a cold wind blows over them which withdraws the bodily heat, the same effects are accomplished on the system.

The first effect of dry, cold air is a sense of numbness and weight, with a peculiar prickling or tingling, and a rush of blood to the surface, giving the skin a lively reddish appearance. If the cold is maintained for any length of time the blood leaves the surface, which becomes now of a pale and whitish aspect, forming a striking contrast to the previous redness. When the cold is suddenly applied and very intense, the skin exhibits a mottled appearance, which is due to the presence of congealed blood in the subcutaneous veins.

Moist cold has a similar effect on the living tissues to dry cold. If the hand is immersed in iced water the blood rushes immediately to the surface, so that the color of the skin increases, which is followed by a marked degree of numbness, and an unpleasant burning and tingling sensation. A reaction comes on in a short time, the blood quits the surface, and the skin becomes bleached and contracts, the tissues underneath also shrink and become painful. There is no difference in the effect of either moist or dry cold, only that the former is more penetrating and its effects are sooner apparent. Those parts of the body that are more directly exposed and in which the circulation is not much protected by fatty tissue, suffer the most from the effects of cold; after exposure for an unusual length of time the toes, feet, heels, fingers, hands, nose, and ears, together with the lips and cheeks are for this reason oftener affected than other parts of the body. Persons whose constitutions are broken down by intemperance, starvation and other privations which lower the power of resistance are more susceptible to this accident.

The first effect of cold in the general system is bracing and stimulating; an agreeable glow is felt over the surface of the body and one feels strengthened and exhilarated. But if the cold temperature is unusually prolonged this agreeable sensation is changed into one of pain and drowsiness; the brain becomes inactive as if under the influence of a powerful opiate or narcotic, and the desire to go to sleep is so strong that it requires the greatest effort to keep awake. To yield to this inclination to sleep would result in slumber that knows no waking, for the blood would now rapidly accumulate in the internal organs, the breathing would become irregular and spasmodic, the nervous functions would soon be suspended and death would ensue from general paralysis. An individual thus exposed, so as to have become drowsy or unconscious and then suddenly brought into a hot room is likely to die from congestion of the brain and lungs, or if he should revive for a short time, the frost-bitten parts will be stricken with mortification. Professor Samuel D. Gross says: "The treatment of frostbite requires no little judgment and adroitness to conduct it to a successful issue. The great indication is to recall the affected parts gradually to their natural condition by restoring circulation and sensibility, in the most gentle and cautious manner, not suddenly, or by severe measures. The first thing to be done is to immerse them in iced water, or rub them with snow, the friction being made as carefully and lightly as possible, lest overaction be produced, as they are necessarily greatly weakened. If no ice or snow is at hand, the coldest well water that can be procured must be used; and if immersion is inconvenient, wet cloths are applied, with the precaution of maintaining the supply of cold and moisture by constant irrigation. Moderate reaction is aimed at and fostered. All warm applications, whether dry or moist, are scrupulously refrained from; the patient must not approach the fire, nor immerse his limbs in hot water, or even be in a warm room. Attention to these precepts must on no account be disregarded, as its neglect would be almost certainly followed by mortification or other disastrous consequences."

(e) Drowning or the submersion of an individual until life is destroyed by suffocation is not an uncommon accident. "The immediate cause of death in drowning," says Dr. Gross, "is suffocation or insufficiency of air. Respiration being thus arrested, the blood is unaerated and consequently unfitted for life, although the circulation may go on for a short time after breathing has completely ceased."

The Navarino sponge divers whose occupation has accustomed them to live under water the extreme limit, average only seventy-six seconds, while the Ceylon pearl divers seldom remain under water with impunity more than two-thirds of that time.

Dr. Gross says: "The period at which a person after submersion may be resuscitated varies very much in different cases and under different circumstances. In some cases, for reasons not always explicable, recovery is found to be impossible at the end of one minute. The chances are never good after submersion of twice this length of time, especially when the water and the air are both uncommonly cold.

"The treatment of apnœa from drowning must be prompt and decided. Every moment of time is most precious. The body being removed from the water to a dry place, is immediately stripped, wiped, and covered with a blanket, especially in cold weather. The mouth, nostrils and throat are cleared of mucus, froth, and any other substances likely to interfere with the admission of air to the lungs; the tongue is to be pulled out at the corner of the mouth, and prevented from falling back upon the glottis; ammonia is rapidly passed to and fro under the nose; and the body is stretched out at full length with the face downwards, the forehead resting upon one arm, for the purpose of allowing any water that may be in the stomach and air passages to escape by the mouth and nose. If these means do not speedily revive the patient, artificial respiration is instituted. For this purpose, the body being placed upon its back, with the head slightly elevated, the arms, grasped just above the elbows, are carried outwards and upwards from the chest almost perpendicularly, and retained in this position for about two seconds, the object of the procedure being designed to promote the introduction of air into the lungs as in natural breathing. They are then lowered and brought closely to the sides of the chest, where they are held for the same length of time, to expel the air, the effect being aided by pressure applied to the inferior and lateral portions of the chest. These alternate movements of elevation and depression from twelve to fourteen times a minute, and are performed with all possible gentleness. As soon as signs of life are observed, dry warmth should be applied to the extremities, the region of the heart, loins, and abdomen, a little brandy and water being administered, or if deglutition be impracticable, thrown into the rectum."

(f) Poisons and their antidotes form an important subject for our consideration, because many of the poisons are among the most useful remedies. The daily accounts in the public press of serious and fatal mistakes in the administration of medicines, are always due to carelessness and very often to criminal negligence.

No package or bottle should be kept about the house without its proper label.

Those that contain poisonous drugs or chemical preparations should be plainly marked Poison, besides the name of their contents.

Vials or packages containing poisonous drugs or chemicals must not be kept on the same shelf and near those medicines that are comparatively harmless.

Always look at the label twice; once before the contents are poured out, and a second time, before the dose is swallowed. Never take medicine in the dark, in the belief that you are certain of the right vial and locality; many a sad accident has occurred from this venture.

Sulphuric, nitric, and muriatic acid cause great heat and a sensation of burning pain from the mouth down to the stomach. Acids are neutralized by alkalies, hence one teaspoonful of washing soda or two teaspoonfuls of bicarbonate of soda dissolved in a pint of water should be drunk as soon as possible: chalk or powdered magnesia mixed with water will also answer the purpose.

Oxalic acid is frequently mistaken for Epsom salts; lime water, chalk or magnesia mixed with water and taken in large quantities are antidotes: then administer emetics, which act more quickly if the stomach is filled with fluids; sometimes the finger run down the throat will excite quick and sufficient vomiting.

Creosote and carbolic acid benumb the stomach so that emetics usually will not act, and large quantities of sweet oil or castor oil should be first drunk; I prefer the former because from one to two pints of it can be taken; after which lime water or a solution of Glauber salt (sulphate of sodium) should be taken; the latter is especially recommended as neutralizing carbolic acid. When circumstances make it possible the stomach pump or india rubber siphon tube should be at once employed.

Alkalies, for example, caustic potassa, soda, lye, strong solution of ammonia, earths and lime are neutralized by drinking vinegar or lemon or lime juice; afterwards milk in water and flaxseed tea.

Arsenic: Give the white of eggs, lime water or chalk and water; tablespoonful doses of carbonate of iron, mixed with water, or calcined magnesia in the same manner, then evacuate the stomach with an ipecac emetic.

Corrosive sublimate: Give white of eggs, or wheat flour mixed with water; afterwards give an emetic.

Alcohol: First cleanse out the stomach with an emetic, then dash cold water on the head and give frequent doses of aromatic spirits of ammonia in water.

Charcoal or coal gas poisoning: Remove the patient into the open air, dash cold water on the head and body and stimulate by passing ammonia to and fro under the nostrils, at the same time rubbing the chest briskly.

· Lead: White lead and sugar of lead should first be treated with alum emetic, afterwards a cathartic of castor oil or Epsom salt.

Nitrate of silver (lunar caustic): Give a strong solution of common salt, and then emetics.

Prussic acid or cyanide of potassium. For this no certain antidote exists, and it destroys life so suddenly as scarcely to allow of use if we had one. When there is time chlorine in solution has been recommended, also water of ammonia and cold affusions.

Opium, laudanum and morphine require the same antidote. If the patient can swallow an emetic should be given; twenty grains of sulphate of zinc and a teaspoonful of powdered ipecac mixed in a draught of water should be given every twenty or thirty minutes until vomiting is insured. A mixture of half teaspoonful of mustard and a tablespoonful of salt dissolved in a pint or quart of warm water is another efficient emetic in these cases. If swallowing is impossible the stomach pump must be used. When the stomach is cleansed out give strong coffee and acid drinks, dash cold water on the head and keep the patient walking.

Belladonna and black henbane: Give emetics, and afterwards a dose of paregoric, and a hot whisky toddy, or a cupful of strong tea.

Nux Vomica and strychnine have no reliable chemical antidote; emetics should first be given, or the stomach washed out with a siphon tube or stomach pump. Chloroform must be employed to control the spasms, then alcoholic stimulants should be freely administered.

Aconite, digitalis, hemlock, lobelia, cantharides, poisonous mushrooms or toadstools, etc., have no certain antidotes. Emetics should be immediately given when any of them are known to have been taken. Animal charcoal is recommended to absorb and render harmless organic poisons in the stomach; teaspoonful doses mixed with water should be given repeatedly, and for those drugs least depressing in their action castor oil is also recommended.

When a prompt emetic is urgently demanded and no drugs of any kind are at hand, large quantities of tepid water should be drunk, say half gallon to a gallon; this distends the stomach mechanically, and by titillating the throat prompt and effective vomiting may be excited; this may be repeated as often as necessary and the stomach thoroughly washed out.

.

CHAPTER XXXII
SOMETHING ABOUT DIET

It has been truthfully said that "many persons dig their graves with their teeth," but, that improper feeding causes many a grave to be dug is also true.

So never feel sorry or disappointed when the family physician makes a professional visit, and fails to write a prescription, but instead, gives you instruction in the art of feeding and nursing the patient.

Food and stimulants support the strength of the system until the struggle between health and disease or between life and death is overcome, and thus cure the patient by not allowing him to starve. There is a large group of diseases for which there are no acknowledged remedies, and in which a properly selected and regulated diet forms the mainstay of successful treatment. This should be combined with healthy, clean rooms, proper ventilation, and other hygienic means which may suggest themselves to the intelligent practitioner.

The patient's fancy for this or that article of diet is no index, as a rule, of what is best suited for him; invalid appetites and cravings are abnormal; they are like that of the chlorotic girl who eats chalk and slate pencils, instead of wholesome food and some preparation of iron.

An aversion to food is also no criterion of the patient's need for nourishment, for the sense of taste is generally blunted or perverted. The desire for food is lost in all diseases of a catarrhal nature of the mouth or stomach, and in those that are characterized by high temperature. In typhoid fever and diseases of a typhoid nature this is always the case.

With children this aversion to food is greater and more general than with adults; and it must be made a rule that their refusal to take nourishment must not be extended beyond several days, otherwise they fail so rapidly in conjunction with the disease as to perish from exhaustion.

The repugnance to food arises from abnormal conditions that are generally localized in the mouth and especially in the parts of the tongue which are supplied by the nerves of taste; these nerves are the lingual branch of the trifacial and the glasso-pharyngeal. But notwithstanding that the food is almost tasteless, when it gets into the stomach it is retained and properly digested and the patient feels better for having taken it. An appetite can be thus cultivated, and after a few days of coaxing or perhaps of forcible feeding, which in children who are failing rapidly becomes necessary in order to save them, the taste and desire for nourishment become natural or restored. Quite often patients beg and plead not to be given food; but in wasting diseases it should be insisted that some at least should be taken (always liquid of course), and when they are sufficiently rational they will always afterward admit that the nourishment did them good.

Liquid food or nourishment and no other is suitable for a sick person; an invalid can drink food when it would be impossible for him to swallow solid material. I have often seen the whim of patients who craved meat indulged; they got a juicy porterhouse steak with the understanding that it was to be thoroughly masticated before swallowing. As a rule, the patient is disappointed with his own bill of fare, and after trying one or two mouthfuls orders the meat taken away with the remark that it is as dry as a chip. But this same person will drink a milk punch, a thin gruel with the yellow or all of an egg beaten into it, with some degree of relish; salt should always be added and indeed, as much as the taste will permit, but sugar should be used as sparingly as possible. Salt is what is needed above all other seasoning; the system requires the chlorides for they are wasted in fevers, but even in health, the chlorides are very essential and salt is the best one we have; salt is the source of the hydrochloric acid in the stomach and one of the most important factors in albuminous digestion.

The saliva is not secreted in sufficient quantity in fever to allow insalivation of food, or to moisten the solid morsel sufficiently to permit its being swallowed without a choking sensation as it glides into the stomach. A person prostrated by disease has not the strength to masticate solid food and that is another reason why liquid food is to be given.

The famous physiologist, Dr. E. Brown-Séquard, is the author of a method for feeding the sick peculiarly his own, namely, that of administering small quantities of food at short intervals. He would give a glassful of milk punch in tablespoonful doses, repeating every ten or fifteen minutes; this method is advised for the treatment and cure of dyspepsia, anæmia, chlorosis, nervous diseases and even organic diseases of the stomach. No particular kind of food was selected for this treatment; butter, milk, cheese, and meats, bread and potatoes were alike to be given in small quantities and at short intervals. One or two mouthfuls even to be eaten at a time, and then repeated in ten or fifteen minutes, until thirty to forty ounces are consumed daily. This system never became a recognized expedient, it is wrong in theory, and certainly in practice; while it may be applicable in isolated cases, they would be so very few that this method of feeding forms the exception and not the rule.

Cases are frequently met with, especially in infants and older children whose digestion has been completely ruined by being fed too often. These cases are not really overfed, because the entire amount in the twenty-four hours, does not exceed the requisite quantity; but giving the food in driblets and at short intervals, causes lactic fermentation, or in plain English, the food sours on the stomach and does not digest, as it would do if a proper time were interposed between each feeding. As soon as the patients are fed at regular and longer intervals, say, from two to four hours, the indigestion corrects itself. During the interval, between the time set for feeding, the children will naturally cry; this is interpreted by the mother or nurse as a sign of hunger, but nothing is oftener further from the truth. The child cries generally for one of three reasons: one of these may be that it wants to be taken up, and dandled or rocked, to which previous indulgences have accustomed it; or it may have pain in the stomach and bowels as a natural result of indigestion or flatulence; or the child may cry from thirst or a sensation of dryness in the mouth and throat; in any event, additional food would only prove injurious. There is no objection against giving nurslings cold water between their meals when they are thirsty or feverish, but warm aromatic tea is so very much superior that I consider it one of the essentials of the nursery. I mean fennel seed tea, of which a sufficient quantity should be prepared every morning to last twenty-four hours; this should be strained and sweetened, then set aside for further use. When the child is restless, between meals, some of the tea should be warmed, and given from the nursing bottle until it is satisfied, for the tea soothes the pain, quenches the thirst and dispels the flatus.

There are also physiological reasons for these longer intervals between nursing; they allow the stomach sufficient time to dispose of its contents before another mess is given to disturb the digestion of former food, which is as yet incomplete. There is another immense advantage in having the length of time between two meals from two to four hours; it allows time for medication and other necessary management of the sick, for sponging off with cold water in fevers, and many other things which are necessary for the patient's comfort and convalescence, and which can only be carried out between the times the nourishment is given. A memorandum should be kept in the sick room and the time and hour noted when everything becomes due in proper order; this avoids confusion and lessens labor.

Digestion is the solution of the food in the stomach for purposes of nutrition. Nitrogenous materials, egg, meat, muscle are digested principally in the stomach, but not entirely so, because the particles of albuminous food which pass from the stomach into the upper portion of the small intestine come into contact with the pancreatic fluid, which is the digestive agent for fats and starches, but which possesses also powerful digestive properties for nitrogenous or albuminous substances and even in a greater degree than the gastric juice of the stomach, which has a strong acid reaction, while the pancreatic juice has an alkali reaction; here is a very interesting illustration how similar digestive processes are accomplished under opposite chemical conditions. The intelligent reader must not fail to observe, from what has been said, that there are two distinctly different digestive processes, namely one going on in the stomach and another equally as important taking place in the small intestines.

Pepsin is the active principle of the gastric juice, held in solution in a clear colorless liquid, principally water; it has a sour taste and a peculiar characteristic sour smell. The length of time required by the gastric fluid to dissolve the food depends greatly upon the minuteness of the division of the solid substances to be acted upon, as well as upon the quantity and quality of the peptic fluid.

The pepsin changes the physical properties of nitrogenous substances so as to make them soluble in water in any proportion and when the albuminoids have acquired this property they are termed peptones; peptones are simply nitrogenous food which has been modified to fit it for absorption and nutrition of the body.

In the tissues of the body there are continual changes going on, termed in technical language tissue metamorphosis; the waste products that are thus formed constitute a group of highly nitrogenized substances, which in a healthy condition of the system are eliminated by the kidneys. These nitrogenized products are urea, urate of soda and uric acid; the accumulation of any of these substances in the blood gives rise to disease; the former is the cause of uræmia and uræmic convulsions, and the latter have been detected in the blood and exudations in cases of gouty and rheumatic disease. The characteristic gouty deposit is urate of soda, due to an excess of nitrogenous elements of the blood. An excess of uric acid constitutes a disease which is first recognized by a reddish crystalline sediment in the urine; the term *lithiasis* has been employed to denote this peculiarity. These lithates are always to be found in the urine of high livers and are due to an excessive consumption of nitrogenous food. The great English authority, Dr. Murchison, looks upon the excessive production of uric acid, or lithic acid, as it is sometimes called, as due to one of two causes and sometimes to both, namely to the excessive consumption of nitrogenous food, or to an inability of the liver to perform its duty, which among other things is to dispose of the nitrogenous waste products. From this point of view lithates or brick dust deposits in the urine are no sign that the kidneys are deranged, but quite the reverse may be true when the kidneys are overburdened in eliminating this excessive waste, for they are performing extra duty, which excess in living or a sluggish liver imposes upon them, and this may excite inflammation in the tissues of the kidneys and develop into what is known as Bright's disease.

This very interesting exposition of the deposit of lithates or gravel in the urine will naturally suggest that when the urine is overloaded with these nitrogenous products nitrogenous food like eggs, cheese, beef, etc., should not be eaten for awhile, and that a vegetable diet should be principally relied upon, thus giving the liver a vacation; the diet should be supplemented with plenty of clean fresh water, and no liquors of any sort should be taken by those whose liver is affected.

Starch, sugar and fat are composed of carbon, hydrogen and oxygen; starches and sugars are termed carbo-hydrates; because the hydrogen and oxygen is always present in them in equal atomic weights so as to represent water; while in the fats the oxygen is considerably less. This is exemplified by comparing the chemical equivalents of starch and cane sugar with those of fats:

Starch	$C_{12}H_{10}O_{10}$	Oleine	$C_{94}H_{87}O_{15}$
Cane sugar	$C_{12}H_{11}O_{11}$	Margarine	$C_{76}H_{75}O_{12}$

When starch is boiled with diluted nitric, sulphuric or muriatic acid for thirty-six to forty hours, it becomes colorless and thin like water, and is converted into a species of sugar. A similar process takes place when starch is taken as food, the diastase of the saliva, and the pancreatic and intestinal juices change starch into *glucose*, in which form it is ready for nutrition.

Cane and other sugars introduced into the system as ingredients of fruits and vegetables are not absorbed as such, but undergo a process of digestion which converts them into grape sugar or glucose; after that they are suitable for nutrition and absorption into the blood, but not before.

The digestion of starches and sugars has been incidentally referred to as not taking place in the stomach but in the upper portion of the small intestine, through the agency of the pancreatic juice which has the peculiar property of converting farinaceous and saccharine matters into grape sugar. But this transformation into grape sugar is not the final product of digestion. In the normal process of intestinal absorption the grape sugar is taken up by the portal capillary vessels and carried to the liver, where under the influence of this organ it is changed into liver sugar or glycogen, and it is as glycogen that it again enters the circulation, to disappear in the lungs. But if the liver from disease or other causes fails to perform this task, the glucose passes through the organ unaltered, and as such again enters the circulation where it acts as an irritant and finally is eliminated by the kidneys in the urine giving rise to the affection known as diabetes.

We have learned that there is a stomachic digestion and an intestinal digestion, the former principally for meats, or that class which are now called nitrogenous foods, while the latter is confined generally to starches and fats. This physiological fact suggested the idea of feeding dyspeptics only on such food as is not acted upon in the stomach, but passes beyond that cavity to become digested in the small intestines, giving the stomach a rest as it were so that it may recuperate and gain strength while the system is being fed by farinaceous aliments. While a superficial glance justified such a procedure, a moment's reflection proves it to be a delusion, and for this reason, that there will be an unavoidable irritation of the stomach which the journey of the farinaceous material occasions in its passage through the stomach, and the insufficient nutritive value of a simple non-nitrogenous diet causes a rapid loss of tissue and bodily strength; hence this course proved itself impracticable and was abandoned. Then again the experiment was tried of putting a certain class of dyspeptics on a purely meat diet; this had one fault common with the former plan; it was also too one-sided, and the system suffered for want of fat and starch, and secondly peptones were not always formed in the stomach from a deficiency of the gastric juice or an impairment of its quality, so that this method was also abandoned.

Fats belong to the starches and sugars as heat producers; they are insoluble in water, and by boiling them in caustic alkali they are decomposed into soap and glycerine. In the cavity of the stomach fats remain unaltered; the heat of the stomach may melt or liquefy them, but in no other way are they changed. They are also digested, like the starches, in the small intestine by the action of the pancreatic juice which possesses the remarkable property when brought in contact with fatty or oily matter at the temperature of the body of emulsifying it, and of converting the fats into a milky, white, opaque looking fluid, by a minute subdivision of the oily particles. This emulsion of the fatty and other substances of the food is termed chyle, and as such, the fatty substances are ready for absorption by the absorbents of the intestinal tract. Experience teaches that a deficiency of fat causes scrofulous diseases, and this class of patients have generally a repugnance for fat; this is another illustration of the unreliability of patients to choose their own food. Professor John H. Bennet first pointed out the usefulness of cod liver oil in consumption and other scrofulous diseases, and directed attention to the value of fat in the nutrition of the body.

Dr. Ferguson made extensive observations on the little children of the factory operatives of Lancashire, Eng. The children were principally fed on tea or water and bread, little or no fat, bacon, butter or cream, and they grew up into puny and stunted men and women, while those who had a bread and milk diet grew into hardier and finer human specimens.

Fat is also an essential food for the brain and general nervous system; the lean are the nervous patients and not the fat and sleek, hence fatty food is considered an important diet for this class of diseases. The brain and nerve fat is called "lecithin" and a little phosphorus enters into its composition. Chronic obstinate neuralgia has often been cured by the administration of cod liver oil.

Milk is the only single article of diet which possesses in itself all the properties to supply the wants of the system, and it may be profitable to give this subject more than passing notice. It is the natural and most wholesome food for the infant when it can suck it from its mother's breast; instinctively the newborn rolls its little head hither and thither in search for this fountain of infantile life and however great the skill of the chemist in approaching the composition of mother's milk, he can never produce an equally good substitute. Milk contains all the principles which are necessary for human food, the nitrogenous, the oleaginous and the saccharine, and these are blended in such proportion that milk is adapted for the complete nourishment of the young and old. In no other single substance supplied by nature does a similar combination exist; it contains the material for the consolidation of bone and for the formation of the red blood corpuscles, by carrying in solution the phosphates of lime, magnesia and iron; in this respect an analysis of milk shows a remarkable similarity to blood. The proportions of the different constituents of milk are liable to great variations and are greatly influenced by the nature of the food.

Dr. Playfair of London, who has made some interesting researches regarding the milk of the cow, has demonstrated that the amount of butter depends in part upon the quantity of oily matter in the food and in part on the amount of exercise which the animal takes; and upon the warmth of the atmosphere in which it is kept. Exercise and cold weather eliminate the oily matter or butter, in the form of carbonic acid and water, while rest and warmth diminish this drain by favoring its passage into milk. On the other hand, the proportion of the cheesy matter is increased by exercise.

In Switzerland, where the cattle pasture in very exposed situations and where, from the rolling of the country, they are obliged to use a great deal of muscular exertion the quantity of butter yielded by the cows is very small, while the cheese is in unusually large proportions; but the same cattle when stall fed give a large quantity of butter and very little cheese.

The character of the food will decide the nature and healthfulness of the milk. The best food for milch cows is bran or middlings mixed with well-seasoned and sweet-cut hay, and this mixture thoroughly scalded and saturated with boiling water; a little flaxseed oil cake, should be added occasionally, for it enriches the milk and keeps the cattle in good condition; during the day the cows should be in the open air; they should not be irritated by dogs, or made to run or trot; these things will affect the milk injuriously. To feed cows on kitchen garbage or swill of any sort will taint the milk so that the offensive odors of the swill can be readily detected, especially after the milk has stood awhile; such milk is particularly dangerous to infants and should at once be discontinued. Distillery slops are often fed to cattle in large cities; these are not only productive of poisonous milk but also injure the cattle so that they become salivated and lose their teeth after a few years of this diet. Brewers' grains are not open to the same objection as whisky slops; a certain proportion of brewers' grains added to the cut food increases the flow of milk. In all large towns there are families who keep one or two cows and who sell the milk as a means of making a livelihood: as a rule these cattle are fed on swill, and not upon the best quality of food, and although this milk is recommended as being pure and one cow's milk, it is as a rule not good, for the stalls and the food do not come up to the requirements for wholesome milk.

I have always found a healthier and purer milk from the dairies run on a large scale, and outside of the centers of population. The cattle look healthier, have better food, good pasturage and pure country air, and if the milk is properly chilled or cooled off before it is poured into the wagon cans, country dairy milk is to be greatly preferred over city milk. The animal heat should have left the milk before it is put into cans for transportation, for it is the animal heat in tightly closed vessels which causes the chemical changes that encourage the development of organic milk poisons or so-called *ptomaines*.

Milk promiscuously mixed from a group of apparently healthy cows is preferable to that of one cow, and for several reasons; the honesty of dairymen is doubtful, for they will not take the extra trouble to keep the milk of one cow apart when the cows are being milked; again tuberculosis or consumption in all its stages is a common disease among cattle, and quite often a milch cow has tuberculosis when she seems healthy. If a child should subsist on the milk from a tuberculous cow, serious consequences would undoubtedly ensue, but if this milk had been mixed with that of thirty or forty healthy cows, the danger of infection would be correspondingly lessened.

Cow's milk should average 12 per cent. of cream; if it contain less than 8 per cent., it is probable that the milk is watered or that it was skimmed. A cream gauge is a cylindrical glass vessel about one and a half inches in diameter and eight inches high, with a capacity of 12 fluid ounces. This tubular measure is graduated so as to make it possible to read off from the top downwards 1, 2, 3, etc., parts or drams of cream which gradually rises to the surface. This glass is filled with the suspected specimen of milk up to the highest mark and set aside for 24 hours, at an ordinary temperature; at the expiration of that time the quantity of cream which rose to the surface of the milk is read off, and in this manner it is easy to see the proportion of cream to the entire bulk of milk tested. Above it was stated that 12 per cent. is an average for good milk, and 14 per cent. is extra good, while 8 per cent. is the lowest that is permissible. If the percentage falls below 8 per cent. it is a sign that the milk has been skimmed, and if the density or specific gravity is below 27 degrees, then it is to be presumed that the milk has also been watered, for sometimes the milk is both skimmed and watered.

The density or specific gravity of milk gives an approximate idea of the quantity of solid matter a given specimen submitted for examination contains, as compared with pure water. The lactometer or galactometer is a kind of hydrometer, but specially graduated to readily read off the density which pure milk should have. Pure milk at a temperature of 55 to 60 degrees should have a specific gravity varying between 27 and 33 degrees and if the sample falls below 27 degrees, it is to be presumed that water has been added. The density of diluted milk is sometimes maintained by boiled starch water; this can be detected by adding a few drops of tincture of iodine, which changes the starch into a beautiful violet blue, also giving the adulterated milk a similar tint.

It must always be remembered that while milk presents itself in a liquid form it becomes a semi-solid in the stomach in the ordinary process of digestion; this change is accomplished by the action of the gastric ferment, curdling the milk. Milk is not a diluent for solid foods and it should never be drank as a substitute for water when other solid food has been eaten. The practice of eating a regular meal of meat and vegetables and drinking milk at the same time invariably overloads the stomach, and if it does not injure the digestion immediately it is sure to do so in time; it also furnishes an oversupply of nitrogenous food, developing an excess of lithates or uric acid, and this burdens the liver and kidneys. If a person is fond of milk it is most excellent as a principal article of diet at a meal, and indeed nothing is better than a bowl of well-prepared mush or a few slices of bread with a pint of fresh milk for either breakfast or supper.

Boiled milk has considerable healing and binding virtues; it may be thickened with a teaspoonful of wheat flour to the pint, and taken quite warm; as a household remedy, it is one of the most valuable in ordinary cases of diarrhœa, but no other food should be taken until the cure is effected.

The milk cure is a well-established and recognized expedient for the relief and cure of a certain class of patients, and as the success of the regimen depends upon an intelligent employment of the fluid, it becomes necessary to enter somewhat into the detail of its administration.

The milk-shake, that is milk shaken in a tumbler or beaten with an eggbeater for several minutes is frequently borne by persons who cannot digest milk which has not been so treated; then again, a teaspoonful of mush or gruel added to a tumblerful of milk and thoroughly beaten, divides the curd mechanically when it forms in the stomach, and so makes the milk much more soluble by the gastric juice.

Milk should never be drank cold, but at a temperature of about 100° F., which is about as warm as it comes from the cow, for cold delays the curdling and hence the digestion of the milk, and gives it time to develop acid or lactic fermentation in the stomach, and this may cause indigestion; a pinch of salt should be added to milk, it assists in its digestion. There must be certain periods at which to take milk, allowing a definite interval for the milk to digest; taking milk in mouthfuls, for instance as a drink instead of water is wrong, for this will ferment and occasion indigestion. The proper length to intervene between each meal of milk is four hours; breakfast 8 o'clock, dinner at 12 o'clock, lunch at 4 and supper at 8 o'clock; if the patient is considerably exhausted, the time between 8 o'clock in the evening and the same hour in the morning may be too long, and if the patient is awake, a meal should be given at midnight.

The quantity of milk which may be taken for one meal is of great importance, for there is the same danger of taking too much of this food as of any other. The average quantity to begin with must not exceed half a pint, and when the appetite is capricious one-fourth of a pint is sufficient. It is now fully established that a grown person can be fairly well nourished for quite a while on one quart of milk in the twenty-four hours.

It is also of considerable importance to the patient that he does not gulp the milk as this would cause it to curd into a large cohesive mass of casein, which would be slowly dissolved or acted upon by the gastric juice, and might give rise to distress from indigestion. If, on the other hand, the patient sips the milk slowly, or eats it with a spoon, the curds will be small and flaky particles which even a weak stomach may digest. There are quite a number of persons who like milk, yet whose stomachs do not take to it, and for these a milk cure might be just the thing. It requires often a great deal of ingenuity to devise a plan whereby the obstacle may be overcome. The first step should be to shorten the interval between each meal and lessen the quantity correspondingly; thus to give the patient the milk every hour would imply that he was to take only one-fourth as much at a time as if he took it every four hours. Perhaps the milk would digest more easily if it were first beaten and slightly seasoned with a pinch of salt, or if a little strained gruel were added to mechanically divide the curd. A soda cracker, toasted bread, or the rind of thoroughly baked wheaten bread is an excellent substitute for dividing the cheesy substance of the milk when it gets into the stomach. They should not be soaked or dipped into the milk and eaten together, but eaten dry and thoroughly masticated until the saliva has reduced the bread to a soft pulp, after which a spoonful of milk should be taken and the bread stuff washed down. The saliva serves another useful purpose besides moistening the bread as it changes the starchy substance into sugar.

In other cases the milk sours on the stomach, and then some antacid or alkali, like lime water or bicarbonate of soda should be added for several days or until the disposition to lactic fermentation has subsided. If notwithstanding every precaution, waterbrash, heartburn, or a heavy oppressed pain in the stomach occurs, or if sourish, slimy secretions are vomited, the milk cure must be abandoned for something else.

Diarrhœal diseases of infants who are fed on cow's milk are caused, in many instances, by germs or spores that get into the milk from lack of proper cleanliness and from the unavoidable exposure of the fluid to the atmosphere of stables and dairy rooms where the milk is handled before transportation to consumers. To obviate the danger of feeding nurslings with infected milk, and to destroy the vitality of germs which find access to the milk, methods have been devised for *sterilizing* the milk. This process was first proposed in 1886 by Professor Soxhlet, and has ever since gained favor with the profession; it consists of exposing the milk to a temperature of live steam or boiling water for about forty-five minutes. In New York City there are two reliable firms which sterilize milk at the dairy in the country and ship it to the city.

In all the methods of sterilization the milk is placed in six or eight-ounce bottles and set on a tray or shelf, which stands above the water at the bottom of a vessel, the cover then applied and the water made to boil forty-five minutes; a perforated stopper is inserted into each flask, admitting of the escape of air and gases at the beginning of the heating process. The stopper may consist of cork with a glass tube in the center, or cotton, or of rubber with a channel a part of the distance on one side. If necessary the family can improve their own apparatus; an inverted tin pan will serve the purpose of a tray to support the nursing bottles, and this placed in the bottom of an ordinary tin vessel with a cover completes the contrivance. The milk is to be prepared as it is to be administered, that is, the proper quantity of water, a little sugar, and the point of a penknifeful of bicarbonate of soda added, and distributed among as many eight-ounce flasks or nursing bottles as the child is fed during the twenty-four hours; thus if fed every four hours the milk should be distributed among six flasks, and if fed every three hours, it would require eight flasks. When the milk has been sterilized, it keeps sweet for an indefinite period at ordinary temperature; the bottle is to be well shaken to mix the cream before the cork is removed and the nipple applied.

When an apparatus or a sufficient number of flasks cannot be readily obtained I have the milk boiled in a fruit jar after the manner of making beef tea, as follows: A quart preserve jar is filled with milk, obtained not later than four to six hours after milking, the cover is lightly put on, to allow the escape of air and gases, and then the jar is put into a vessel, on the bottom of which an inverted pan has been placed so that the preserve jar does not rest on the bottom of the vessel where the heat would crack it; the vessel is then to be filled a third with water, and this boiled for an hour, after which the jar is carefully closed, as in preserving fruit, until wanted for use. The milk should be kept in a cool and clean place, and only as much measured out each time as is required for one mess, after which immediately close the jar. The water that is to be used for diluting the milk must have been thoroughly boiled; it is always better to prepare and dilute the milk before sterilizing it for very young infants, but when they are a year or more old, the boiling water may be added at each meal.

The casein, which is the curd or coagulable part of milk, differs greatly in its physical property in the milk of the cow from that in human milk. Mother's milk curds in *soft flaky coagula* which are readily dissolved in the infant's stomach, while cow's milk curds in a semi-solid conglomerate coagulum which the cavity of the child's stomach is often unable to tolerate nor the gastric juice to penetrate and dissolve. It is this heavy curd which forms the main objectionable feature of cow's milk as a substitute for that of the mother. This can be greatly modified by first thoroughly beating or churning the cow's milk with an egg beater, and afterwards scalding it as above described; the milk treated in this manner curds light and flaky. But it must not be presumed that the physical characteristic of casein is the only peculiarity of cow's milk in comparison with mother's milk, for this is not so; it also differs in quantity, that is, mother's milk has less of casein, a fact which may be better understood by the following chemical analysis of both:

	Human milk.	Cow's milk.
Water	87.09	87.00
Casein and albumen	2.48	3.72
Fat	3.90	3.66
Sugar of milk	6.04	4.92
Phosphatic salts	0.49	0.70
	———	———
	100.00	100.00

There are some children who are unable to digest cow's milk in any form, either from a peculiarity of constitution, or from a derangement of the digestive apparatus; the milk, no matter how prepared, passes through them curdled, in lumps and undigested; to continue feeding infants on milk, notwithstanding this symptom would in all probability sacrifice the life of the child. If curds persist in the stools milk is to be withheld for a time, and crushed wheat, barley gruel or other diluents should be given alone or in combination with the thoroughly beaten white of egg. This treatment must be continued for several days and in some cases for several weeks.

Whey prepared from sweet and pure milk has often been borne by delicate and suffering infants, when nothing else could be retained. An examination into the chemical composition of whey reveals astonishing nutritive virtue, which it holds in solution; the following table shows the proportional constituents in one hundred parts:

Water	93.31
Nitrogenous matter	0.82
Fat or butter	0.24
Sugar of milk	4.98
Fixed salt	0.65

When the whey is the product of soured milk, 0.33 or more of lactic acid is to be added to this analysis, and the same amount deducted from the sugar of milk. Essence of pepsin will curd lukewarm milk, not warmer than can be agreeably borne by the mouth; a temperature higher than one hundred and fifteen degrees Fahrenheit destroys the curdling principle of the pepsin. The quantity of essence of pepsin to be used to the pint of milk depends on the strength of the preparation; usually a teaspoonful or two is added and stirred just enough to mix; let it stand till firmly curded, then beat up with a fork until the curd is finely divided; now strain and the whey is ready for use; it should be sweetened a little; sugar of milk, if pure, would be the best, otherwise white cane sugar may be used. A newborn babe will require a tablespoonful to begin with, every two hours, always slightly warmed. It is particularly essential to keep everything clean, especially the tube and nipple; these are to be brushed and cleaned after each meal, and then laid on a clean dry plate for future use; the nursing bottle too must be rinsed and drained. The prevalent custom of keeping the tube, nipple and bottle in water after they are washed is a bad one, for to have them sweet and pure they should be allowed to dry out between times.

Condensed milk is often a valuable substitute for fresh cow's milk; its utility, is probably due to the employment of heat in its manufacture, which destroys the germs or spores that find their way into all milk, and to the scalding of the casein which modifies its physical character so that it no longer curds into large lumps when in the stomach, but into smaller flakes. There are different brands in the market, and even the best of them may be too old and shop worn; they then become thick and dark in which condition they are no longer fit for infants' food. The Eagle and Anglo-Swiss are among the best varieties; others contain too much sugar, while some are adulterated with starch or flour. A heaping teaspoonful of condensed milk to a teacupful of warm water, previously boiled, is the average strength, although better results are obtained when a thin gruel of corn starch or arrowroot is employed instead of plain water; when the child grows older cracked or rolled oats or graham flour may be substituted for the arrowroot. The gruel is prepared in the following manner: take half a teacupful of oatmeal or graham flour, saturate first with cold water, then stir slowly into three pints of boiling water; add a pinch of salt and boil over a slow fire for three-quarters of an hour, stirring constantly so that it will not scorch on the bottom; then strain, and if it has boiled down to less than a quart of gruel, add a sufficient quantity of boiling water through the strainer to make it measure a quart.

The gruel is to be prepared fresh every morning, and the above quantity will last about twenty-four hours. It should be kept in a porcelain or glass pitcher covered with a napkin, and set aside in a clean cool place. At regular mealtimes take out the required quantity, warm in a little agate saucepan, kept only for this purpose, and when warmed add the condensed milk, stirring until it is dissolved. This makes a fine cream-like food, agreeable to take and very nourishing if well borne by the stomach. The stools may become too loose at times from the oat or wheaten gruel, then this gruel should at once be changed for that of corn starch or arrowroot until the bowels are regulated again, and when that is done it may be advisable to return to the oatmeal or cracked wheat. The exercise of a little judgment and close observation in feeding a child will contribute greatly to its well-being; any diarrhœa or disturbance of the digestion must at once receive prompt attention and this can often be accomplished by change of food; to allow these disorders to run for any length of time is to invite serious consequences.

Adults or grown persons have also their share of stomach troubles; as a rule they eat too much, too fast and do not masticate their food sufficiently. It is not so much what a person eats, but how he eats, not so much quality as quantity.

After an exclusive dietary of milk dyspeptics should gradually return to a mixed diet, that is a regular dinner once a day; but eat slowly and masticate thoroughly; thus one eats rarely if ever too much. When the food is bolted, it makes little or no impression on the nerves of taste, nor does it appease the sense of hunger, and the only indication of satiety is a feeling of fullness.

As to the time of taking one's dinner that depends altogether on the occupation and habits of the individual. In dyspeptics in whom the digestion is slow and the circulation sluggish the principal meal or dinner should be eaten at noon; this gives opportunity to move about, stimulating the circulation, hence increasing the absorption to its highest point. If a man eats his dinner in the evening and afterwards goes out into society or attends amusements the late dinner is not objectionable. But if a person is worn and tired out at supper and then eats a hearty meal, and lounges around the room the remainder of the evening, reading the newspaper or otherwise inactive, he is quite likely to feel distress from what he ate, and sure to experience occasional bilious spells; nightmare disturbs his sleep and he awakes in the morning unrefreshed, languid and dull. It is better for such persons to eat their dinner at noon, and retire early on a very light supper.

Beef tea became very popular at one time as a nourishment for the sick, and there can be no doubt that many patients who were stricken down with different acute diseases slipped into their graves, because beef tea was relied upon with a belief that it was a sufficient nourishment. Observation and careful researches on the subject have proved conclusively that the nutritive value of beef tea as ordinarily prepared, that is chopped beef put into a bottle and boiled in a water bath for three or four hours, has been greatly exaggerated. The process of boiling the beef has no other effect than that of drawing out the watery substance of the meat. The phosphatic salts that are contained in the meat are also extracted with the serum which holds them in solution. The natural albuminoids (musculine) which constitute the real nutritive element of beef are congealed and surrounded by the fibrous tissue—that part which snarls up and renders the beef gristly and tough. Yet as a nutritive stimulant, beef tea possesses at times considerable value; it is an excellent vehicle sometimes, for instance an egg thoroughly beaten and added to a cupful of warm beef tea is a desirable form of liquid food for invalids.

Eggs constitute a highly nitrogenized food and their nutritive value is even greater than that of stall-fed beef. The subjoined tables of chemical analysis give the definite quantity of each constituent that is contained in one hundred parts of egg and beef:

	Stall-fed Beef.	Egg.	Lean Beef.
Phosphatic salt	0.5	1.0	1.5
Albuminoids	10.5	15.0	17.5
Fat	45.0	12.0	6.0
Water	44.0	72.0	75.0
	———	———	———
	100.0	100.0	100.0

If we compare the analysis of egg with that of milk, a remarkable similarity will be observed, save one exception, namely the carbo-hydrate sugar of milk is lacking in egg, and in order that eggs have the same property of nourishing the body as milk, this element may be readily supplied by eating a little bread. The writer is familiar with the history of a case in which a patient was kept on an exclusively egg diet for five months, and during this time he increased his weight thirty-eight pounds; he consumed eight eggs and twelve ounces of bread a day.

We hear considerable unfavorable comment in regard to hard-boiled eggs, and indeed for good and sufficient reason, but the indigestibility of the hard-boiled egg is not due to any change in the nature of the albumen because it is boiled; the cause is entirely mechanical. The reason is that a hard-boiled egg is not sufficiently divided by the ordinary process of mastication to allow the gastric juice to attack it from all sides; if it were finely pulverized either by the teeth or otherwise it would be as readily digested as a soft-boiled or raw egg.

A raw fresh egg that is thoroughly beaten with an egg beater is the most readily digested food that there is. The author has known dyspeptics who could not digest any other kind, and by adding a pinch of salt and half to one tablespoonful of whisky after it is thoroughly beaten, it is certainly one of the most valuable foods for a certain class of stomach troubles that can be recommended. Patients whose digestion is very weak should begin with one egg every four hours until four eggs are taken during the day; when the strength increases, two may be taken for breakfast, and one for each meal the rest of the day; after the lapse of a few days another may be added to the second meal, and so the number gradually increased until eight are consumed; prudence would not go beyond this number lest an excess of nitrogenous matter overtax the liver and kidneys to eliminate it from the system and this result in other complications.

Dyspeptics, more than others, must avoid overtaxing the digestive organs, and while the stomach is sensitive and for a long time afterwards, they must avoid solid food.

The quantity of bread must also be jealously guarded; while the stomach is very sensitive and weak it had better be entirely suspended and when resumed no more than three ounces should be eaten at each meal to begin with. For those dyspeptics whose stomachs possess average digestive power, and who require a nourishing and readily digestible meal, the writer would recommend for breakfast a milk gruel to which a raw egg has been added: he directs that four tablespoonfuls of oatmeal mush be mixed with three-quarters of a pint of warm milk and this worked through a tin strainer by means of a potato masher; to the milk gruel so obtained and again moderately warmed, a raw fresh egg is added, which has been previously beaten to a foam, and then the whole mess is again beaten together, seasoned with salt and served in a bowl.

Medicines should play a very minor part in the treatment of dyspepsia; the artificial pepsin preparations are all overrated and their supposed efficacy is due to a careful and regulated diet rather than to the virtue of the pepsin. If the bowels are costive and if the stomach is sour and feels oppressed, prescription No. II will materially relieve these symptoms.

A person who is suffering from indigestion must above all things learn to discipline himself; when that has been once accomplished the task of carrying out an appropriate diet will become an easy one, and restoration to health and strength will be the reward.

INDEX

Digestion,

of fats and starches,

Diphtheria,

Disease is as much a vital process as health,

Diseases of children,

that are conjured up in the minds of susceptible persons,

Disinfection of the lying-in woman in Germany,

Dispersing electrode,

Divided skirts,

Dobell, Dr. Horace,

Drowning,

treatment for,

Drug diseases of Hahnemann,

Drugs are physical agents,

Düvelius, Dr.,

Dysmenorrhœa,

prescription for,

inflexion,

Dyspepsia, or indigestion,

Dyspeptics,

EGGS,

Elastic garters,

Electricity in diseases of women,

as a remedy,

in catarrhal inflammation,

in subinvolution,

medical,

without puncture,

Electrodes and poles,

Electro-puncture,

Emergency treatment in sudden accidents,

Endometritis,

In the realm of thought there is no monopoly,

Indigestion,

Infants fed on cows' milk,

overfeeding of,

Infection,

gonorrhœal,

innocent,

Inflammation,

of the womb,

chronic,

Interpolar regions,

Intra-abdominal pressure,

Involution,

Iron pills in chlorosis,

KNEE-CHEST posture,

in relaxed vagina,

in falling of the womb,

LAITY, object of educating the,

Landois, Prof., on the curative force in the lower animals,

Laws on abortion,

Leucorrhœa,

Little girls, muco-purulent secretion of the vagina,

Lochial discharge,

Lung fever,

Lying on the back after confinement,

MALTHUS, law of,

Man, instinctive desire of,

Mania for cutting operations,

Marital excesses, and prevention of conception,

Marital excesses the mainspring of disease,

Married women exposed to infectious contamination,

Martin, Dr., of Chicago,

papillated growths and mucous polypoids,

Urinary fistula,

Uterus,

anteflexion,

anteversion,

changes after confinement,

measurements after confinement,

natural position and support,

prolapsus, or falling of the,

retroflexion,

retroversion,

treatment for prolapsus,

versions and flexions,

VAGINA,

catarrh of,

catarrh in children,

acute and chronic inflammation of the,

gonorrhœal infection of,

knee-chest posture in catarrh of the,

relaxed, mistaken for falling of the womb,

Vaginal douches after confinement,

Vaginal injections, directions for their use,

Versions and flexions due to abortions,

Virchow, Prof., theory of inflammation,

WARMING a dwelling,

Weapon ointment,

What is mind-cure?

What is termed mind-cure is not mind-cure,

When the soul becomes associated with the body,

When to begin to train mothers,

Whey,

While in childbed,

Whites,

Whom to teach,

Whooping-cough,

Why crowd our girls into the profession?

Winter cough,

Wives who become delicate and nervous,

Womb,

tear or laceration of,

Women's rights vice women's wrongs,

Women, after getting up from confinement,

Worms,

Wounds,

contused,

incised,

lacerated,

poisoned,

punctured,

ZIEGLER, Prof., on infection,